Talma

Talma as Néron in *Britannicus*
A portrait by Delacroix

TALMA

A Biography of an Actor

by

HERBERT F. COLLINS

FABER AND FABER
24 Russell Square
London

First published in mcmlxiv
by Faber and Faber Limited
24 Russell Square, London W.C.1
Printed in Great Britain
by Ebenezer Baylis and Son Limited
Worcester, and London
All rights reserved

For

WINIFRED

Foreword

Apart from one holograph letter, all material used for the making of this book has been found on the printed page. In writing this biography of Talma, the first to be undertaken in English, the author has encountered all the difficulties that surround the life of a dead and gone actor. He has tried to stick to verifiable fact, to avoid at all costs flights of fancy, and if here and there a love for the theatre may have engendered some emotional warmth, the fastidious reader will doubtless apply a cool corrective. The papers in the Fonds Rondel at the Bibliothèque de l'Arsenal, the intimate letters and jottings in the Fonds Lebrun at the Bibliothèque Mazarine, the early biographies and memoirs which sprouted immediately after Talma's death in 1826, the theatre historians' renewed interest in him around 1885, the plays in which he appeared and the newspaper reports of the tragedian's acting throughout his stage career, have formed the basis of this book.

Two matters should be mentioned. The names of the characters played by Talma remain in their French form. Racine's Oreste and Achille connote dramatic values different from those which apply to the corresponding heroes of classical Greek tragedy. Again, dates given according to the tiresome revolutionary calendar have for the sake of clarity been transposed to orthodox chronology.

The author wishes to express his thanks to his friend and former colleague, Miss L. L. Ross, M.A., who read the manuscript and made valuable suggestions. Debts also extend to Mr. B. W. Winkless, B.A., to Mlle Marthe Chalmel of Paris and to Mr. A. van Smevoorde of Lille University who so generously helped him to much useful material. Finally there remains Mme Sylvie Chevalley, Bibliothécaire-Archiviste of the Comédie-Française, who with exemplary patience and courtesy made available to him her own

Foreword

scholarly knowledge of the French Theatre and much vital information about the actor's final appearances in Paris.

Thanks are also due to Mr. J. P. T. Bury of Corpus Christi College, Cambridge, for permission to quote from *An Englishman in Paris, 1803*.

HERBERT F. COLLINS

Goring-by-Sea, 1963

Contents

Contents

PART THREE

Under the White Cockade

PART FOUR

Apotheosis

Illustrations

Part 1

Son of the Revolution

CHAPTER 1

The Talma Forbears

Beside a secluded path in the vast Parisian necropolis of Père-Lachaise stands a severe tomb of strictly classical design, bearing on its marble frontal the name Talma. No other details are vouchsafed the onlooker. Clearly those who erected this monument were convinced that the mere unqualified name of France's greatest actor would awaken in the mind of the idlest passer-by such a trail of theatrical glory that would do honour to the tragedian who lies buried in that hallowed ground. For Talma is the one inevitable name in any estimate, however brief and modest, of French acting. Here in England under similar circumstances we should invoke the name of Garrick, and Talma, like his great English counterpart, made a contribution to the theatre of his time that went far beyond his own brilliant performances before an admiring public. A Frenchman might perhaps, thinking of Molière's well graced troupe, pause on the name of Michel Baron, a player whose greatness had done much to raise the status of the acting profession in France; he might linger too over Voltaire's idol and ideal interpreter, Henri-Louis Lekain, whose death occurred in 1778, nine years before Talma made his début at the Comédie-Française, and whose memory was enshrined in so many brilliant impersonations that the young actor had much to endure in the way of unfair comparison. Great as undoubtedly were Baron and Lekain, Talma, the child of the French Revolution and the friend of Napoleon Bonaparte, was in the judgment of the finest minds of that stimulating age the outstanding innovator and artist in the French theatre.

Well might the gravestone in Père-Lachaise bear none of the usual details. Even allowing for the spirit of a flamboyant age, when Lamartine could write of another tomb at Saint-Helena 'here lies nameless', the date of Talma's birth was still a matter for dispute during his lifetime. Four contemporary chroniclers had placed his arrival in this world on different dates: 'Talma

(J.-F.) born in London on January 17th, 1766'; 'François Talma born in Paris on January 15th, 1760'; 'Jos.-Franç. Talma born in Paris on January 15th, 1767'; 'Talma (*tout court*) born in Paris in the month of January, 1762'.[1] This uncertainty about his age gave the actor immense pleasure. 'How old am I?' he would say. 'I played Othello last week and I was as old as he. Tomorrow I shall act Oreste and my years will be his.' Yes, he would muse, how old is an actor? When pressed about his date of birth, his own vanity decreed that he saw the light of Paris on January 15th, 1767. No wonder he said on the last day of his life: 'People will be surprised when they learn my age.'

What then are the facts? Happily Talma's birth certificate was available at the late fourteenth century church of Saint-Nicolas-des-Champs, just across the rue Réaumur and immediately south of the Arts et Métiers. This document states that 'on Saturday January 15th, 1763, was baptized François-Joseph born that very day, the son of Michel-François-Joseph Talma, confidential agent, and of Anne Mignolet his wife, domiciled in the rue des Ménétriers.' The godfather was Philippe-Joseph Talma, uncle of the child; his godmother was his aunt, Marie-Thérèse Mignolet.

Who were these Talma? It can be established beyond dispute that the actor's grandfather was born at Poix-du-Nord in 1700, where he lived until his death in 1782. He married Marie Cathérine Hardy and from their union sprang thirteen children, three girls and ten boys, of which the actor's father was the sixth. In accordance with the custom of the times, this child Michel-François-Joseph Talma was baptized in the parish church on his birthday, February 10th, 1733. He is described as the legitimate son of François-Joseph Talma and of Marie-Cathérine Hardy his wife, '*simple paysan et habitant de cette paroisse*', born on that same day about three o'clock in the morning. The godparents were Michel-François Deullin, a native of Poix and a trooper in the King's Regiment, and Marie-Françoise-Joseph Talma, daughter of Jean-Baptiste and Marie Deullin, a parishioner of Poix. The father did not attend the ceremony.

---

[1] Cited by Regnault-Warin, *Mémoires historiques et critiques*, p. 15. Regnault-Warin, Moreau and Duval all give the correct date, Jan. 15th, 1763. P. F. Tissot in his *Souvenirs historiques sur la vie et la mort de F. Talma*, p. 8, gives Jan. 15th, 1760. In *Souvenirs historiques sur la vie et la mort de Talma d'après les documents donnés par lui-même*, Bruxelles, Tarbier 1826, and in the *Notice historique sur la vie de Talma*, Bruxelles, A. Delavault 1827, the birth date appears as Jan. 17th, 1766. The Leipzic publication has not been traced.

These facts, fully documented, make clear that the Talma family had modest peasant origins in the soil of northern France and obviously belonged to the Catholic faith. A family so large and so poor would give every encouragement to its fledglings to leave the home nest and seek a livelihood in more profitable places. The actor's father, Michel-François-Joseph, must at some time have made his way to Paris, where he served as *valet de chambre* to an English gentleman and having won his master's favour was promoted to the position of '*homme de confiance*', an expression difficult to translate today but indicating clearly an upper, trusted servant. Among his gifts this Talma claimed some knowledge of human anatomy which, allied to a certain manipulative dexterity, enabled him in those credulous and accommodating days to undertake among his other duties the delicate task of extracting teeth. At the age of twenty-seven he had married, on April 29th, 1760, Anne Mignolet, his senior by one year, the daughter of Pierre Mignolet and Marguerite Trouvé, living in the rue des Ménétriers where the tragedian was born.

All his life the actor was conscious of bearing an unusual name. At the very height of his fame, he received a letter from a learned young Dutchman of Engervirum in Friesland, Aretius Sibrandus Talma, who asked if he might claim kinship with the eminent tragedian. Talma, in a charming and witty reply from Paris, dated June 15th, 1822, referred to his father's family established in French Flanders 'at six leagues from Cambrai', and proceeded to tell with his own innate romanticism how a son of the Emperor of Morocco had sought him out, believing him to be of Arab descent. Talma in Arabic means 'fearless' and Talma's vivid imagination led him to believe that a Moorish family had settled in Spain, had embraced Christianity and, in the days of the Spanish occupation of the Netherlands, had journeyed to Flanders where they remained. However, the fact that there were many Talmas in Holland tended to upset these oriental fancies and in more serious moments the actor was prepared to accept the probability of a Dutch ancestry.

Talma's father showed himself a man of enterprise. While still in the service of his English master, he set up on his own initiative a dental practice in a house in the rue Mauconseil, where a limited circle of well to do clients conferred their patronage. So successful did this venture prove that the aspiring dentist's brother, Philippe Talma, joined forces. This Philippe Talma submitted to a strict professional training which his most progressive and enlightened tract, *Necessary Instructions for the Care of the Teeth*, published in 1770, proclaimed. His brother, even by the lax standards of those days, did not altogether escape the odium which attaches to the charlatan. Evidence is not lacking that the actor's father in the rue Mauconseil ran counter to the interests of a more established and better qualified dentist, who at one time threatened the interloper with legal proceedings and the dangerous word '*brevet*' was bandied about. So useful had Michel-François-Joseph Talma become to his English master that, when this gentleman returned to London, his trusted servant accompanied him.

It is at this point that the biographer of Talma begins to tread uncertain ground. It is impossible to establish with precision the date of this emigration. It may well have been about 1768. We know for sure that the actor's father lived as a practising dentist from 1770 to 1780 at 13, Cavendish Street, to which fact certain fanciful minds add that the future tragedian 'in the garret of this house qualified himself for the profession he was burning to pursue'.[1] Another writer claims that Talma's father practised his calling in Halkin Street, Belgrave Square, quite a possibility after 1780 but unverifiable because no rent roll of Halkin Street was in existence until 1808, by which time Talma's father had departed this life. While there are many legends concerned with the actor's infancy—some of them certainly encouraged in later life by Talma himself—the truth about what happened to him immediately after his father's journey to London is indeed hard to come by. Henri d'Alméras, editing in 1904 Regnault-Warin's *Mémoires sur Talma* which were written in 1826, the year of the tragedian's death, states categorically in an appendix: 'Until the age of nine Talma, who had not been taken by his father to London, where he exercised his profession as a dentist, was left with one of his aunts. This period of his life was spent entirely in the hamlet of Vagnonville, part of the commune de Poix. It is said that he planted an apple-tree there which still flourished in 1830.'[2] We know that Talma, late in his lifetime, attended gatherings of the '*Enfants du Nord*', and in those days he took care to refer to an ancient Château Talma of which he contemplated the purchase and which was situated in the *arrondissement de Cambrai*, near the Saint-Quentin canal. Other testimony prefers that the

---

[1] Cunningham, *London. A Comprehensive Survey*. P. 450.
[2] D'Alméras, *Mémoires sur Talma*. P. 310.

child remained under the care of his uncle in Paris, where his father had arranged for him to receive a good education with much emphasis on drawing, an interest that lingered with Talma all his life. Mlle Flore, a gay and spritely *comédienne* of those days, states in her reminiscences that she, with the young Talma and one Mira, destined to become the celebrated Brunet of the Théâtre des Variétés, attended a little school situated in the cul de sac de la Bouteille, rue comtesse d'Artois, conducted by M. Vaperot, a pedant of the lowly sort. She asserts with an actress's superb disdain for dates that she and the boy Talma got into trouble one day for inking their faces and acting a short scene from *Andromaque*. When discovered, Talma is alleged to have hurled at the irate schoolmaster Racine's sonorous line: *Souffrez, au nom des dieux, que la Grèce s'explique*. One can certainly accept as fact that the boy was placed at the Collège Louis-le-Grand and, during his studies there in 1772 when barely ten years of age, he acted the part of Messenger in the school play *Tamerlan*, a tragedy written on the austere classical model by a master, M. Verdier. Talma's task in Act V was to give an account of the hero's death and the young actor, starting in measured tones, so warmed to his tragic mission that at the end of the *récit* he collapsed in tears and shaking sobs, creating thereby a profound impression upon his audience. A letter, still extant and addressed to the father of a seventeen year old boy, Sulpice H., who played the title rôle, lavishes high praise upon this amazingly mature and emotional performance from so young a boy. The writer of this letter drew attention to little Talma's intelligence and sensitivity, qualities that were never to fail the actor in subsequent professional appearances. This *'journée de Tamerlan'*, firmly fixed in 1772, was later to prove a decisive influence in the boy's choice of a career.

Regnault-Warin, who in 1826 claimed a twenty-five years' close friendship with Talma, maintains in his biography that, after his schooldays at Louis-le-Grand, Talma passed on to the Collège Mazarin where on the staff as a teacher of rhetoric was the Abbé Geoffroy, who, as we shall be forced to note, exchanged at a later date schoolmastering for dramatic criticism. Viewed objectively this enrolment at the Collège Mazarin seems a little shadowy and Regnault-Warin's account of how Geoffroy advised an inexperienced colleague to ignore utterly, 'in fact to obliterate from sight and mind' the lazy, exhibitionist pupil that Talma had become, may well have been inspired by later relations between

critic and actor. Geoffroy's prescription we are told brought the
young student to his senses. Talma's heart was not in his lessons.
He had discovered the Comédie-Française and alongside the
classical masterpieces of Corneille and Racine drank in such contemporary productions as Lemierre's *Guillaume Tell*, de Belloy's
Le Siège de Calais and—experience most pregnant of all—the
timid adaptations by one Ducis of the plays of a drunken savage
named William Shakespeare.

As one examines these diverse accounts of Talma's boyhood,
all purporting to come from people who claimed to know him and
even to have shared some of his schoolday experiences, it seems
more than probable that Talma, as a very small boy, went with
his father to London, where he may have received some schooling
at the establishment of a Mr. Prendergast in Duke Street, Manchester Square,[1] reasonably near to the family home in Old
Cavendish Street. Aubert de Vitry, who described himself as
Talma's *'camarade d'enfance'*, asserted that his friend came from
London to Paris when he was nine years old. As Vitry formed
part of the audience for *Tamerlan* in 1772, his evidence seems to
bear out the facts. Talma certainly was at the Collège Louis-le-
Grand in 1772 and received there and no doubt elsewhere a
French education until such time as his father recalled him to
London to prepare for a dental career. Talma himself offers no
help to sort out these obscure happenings. At the very height of
his brilliant success as an actor, he paid in 1817 a professional
visit to London where he told all and sundry that he had been
born in the English capital of French parents and that until the
age of seventeen he had received his education at Mr. Prendergast's academy. Anything more patently false it would be difficult
to imagine.

[1] Cunningham, *London. A Comprehensive Survey.* P. 203.

CHAPTER 2

The London Connection

Talma's life with his father in London is poorly documented. It is difficult at this distance of time and on the data available to state precisely when Talma, after his schooling in Paris, rejoined his father in London. All accounts agree on the prosperity of Talma *père*, whose dental skill and progressive methods earned for him a wide circle of aristocratic clients. Exactly where he did his business after 1780 cannot be ascertained, but here and there a fleeting reference to the West End and to Hyde Park might point to a house in a fashionable quarter, possibly in Halkin Street. His patron Lord Harcourt emerges quite substantially from the shadows. This friend of the Talmas was the second Earl of Harcourt, George Simon, who had been Member of Parliament for St. Albans 1761–68 and, like all his kin, was very close to the royal circle. He became Master of the Horse to Queen Charlotte and until his death in 1809 enjoyed the boon companionship of the Prince of Wales. He was most certainly an assiduous patron of the dentist and has been frequently identified as 'the English gentleman' whom Michel-François-Joseph Talma served in Paris first as *valet de chambre* and later as *homme de confiance*. Lord Harcourt did much to advertise the improved dentistry of his French protégé and even succeeded in interesting no less a person than the Prince of Wales. It is more than probable that decently conducted struggles with Florizel's molars led eventually to Talma *père*'s attendance as surgeon-dentist upon His Britannic Majesty, King George III.[1]

The young Talma's arrival in England meant an apprenticeship in dentistry under his father's direction. It had been decided that François-Joseph would, in the ripeness of time and experience, take over this flourishing, lucrative practice. In later life Talma made no secret of his aversion from such a plan and, although he

[1] Mr. R. Mackworth-Young, Librarian, Windsor Castle, has established the fact that Talma *père* held no royal appointment.

23

gave every indication of falling in with his father's wishes, he looked around to find an outlet for his acting vocation. It did not take him long to discover a dramatic society organized by members of the French colony in London. The amateur actors had specialized in short drawing-room plays. It was the age of the *comédie-proverbe* and Carmontelle's elegant playlets were much in vogue. We learn that what the French in that day called '*variétés*' and the English 'plum-puddings' seemed to absorb the attention of these amateur actors and that in one of their programmes Dumaniant's *La Guerre ouverte* allowed Talma to taste the sweets of early success, with a sparkling performance of a Provençal marquis desperately in love. Very creditably this French fellowship of players decided to extend their range and, venturing beyond the neat production of drawing-room '*proverbes*', to include in their *répertoire* some of the tragic masterpieces of the French stage. A policy so ambitious enabled the young London dentist, already popular as a polished comedian, to stir innate tragic fires by rendering some of the great rôles of the French classical theatre, Cinna, Néron, Oedipe and Oreste. His performances of these major parts made him the talk of that London where French was understood and appreciated. Lord Harcourt brought with him an entranced spectator, the Prince of Wales, and we hear that both gentlemen, as a result of such an experience, 'were overcome by the nobility of the French theatre'. Naturally Talma's renderings of these great classical parts could only be immature. His acting carried every precocious fault, exaggeration, mistimed outbursts, overheated imagination; briefly there was everywhere a lack of control. But nothing succeeded like excess. The divine fire was there, and however unsteady the flame its warmth went out to the audience.

The young Talma was not exclusively occupied, however, with his amateur actor compatriots. He set himself to master the English language, which he did with a fluency and an absence of foreign accent that amazed his hearers. He frequently went to the theatre and, although he missed David Garrick, he thrilled to the performances of that redoubtable brother and sister, John Philip Kemble and Sarah Siddons. Drury Lane and Covent Garden made him realize that Shakespeare must be acted with warmth and poetic feeling and also made him understand how wholly inadequate were Ducis' timid adaptations of such vivid, pulsating, dominant plays as *Hamlet* and *Romeo and Juliet*. He saw that the half had not been told him. Then there were his books also. As an avid reader he devoured the works of Milton, Pope, Thomson, Addison, Otway and, of course, Shakespeare. In any estimate of Talma as an artist, this English influence should not be minimized. To the end of his days his bedside books were *Shakespeare's Dramatic Works with Explanatory Notes and a Shakespearean Index* by Sam Ayscough, London 1790, and, acquired at a much later date, William Hazlitt's *Characters of Shakespeare's Plays*. So complete had become his mastery of the English tongue that the Prince of Wales offered to secure for him a contract to appear at one of the patent theatres, either Drury Lane or Covent Garden. To the accommodating Lord Harcourt fell the task of disclosing this suggestion to Talma's father who, whether by diplomacy or by genuine desire to acquiesce, put up no obstacles to the royal proposal.

The footlights of Drury Lane or Covent Garden were not destined to illumine the acting of François-Joseph Talma. The young stage aspirant was packed off to Paris to study anatomy at the École de Médecine and to practise dentistry in the cabinet of his uncle in the rue Mauconseil. Before we accompany Talma on his return to Paris, believed to have taken place on March 27th, 1784, some reference should be made to a highly romantic episode, often brought forward as an explanation of Talma's apparently sudden departure from London. The young Frenchman, through the agency of an unknown German-speaking servant, was invited to pay a secret visit to a lady in St. James's Palace. In a mysterious note, signed with the initial C, she expressed a desire to hear him recite to her privately Orosmane's passionate verses from Voltaire's tragedy *Zaïre*. Talma, scenting adventure of a possibly amorous kind, obediently followed his guide across Blackfriars Bridge and duly made the Arab hero's declaration of love to '*une très grande dame de Brunswick*', rather imperfectly concealed behind a screen, whence came prolonged sighs and something akin to voluptuous movement. When a small white hand was thrust forward, Talma's lips met it with more ardour than respect, but alas! the word 'enough' was pronounced by its owner with a grim finality, whereupon the young man was led away by a desiccated dowager and duly dismissed. Three days later there appeared in a scandal sheet called the *Evening Post* an article which purported to describe how a handsome young Arab named Amlat, on pretext of giving a recitation, had penetrated the private apartments of a great lady of Brunswick, the wife of a prince who in rank was second only to '*le sultan*'. The prince's sudden return to the Palace put an abrupt end to the poetry reading and the writer of the article concluded with a veiled threat. A day or so later that threat showed itself in a challenge to a duel which young Talma received, during a presumably chance encounter in Hyde Park, from an Englishman who, outraged by the *Evening Post* scandal, had seen through the flimsy Amlat anagram. One can imagine with what pride the highly imaginative and socially vain Talma would recount this cock-and-bull story around Parisian dining-tables when in reminiscent mood he talked of his London days. The fragrant note initialled C, the lady from Brunswick and the wife of a prince second only to a king, could have an added significance and topicality at a time when all Europe simulated suitable horror at the indiscretions of Caroline, Princess of Wales. But Talma's tale collapses utterly. Caroline of Brunswick did not set foot in England until she landed at Gravesend on April 2nd, 1795, when Talma, in Paris at that time, had more to think about than clandestine assignations in St. James's. Although a French scholar as late as 1928 [1] identifies the lady of the adventure as '*la duchesse de Brunswick*',[2] no evidence of a personage so illustrious exists in the court circulars of the time.

Talma's second wife, Caroline Vanhove, hints in her memoirs that during this period there were dissensions in the Talma household. We know that Talma had a younger brother, Jean-Joseph Talma, and two sisters, Anne-Gertrude and the beloved Euphrosine, who was at a later date to marry the painter Louis Ducis, son of the dramatist. It may well have been a family quarrel that induced Talma to follow his mother to Paris, where his dental studies both at the École de Médecine and in the rue Mauconseil would be supervised by his uncle Philippe.

---

[1] Guy de la Batut, *Talma. Correspondance*, p. 47.

[2] Princess Augusta (1737–1813), sister of George III, married Charles William Ferdinand, Hereditary Prince of Brunswick, in 1764. She became Duchess of Brunswick in 1780. Her much younger sister, Caroline Matilda (1751–1775), married Christian VII of Denmark. There was no Caroline of Brunswick in England until 1795.

CHAPTER 3

Return to Paris, March 1784

Talma in those last days of March 1784 returned to a Paris where the teachings of Voltaire, the *Encyclopédistes* and Jean-Jacques Rousseau were beginning to crystallize and leave their politically active deposit in young forward-looking minds. Barely had he settled in with Uncle Philippe in the rue Mauconseil than the daring situations and the even more daring dialogue of *Le Mariage de Figaro*, a comedy by one Beaumarchais, a watchmaker's son if you please, stirred the capital and dismayed the gentlemen of the royal bedchamber who were answerable to His Majesty King Louis XVI for the direction of the Comédie-Française, where this challenging play had been performed on April 22nd. Clearly there were stirrings beneath the surface of that elegant life which centred still in the Marais and the Palais-Royal. The cracks were yet fully to be revealed and for Talma, paying little heed to the signs of change, life was strenuous indeed. There were of course lectures, dissections, bleedings and operations to occupy him at the École de Médecine and this relatively grim routine brought to light something of Talma's sensitivity. He would faint even at dissections and this traffic with human corpses left him strangely obsessed. His second wife[1] tells us that all his life he claimed to see the skeleton beneath the living flesh and often, as he acted before his crowded audiences, he would muse how fleeting was the life of those spectators and how ignominious would be their final dissolution. Such macabre speculations allied to a deep-seated sensitivity explained for many of his later ad-mirers the heightened sense of poignant reality he brought to his great tragic creations, *Hamlet* especially. 'Alas, poor Yorick' was for him fraught with a terrible meaning.

Apart from these anatomical studies there were however certain compensations. Uncle Philippe's clientèle was fashionable and included Madame de Genlis, who was most anxious that the

[1] Caroline Talma, *Quelques Particularités*. Section XIV, pp. 300, I.

27

young dentist should accept the protection of the Duc de Chartres and ply his pincers in the ducal apartments of the Palais-Royal. This proposal came to nought. Talma's father in a letter from London dated September 6th, 1785, strongly advised his son not to barter his professional opportunities in the rue Mauconseil for the profitless honour of a sinecure in the Palais-Royal. And Talma *père* was right. In his uncle's circle the nephew met all sorts of interesting patients, even actors and actresses. Mlle. Flore[1] tells us that uncle Philippe had in his professional care the teeth of the whole company of the Comédie-Italienne, a responsibility that gave both uncle and nephew an entry backstage where she, as a member of this lighthearted troupe, renewed the acquaintance begun years before in M. Vaperot's school. The *théâtre* began to loom large in young Talma's life. Lord Harcourt, that powerful English friend, had asked his young protégé to put before Molé, soon to become in 1786 Doyen of the Comédie-Française, a scheme whereby that illustrious theatre would send to London a permanent company of actors to play in French a classical *répertoire*. The Prince of Wales promised to become a founder subscriber. Unfortunately Molé thought the scheme impractical, but at least it had from Talma's angle the merit of bringing him in contact with a leading personality of that great theatre. In any case he had become a regular playgoer, eager to meet the *vieux amateurs* of the parterre and to hear their memories, especially of Lekain and of those two great tragediennes Mesdemoiselles Clairon and Duménil. In connection with these early theatre-going days, a remark made by Talma on Larive's performance of Oreste in Racine's *Andromaque* deserves to be remembered. Asked by a connoisseur of acting what he thought of this rendering by Lekain's immediate successor as *chef d'emploi* for tragic rôles, the young man replied: 'If I ever played that part, I would perhaps not do it so well but I would do it differently.'

The struggle between the stage and dentistry still raged in the breast of young Talma. He had however to walk warily. In London was a dentist father pouring out in his letters professional advice and so obviously taking for granted his son's following his own career. In Paris his actor friends became more and more important and one, Dugazon, a Marseillais by adoption and a brilliant exponent of comic servants at the Comédie-Française, brought to his notice the founding on June 18th, 1786, of the

[1] Mlle Flore, Mémoires, pp. 9, 10, 11.

École Royale de Déclamation, later to become in 1793 Le Conservatoire. Talma, still continuing to practise dentistry, was accepted as one of its first pupils on July 13th, 1786, on the strength of his reading of the part of Xiparès in Racine's *Mithridate*. Here he remained as a student until May 31st, 1787, and during that period had the good fortune to sit at the feet of three remarkable teachers: Molé, now Doyen of the Comédie-Française and the creator of Ducis' *Hamlet*, Fleury, whose polished performances in Molière and Marivaux were always outstanding attractions at the same theatre, and of course Dugazon. During his student days at the École Royale de Déclamation Talma rehearsed no fewer than 180 parts from the classical repertory.

It is, however, important to indicate something of the instruction Talma received from these ornaments of the French stage. Dugazon, who took the Tuesday class, always insisted upon cultivating an actor's own resources independent of the author whose rôle he was called upon to interpret.[1] He taught the need for pantomime, the relevance of gesture, the technical skill to keep interest alive during gaps in the dialogue and above all the art of listening. He would say: 'The art of listening to each other with interest, to indicate facially the exchange of reciprocally felt emotions, to enter into the feelings of the actor playing opposite, this is indeed the acme of silent playing, the triumph of intelligence and the most abundant source of sensitivity.' Dear Dugazon, who throughout his life was Talma's devoted friend, claimed with true Marseillais exaggeration that he could move his nose in forty different ways and thus had at his disposal forty different facial expressions. The Thursday class fell to the corpulent Molé, a mannered tragedian reared in the pompous classical school but a well-graced actor withal. His versatility enabled him to assume leading rôles in comedy. His teaching and his own personal attitude to acting were to provide an admirable corrective to the exuberance of his student who, like the youth of that generation, was all afire with the new theories of Rousseau, firmly convinced that a blind obedience to Nature should be an actor's only guide. Molé was the apostle of faultless technique which enabled an actor to repeat the same performance night after night and to achieve complete credibility, even when living on the prompter's words. He was a fervent exponent of Diderot's *Paradoxe sur le*

[1] Regnault-Warin, *Mémoires sur Talma*, pp. 64 et seq. A. Copin, *Talma et la Révolution*, pp. 13, 14.

Comédien, ever insisting that Art must oust Nature with her hit or miss methods and in her own undisputed right dominate the contrived world of theatre.[1] Molé's contribution to Talma's acting can be summed up in a single word, control. Fleury taught on Saturdays.[2] Here came a fine artist, aristocratic of bearing, a veritable *talon rouge* and yet, in the sense the world gives to the word, totally uneducated. His father was the proprietor of the theatre at Nancy and the normal academic apprenticeship did not come his way. But oh! the polish of his playing! He was a master of mannered comedy, one whose rendering of that gigantic part of Alceste in *Le Misanthrope* ranks high in the annals of France's great national theatre. With his students, Fleury worked on their intelligence and sensitivity. For him the nuance was all important but he always stressed that delicate shades of meaning did not come to a part without effort. Talma was never to forget this master's insistence upon *'omnia vincit labor improbus'*. Fleury emphasized too that the good manners of human behaviour must permeate the *convenances* of the stage. His ideal was the smooth, polished performance and to achieve this an actor must have style. He is reported to have said to his student: 'You, M. Talma, have not so many difficulties to overcome as flights of fancy (*écarts*) to control. Happy is he in the arts who sins only by excess.'[3]

To English-speaking lovers of the theatre it seems almost fantastic that such a training could be given to young French players in 1786. Above all they were taught to speak and, no matter how humble their origin, they certainly acquired a perfect French. They learned that the art of declaiming the alexandrine depended upon moral as well as physical qualities. Inadequate breath control chilled the genial current of the classical line and robbed it of its real value. Only an enunciation complete in its physical and technical mastery could bring to Racine's poetry full significance and deep feeling. Art and artifice, polish and style, intelligence and *sensibilité*, facial expression and mime, to say nothing of the actor's disciplined surrender to the total demands of a play in performance, these were some of the lessons Talma learned under masters at an academy that only a national theatre, conscious of its traditions and of its duty to posterity, could so fittingly provide.

[1] Regnault-Warin, *Mémoires sur Talma*, pp. 65 et seq.
[2] Ibid, pp. 102 et seq.   [3] Regnault-Warin, *Mémoires sur Talma*, p. 109.

Outside the theatre school and the dentist's consulting room Talma led an exciting social life. We find him mingling with lawyers whose need to stimulate their own oratory through '*cours de rhétorique*' provided a common interest in declamation; he was now rubbing shoulders with the theatre personalities of that time; perhaps most fortunate for later development were his contacts with musicians, painters and sculptors. In Jacques-Louis David, the artist later to become a member of the Convention and official painter under the Revolution and the Empire, Talma found deep and lasting friendship [1] and an influence which was to make itself felt profoundly in his acting. David's studio in the rue de Seine was to become a rendez-vous for all artists and politicians who believed in the new ideas beginning everywhere to stir and to presage the revolutionary storm. Although Talma liked to call himself an *enfant de la Révolution*, it was the neo-classicism of David rather than the noisy affirmations of political slogans that profoundly influenced the actor student. Through David's eyes Talma saw how Greek and Roman heroes should dress and move against a background of Athenian and Roman life to which, at that date, the French theatre had paid little heed.

Of course there were love affairs, but the amours of one so handsome can interest us only as they affect his work in the theatre. Under circumstances truly romantic Talma became acquainted with a young lady, destined to become Louise Desgarcins, who was in the habit of reciting Racine to her mother in a secluded part of the Jardin du Roi, not far from where Buffon's house stood and which today is known as the Jardin des Plantes. [2] The reader must be spared Regnault-Warin's highly coloured and detailed account—it runs to eighty-three pages—of this idyllic platonic association. Talma persuaded this young woman—blessed with a lovely voice but compelled because of some affection of the chest to wear a veil—to discard her disfiguring trappings, to breathe clean air and by more skilful medical treatment to regain her strength. When a woman student at the École, due to play Atalide in Racine's *Bajazet*, was stricken with sudden illness, Talma brought Mlle Desgarcins, who knew the part, to fill the gap. This the modest young lady agreed to do on condition that she retained her veil. As the play has a Turkish setting, the veil seemed not unduly out of place. However, in her big emotional

---

[1] A. Copin, *Talma et la Révolution*, p. 17.
[2] Regnault-Warin, *Mémoires sur Talma*, pp. 140 et seq.

scene with Roxane, she accidentally let it fall and, revealed in all her beauty, gave a display of such emotional power that carried her to the point of collapse. This event decided Mlle Desgarcins' career for, with the powerful aid of M. Malesherbes, a one-time Minister of Finance who had befriended both mother and daughter, she enrolled as a student at the École Royale de Déclamation and subsequently made a successful début at the Comédie-Française.

Before making his final decision to abandon dentistry, Talma on Dugazon's advice undertook to appear before a paying audience in a little theatre that Doyen, a house painter, had constructed in the Marais, to be precise in the rue Notre-Dame-de-Nazareth. [1] Doyen was fanatically interested in the theatre and his '*petit spectacle bourgeois*' was sympathetically regarded by such actors as Molé, Fleury and their colleague Vanhove who played *pères nobles* at the Français. It was before the highly critical audience that Doyen never failed to assemble that Talma made his bow as Achille in *Iphigénie en Tauride*, not to be confused with Racine's *Iphigénie*, but a very conventionally patterned piece of stage mechanics by a certain Guimond de la Touche, an unfrocked Jesuit. Despite the applause of the audience and the encouragement of his friends, Talma was thoroughly dissatisfied with his performance. This initial effort served at least to reveal to Parisian playgoers his virile beauty of form and face, his graceful carriage and his exquisite delivery of the verse. But Talma still doubted his powers; not for nothing was he the son of a father from the Nord and a mother from Lorraine. Still greater became his indecision when Mlle. Sainval of the Comédie-Française, who after a sensational début had failed to justify her early promise pointed out how mad it would be to give up a secure, lucrative profession to risk the hazards of unemployment and the caprice of a fickle public. [2] On the other hand came Mlle Fleury, [3] no relation of Talma's teacher but a popular actress of the same theatre, to convince him that he had the necessary talent and to beg him, Dugazon seconding her every word, to obtain the necessary authorization for his début at the Comédie-Française. This the devoted Dugazon undertook with all commendable speed. Mlle Fleury's encouragement was decisive. Talma chose the stage.

[1] A. Copin, *Talma et la Révolution*, p. 14. *Mémoires de Mlle Flore*, pp. 447, 448.
[2] Regnault-Warin, *Mémoires sur Talma*, p. 225.   [3] Ibid, p. 225.

CHAPTER 4

Début at the Comédie-Française

On November 21st, 1787, François-Joseph Talma aged twenty-four made his début at the old Théâtre-Français, where stands today the Théâtre de l'Odéon, in Voltaire's *Mahomet*, playing the rôle of Séïde before a very well filled house worth 3,403 livres, 8 sols.[1] It is not difficult to understand why the young actor chose Séïde for this great ordeal. It was a most effective, even showy part. Voltaire makes his young religious fanatic Séïde, under the influence of the charlatan Mahomet, kill Zopire, who turns out to be not only his own father but the father of his beloved Palmyre. Séïde, torn between fanaticism and a loathing of murder, endures before the awful deed an agony of mind which carries him to the point of frenzy in which he sees supernatural omens, a ghost, moving shadows, blood red flashes of light in the gloomy recesses of the altar where his victim stands. This makes a terrific situation with an Act Five to dispose of all the horror and confusion the murder of Zopire has evoked. Here indeed was a part to get one's teeth into and Voltaire's hatred of religious intolerance was something to which Talma all his life would subscribe. Making a considerable advance upon his first effort, Talma repeated his performance of Séïde four days later on November 25th.

The faithful Dugazon had warned his young protégé not to be carried away by applause. Had not Lekain and Fleury been hissed in their time? Aim at the highest, he advised. Give of your best but you must make an impression and arouse a sense of curiosity in the spectators. If you can bring vigour and truth to your performance, you will win the approval of all.[2] We may be quite sure that Talma did all in his power to carry out his master's advice, but it must be confessed that his débuts were in no way spectacular. He had earned a modest success. At a time when dramatic

[1] *Archives de la Comédie-Française.*
[2] Regnault-Warin, *Mémoires sur Talma*, p. 276, 277.

criticism tended to extend its space upon the play rather than upon the acting, we find the Abbé Duviquet writing in the *Journal de Paris*, November 22nd, 1787: 'The young actor who made his début yesterday in the rôle of Séïde in the tragedy *Mahomet* gives every promise. He has moreover every physical advantage that it is possible to desire in an actor for *jeune premier* parts—figure, face and voice—and rightly the public applauded him, especially in the first three acts. The fourth requires an abandon and a mastery of miming rarely found in the range of a beginner; but we believe that with hard work this actor can hope for brilliant successes.' Let us not forget that the highly adulatory even absurdly flattering notices of some of our contemporary critics had not been invented. Parisian playgoers would interpret this opinion as cautious encouragement to a young man of promise.

Talma's official débuts continued through November and December. On November 27th he appeared as the Young Brahmin in Lemierre's *La Veuve du Malabar*, a part in which the young actor was called upon to show lofty philosophical detachment, a love of independence and a hatred of fanaticism and superstition. Two days later, November 29th, he gave a taste of his quality in comedy, playing on the same evening Euphémon in *L'Enfant prodigue* and Valère in *L'École des Maris*. Early December saw him as Saint-Albin in *Le Père de Famille*, an exacting part that called for a passionate outburst and the portrayal of an ensuing crazed mind. On December 22nd he played Pylade opposite the fixed star Larive as Oreste in *Iphigénie en Tauride*. After the performance, in Larive's dressing-room were gathered the playwrights Ducis, Lemierre and Palissot as well as the Abbé Duviquet.[1] All these judges were unanimous in the praise they accorded to Talma's handling '*avec beaucoup de vérité*' of the significant *jeune premier* part. On December 26th the young actor's débuts came to an end. After a very creditable rendering of the testing rôle of Égisthe in Voltaire's *Mérope*, Talma was received on that same day as *pensionnaire du roi*, a junior member of the Maison de Molière, with the precisely stipulated functions of playing third parts.[2] To be received for '*les troisièmes rôles*' was certainly no overwhelming triumph; it was at least an honourable success.

An interesting sidelight is thrown upon Talma's débuts by

[1] Regnault-Warin, *Mémoires sur Talma*, p. 284.
[2] *Archives de la Comédie-Française.*

Bachaumont in his *Mémoires Secrets*. He writes: 'He (Talma) achieved success in comedy and tragedy. To natural gifts he adds attractive features, a sonorous and sensitive voice, a pure and distinct enunciation. He himself feels and makes his audience feel the beauty of the verse; his bearing is manly, his movements are natural. Above all he is always in good taste and has no affectation. He imitates no actor and plays in accordance with his own feelings and his own resources.' M. Regnault-Warin disputes the sonorous voice. With twenty-five years' first-hand experience of Talma's acting behind him he states: 'Never in our opinion had he a sonorous voice but within its own range it was penetrating, slightly vibrant, sensitive and therefore tragic'.[1] All subsequent evidence goes to show that this is a sound judgment. Talma never had the consciously beautiful voice of the elocutionist; he possessed the powerful, flexible instrument of the actor. While dealing still with the *débutant* we should record that Ducis was convinced from the very start that Talma was a great actor and that he clearly saw in his playing those qualities that he himself knew were required for the great Shakespearean rôles his own pallid adaptations would provide. Yet Ducis' opinion is of interest. He discerned something of an English quality that would help Talma to project French tragic acting out of the rut into which it had fallen during this latter part of the eighteenth century. And what, may one ask, of the final arbiters, the parterre, the paying public? At this stage the record runs: 'He had his following, his art was enjoyed, he was appreciated.'[2]

[1] Regnault-Warin, *Mémoires sur Talma*, p. 281, footnote.
[2] Regnault-Warin, *Mémoires sur Talma*, p. 283.

CHAPTER 5

Difficulties in a National Theatre

The time has come to look a little more closely into the affairs of this great organization, the Comédie-Française. The theatre was founded in 1680, when the players at the Hôtel de Bourgogne joined forces with the members of Molière's various troupes who, after the playwright's death in 1673, had had a somewhat chequered history. Thus was founded, with royal consent, the Maison de Molière, a name still in use, and bestowed as a tribute to the memory of that supreme artist. The theatre however, early in its history, acquired the name of the Comédie-Française in order to distinguish it from the much longer established Comédie-Italienne. This newly formed Théâtre-Français was in essentials a *société* or a fellowship of players. Its actors were graded in two categories, the *pensionnaires* and the *sociétaires*.[1] The *pensionnaires*, as we have seen in Talma's case, were generally the *débutants*, engaged at a fixed salary to play specified parts as they would have been in any other theatre. The *sociétaires* were really the co-proprietors of the dramatic enterprise called the Comédie-Française. It was they who controlled the theatre either by decisions taken in general assembly or through a *Comité* composed of a few members, elected by the other *sociétaires* and instructed to carry out special duties, among them the reading of new plays. As regards remuneration the *sociétaires* received fees (*des feux*) for each performance and at the end of the year a share (*une part entière* or *une fraction de part*) in the net profits earned. The number of shares available, *parts entières*, during the latter part of the eighteenth century, varied from 34 (21 men, 13 women) to 23, and the exact fraction of a share to be allocated to a newly accepted *sociétaire* would be determined by the *Comité*, according to the player's length of

---

[1] Sylvie Chevalley, Bibliothécaire-archiviste de la Comédie-Française. The first official use of the term *sociétaire* occurs in Napoleon's Acte de société signed by the actors on April 17th, 1804.

experience, notoriety, influence, talent or zeal. *Une part entière* was considered the highest distinction the theatre in France could confer upon any actor or actress. After twenty years' service a *sociétaire* qualified for a pension and a farewell benefit performance.

Royal patronage loomed large in the affairs of the Comédie-Française. It would be erroneous to suppose that the *sociétaires* exercised a completely autonomous control. There were the court functionaries to reckon with, the *gentilshommes de la chambre du roi*. These gentlemen of the bedchamber acted as something more than liaison officers between the Comédie and the King. Under the ancien régime their power over the theatre was supreme. Royal interference during the reigns of Louis XIV, Louis XV and even in the less autocratic and more uncertain days of Louis XVI and Marie Antoinette, weighed very heavily upon the *sociétaires*. The gentlemen of the bedchamber could and did play a preponderating part at the Théâtre-Français. They could imprison actors and actresses at Fors l'Evêque for indiscipline, with M. le Lieutenant-Général de Police giving the immediate order. They could further opportunities for débuts, working upon the Minister of the Interior, whose authorization was essential before any newcomer could appear. They could advance the fortunes of an actress—the commerce of love and of the theatre had a common currency at their disposal. They could cause plays to be withdrawn and others to be produced. They could persuade the King to grant pensions to favoured players. In 1787 M. le Maréchal, duc de Duras, *premier gentilhomme de la chambre du roi*, was the all-powerful functionary. It is noteworthy that, thanks to the personal preference of Marie Antoinette, comedy flourished in court circles and the oft commanded team from the Théâtre-Français as a result of such favours began to assume almost excessive royalist pretension, little dreaming of the troubles to come. The gentlemen of the bedchamber cared little for the ever increasing vogue for tragedy which gave authors like Voltaire opportunities well and truly taken to deride tyrants, challenge kingly power and unmask political intrigue. Certainly the new ideas of the *philosophes* failed to fit in with the nicely graduated society of Versailles, whose types still live abundantly in the comedies of Molière, Regnard and Marivaux.

Formidable obstacles stood between the eager Talma and his burning desire to act the great tragic rôles. He soon saw that the

Comédie-Française was a hierarchy in which seniority appeared to be the massive qualification. For every type of part there was a recognized leading player, a *chef d'emploi*, and almost always a senior member of the company. There were *chefs d'emploi* for tragedy kings, for *jeunes premiers*—*jeunes* by the way had no real chronological significance—for principal confidants, for heavy fathers, for valets, for queens, for young princesses—dowagers not debarred—for coquettes, for soubrettes, for character parts (*rôles marqués*) and so forth. Then came the seconds, those actors who had second claim upon a part, and after them there were the *doubles* or understudies. In such a world rivalries and jealousies abounded. *Pensionnaires* intrigued to become *sociétaires*, *sociétaires* fought progressively for the coveted *part entière*. Understudies grumbled either because they were denied opportunity to appear in worthwhile parts or because they were exploited at short notice to replace tired or lazy actors. In the green-room could be heard the lamentations of the playwrights, railing against a classical repertory that selfishly held the stage to the exclusion of contemporary effort. Quarrels, factions, fleeting alliances occurred all too often. Talma, a mere newly received *pensionnaire*, was not going to find life easy within those august portals.

It was not long before he realized that brief and few would be his appearances on the stage of the Théâtre-Français. In tragedy the *chef d'emploi* was Lekain's immediate successor, Jean Mauduit, known as Larive, whose service went back to December 3rd, 1770, when, as a pupil of that high priestess, Mlle. Clairon, he made his début as Zamore in Voltaire's *Alzire*, with the instructress ensconced in the prompter's box to direct his every line, whispering advice on voice, gesture and movement. As Baron Grimm tells us in his *Correspondance*, Larive was an essentially mediocre performer who relied upon a booming voice and a good figure. Nevertheless he clung tenaciously to his rights and privileges. Molé, to whom reference has already been made, was now Doyen. After the failure of his début, on November 7th, 1754, he had endured exile in the provinces until his triumphant return on January 28th, 1760. His versatile playing, both in comedy and tragedy, won for him certain prescriptive rights over particular major rôles. There was also Monvel, a really brilliant actor, all fire and intelligence, but whose cerebral gifts were not equally balanced by physical attributes. His first appearance on April 28th, 1770, was hailed as an earnest of future outstanding

successes, but he became so impatient at being kept subordinate to
Larive and Molé that he obtained permission from the *Comité* to
undertake tours as far away as Sweden, in which country he remained nine years. Junior to these three chief custodians of all
tragic rôles were Saint-Prix, who was engaged as an understudy to
Larive, and Saint-Fal, a 'second' for tragic parts. Both Saint-Prix
and Saint-Fal were received in 1782; both were by no means without talent and gave every promise of success if and when opportunity knocked at their doors. Nor must martial Naudet be forgotten, a giant in inches if not in dramatic worth, who had joined
the company three years before Talma and combined with his acting responsibilities a military command in the Garde Bourgeoise.
Inadequate as an actor, he was a touchy, quarrelsome man, swift
to action with fists or sword. There was also Vanhove, quite a
character this fellow, who monopolized the *pères nobles*. With such
a number of senior colleagues, all eager to assert their claims,
Talma might well wonder what chance had he, an essentially
tragic actor, gifted physically and intellectually, to give a taste
of his quality in a major rôle.

It would require too much of the reader's time and patience
if an exact account of the ladies of the company, their histrionic
talents, their amorous adventures, their intrigues and their
jealousies were to be attempted. It will suffice to say that acting
ability alone rarely proved an adequate passport to the *sociétariat*.
This was for actresses the age of the powerful protector and the
gentilshommes de la chambre did not scruple to press their advantages.
The performances they had in mind differed somewhat in scope
and character from the more orthodox services required by Thalia
or Melpomene. At the time of Talma's entry, the great Louise
Contat queened it in comedy. She was judged by admirers and
critics alike a truly polished comédienne, and the fact that she
bore three children out of wedlock to three of her many aristocratic lovers might indicate carelessness but was otherwise
deemed quite irrelevant to her status. When Célimène was not
gracing the boards of the Comédie-Française, she lived lavishly in
her château at Ivry, which her *part entière*, augmented by a pension
of one thousand livres from the King, failed fully to maintain.
The really outstanding tragic personality was Mlle Raucourt,
who, since 1779, on the instruction of the Duc de Duras, had had
first claim on all the tragedy queens. Mlle Raucourt's private
life was a public scandal. An avid Lesbian, she lived with the

infamous Madame Souck, a German of horribly depraved morals who, like the actress, wore male attire: by their disgraceful behaviour in public places these two women shocked a generation that was not easily upset by sexual deviations.[1] Nevertheless Mlle Raucourt was a remarkable tragic actress, the last representative of the imposing Clairon tradition.[2] Off the stage she was masterful, overbearing, ever difficult. Male colleagues in violent disputes with her were goaded to address her: 'Ah! Monsieur.' Before an audience she showed herself majestic, proud and often deeply moving. In such exacting parts as Cléopâtre, Médée, Jocaste and Agrippine, her contemporaries voted her unsurpassed. As we shall see later, she and Talma fought many battles and shared many triumphs. Two other ladies must be mentioned at this point. Dugazon's sister, Madame Vestris, who had married the brother of 'the god of the dance', when not quarrelling over parts with her hated rivals, the two demoiselles Sainval, could always be trusted to give a powerful rendering of any tragic rôle. The other actress, Caroline Vanhove, daughter of the good old stager already mentioned, staggered Paris by her débuts in 1785 when, as a mere child of fourteen, she played with astonishing success Racine's Iphigénie. So brilliant was her acting, enhanced by beauty of face and voice, that her débuts were prolonged beyond the normal term for box-office reasons. Even the great Contat took umbrage at such popularity, but not for long. The queen of comedy had noticed that Caroline was inclined to overdo her actions and she persuaded the young artiste to act with a cotton thread tied to her wrists, which Louise herself, stationed in the wings, sharply jerked at times to remind the novice that rather less exuberance of gesture was desirable. Of course we shall meet many more interesting ladies, but in a life of Talma the women who affected his playing must claim prior attention.

With such an established organization which, in spite of all abuses, had at its disposal the best of contemporary talent, the Théâtre-Français had as its first duty to keep alive by constant revival the great classical *répertoire* of the seventeenth century and what looked like surviving from the first half of the eighteenth. We are dealing with an age when comedy and tragedy were two rigidly separated genres and the mere idea of their

---

[1] Émile Campardon, *Les Comédiens du Roi*, pp. 249, 250, 251, 152.
[2] Talma's last tribute at the time of her burial on Jan. 17th, 1815.

mingling in one and the same play repelled critic and playgoer alike. If comedy, thanks to the liberating example of Molière and the innovations of Marivaux, enjoyed a somewhat more flexible development, the canons for tragedy were strictly and narrowly applied. French classical tragedy received its form and its highest expression in the masterpieces of Corneille and Racine, who bequeathed to their successors perfect examples of the five act play, tautly bound by the Aristotelian unities of time, place and action, written in rhyming alexandrines around a subject drawn from Greek or Roman history or mythology. The rare exceptions to this *'merveilleux païen'* in the seventeenth century can be seen in Racine's one excursion into a Turkish environment with *Bajazet* (1672), and his preoccupation with the Old Testament in *Esther* (1689) and *Athalie* (1691). Within the framework of this highly restricted form, Corneille had portrayed the Roman super-man, often at grips with love and duty in political problems; Racine exploited a penetrating analysis of love intrigues which, credible in an ancient Greek setting, reflected more accurately the silken dalliance of the Sun King's court at Versailles. To these flawless masterpieces the *semainier* responsible for drawing up the week's playbills could add the complicated and psychologically feeble plays of Crébillon, notably *Rhadamiste et Zénobie* (1711), and many of the experiments in tragedy of Monsieur de Voltaire who, having viewed with disapproval the emancipated plays of William Shakespeare, nevertheless thought that the narrower confines of Corneille and Racine might with advantage be ex-tended. This he proceeded to show by recourse to the Middle Ages and even to such remote civilizations as Peru and China for his subject matter. Again, he quickened the pace of his dramas, often with implausible plots, adding to them all the excitement of armed crowds, ghosts and occasionally a murder, in defiance of erudite strict decree that never should the stage be stained with blood. So much for the repertory of tragedy.

New plays of course had to be produced and the predominance in literary circles of the ideas of the *philosophes* encouraged poets to turn their attention to Roman politics and Greek tyrants, where telling parallels could challenge, without too much danger from the censorship, the corrupt government of the Ancien Régime. These contemporary plays as we shall see were often the mere dead bones of Cornelian and Racinian prototypes and, if occasionally a timid innovation appeared, the lamentable absence of that penetrating psychology and high moral purpose, the very hallmark of their seventeenth century masters, made the literary children of Marie-Joseph Chénier, Népomucène Lemercier, Gabriel Legouvé and Jean-François Ducis seem still-born babes offered to a heedless posterity. The inflated, grandiose quality of the dialogue, *le style noble*, which required princess and serving-maid to speak the same high-falutin language, rolled from the player's tongue in stilted, sing-song delivery. Of course great parts like the Cornelian rôles of Cinna, Auguste, Horace, Polyeucte and the Racinian protagonists Oreste, Néron, Mithridate, Joad, remained ever powerful magnets to attract the mettle of the ambitious actor. The time too had come for such terrific parts to be revitalized in performances less stereotyped than the conventional routines accorded them in 1787. Talma earnestly thought so. But when, he asked himself, would he ever get an opportunity to endow them with nature and truth?

CHAPTER 6

Talma's Costume Reforms

After the excitement of his début, Talma endured some wearisome months. It irked this newly accepted *pensionnaire du roi* to find there was so little call upon his services for, apart from occasional appearances in quite minor rôles, he was given no real chance to display his undoubted talents. To his great credit the young actor spent much of his enforced leisure in serious study. He nourished a real passion for antiquity and, fired by David, that ardent apostle of *néo-classicisme*, he devoted those energies yet untapped by the theatre to earnest research in the field of Greek and Roman life, with a particular emphasis upon costume. It will be remembered that the eighteenth century in its middle flight saw the uncovering of Pompeii, and the writings of the French *savant*, the abbé Barthélemy, and of the German archaeologist, Winkelmann, opened up for that generation new vistas of knowledge and thought about the ancient world.

In French tragedy local colour had yet to be born and only the references in text to classical history gave these tragic themes any local significance. The players entrusted with such parts paid little heed to veracity of costume or décor. An actor's stage wardrobe at that time consisted mainly of clothes extravagantly cut, showily decorated and strictly in contemporary styles. We know of the first timid departures from such dressing, devised by Lekain and Mlle Clairon,[1] who to their great credit suppressed the monstrous *hanches*, those horse-hair hip pads, which were fastened to the figure so that the contemporary costume would stand out in an imposing way and give its wearer the impression of 'filling the stage'. With the suppression of the *hanches* came the disappearance of the *paniers*, which all too long had forced upon Agrippine and Phèdre the mincing gait of the eighteenth-century salon. On August 20th, 1755, occurred the noteworthy production

[1] Lanzac de Laborie, *Paris sous Napoléon*. Le Théâtre-Français, p. 24. Germain Bapst, *L'Histoire du Théâtre*, pp. 463, 464.

of Voltaire's *Orphelin de la Chine* with Lekain as Gengis-Khan and Mlle Clairon as the heroine, Idamé. Here was a play that went far beyond Greco-Roman frontiers and Voltaire, anxious to add a touch of chinoiserie to his scenes, generously waived his royalties in order that they might be passed on to the actors to purchase costumes more in keeping with the spirit of his tragedy.[1] Very discreet however were the innovations achieved. A few mandarin hats, an occasional close-fitting long silken gown and a flutter of peacocks' feathers hardly transported the spectators to the city of Cambalu, the ancient Pekin. Still it was a beginning. Elsewhere Marmontel in the *Encyclopédie* and other publications railed against the appalling anachronisms permitted on the French stage. He wanted to know why the barbaric Gustavus Wasa should emerge from a cavern in Dalcarlia immaculately clad in a sky-blue suit trimmed with ermine. Larive, Lekain's successor, had grave doubts about the rightness of playing Caesar in a full-bottomed powdered wig, satin breeches and red-heeled shoes. Despite such questionings, stage costume before Talma's reforms took little account of the period of the play. Garments were spangled and fringed. Gloves had become such a vital necessity to an actor's by-play that he refused to discard them. Néron, Mithridate, Oreste waved huge feathered hats and we know that old Vanhove wore indiscriminately for all his Greek and Roman parts a cuirasse of green velvet enriched with golden sequins and heavily decorated with a design of cannons, drums and rifles.[2] The sceptre reserved for the actor playing the title rôle in *La Mort de César* bore the fleur de lys.

To add to the reformers' difficulties, the Court had very definite views as to how a player should be attired. An unpowdered actor dispensing with a wig offered an affront to His Majesty whose *sociétaire* or *pensionnaire* he was. Larive on one occasion was sharply reproved by an *Intendant des Menus Plaisirs* for daring to appear in the royal presence with his hair unpowdered and his arms bare.

The way of historical accuracy was indeed hard, as Talma himself would soon find. Restrained designs and appropriate materials, essential if any sense of the period were to be conveyed, stood a poor chance against the flaunting silks and velvets of the latest fashions. Early in January 1789, Talma had been cast for the seventeen-line part of Proculus, a military tribune, in Voltaire's

[1] Germain Bapst, *L'Histoire du Théâtre*, pp. 466, 467.
[2] A. V. Arnault, *Les Souvenirs d'un sexagénaire*, Vol. I, pp. 273, 274.

Brutus. Dressed for the part, he had to cross the green roo[m] his way to the wings. Louise Contat, surrounded by her fri[ends] caught sight of him and uttered a cry that has become legen[d] in the annals of the French theatre. 'Look at Talma! How ugly he is! He looks just like one of those old statues.'[1] Here came Talma's moment of triumph. Unfurling the scroll he carried in his hand, he showed her David's sketch of his costume, Roman toga and footwear to be worn and his own hair. When he took his place on the stage beside breeched and bewigged Brutus, Titus and Valerius, the parterre gasped its astonishment and then burst into frantic applause.

From that night onwards, Talma dressed his part in strict conformity with the period of the play. He remembered his London play-going days and recalled how Mrs. Bellamy, Macklin and Kemble by their costumes made every effort to evoke a vanished past. The approval with which the parterre greeted Talma's innovation compelled the *Comité* to pay a little more attention to this aspect of production. There were indeed die-hard opponents. Replenishment of wardrobe was no light expense for an actor. Old Vanhove went so far as to describe Talma's reforms as 'mad'. 'Tragedy no longer exists in France,' was his remark on being confronted with a print from the Bibliothèque Nationale for his costume as Burrhus in *Britannicus*.[2] When the costume arrived, finding no pocket for his handkerchief, he turned angrily to the wardrobe master: 'Do you know, sir, that for more than thirty years I have played tragic parts and that I have always had pockets and shall always have them? Did not the Romans ever wipe their noses? Or do you claim that they wiped them with their fingers?' The old boy got two pockets, one for his handkerchief, the other for his snuffbox.[3]

With the passing of the years this reform of stage costume was to be one of the great contributions Talma made to his profession. He received inestimable help from David, Girodet and Gros, painters determined to obliterate the falsity of the so-called classical pictures of Vanloo, Boucher and Watteau. In addition, he ransacked museums, studied collections of old prints, noted the decorations on vases, the effigies on old coins. The following letter shows how he borrowed from museums.

[1] Regnault-Warin, *Mémoires sur Talma*, p. 307.
[2] E. de Manne, *La Troupe de Talma*, p. 98.
[3] E. de Manne, *La Troupe de Talma*, p. 32.

This day, the eleventh of Fructidor in the year II of the French Republic, one and indivisible, the Citizens Varon and Picault, members of the temporary Arts Commission, by virtue of powers entrusted to them, called to reclaim a marble foot with tragic sock, which had been lent to me by Citizen Monge, curator of the antiquities section of the former Church of Sainte-Geneviève; the aforesaid foot I promise to send back to the Conservatoire of the Arts Museum, together with a Spanish helmet which I have told them belongs to the same section.

Paris this II Fructidor, year II of the French Rep. one and indiv. (*28th Sept.* 1793)

FRANÇ TALMA.

On September 23rd, 1794, Talma and Monvel shared the leads in Lemierre's old fashioned piece of stage carpentry *Guillaume Tell* (1766). Through the courtesy of the officials of the Helvetic Republic, they studied a medal struck shortly after the hero's death in order that their costumes should conform historically. Those who saw this production affirm that Tell and Gessler were suitably dressed but that the smaller parts and supers were rigged out in contemporary comic opera silks and satins.[1]

Towards the end of his career, when Talma came to write *Réflexions sur Lekain et sur l'art théâtral*, he looked back upon this struggle to reform stage costume. 'I became a painter in my fashion; I had much obstinacy and prejudice to overcome, less from the public than from the actors; finally success crowned my efforts; and without fear of presumption I can say that my example exerted a great influence upon all the theatres of Europe.' He would remind the actor careless of historical detail that 'the theatre somehow must offer to young people a living course of history. Does not such negligence rob it, in their eyes, of its real nature? Does it not give them altogether false ideas about the life of peoples and about the characters tragedy seeks to recreate?'[2]

Let us return to the young actor at the Comédie-Française. In the round of small supporting parts from the classical repertory Talma, between July 4th, 1788 and March 6th, 1789, was entrusted with four *créations*, parts in four brand new plays. Oddly enough, all four rôles were in comedies, all now quite forgotten, but interesting to us as evidence that senior colleagues stood between him and any opportunity to act contemporary tragedies. His Clitandre in *La Jeune Épouse*, a comedy by Cubière, did not set the

---

[1] Germain Bapst, *L'Histoire du Théâtre*, p. 516.
[2] Regnault-Warin's reprint of Talma's *Réflexions sur Lekain*, p. 519.

Seine on fire. On September 13th, 1788, he appeared in the not
very exciting part of Le Chevalier Tristan in André de Murville's
Lanval et Viviane, a 'heroic comedy' which Grimm tells us 'in
spite of a few pretty verses seemed cold and dull'. A more
exciting chance came with Le Comte d'Orsange in *Le Présomptueux* by Fabre d'Églantine, an acknowledged wit of the day.
Unfortunately a rough house for its first night, January 7th,
1789, demonstrated through paid bullies that the play owed too
much to Colin d'Harleville's *Châteaux en Espagne,* a work
scheduled for production in the following February. Despite the
brouhaha of conflicting *claques,* Talma attracted notice by his
portrayal of the lively Provençal nobleman. In Dezède's threadbare comedy, *Les Deux Pages* March 6th, 1789, Talma, in the tiny
part of the English valet, astonished Paris by his wonderful
English accent and by the amount of laughter he aroused by his
skilful playing. His days as *pensionnaire* drew to a close because on
April 1st, 1789, François-Joseph Talma entered the ranks of the
sociétaires, but only to play *'les troisièmes rôles'.*

CHAPTER 7

Political Divisions at the Comédie-Française

U nder the Ancien Régime it was customary for the Théâtre-Français to close its doors before Holy Week and re-open with the next year's programme after a three weeks Easter recess. At closure and re-opening the public were addressed from the stage by a *sociétaire* instructed to express the *Comité*'s gratitude for past favours and the hope of their continuance during the following season. When the theatre re-opened on April 20th, 1789, Talma as the most junior *sociétaire* was deputed to deliver what the actors called '*le compliment*', on this occasion a speech written by the contemporary dramatist, Marie-Joseph Chénier. It should be remembered that this re-opening of the Comédie-Française with *Athalie* and Chabanne's slight comedy *La Matinée à la mode*, occurred at a time when the capital was much disturbed. A spirit of revolt was in the air. The States-General had been summoned; the notorious '*brigands*' made the streets unsafe and seven days later on April 27th, all too near the theatre, an out-of-hand crowd fired the house of the grasping wallpaper manufacturer, Réveillon, in the Faubourg Saint-Antoine. Here were the first drops that presaged the revolutionary storm.

Talma, very conscious of his responsibilities, proceeded to deliver from the footlights a speech that differed considerably in tone and content from the sugary orations to which the public had long been accustomed. Chénier was of the stuff of which revolutionaries are made. After a few conventional remarks about the glory of the national theatre, its educative rôle and the intellectual pleasure it gave to a public generous with its support and applause, he put into the mouth of the young Talma veiled references to existing discontents, which the censor never allowed to appear in the printed text of the speech. The following passage gave particular offence:

Never does your support become more precious, never must we (actors) desire your applause more fervently than when besides being a sign of good taste, they are also proof of good sense and an expression of public feeling. At what time, Gentlemen, are we to be allowed to give utterance to this opinion and to proclaim it before a numerous and worthy assembly if not at the present moment when, at the call of a popular prince, the fatherland is born again and sees, united around its cradle, all the virtues of the citizen? You know, Gentlemen, how the image of all these virtues is recreated here before your eyes every evening in plays of which we are the interpreters, exactly as the seed of those same virtues existed in the mind and talent of their industrious authors. Therefore let us be allowed to share in their triumph which still more is yours, Gentlemen, by the agreement of your views with theirs.[1]

Contemporary accounts assure us that Talma delivered the speech most gracefully and called forth enthusiastic applause from the whole audience. Back stage the same unanimity did not obtain. Political events were moving fast. The *sociétaires* were sharply divided. The majority, the *rétrogrades, les aristocrates*, looked to the Court and saw none of the virtue in the new trends Chénier advocated so earnestly. They shut their eyes to what was happening around them; on the other hand, Talma, Dugazon, Mme Vestris and Mlle. Desgarcins, now a member of the troupe, were the *avancés, l'escadre rouge*. The revolutionary spirit proved a great stimulus to Talma who, without its inspiration, might so easily have vegetated in minor rôles. In a private letter[2] he said that he saw history made before his eyes; he beheld living tragedy and every event of which he was a witness gave him food for thought which he turned to the profit of his art. Playwright Chénier might well try to indicate through the persuasive voice of Talma impending change. He himself was busy revising his tragedy *Charles IX*. As preface to this play he wrote a 'Dedicatory Epistle to the French Nation', which makes all too clear the political feelings and ideas that animated its author. The following paragraphs deserve quotation.

Frenchmen, my fellow citizens, accept the homage of this patriotic tragedy. I dedicate the work of a free man to a nation become free. . . . Dictatorial authority you have brought to naught; you will achieve laws and moral standards. Your theatre must change with all the rest. A drama of mincing fops no longer suffices for men and citizens.

[1] Quoted in full by A. Copin, *Talma et la Révolution*, pp. 31-33.
[2] E. de Manne, *La Troupe de Talma*, p. 100.

More exalted still reads his peroration.

Spiritual, industrious, magnanimous nation, you have deigned to receive the first fruits of an undeveloped talent which will always be consecrated to your service. Support me in this difficult career which I wish to complete. Henceforward I have as implacable enemies all those who owe their lives to prejudice, all those who regret slavery. As my friends I must have all who love the fatherland, all true Frenchmen. You are setting a great example to the world. The remains of the feudal structure will soon collapse beneath the efforts of the august assembly which represents you. Your excellent Constitution is based upon equality. We shall see those titles disappear, those anti-social distinctions, those ridiculous differences that one has unblushingly recognized between man and man, between land and land. If tyranny or slavery dares to show its head, let your stage administer a just punishment, rivalling in every way the Athenian theatre. But it is incumbent upon you, upon the country, to protect the citizen poets who enter those glorious lists to bring low the enemies of the Nation.[1]

[1] M. J. Chénier, *Charles IX, Préface, Épître dédicatoire à la nation française.*

CHAPTER 8

L'Affaire 'Charles IX'

Chénier's five-act tragedy, *Charles IX ou l'École des rois*, actually written before the outbreak of the Revolution, had been accepted some time earlier for production by the *Comité*. The Fall of the Bastille, July 14th, 1789, the King's enforced return to Paris on October 6th, were such significant and turbulent manifestations of the growing discontents that Chénier revised his text, bringing it more in line with the uneasy mood of the times. The more reactionary members of the Comédie-Française expressed some concern about the suitability of the play they had already planned to present and their fears were reflected in a major casting problem that arose. The tragedy's central theme was of course the massacre of the Huguenots on St. Bartholomew's Eve 1572, at the order of an evil king, in fact a perfect example of that religious intolerance against which Voltaire and the *philosophes* had so long railed. Again, the comparative modernity of the events portrayed challenged the firmly established canon that tragic themes should be drawn from ancient history. To the actors, those *rétrogrades*, it seemed an uncomfortable play from every angle. Chénier was anxious that the title rôle of the weak, highly strung and mentally unbalanced Valois King should be played by Saint-Fal, a rising tragedian reared in the old school, who to his chagrin flatly refused the part. Like many of his colleagues he took fright at the play's revolutionary sentiments and had taken note that Mirabeau, in a recent inflammatory speech to the Parisians, had made the following allusion: 'I see from this rostrum the window from which the infamous Charles IX fired upon his subjects whose crime was to worship God in a different way from his own.' Saint-Fal saw himself being booed by the parterre as '*l'infâme Charles IX*' and contented himself with the safer but less prominent part of the King of Navarre. When his understudy showed no inclination to act the rôle, Talma, strongly urged by Madame Suin,[1] an ageing actress who played elderly confidantes, agreed to accept the unwanted part.

At long last opportunity knocked at Talma's door. As a play, Chénier's *Charles IX* interests us today only because of its relevance to a great actor's career and its revolutionary propagandist value. The *Comité* put up a good cast with Saint-Prix as the bigoted Cardinal de Lorraine, Naudet acting much against the grain as Coligny, and that most competent *tragédienne* Mme Vestris, as the wily Cathérine de Médicis. After stormy rehearsals, from which political partisanship was by no means excluded, *Charles IX* was finally produced on November 4th, 1789.

This night proved a turning point in Talma's career. He had studied that nervous poltroon of a King to the very last detail. His make-up reproduced the mongolian eyes, the thin-lipped, tightly drawn mouth of the tyrant with such success that David told him he looked like a portrait taken down from the walls of the Louvre.

His costume was historically accurate in every particular. Add to this, his sensitive playing. His emotional outbursts, running the whole gamut from childish petulance to frenzied horror, brought to the mannered acting of his day, with its monotonous chanting and stereotyped gestures, a new conception based on nature and truth, in fact a new life. Like our own Kean, yet to arrive, he showed he could command the lightning-flash to dispel the foggy gloom that all too often enveloped contemporary tragic acting. And what panache was his! He could preen, he could strut in that decadent Valois Court. He could arouse horror, inspire terror and hold an audience frozen in the hollow of his hand. From his lips Chénier's pedestrian verse rang out like a tocsin. All who saw his performance realized that something vital, something new had come to the French stage.

Not only did this man enthral them with his voice, he gripped them with his by-play, with his silences, with his least movements. Such sophisticated leaders of theatrical opinion as the Marquis de Ximénès and M. Grimod de la Reynière hailed him as Lekain's true successor. The parterre went mad with enthusiasm. This Charles IX, tyrant, hypocrite, weakling, held them as in a vice. The play was a prodigious success; for Talma a personal triumph.

[1] Regnault-Warin, *Mémoires sur Talma*, p. 337.

L'Affaire 'Charles IX'

A spectator present at the first performance wrote: 'The art with which he expressed weakness, hypocrisy, cruelty, the terrible amalgam that goes to make the character of Coligny's murderer; the scrupulous accuracy of his costume and especially his dumb-show produced a deep impression.'[1] The same anonymous critic however noted a tendency to shout, which he was prepared to excuse on the grounds of inexperience. Louise Fusil, an eminent actress in her day, who saw the play later in its run, said in a letter addressed to Mme Lemoine-Dubarry at Toulouse, dated May 10th, 1790: 'I went yesterday to the Théâtre-Français to see that play *Charles IX*, of which I had heard so much talk; it is the first important part that Talma has created. I had a great desire to know this actor and to talk with him. The opportunity came and I seized it eagerly. He has such a love for his art that he never misses a chance to practise it; and as he plays comedy in a very delightful manner he is often asked to give performances at Versailles and at St. Germain. People come out from Paris to see Talma in the great parts he does not play at the Comédie-Française.'

Charles IX was set for a prosperous run. It took its place in the repertory and played to packed houses. Back-stage, things were not easy for Talma. He had committed the crime of being too successful in a part whose possibilities his mortified colleagues had signally failed to divine. They loathed the play for its revolutionary tone and felt traitors to the royalist cause when one of their flock in Act III had to declaim:

> *Laissons faire le temps; à la grandeur du trône*
> *On verra succéder la grandeur de l'état:*
> *Le peuple tout à coup reprenant son éclat,*
> *Et des longs préjugés terrassant l'imposture,*
> *Réclamera les droits fondés par la nature;*
> *Son bonheur renaîtra du sein de ses malheurs;*
> *Ces murs baignés sans cesse et de sang et de pleurs,*
> *Ces tombeaux des vivants, ces bastilles affreuses,*
> *S'écrouleront alors sous des mains généreuses:*
> *Au prince, aux citoyens imposant leur devoir,*
> *Et fixant à jamais les bornes du pouvoir,*
> *On verra nos neveux, plus fiers que leurs ancêtres,*
> *Reconnaissant des chefs, mais n'ayant point de maîtres;*

[1] Regnault-Warin, *Mémoires sur Talma*, pp. 342, 343.

Heureux sous un monarque, ami de l'équité,
Restaurateur des lois et de la liberté! [1]

No, it was too much! What gall was theirs to hear that wild applause when Talma, as the anguished monarch, sees in a vision at the end of the play the parade of his victims and sobs out in stricken remorse:

J'ai trahi la patrie et l'honneur et les lois:
Le ciel en me frappant donne un exemple aux rois. [2]

It should be added that their gall was sweetened by the box-office returns.

Even after thirty-three triumphant performances *Charles IX* gave every indication of its prosperous continuance. A deputation of bishops, alarmed at the play's hold upon the people and doubting the prudence of a nightly assassination of Admiral Coligny at the instigation of King and clergy, petitioned Louis XVI for its withdrawal in the interest of public morals. Their request was duly granted. For Chénier this meant severe financial loss. The suspension of *Charles IX* also deprived Talma of his only acting opportunity and forced him back to the weary round of minor parts. He had tasted success and had won a legitimate acclaim. Was he, at a time when all forces were stirring to challenge privilege and tyranny, to take this decision with meek resignation? Evidence is not lacking that this *enfant de la Révolution* sought out Mirabeau and begged his intervention. [3]

We enter upon a phase when the affairs of the Comédie-Française, now renamed, out of compliment to the Revolution,

[1] Time will tell; to the grandeur of the throne
 There shall succeed the grandeur of the state,
 And when the people, glorious again,
 Shall banish every prejudice and lie,
 And repossess themselves of natural right.
 Then shall these living tombs, these dread bastilles,
 Crumble to dust beneath their generous hands
 Which give to prince and citizen their duty
 And fix for ever the limits of their power.
 We shall see our heirs, prouder than their sires,
 Respecting leaders but yielding to masters none,
 Happy beneath a justice-loving king
 Who gives them back their liberty and laws.
[2] I have betrayed my country and its laws:
 May my sad fate make other princes pause!
[3] Regnault-Warin, *Mémoires sur Talma*, pp. 348, 349. A. Pougin, *La Comédie-Française et la Révolution*, pp. 14, 15, A. Copin, *Talma et la Révolution*, p. 44.

the Théâtre de la Nation, require a deal of sorting out. So many conflicting reports are available, all tinct with political partisanship, that the truth is hard to come by. Only by the stepping stones of indisputable facts can we hope to emerge from this morass. Talma it is true had opportunities for contact with the Comte de Mirabeau, the elected representative of the Tiers-État of Aix-Marseilles in the States-General; the oratory and leadership of this aristocratic liberal made him very quickly a dominant personality in the newly formed revolutionary National Assembly. During those crucial months, June and July, that saw the suppression of *Charles IX*, Mirabeau was living in the rue Chantereine in a house belonging to Julie Careau, whom Talma was before long to marry. At this time Mirabeau had in the capital for the Fête de la Fédération 400 of his Provençal supporters, his *fédérés*, and the City of Paris was at pains to entertain these delegates from all parts of France with parades, theatrical performances and banquets. On July 14th, to mark the first anniversary of the Fall of the Bastille, the Comédie-Française put on a short topical play by Aude called *Le Journaliste dans les Ombres*, in which Talma played Jean-Jacques Rousseau with a make-up so startlingly accurate that Grimm was moved to record that in veracity it excelled the actor's appearance as Charles IX, adding that 'the living copy was so true that one was almost tempted to accept it as the original. You could have believed you saw the Genevan sage in person.'[1] This little *pièce de circonstance* again brought Talma to the fore but, with *Charles IX* banned, he had no longer an adequate outlet for his abilities. Really Mirabeau must do something. He was not slow to act.

On the night of July 21st the parterre of the Théâtre de la Nation was invaded by the *fédérés* from Provence. The playbill announced a performance of *Le Réveil d'Épiménide*, a comedy by Flins des Oliviers, in which Talma had created the part of d'Harcourt. When the curtain rose, immediately there were yells, full throated Marseillais yells, for *Charles IX*. On the stage were Naudet, Talma and Mlle Lange. Pandemonium continued until one member, some say Mirabeau himself, others a *fédéré* named Sarrazin, obtained sufficient silence to read from a paper a formal request that the actors should perform Chénier's play. Naudet stepped to the footlights and, addressing the unruly audience, declared that it was quite impossible to act *Charles IX*. Mme

[1] Regnault-Warin, *Mémoires sur Talma*, p. 354, footnote.

Vestris, he said, was ill and M. Saint-Prix, who played the Cardinal, was suffering from erysipelas in his leg. Far from appeasing the audience, Naudet seemed, by his casual dismissal of their request, to inflame them still further. More threatening became the shouting. The actors were roundly accused of a lack of patriotism. At this point Talma, with a sign that he had something to say, quelled the din and addressed the audience. 'Gentlemen, Mme Vestris is indeed indisposed, but I can promise you she will play and give you proof of her zeal and patriotism. As for the part of the Cardinal, since M. Saint-Prix is quite unable to act, one of our colleagues will read it in his absence, if you agree, and in this way it will be possible to perform *Charles IX*.'[1] Talma's suggestion aroused frantic applause and the Comédie-Française had to bow before the storm with what grace it could. Amid the ensuing disturbances a certain gentleman named Danton was[2] arrested and conducted to the Hôtel de Ville. The following day July 22nd, Mme Vestris, despite a sore throat, took great joy in appearing as Cathérine de Médicis and the part of the Cardinal was read by Grammont.

The performance of *Charles IX* was indeed tempestuous. Not all members of the audience showed sympathy with the *fédérés*, and some of them during the play persisted in keeping on their hats, which studied rudeness called forth further protests. Quarrels were rife everywhere and armed force had to intervene. Despite the hubbub and constant interruptions, both play and players were most enthusiastically applauded, and Talma, the hero of the evening, enjoyed a special recall.

Peace with the public meant war in the green room. Matters could not be left there. The issues at stake went far beyond the performance of a play by the Comédie-Française. Mirabeau's intervention alone endowed the incident with a political significance which the general public was quick to realize. The press according to its political colour took sides. Some applauded Talma's conduct and saw sinister forces of reaction entrenched in the Théâtre de la Nation; others felt that the young tragedian, by taking too much upon himself, had compromised his colleagues. The actors themselves were convinced that Talma, abetted by Mirabeau, had engineered the whole business merely to repeat his resounding success. The military-minded Naudet, furious

[1] A. Copin, *Talma et la Révolution*, p. 40.
[2] Regnault-Warin, *Mémoires sur Talma*, p. 353.

at being contradicted in public by a junior *sociétaire*, sought satisfaction in a duel, in which both combatants suffered slight wounds.
Even then honour was not satisfied. Talma with opposition all
around him wrote to Mirabeau: 'I appeal to your goodness, Sir,
to clear me of the calumnious charges my enemies are at pains
to spread abroad. According to them it is not you who asked for
Charles IX; it is I who by intrigue forced my comrades to perform
this play. Hired journalists assure the public of everything their
own malice dictates. If you do not give me permission to tell the
truth, I shall remain under an accusation they hope to turn to their
advantage. I therefore beg you, Sir, to allow me to undeceive the
public which a hundred enemy voices seek to turn against me.
(Signed) Talma.'

Mirabeau replied. 'Yes certainly, sir, you can say that I asked
for *Charles IX* in the name of the Provençal delegates and also
that I energetically insisted upon its being given; you may say this
because it is the truth and a truth in which I take pride. The degree
of loathing which the actors have shown in this instance, at least
if one is to believe rumour, was so discourteous to the general
public and was moreover based upon so-called reasons quite outside their normal competence; they have not the experience
to decide whether a play, legally performed, is or is not inflammatory; the importance they gave to its request and refusal
was quite extraordinary and tactless; finally, they had so very
explicitly told me personally that they would yield only to the
expressed wish of the public that I felt bound to spread abroad
their reply. The wish was expressed and badly received, so one is
assured; the public wanted to be obeyed. That is a fairly straight-
forward matter when it pays for its seat and I see no grounds for
surprise. That they (the actors) should seek to make you or anyone
else responsible for so spontaneous a happening is but the petty
dregs of their childish rancour to which you in your turn would
be wrong, in my opinion, to attach any importance. For all time
there is the truth which I gladly sign, as well as the expression of
my regards with which etc. etc. (Signed) Mirabeau *l'aîné*. Paris
27th July 1790.'

These two letters, written in the heat and burden of the affray,
were not published until August 11th, 1790, when both appeared
together in the columns of the *Chronique de Paris*. Camille Des-
moulins in his very ultra newspaper *Les Révolutions de France et
de Brabant* made much of the *affaire 'Charles IX'*, going so far as to

accuse Naudet of violently assaulting both Talma and Chénier. The latter in a statement to the *Chronique* dated August 29th denied the whole story. Talma however in his version to the same journal on September 1st referred to an attack upon his person by Naudet before a performance of *Tancrède* some six months previously and added that the hatred his own political views had aroused in '*les noirs*' forced him to carry arms in self-defence. All these letters are mere fragments in a publicity campaign, where *le sieur* Naudet and *le sieur* Talma showed, by their retaliatory brochures, a deeply rooted animosity.

The question must be asked, even if it cannot be satisfactorily answered. Was Talma the real instigator of these disturbances over *Charles IX*? Mirabeau's letter would seem to be decisive. Mention must be made of another letter that Talma always quoted to exonerate himself, a letter from one Barthélemy,[1] commanding the Marseilles detachment of the National Guard, in which the writer thanked the actor for so zealously backing '*la demande de nos Provençaux*' and, with adulatory references to Talma's own performance, asked him to convey the *fédérés*' gratitude to his colleagues who had contributed to so fine a rendering of a truly national play.

[1] A. Pougin, *La Comédie-Française et la Révolution*, p. 20.

CHAPTER 9

Talma Suspended

After all these years it seems a little strange that the Parisians, caught up in the throes of a revolution, could still find time to interest themselves in these backstage jealousies and quarrels. Such however was the case. The newspapers reported at length, matching their comments with their own political colours, and in addition the presses poured forth a number of recriminatory documents. The Comédie-Française at the very centre of the storm could not ignore a situation fast becoming impossible. The *Société*, of which Talma was a junior member, felt that sanctions should be taken against an irresponsible colleague. In the absence of Molé, the Doyen, Fleury on July 23rd convened a meeting of the *sociétaires*, which he opened by referring to a conspiracy against the Comédie-Française. Dugazon, a rather late arrival, is alleged to have opened the door just as these remarks were being made and, in a moment of unquenchable fun, to have taken up Fleury's phrase by impersonating a newsboy crying: 'Great conspiracy discovered! Something strange, something new!' This hilarious entry Fleury years after always denied, but others agreed that the laugh Dugazon so easily raised did nothing to reduce tension in the assembled group. Fleury and his associates, particularly Naudet, Mlle Contat and Mlle Raucourt, had too many bones, artistic and political, to pick with their young colleague. They remembered how, when the current season opened in the preceding April, Talma, working in connivance with Chénier, had agreed to deliver the opening speech which the author of *Charles IX* had spiced with so much innuendo and revolutionary salt that the actors, after rejecting it wholly, arranged for Naudet to deliver a more innocuous compliment which received municipal approval on April 12th. When Naudet took the stage to give a more conventional address to the public, he was greeted with shouts for Talma and to his amazement saw flutter from the upper galleries a shower of printed leaflets bearing the speech that Talma was not allowed to make. Fleury and his friends declared that this printed version carried the following dangerous words: 'A few members of the Comédie-Française are oppressed by aristocratic vapours but great evils call for great remedies.' When this charge against Talma was finally made public, in a brochure[1] issued by the actors to justify their action against him, both Chénier and his collaborator hotly denied the charge of dropping leaflets inside the theatre, but they had very grudgingly to admit the distribution of a few copies at the doors. On that September afternoon, despite every effort the faithful Dugazon made on Talma's behalf, Fleury and his friends secured the suspension of François-Joseph Talma from any public performance in the Théâtre de la Nation. For them he was '*un mauvais associé*' whose service at the Comédie-Française compromised them all.

Partisans eagerly leapt forward to support the disgraced player and were determined to refer the matter of his expulsion to the National Assembly. As a *sociétaire*, Talma had certain inalienable rights, but his colleagues, by refusing to appear with him, knew he was completely silenced. Dugazon suggested that he might act at another theatre, but in true dog-in-the-manger fashion the *sociétaires* reminded him of the binding force of Talma's contract. The general public however found ways and means of making their voice heard. At every performance the cry of 'Talma, Talma' was raised and on September 16th a real manifestation was staged. The newspapers tell us that on that night 2,000 partisans, organized and equipped with whistles, entered the theatre and demanded Talma's return. The actors, poorly represented by a few friends in front, who were silenced by threats and blows, decided before this seething crowd to make an announcement, assuring those present that an official statement about M. Talma would be made the following night. On September 17th *L'École des maris* was to be performed. The curtain rose. Fleury, dressed entirely in black, faced a restive, determined audience, even more numerous and unruly than that of the preceding evening. 'Gentlemen,' he began, 'my Society, persuaded that M. Talma has betrayed its interests and compromised public order, has unanimously decided to have no further relations with him until the whole matter has been judged by authority.'[2] These brief, high-

[1] *Exposé de la conduite et des torts du sieur Talma envers les comédiens français.*
[2] A. Copin, *Talma et la Révolution*, pp. 57, 58.

handed words did not satisfy the tragedian's friends. Uproar ensued. The sight of Dugazon, rushing on the stage, produced a momentary lull during which he, in his turn, addressed the crowd. 'Gentlemen,' he cried, 'the Comédie is going to pass against me the same vote of censure as against M. Talma. I denounce the whole Comédie; it is false that M. Talma has betrayed the Society and compromised public safety; his crime lies in having told you that *Charles IX* could be played, and there you have the whole matter.' After these damaging words Dugazon deemed it prudent to disappear, quite unmindful of the fact that he was due to play a leading part in *L'École des maris*![1] The parterre, stirred to further wrath by his speech, demanded that Fleury should read the terms of the vote of censure taken by the *sociétaires* against Talma. To this insistent demand Fleury acceded, but so great was the din that armed force had to be called in. Unfortunately the soldiery could not restore order for the stage performance because Dugazon was nowhere to be found. With no play in prospect the audience got completely out of control, smashed up seats, invaded the stage destroying everything it found there, climbed up into boxes and finally marched, a yelling mob, from the Comédie-Française (then on the site of the Odéon) across the river to the gay lights of the Palais-Royal quarter. Well might Fleury write: 'We knew that Talma had supporters. We discovered that he had behind him a whole people.'[2]

Bailly, Mayor of Paris, a man of the highest probity, who enjoyed universal esteem, felt in view of these happenings that the time had come for the Municipality of Paris to intervene in the affairs of the Théâtre de la Nation. The uproar created on September 17th could not be tolerated; public order must be preserved. Dugazon had been fined and confined eight days to house arrest for deserting his post and thus adding to confusion in the theatre. Bailly was determined to do everything in his power to persuade the *sociétaires* to reinstate Talma, but even his patience came near to exhaustion when the *Société* sent Grammont to complain to the Gentlemen of the Bedchamber. The Mayor then summoned the adamant actors to appear before him, but his suggestions for a peaceful solution yielded no results. Meanwhile, the general public, by its clamouring for Talma, made abortive every performance at the Comédie-Française. The actors foolishly

[1] A. Pougin, *La Comédie-Française et la Révolution*, pp. 34, 35.
[2] A. Copin, *Talma et la Révolution*, p. 56.

tried to counter this situation by a wholesale distribution of free seats to trusty friends, a policy which drew from the *Chronique de Paris* in its issue of September 25th, 1790, the following comments: 'The actors of the Comédie-Française have decided no longer to recognize the Municipality's authority and have resolved, if they should be forced to such obedience, to return the keys of their theatre to the King. . . . If all the corporations in the kingdom despised municipal authority and the people's magistrates, if they wished to recognize no power other than that of the King, the counter-revolution would have been achieved. The young aristocrats have deserted the Opéra for the Comédie-Française and this place is now becoming a hotbed of rebellion and aristocratic privilege.' Here indeed was a danger signal.

Bailly, cutting a tiresome Gordian knot, decided to reinstate Talma by a municipal decree dated September 24th, 1790, and accordingly placarded Paris with the Municipality's writ. The actors remained intransigent. The performance of September 26th was attended by an audience so quickly out of hand that Bailly himself came down to the theatre and from a box made an earnest plea for order. His own personal popularity assured a hearing for the play. Such open defiance of his orders could not be tolerated. Persuasion had failed and the Mayor of Paris in the interests of public safety closed the Théâtre de la Nation.

Only such a prompt and decisive step brought the actors to their senses and, as a result of the ensuing rapid *pourparlers*, Talma returned to the Comédie-Française on September 28th to repeat his resounding success in *Charles IX* for the thirty-fourth time. His popularity was enormous and prominent in his triumph were his devoted friends, that very leftish sister and brother, Mme Vestris and Dugazon.

As may well be understood, Talma did not return to a bed of roses. Frigid toleration awaited him. His reappearance in the green room was utterly repugnant to Mlle Contat, who flounced and fluttered with her courtly grace, and of course to Mlle Raucourt, whose virile stampings and manly indignation indicated clearly her own feelings. In the face of Talma's overwhelming success both actresses felt constrained to talk of resignation, a threat they ultimately carried out. They would not act in the same theatre with him. Their example was followed by Mlle Sainval who of course loathed Mme Vestris. If Talma was having a bad time backstage, his colleagues were constantly under fire in the newspapers to which Palissot, a very progressive *littérateur*, had lent his violently satirical pen. The actors were really in a bad way and in an effort to ingratiate themselves with the public they gave on October 9th a benefit performance for the widow of Jean-Jacques Rousseau. Talma did nothing to improve the situation. Always a vain man, his head had certainly been turned by the public's excessive adulation. At this most uncomfortable period he demanded an '*emploi*', that is the contractual right to play specified leading parts.

Unfortunately for the tragedian, Chénier decided to withdraw *Charles IX* from the *répertoire* of the Comédie-Française. He had very good reasons for this course of action. He feared that the *Société* might put his play in the bill on two consecutive nights or over a period of three, when revolutionary entertainments elsewhere would ensure poor houses and also, on the grounds that the tragedy had failed to attract, the Comédie-Française would automatically acquire the copyright of *Charles IX*. This disgracefully unfair condition was one under which the contemporary dramatist had long groaned, and with reason, because the Comédie-Française was not over-scrupulous in invoking such an iniquitous regulation. Once possessed of the copyright, the *sociétaires* would restore the play to the bill at a more favourable moment and, without any deduction for a mere author, pocket the entire proceeds. The actors knew that in Chénier's tragedy they had a sure-fire success and had announced performances of it on September 30th and October 3rd, a Thursday and a Sunday when bumper audiences might be expected. Chénier, in as bad odour with the actors as Talma himself, safeguarded his property by its withdrawal, thus leaving his friend without a single prominent part. Until the end of that theatrical season, April 10th, 1791, Talma was given no opportunity to act a worth-while part in the classical repertory and, more galling still, was entrusted with no creation in a new play.

In a letter to his friend Coupigny in San Domingo, dated December 25th, 1790, [1] Talma gives his own version of life at the Comédie-Française during this period. After lyrical praise for the changes wrought by the Revolution, in particular a just reappraisal of the glory of Louis XIV, he proceeds to deal with his own career. 'My successes in my débuts have been fairly distinguished and since my entry to the profession the public has given

[1] Guy de la Batut, *Talma: Correspondance*, pp. 161–164.

every evidence of its great kindness to me. Never have I endured the mortification of the slightest hostile murmur. I have played among others several new parts which earned me the public's most flattering opinions, especially the part of Charles IX in the tragedy of that name. But these successes have also stirred up against me many enemies among the tragi-comic specialists. You know that is the political swing in this little state; if the public likes you, your comrades hate you. The advent of the Revolution created a diversity of political opinions among the members; on that score, quarrel after quarrel. I stood up for the public, but those ladies and gentlemen, the ladies especially, were for the Gentlemen of the Bedchamber. Tempers rose and war started with a stage duel between myself and *le sieur* Naudet who, as you probably know, plays comedy like a mendicant friar and tragedy like a recruiting sergeant. Long live the federal entertainments!' Thereupon Talma recapitulates in exact detail the events we already know. This letter is of real interest to any biographer of Talma, because it establishes beyond doubt his intense fervour for the Revolution and his uneasy relations with his colleagues.

The National Assembly, prodded by Chénier, began to cast a malevolent eye upon the Comédie-Française. In response to a petition from dramatists, this revolutionary body on January 13th, 1791, decreed that plays could no longer be regarded as the exclusive property of the Comédie-Française and, in a way more damaging still to the prestige of the *Société*, that all masterpieces in the classical *répertoire* could be performed in any theatre. Here was indeed a blow at a much cherished monopoly. Competition became a possibility. The *sociétaires* would have to be on their toes. They persuaded Mlle Contat and Mlle Raucourt to withdraw their resignations and bring their strength to a company that still ignored the talents of Talma. Louise Contat opened on January 15th, 1791, in *Le Jaloux sans amour* and *Le Mariage secret* and the following day Françoise Raucourt thundered out Clytemnestre in *Iphigénie en Aulide*.

Talma's life at the Comédie-Française had become a blank. With other managements in Paris now empowered to revive classical tragedy, he began to feel that there were other stages to conquer. Dugazon urged him to leave, but the *Société*, getting wind of such advice, threatened a lawsuit and talked of laying hands on Talma's costumes and properties. The latter step Dugazon prevented by a neat stratagem. He dressed eight supers as lictors and, having instructed them to carry four large baskets from the wardrobe room, he marched them to Talma's dressing-room where, under his orders, wigs, costumes, cuirasses, helmets, arms of all kinds were duly packed. He draped the baskets with togas and cloaks and himself, garbed as Achilles with visor low, carrying shield and lance, led his heavily laden Roman band through a group of wondering *sociétaires* to the outer door and finally to the safety of the Palais-Royal. Talma's stock in trade was safe and all Paris laughed. The Comédie-Française dared not face further ridicule by any kind of retaliatory action.[1]

[1] A. Copin, *Talma et la Révolution*, p. 67.

CHAPTER 10

Rue de Richelieu

In the rue de Richelieu, which revolutionary zealots were later to rename the rue de la Loi, stood a new handsome theatre with a capacity of 1,600 places, opened in 1790 as the Variétés-Amusantes, but more commonly referred to as the Théâtre du Palais-Royal. Two very enterprising managers, Gaillard and Dorfeuille, who had already made a great success of the Grand Théâtre at Bordeaux, arrived in Paris to take over the new theatre, which occupied the exact site of today's Comédie-Française. Their artistic susceptibilities were really jarred by the second-rate comedies and melodramas which it had been that theatre's policy to present. They wished to aim at higher standards and the National Assembly's decree allowing plays from the classical repertory to be performed anywhere in Paris inspired them to engage a first-class company, capable of tackling the masterpieces of Corneille and Racine. Events will show that Chénier was at their elbow. When the Palais-Royal closed for the Easter recess on April 12th, 1791, Saint-Clair, the actor entrusted with the compliment to the public, informed the audience, mentioning no names, that plays by new authors as well as the works of Corneille, Racine and Voltaire would be performed on their stage where Molière alone had reigned. 'To this end,' he added, 'we summon to our aid talents already known, already loved by the public and that a precious tradition has made familiar with the masterpieces of our great dramatists.'[1]

During these weeks of closure arrangements were made for Talma, Dugazon, Grandmesnil, Mme Vestris, Mlle Desgarcins and Mlle Lange to leave the Comédie-Française, and to transfer their services to Gaillard and Dorfeuille's new theatre, which the proud managers promptly called the Théâtre-Français de la rue de Richelieu. There the fugitives joined forces with that brilliant *sociétaire*, Monvel, returned from Sweden, who had

[1] A. Copin, *Talma et la Révolution*, p. 70.

persuaded a most accomplished comedienne to follow him, Mlle Candeille, expert in coquette rôles. With these newcomers must be grouped Antoine Michaud, an actor endowed with the *vis comica* and known to the Parisians as Michot. Here was indeed a galaxy of talent and one, to the dismay of Molé and Fleury, well able to compete with their Society.

The new Théâtre-Français advertised its opening for April 25th, forestalling the Comédie-Française which would resume operations on May 2nd. The play chosen to inaugurate the new season was Chénier's tragedy *Henri VIII*, which had actually been in rehearsal at the Théâtre de la Nation until its withdrawal by the author. After an unforeseen delay, doors opened in the rue de Richelieu on April 27th when, with *Henri VIII*, *L'Épreuve nouvelle* by Marivaux, shared the bill. A packed expectant audience awaited the Chénier play. Distributed throughout the house were the *sociétaires* and their friends. They of course knew the play intimately and knew also exactly where to destroy its pathos by mocking jeers. Although they were responsible for several ill-natured interruptions, Talma in the title rôle, with Mme Vestris as the unfortunate Anne Boleyn and Mlle Desgarcins as Jeanne Seymour pulled the play through to a successful conclusion. Performance had however revealed that an actor, vocally inadequate for the important part of Cromwell, would have to be replaced by Monvel and that the child cast for Princess Elizabeth required an immediate substitute. Yet in spite of these weaknesses, mercilessly exposed by the cabal, when the author's name was announced at curtain fall, it was greeted with wild applause. A grim fate awaited however the Marivaux trifle. Let it be remembered that the Comédie-Française, with the talents of Louise Contat, Molé, Fleury, Dazincourt at its disposal, could always produce a brilliantly integrated comedy team to tackle Molière, Regnard and Marivaux. Although the new troupe certainly numbered two ripe comic actors, Dugazon and Michot, both excellent when cast as valets, and a brilliant comedienne Mlle Candeille, it had yet to acquire the really smooth, finished performance. Even friendly critics admitted that *L'Épreuve nouvelle* was poorly rendered but, if it released a mild version of pandemonium, its failure did not detract from the success Gaillard and Dorfeuille's enterprise had achieved with *Henri VIII*.

What of Talma in his second major part? The critics agreed that *Henri VIII* was a dramatic play, full of strong situations, and both scenically and from the literary point of view superior to *Charles IX*. Talma's meticulously accurate historical costume and make-up, his seductive yet robust wooing, his outbursts of senseless wrath, his portrayal of crafty statesmanship and his fine assumption of kingly power, all provided a full length portrait of the English monarch to which his early London background brought knowledge and feeling. He went all out for 'nature' and poured a warm humanity into some very pedestrian alexandrines which Larive and his minions would have lugubriously chanted.

Mme Vestris wrung all hearts as the unhappy Anne and Mlle. Desgarcins, in perhaps the greatest performance of an all too short career, by her touching, sensitive and sweet playing of Jeanne Seymour, brought tears to the eyes of the spectators. The *Chronique de Paris* of April 29th, 1791, commiserated with the actors in *L'Épreuve nouvelle* because of the organized stormy reception, but even with this handicap Dugazon emerged as *l'excellent Dugazon*.

Apart from their reviews of *Henri VIII*—another tyrant king like Charles IX and therefore good revolutionary propaganda— the newspapers made much of the competition that the Comédie-Française would now be compelled to face. That active publicist, Palissot, an ardent admirer of Talma, reminded the *sociétaires* that the new venture owed its inception to their own disgraceful treatment of the interpreters of *Charles IX*. Well might they turn pale and tremble before such redoubtable opposition. Instead of organizing cabals, let them strive worthily to emulate the Théâtre de la rue Richelieu. To this diatribe the Comédie-Française made the following brief retort: 'Our reply will be brief but to the point. M. Palissot is a charlatan.' Nor was Chénier silent. Ever eager to strike at his old enemies, he addressed them in a letter to the *Chronique de Paris* dated May 10th, 1791. 'Yes, you are the people who disturbed the first night of *Henri VIII*, working with aristocrats and courtesans. Yes, the actors and actresses of your theatre, their lackeys and the lovers of these young ladies, even their creditors, your *ouvreuses* and your call-boys, turned up for this performance not out of any spirit of curiosity.' Clearly vivid pens were at the disposal of the new theatre and the monopoly that the Comédie-Française had so long enjoyed was now at an end. Competition between the two groups became unpleasantly keen and certain differences in the dramatic fare each offered and in the audiences for whom it was served could not escape attention. Talma and his colleagues undoubtedly bore the palm where tragedy was the staple entertainment. Their audience was much more revolutionary in spirit, seeing in the procession of tyrants, kings and political dictators appropriate comment upon their present day problems. In the faubourg Saint-Germain, the Comédie-Française excelled in comedy, where a conservative, even reactionary public delighted in all the formal grace and the polished society of the Ancien Régime. The new theatre pulled in the defenders of the *sans culottes*; the old establishment continued to click *les talons rouges*.

Even after so stormy a start, popular success assured for *Henri VIII* constant repetition during that initial season. On April 30th, to the discomfiture of their rivals in Saint-Germain, the Théâtre-Français de la rue de Richelieu scored an unquestionable triumph with a revival of *Le Cid*. Talma could now essay the great tragic rôles of the classical repertory. Had not the National Assembly deprived Larive and his satellites of their exclusive right to play the heroes of Corneille and Racine? With Monvel as Don Diègue, Mlle Desgarcins as Chimène, Talma revelled in the opportunities that the part of Le Cid gave to him. To Rodrigue he brought his own male beauty, his superb diction—everywhere praised—and all the panache that befits a Spanish lover and hero. He did not altogether escape the charge of monotony, especially in the delivery of the *récit*, seventy-three rhyming alexandrines long, in Act IV, where Le Cid describes his victory over the Moors at sea. Paris had seen many performances of *Le Cid*, but this revival astonished by its vigour, its colourful décor and its sense of period. Monvel was an impressive father to Rodrigue and Mlle Desgarcins pleased by a quality of heart-rending sincerity as Chimène. The new enterprise had been launched on a tide of success. A beautiful theatre, situated in the frequented Palais-Royal area, had many advantages over an old building tucked away in an almost residential quarter. Talma, housed in the very centre of pleasure-loving Paris, could look forward to playing Néron, César, Achille, Oreste, rôles he had long hankered to play. Within a few months, from an enforced and frustrating obscurity, he had leapt to the top of his profession. In the artistic world of the capital he was already a power and his friendship with David gave him an entrée to salons where, despite revolutionary disturbances, men and women of cultivated taste could still meet and discuss, as only the French can, the contemporary arts and the political scene so irrevocably unfolding before their eyes. One salon had already attracted the actor's attention. Of this we must now speak.

CHAPTER 11

Enter Julie Careau

No actor however dedicated to his art lives his life entirely in the theatre. Talma certainly provided no exception to this dictum. Reference has already been made to his passionate interest in antiquity and, if we are to believe the somewhat spiteful memoirs of his widow, his years in Paris immediately after his return from London were singularly free from amorous entanglements. Madamme Talma attributed this indifference to women either to a preoccupation with intellectual pursuits or to rather poor health. She adds: '*l'étude le captivait tout entier*'.[1] We have already noted his platonic friendship with Mlle Desgarcins, but his widow—she is our only source of information during this undocumented period of the actor's career—states that there was a most hectic liaison with a beautiful girl from Languedoc, who gave him not only a daughter but all the torments that can beset a jealous lover. Talma's desire to marry this fickle southerner was thwarted by his family. For one fleeting moment we glimpse him, parading the streets of Paris one night in dire despair, his babe in his arms, that his mother received and somehow consigned to oblivion. That he could be wholly indifferent to feminine charms is borne out by the story of a beautiful English girl with whom, at his father's urgent request, Talma shared his Paris flat. Although these young people used the same key for six months, the young lady returned to London completely fancy free, to the amazement of Madame Talma *veuve*.[2] Certainly study provided the great incentive to his work as an actor.

After his acceptance by the Comédie-Française, life, for lack of material means, began to prove hard for Talma. His salary as a *pensionnaire* was not large and his was no frugal existence. London had given him opportunities to mingle with the nobility. His ideas for accurate stage costume, when carried out, cost a great

---

[1] C. Talma. *Particularités*. pp. 282, 283.   [2] Ibid. p. 284.

deal. His cult of the antique led him to indulge in expensively designed furniture and ornaments. Hospitality he offered lavishly. It was said that his table was open to all comers. Rather naïvely he imagined his finances were in order because every day he kept meticulous account of each debt incurred. Alas! never was there any effort made to pay them. His promotion to the rank of *sociétaire* helped to bolster up his failing credit, but extravagance in the theatre and in his social life proceeded unchecked.

It was under these financially difficult circumstances that Talma, probably in the spring of 1789, first appeared in the salon of Julie Careau. This extraordinary woman, essentially a product of the eighteenth century, had won for herself something of a position in the bohemian society of pre-revolutionary Paris. She was the daughter of Marie Careau, a *fille d'amour*, and a certain François Proch, who in a very belated way recognized her on August 6th, 1801. Julie was born in Paris on January 8th, 1756, and was baptized at Saint-Eustache. She had risen from the streets and, as a child dancer at the Opéra, was soon initiated into the cult of *la haute cocotterie*. In 1789 she was a woman of substance and owed her fortune to a series of rich protectors. Before Talma met her, she had been the mistress of the Vicomte de Ségur and of the Comte de Narbonne; she had had out of wedlock three children by three different fathers. Yet this remarkable woman by her intellect and charm attracted and retained the friendship of such eminent men as David, Chamfort the moralist, a bevy of dramatists Arnault, Ducis, Chénier, Legouvé and Lemercier, the composer Méhul and such political leaders as Mirabeau, Vergniaud, Gensonné, Gaudet and the young Roederer, at that time one of the editors of the *Journal de Paris*. Apart from a few actresses like Louise Fusil women did not figure conspicuously in Julie's house in the rue Chantereine, a property she had acquired for the sum of 50,000 livres as long ago as 1780 from Perraud de Montreuil, architect to the Comte d'Artois.

To this woman, seven years his senior, Talma was immediately drawn. Julie, *à l'âge des grands amours*, passionately reciprocated his admiration. Her political views coincided with those of the actor. She was a true daughter of the *philosophes* and was devoted to the Gironde faction. Talma's widow maliciously stated that she was twenty years older than her young admirer and that his affections centred mainly on her income of 40,000 livres. This simply is not true. Aspasia and Roscius were certainly in love and

Julie Careau, Talma's first wife

here was the woman who would stimulate the actor's imagination and widen his social horizon. Regular indeed were Talma's visits to the gatherings in the rue Chantereine. He proposed marriage and to his joy was accepted. On April 30th, 1790, the marriage contract was drawn up at No. 6, rue Chantereine in the presence of four witnesses by the lawyer Martinon. Talma undertook to bestow 10,000 livres upon the bride and she, in addition to her income and the house where she lived, brought two other substantial properties. As the married couple would own all property jointly, Talma's financial position, so menaced by debt, improved immediately.

But of course they had to marry. At that time Talma lived in the rue Molière, in the parish of Saint-Sulpice. Very properly he requested the curé of that church to publish his banns of marriage, in which he described himself as '*comédien*'. At once this ecclesiastic made difficulties. He refused not only to publish the banns but also to be a party to any solemnization of marriage as long as Talma described himself as an actor. On this point the Church was obdurate. From the days of Molière, whose Tartuffe was never forgiven, all too many cases could be cited to illustrate the clerical attitude to the theatre. If Talma would describe himself as a musician, the sacrament of marriage could be vouchsafed. Although the Parisians had destroyed the Bastille a year before, the Church was still able to enforce so mean and petty a regulation. The curé of Saint-Sulpice would never yield to a man who, by his impersonation of Charles IX, had heaped much odium upon Holy Church. Well might one cry: 'Whaur's yer Declaration o' the Rights o' Man?' No actor is averse from publicity and Talma conformed to the propensities of his kind. On July 12th he first carried his grievance to the National Assembly, calling upon that body to secure his right as a citizen to Christian marriage. His letter, published in the *Moniteur* on Tuesday July 12th, 1790, contained the following: 'I prostrate myself before God, I profess the Catholic religion, apostolic and Roman. . . . How can this religion authorize profligacy?'

That the National Assembly espoused Talma's cause can be shown by quoting in full Mirabeau's brief note. 'Your business comes up tomorrow morning, my dear Talma. A secretary will read your petition. You must be at the National Assembly by ten o'clock at the latest. Good evening, good night and kiss in my name your hostess's pretty hand.' Sunday evening (July 18th?)

Talma's ringing phrases were duly read from the tribune. His complaint was referred to the *Comité ecclésiastique* and there the matter dragged on for some time. Sieyès, that hero of the Tennis Court Oath, makes this abundantly clear in his letter to Talma of October 15th, 1790. 'I have the honour to send Monsieur Talma the report the ecclesiastical committee proposes to issue with reference to his marriage. One must not dwell upon its tone, its style, its thoughts, its reasoning; they all still reek of the manners of the eleventh century. But the elements of a good law are to be found there and it is something gained that the *jansénistes* have been persuaded to put it forward. Monsieur Talma, like ourselves, will understand that the National Assembly, unable to deal with a particular case, must go back to general principles and from them deduce a general law; it will, in truth, be an excellent law which, separating from religious matters all that concerns a citizen's status, will rescue from the yoke of clergymen's opinions the most important of all civil acts.

I beg Monsieur Talma to accept my compliments and the expression of the very sincere wish I offer for the termination of his business.

Since I have seen your Julie, I understand more easily your impatience.'

Despite the promises the above letter seemed to offer, Talma made no headway at Saint-Sulpice. The matter was now becoming urgent. Julie was an expectant mother. Talma fought the battle for his profession as long as he could. April 1791 was indeed to prove a memorable month for him. On its second day Mirabeau's death plunged all France into the deepest gloom. This national disaster both Julie and her intended husband could claim as a personal loss. The actor owed much to the great man for his support over *Charles IX*; Julie knew the statesman as a habitué of her salon and also as the tenant of her house in the Chaussée d'Antin where he died. A catastrophe of such magnitude dwarfed, even in ardent revolutionary circles, Talma's clamour for Christian marriage. Paris had other things to think about. However, when he was in the throes of rehearsal for *Henri VIII*, on April 19th, 1791, François-Joseph Talma, *bourgeois de Paris*, aged 28, led the demoiselle Louise-Julie Careau, whose age was erroneously given as 25(!), to the altar of Notre-Dame de Lorette, where M. Lepipe the *vicaire* pronounced the nuptial benediction. Twelve days later, on May 1st, 1791, in the same church, Talma and Julie's twin sons,

Henri-Castor and Charles-Pollux, born the previous day, were baptized by the same M. Lepipe. At this christening ceremony, prominent as god-parents were the faithful Dugazon and the 'melting' Mlle Desgarcins. Madame Talma *veuve* recorded the baptism of her predecessor's twins with all the self-righteousness of outraged indignation. She refrained from any mention of Julie's marriage contract, duly signed and sealed twelve full months before the birth of the boys. This dispute over his marriage was Talma's first brush with the Church. It would not be his last.

Once installed with his wife and two sons in that very charming house in the rue Chantereine, life took on for Talma a greater ease and more exciting social contacts. Julie of course remained the gracious hostess, eager above everything to further her husband's brilliant career. If, before her marriage, her salon had been mainly political in its tone and personalities, once she was Madame Talma she did everything to attract dramatists, painters and scholars to her reunions.

A word is due about the house itself. It was a compact town mansion, such as the wealthy bourgeois built in an eighteenth century undisturbed by revolutionary fears. It stood foursquare in that pleasant avenue, with its two storeys surmounted by a mansard roof. A flight of circular steps, flanked by two stone lions, led to the entrance. Beyond the vestibule the ground floor contained a beautiful oval dining-room, a small ante-room used as a boudoir; from the dining-room one passed to a commodious drawing-room, graced by a handsome chimney-piece, from which a glass door led by an outside stairway to the garden. Adjacent to this salon was a smaller room, interesting because when Julie sold the house to Josephine it was here that Napoleon worked. By a narrow spiral staircase one reached the upper floor, where the rooms almost exactly reproduced the shape and dimensions of those on the ground floor. We know that the upstairs oval apartment was Talma's bedroom. It will be readily understood that the Etruscan and Roman decorations, which the house had in plenty when the Bonapartes took possession, owed much to the actor's taste for antiquity.

The second Madame Talma's book of memoirs includes a very malicious account, inserted no doubt to denigrate her predecessor. She gives a picture of a neglected Talma[1] who, fleeing from the political discourses of the salon, took refuge in the kitchen, where

[1] C. Talma, *Quelques Particularités*, p. 292.

an old, good-natured cook nourished him with bouillon and where, in the fireside corner, the actor found a little peace to study his parts. Two points can surely be deduced to prove the falsity of such statements. Like most actors, certainly all the great ones, Talma was the complete extrovert. Can one really see him skulking wearily below stairs to the kitchen when in the drawing-room Arnault, Lemercier, Legouvé and Ducis were discussing and reading their newest plays? Another point. All his life Talma was very short-sighted. The possibility of blindness became later something of a nightmare for him. Is it likely that in the glow of the firelight, reinforced only by the tallow candles of an eighteenth-century underground kitchen, he would regularly study his scripts? No, much too thrilling was the discussion in the drawing-room and in such exchanges the lady of the house always acquitted herself with distinction. Benjamin Constant, writing years after Julie's death in 1829, reminds us how irresistible were Julie's wit and charm. 'She would speak of love with all a woman's delicacy but with the sense and thoughtfulness of a man.' In that highly intelligent company Talma would have his say. Besides, he was deeply in love with his gifted wife.

The Théâtre de la rue de Richelieu absorbed fully his working day. There he toiled with an almost frantic energy. Two considerable successes had already been won when on May 21st he presented a third, Voltaire's *Brutus*. This was in every sense a quite memorable production. In Talma's company was an actor who painted, one Boucher, and his help over scenery and properties proved of inestimable value. As for the acting, Talma played the title rôle with Monvel as Titus and both men earned superlative praise. Voltaire's political thesis[1] proved exactly to the taste of the theatre's leftish following and the accuracy of the décor and costumes down to the last detail, not only expended on leading parts, made this performance a consistently true and vivid evocation of ancient Rome. This success came at the right moment. In the ding-dong struggle between the two theatres, the *sociétaires* had launched on May 29th a new tragedy, *Marius à Minturnes* by Julie's friend, twenty-one year old Arnault, which offered a

---

[1] Some idea of Voltaire's anti-monarchical thesis can be gauged by the following lines in this play:

J'ai tenté par degrés d'effacer cette horreur
Que pour le nom de roi Rome imprime en son coeur. . . . (Act III Sc. ii.)
Je porte en mon coeur . . .
La liberté gravée et les rois en horreur. (Act II Sc. ii)

serious challenge to the alleged superiority of the rue de Richelieu players in this genre. Paris hailed Arnault's play as a great success. As Marius, old Vanhove, none too accurately garbed and, according to the author, far from intelligent in his reading of the part, nevertheless shared honours with Saint-Prix making his first hit as Le Cimbre, with Saint-Fal as Mutius.

If the company in Saint-Germain crowed over their Arnault triumph, the actors in the Palais-Royal retorted with a high-spirited performance of Fabre d'Églantine's comedy, *L'Intrigue épistolaire*, on June 15th, 1791. Talma, himself taking the comic part of Cléry, cast the play brilliantly with Grandmesnil, a fine exponent of the witty, polished line, Dugazon, funniest of valets, and Mlle Lange as the heroine, Pauline. Mlle Lange had the distinction of playing lead in four consecutive plays by Fabre d'Églantine, quite the best writer of comedy in that somewhat sterile period. Here was indeed a successful challenge in a genre that Parisian playgoers thought was better served in the Théâtre de la Nation.

L'Intrigue épistolaire had barely embarked upon its promising run when political events emptied the theatres. It will suffice to remind the reader that on June 20th and 21st occurred the King's flight to Varennes, and on June 25th his return to Paris virtually a prisoner. July was punctuated by a wonderful street pageant on the 11th, the apotheosis of Voltaire at the Panthéon; on the 14th there was the second *Fête de la Fédération*; on the 17th blood flowed in the Champ de Mars. Here was in truth an opposition compared with which the efforts of the *sociétaires* seemed negligible. It is against this disturbed background that Talma and his colleagues were called upon to act. For Julie's friends of the Gironde faction, the impassioned oratory and the mounting influence of the 'sea-green, incorruptible' Robespierre brought a particular menace. Why go to the theatre when drama stalked the streets?

The theatres bravely kept their doors open but takings fell alarmingly. Ducis, always a fervent admirer of Talma's abilities, brought to the rue de Richelieu his tragedy, *Jean sans Terre*, an adaptation of Shakespeare's *King John*. Professor F. C. Green in his valuable critical survey of French and English literary ideas in the eighteenth century, *Minuet*[1], very properly described Ducis' adaptation as a 'travesty' of the English chronicle play. Ducis

[1] F. C. Green, *Minuet* p. 111.

certainly knew how to inoculate the original with a revolutionary virus. Jean is a tyrannical monarch, at pains to defend his throne against the intrigues of Arthur, the people's favoured claimant. All the odium that kingship can carry, all its ridicule too, Ducis poured upon a puppet, Jean sans Terre. Talma, whose love of Shakespeare we already know, jumped eagerly to play a part his most enthusiastic admirers voted '*un rôle atroce*'. The opening night was June 28th, 1791. In this lifeless five-act tragedy, so typical of the accepted form of its day, Talma acted with his nerves; he shouted and poured unrestrained emotion into this sawdust king, only interesting to the French as a symbol of royal tyranny. A newcomer, Mlle Simon, played Constance; to her and to Monvel as Hubert fell some very maudlin, sentimental speeches. When right had triumphed and had brought low the dark deeds of hereditary kingship, Hubert devised an appropriately lingering death for '*le tigre Jean*'. On the first night the audience lost interest after the blindness of Arthur. Ducis, nothing daunted, reduced his five acts to two in an effort to compress and heighten his plot, but even such curtailment did not save the play. It promptly disappeared from the repertory.

Sandwiched between his creations in some hazardous new plays, Talma found compensation in certain established successes that reflected exactly the spirit of the times. Sharing leads with Monvel, he appeared to good effect in Voltaire's *La Mort de César*, Debelloy's *Le Siège de Calais* and Lemierre's *Guillaume Tell*, all three making a very dramatic plea for liberty. As Brutus and Tell, Talma earned high praise, but at that particular time dramatic criticism was almost non-existent. Political personalities, the oratory of the tribune, the decrees that were endlessly promulgated, swamped the newspapers, leaving little if any space for a record of aesthetic delights in the theatre. These are bad years for the stage. We shall see the coarsening effects of these chauvinistic audiences upon actors called to project much ultra-patriotic bombast. Law-abiding thoughtful playgoers gave place to political hotheads, who used the parterre as a stamping ground for extremist interests.

Hope in the theatre springs eternal. Ducis' setback was followed by Chénier's dramatic reconstruction of *l'affaire Calas*, a case of monstrous injustice that Voltaire publicized, to his eternal credit and to the shame of his generation. Jean Calas was broken on the wheel as the murderer of his son on the judgment of bigoted Catholics, who accused the father of preferring to see his son dead rather than renounce Calvinism for Catholicism. Voltaire, by an examination of the records, proved the charges without any foundation. In Chénier's conventional tragedy, *Jean Calas*, produced on July 6th, 1791, Talma played Lasalle, the examining magistrate. Chénier could always be relied upon to support Protestantism against Catholic intolerance and, if his play did not hit the target of success, it at least passed muster. The management decided on September 2nd to revive Talma's early triumph *Charles IX*, which signally failed to repeat its former success. The Revolution was moving fast and writers, to compete with the tribune, must wield more venomous pens where kings were concerned. October 3rd saw André de Murville's exotic tragedy *Abdelazis et Zuliéma*, with Talma and Mlle Desgarcins in the title rôles of two thwarted lovers. The following month, November 26th, the rue de Richelieu offered Dumaniant's adaptation from the English, *La Vengeance*, in which Talma as Alonzo had a part made to measure and one that provided him with an early sketch for Othello, wildly jealous of Mlle Desgarcin's Roxane. Success however, despite exciting acting and beautifully accurate costumes and décor, tapped only gently at the door of the Théâtre de la rue de Richelieu. In an effort to flaunt the theatre's newfound liberty, La Harpe's drama *Mélanie*— its subject matter forbade its pretensions to sacrosanct tragedy— was produced on December 7th. Written in 1770, it had been suppressed by the censorship because it dealt with the enforced profession of religious vows, a situation that Talma, as the distracted lover Monval, exploited to the full with the aid of '*la touchante Desgarcins*' as Mélanie, the reluctant nun.

Today these new plays of 1791 can have only the faintest shadow of academic interest. They achieved performance mainly because of the revolutionary fervour they exuded and of the big acting chances they offered a young ambitious player. M. Manne,[1] in his *La Troupe de Talma*, is hard put to it to make some review of Talma's quality as an actor at this period. He states that in these new plays Talma was 'above all praise'. He goes on to say that in Ducis' work Talma found his first Shakespearean inspiration which would raise him above every rival. Although cast mostly for jeune premier parts, he already showed his astonishing power to delineate strong emotion and con-

[1] E. D. de Manne. *Op. cit.* p. 102.

79

centrated passion. He could grip, nay hypnotize, an audience by the urgent, forceful and ever audible delivery of his lines, so different from the slip-shod, sing-song elocution of his contemporaries.

CHAPTER 12

Marat disturbs a Party

The year 1792 opened disastrously for the Paris theatres. With the revolutionary storm breaking everywhere with redoubled force, audiences shrank to negligible numbers. Orators of such varied styles and attitudes as Gensonné and Guadet, the Girondins, Danton, Robespierre and Marat, the Jacobins, thundered from the tribune. Warmongers were busy and enrolments for the National Guard mounted ominously. Dumouriez made his voice heard at the Ministère des Affaires Étrangères. Against this background of national tension, Chénier's *Caius Gracchus* saw the footlights in the rue de Richelieu on February 7th. In this tragedy, where the author expounded for revolutionary satisfaction the agrarian problems, patricians' privileges and the colonial extension of ancient Rome, Talma played *à succès* Fulvius Flaccus. How embarrassed he, the stickler for historical accuracy, must have been when a member of the first night audience carried a motion that the play should be interrupted for a ceremonial unfurling of the national flag! Prudent actors took care to wear the tricolour cockade.[1] From this play six words enjoyed current quotation: '*Des lois et non du sang!*' (Laws and not bloodshed!') It is noteworthy that after this incident Talma's appearances on the stage became less frequent. Audiences too easily got out of hand.

If business was bad at Talma's theatre, the plight of the Théâtre de la Nation was even worse. Public temper had driven the *sociétaires* to drop from their repertory such tried favourites as *Mérope*, *Didon*, *La Partie de Chasse de Henri IV* and even *Athalie*. Comedy of course was their staple attraction but laughter was not in the Parisian air. War was imminent, for had not the coalition of the Kings of Europe threatened to destroy the Revolution? In that spring and summer of '92, the spate of events seemed almost to overtake time itself. The newsboys yelled

[1] Germain Bapst, *Histoire du Théâtre*, p. 518.

portentous tidings. Declaration of war against Austria, the dismissal of the King's bodyguard, the Paris camp, the Country in danger, the attack on the Tuileries, imprisonment of the Royal Family in the Temple, the Fall of Longwy, the Fall of Verdun, the September massacres, a quite absurdly inadequate catalogue of that summer's crowded happenings. No wonder interest in the theatres waned! Their only *raison d'être* seemed to be to give, during that hectic August, benefit performances for the widows and orphans '*de nos frères*' killed during the assault on the Tuileries. After the awful September massacres in the Paris prisons, the Municipality closed all theatres in the capital. Dark indeed was the outlook.

At long last came the dawn. On September 22nd, 1792, Paris rang with news of the victory of Valmy, a battle destined to prove decisive in the history of the world. Dumouriez and Kellermann had routed the invading Prussians and had saved the fatherland. Only two days previously, at the very time of the cannonade, the National Convention met for the first time to elect its officers. For a brief respite the sinister drum-taps and the ominous tocsin ceased to make the revolutionary night hideous. The capital gave itself up to frenzied joy. Talma's theatre timidly opened its doors on September 27th. Our spotlight must move however from its stage to a quite extraordinary event in the rue Chantereine.

With the Champagne frontier assured against the invaders, Dumouriez took a few days' leave to confer in Paris with his political chiefs on the future conduct of the war. He arrived on October 11th, at variance with the Girondins and loathing the Jacobins. Danton welcomed him at the Jacobin Club, but of course victory pardons sins. What more natural for the hero of the day than to seek relaxation in the theatre and enjoy the hospitality of its bohemian world? Talma and Julie had even extended their floor space by the erection of a marquee in the garden in order that the entertainment they planned for the victor of Valmy could be enjoyed by their political and theatrical associates. [1] Marat, the People's Friend, got wind of the affair and with partisans Montaut and Bentavolle gate-crashed the party. Let us look at Marat's account of this social occasion in the *Journal de la République française* of October 17th, 1792:

[1] Chénier, Méhul, Millin, Langlès, Rieuffe, Roland, Garat, Monge, David, Ducis, almost all the deputies of the Gironde faction and many actors and actresses (Mme Vestris, Mlles Desgarcins, Candeille) were present.

We knew he had returned from the Variétés;[1] we went to seek him at the D. Cypher Club where we had been told he was to go; all in vain. Finally we learned he was to sup at Talma's little house in the rue Chantereine. A line of carriages and brilliant illuminations showed us the Temple where Thalia's son was entertaining a scion of Mars.

It is important to dwell on these lines because Adolphe Thiers, writing in his *Les Girondins* before 1827, erroneously placed this incident *chez* Mlle. Candeille, an actress in Talma's company. Marat continues:

At the entrance was Santerre, general of the Parisian army, acting as lackey, presenting the guests. He announced my name in a loud voice which much displeased me because it caused some personalities, interesting to know, to disappear. However I saw enough to get the hang of the plot. I shall not mention a dozen fairies whose purpose was to decorate the feast. Perhaps politics was not the purpose of their presence there. Nor shall I mention the officers who were paying court to the great general, nor the former aristocratic lackeys who, in the uniform of aides de camp, brought up his rear. Finally I shall not mention the master of the house who in his stage costume mingled with them all.

He then proceeds to name some of the important members of Julie Talma's salon he found there, adding:

. . . all henchmen of the Federal Republic. Before giving any account of our talk with Dumouriez, I pause here a moment to make with the judicious reader a few observations which will not be irrelevant. Can one conceive that this Generalissimo of the Republic, who allowed the King of Prussia to escape at Verdun and who made terms with the enemy he could have forced into his own camp and compelled to lay down their arms, instead of encouraging their retreat, should have chosen so critical a moment for the armies under his orders to frequent playhouses, court popularity, and for himself to indulge in orgies in an actor's house with ballet-girls from the Opéra?

Dumouriez has covered up the secret motives that bring him to Paris by pretending to discuss with ministers the plan of his campaign. What! with a Roland, monastery scullion and mean sneak who knows only dirty, underhand lying and sharp practice?

And on he goes heaping vituperation upon Julie's guests.

Dumouriez has come to ally himself with the leaders of the clique

---

[1] The old name of the Théâtre de la rue de Richelieu.

which is intriguing to set up the Federal Republic; that is the object of his escapade.

Upon entering the drawing-room where the banquet was laid, I noticed that my presence disturbed the general gaiety; that is easily understood when one reflects that I am the scarecrow of the fatherland's enemies. Dumouriez especially seemed disconcerted; I requested him to come with us into another room for a few minutes' private conversation.

Up to this point, our main sources, Marat, Dumouriez and the actress Louise Fusil all agree. Differences now follow. In his version Marat trounced Dumouriez for his conduct and demanded to know why two battalions of volunteers had been severely punished for cutting the throats of four deserters, Prussians according to Dumouriez, émigrés according to Marat. With threats to refer the matter to the Convention, Marat and his two companions took their leave. Before his departure he noticed that Dumouriez's officers had bared their swords and carried them at the shoulder. If, said Marat, this stupid farce was meant to intimidate him, then the general and his lackeys had strange ideas of liberty. Came the parting shot: 'Have patience, gentlemen, we will teach you to know it.'

In the Dumouriez *Mémoires*, written actually by Berville and Barrière, the brush with Marat takes place differently.[1] 'The general, scornfully eyeing him up and down, answered: "Ah! you are he they call Marat. I have nothing to say to you." And he turned his back.' It was at that point that the warm-hearted mulatto, the Chevalier Saint-Georges, famous as a swordsman in his day, had to be restrained from throwing himself upon Marat. Dumouriez, unaware of the identity of Marat's two companions, Montaut and Bentavolle, conversed with them in a reasonable way. They of course withdrew with their master.

In a letter sent next day, October 17th, to her friend Madame Lemoine-Dubarry, Louise Fusil gave an eye-witness account of these events. 'I saw Marat for the first time in my life and I hope it will be the last. But, if I were a painter, I could do his portrait, so much did his face impress me. He wore the carmagnole and around his head a dirty red bandana handkerchief, in which he had probably slept for a very long time. Greasy hair slipped beneath it in strands and round his neck was a choker loosely tied.' She

[1] Berville et Barrière, *La Vie et les Mémoires du Général Dumouriez*, Vol. III, pp. III, 114, 115.

adds that Marat expressed surprise at finding Dumouriez in such a house, 'surrounded by concubines and counter-revolutionaries'. This proved too much for Talma. 'Citizen Marat, by what right do you come to my house to insult our wives and sisters?' 'This house is a hotbed of counter-revolution,' retorted Marat. We are told he went away uttering the most awful threats.

That irrepressible joker, Dugazon, brought laughter to the interrupted party. He found a perfume-brazier and with burnt sugar proceeded to purify the air in the wake of the malodorous Marat. During supper he improvised a most amusing scene between an Austrian soldier at cross purposes with his captor, a French sergeant. The evening ended in hilarious laughter. Dumouriez soon slipped off to rejoin his forces in Belgium where, on November 6th, at Jemappes, victory again crowned his military leadership. Talma and his friends remained in Paris to hear the newsboys shout, hawking that scurrilous broadsheet *L'Ami du Peuple*; 'Party given to the traitor Dumouriez at Talma's house, with the names of conspirators who had plotted to assassinate the People's Friend.'

Not only upon Dumouriez was that November of 1792 to bestow success. The 26th day of that month saw Talma in the terrifying rôle of Othello. Ducis, working on Shakespearean material more dramatically intense than *King John*, had produced a workmanlike adaptation which unfortunately sacrificed the original poetry and fire to the stereotyped 'rules' of French tragedy. He tells us that he felt constrained to make Othello ochre-coloured, lest a blackamoor should outrage the feelings of a French audience. In his hands the character of Iago, renamed Pézare, underwent a quite disastrous change from a psychological point of view. Ducis feared the public would never accept the 'execrable character' of such 'frightful suppleness', 'this serpent'. 'I am quite persuaded,' he says in his preface, 'that if the English can quietly observe the manoeuvres of such a monster, the French could not for one moment suffer his presence, much less watch him reveal the whole scope and depth of his villainy.' So Pézare (Iago) becomes a false friend whose deceits are unmasked only towards the end of the play. Such an interpretation makes nonsense of Shakespeare's character. Desdemona is rechristened Hédelmone, a name very convenient for rhyming alexandrines where '*soupçonne*', '*ordonne*', '*donne*', as Vigny pointed out,[1] could

---

[1] *Le More de Venise, Préface*, p. x.

be so easily pressed into service. This lady writes under duress a compromising letter and parts with a diadem to Othello's young friend, Lovédan, a pale shadow of Cassio. Othello, at the instigation of Pézare, stabs Hédelmone with the classical poignard. Such mundane matters as a handkerchief, Cassio's drunkenness, the smothering of Desdemona, have all been 'ennobled' or excised in accordance with French taste. And yet, how brave of Ducis to follow Shakespeare by setting his last scene in his heroine's bedchamber! This was a terrific innovation. Tradition, ever fearful of violence on the stage, required a *récit* of Hédelmone's murder. The audience must not see too much. From the very start of his version, Ducis gives Othello a reputation for insensate jealousy, which robs the character of those exquisitely subtle gradations of suspicion and agonized fear, inseparable from Shakespeare's Moor. Some concessions were made to the parterre. Othello was the stout loyalist at grips with decadent and treacherous nobles, prominent among whom figured Odalbert (Brabantio), the heroine's father. One further point. Ducis, no doubt recalling the fate of *Jean sans Terre*, wrote an alternative ending. In the nick of time the murder of Hédelmone is averted and Othello generously pardons Pézare.

The play as acted by Talma in the title rôle, Monvel as Pézare and Mlle Simon as the tearful heroine was a huge success. Well might Ducis load his letters for years to come with fulsome apostrophe, '*Oh, mon filleul, mon Othello!*' Coming as it did at the end of a most difficult theatrical year, when sparsely attended and frequently interrupted performances had done little to develop a serious actor or to encourage an aspiring playwright, *Othello* restored Talma to the fulness of his reputation. His playing of the Moor made plain his bent for '*ces rôles terribles*', a bent that both actor and public tended later to exploit. This tour de force was unquestionably a milestone in his career. All who worked with Talma, actors and especially authors, marvelled that a man so terrible in his portrayal of wrath, jealousy, passion and all the phases of a mind deranged, could immediately at curtain fall become himself, the kindly, dedicated student of life and letters. Talma believed that the true actor should play parts remote from his own personality. He knew that his acting strength could run the gamut from an all-pervading melancholy through passion in all its stages to a boundless ferocity. In Othello, Ducis gave Talma a part that he would retain all his life. Years later, when he was asked to give a taste of his quality in the drawing-rooms of the great, he would play without make-up or costume 'the great jealousy' scene from *Othello*, and Madame de Rémusat tells us that all present were overwhelmed by his 'unspeakable emotion'. The news of his triumph in this exacting rôle reached London. His father, writing on Christmas Day 1792, while congratulating him upon his great success in a new play, included a word of warning about his health, an interesting indication of the great nervous strain to which such major rôles subjected Talma. The matter of the tragedian's health will engage our attention later.

CHAPTER 13

Arrest of the Sociétaires

W hile Talma was astounding audiences in the rue de
Richelieu with all the agonized tortures of his Othello,
Paris was staging close at hand another tragedy that
would move the world. The King's trial began on Wednesday
December 26th and on Friday January 18th, 1793, the son of
St. Louis was condemned to death. Three days later he was
guillotined in the Place de la Révolution. These bald statements
of indisputable fact throw into remarkable relief happenings at
the Théâtre de la Nation. On January 3rd the *sociétaires*, incredibly
blind to the political consequences of Robespierre's dictatorship,
launched Laya's *L'Ami des lois*,[1] *véritable oeuvre de combat*, and a
quite bitter satire against the extremism of the Jacobins. Fleury,
Dazincourt, Saint-Prix, Saint-Fal, old Vanhove and Mme Suin
were in the cast and the audience quickly recognized in the characters of Nomophage and Duricrâne, Robespierre and Marat, who
were not spared by the author as objects of hatred and repulsion.
The enthusiastic reception the play received indicated much
anti-Jacobin feeling in the audience. The *Gazette Nationale*
commented thus: 'L'Ami des lois* strives to enlighten the people
as to their real interest, to show them the crimes licence and
anarchy bring in their train, to lead all citizens toward a
common goal, public prosperity, which will never exist without
government, without order, without a respect for law.' Strange
to relate, the early performances of this bitter attack on tyranny
were well received and the following lines never failed to evoke
applause:

> *Que tous ces charlatans, populaires larrons,*
> *Et de patriotisme insolents fanfarons,*

---

[1] A. Pougin, *La Comédie-Française et la Révolution*, pp. 71–98.

Purgent de leur aspect cette terre affranchie!
Guerre! Guerre éternelle aux faiseurs d'anarchie. [1]

Such enthusiasm was not to the taste of *Père Duchêne. Numéro* 208 of this slangy, ultra-republican rag put the question: 'Can we allow that, before our face and under our very nose, patriots should be so insulted? Have we no longer blood in our veins?' So the Commune got busy and, despite Laya's brave protest, forbade the performance of *L'Ami des lois* on January 12th, but the *sociétaires*, flouting that order, tried to give the play on that night before a noisy, divided parterre. By some odd, inexplicable paradox, the Convention took a different line. It authorized the play's performance. Crowds gathered outside the theatre, sensing a coming storm. The Commune replied with an order to close all theatres in Paris, which Roland, Minister of the Interior, promptly countermanded. On January 14th the playbill read *L'Avare* and *Le Médecin malgré lui.* Still the public clamoured for *L'Ami des lois.* The actors feared the consequences of acting in a play not officially advertised. On that night however neither of the Molière comedies was performed; *L'Ami des lois* was READ '*au milieu des transports du plus vif enthousiasme*'. The Théâtre de la Nation, in a mood of appeasement, gave a further performance, the proceeds of which went to the war fund. Dazincourt, fully aware of the mobilized Jacobins, begged audiences from the stage not to request a play that might have dire consequences for the actors.

Meanwhile the *sans culottes* enjoyed themselves in the rue de Richelieu. But under what conditions? Talma and his colleagues had often to endure quite disgraceful scenes in order to safeguard their calling and their lives. Crude, patriotic plays like *Le Général Dumouriez à Bruxelles* or *Les Vivandiers* appealed to the worst, jingoistic instincts. Spectators, duly fired by such claptrap, would clamber on the stage and dance the carmagnole or sing raucous, revolutionary songs. The cast were often terror-stricken, but one actor, Alexandre, and the scenic designer, Boucher, earned notoriety by their excessive Jacobinism. For such noisy, ill-disciplined mobs the classic répertoire of Corneille, Racine and Voltaire meant nothing. Chénier on February 9th offered *Fénelon*,

[1] Let all these humbugs, lowborn knaves,
And haughty braggarts with their patriotism
Purge from their sight this liberated earth!
War, everlasting war upon agents of anarchy.

a violent attack against nuns and their spirit of vengeance. Talma played Delmance opposite Monvel's Fénelon but, if the play passed muster for its uncompromising anti-clericalism, its seventeenth-century atmosphere which Talma was at pains to evoke seemed, in the Paris of Robespierre, remote and tame. With no classical revivals and only a lukewarm reception for *Fénelon*, Talma's appearances at the Théâtre de la Révolution, now to be known as the Théâtre de la République, became even more rare. From the managerial point of view, the most important feature of the theatrical year of 1793 was the suppression of the annual closure at Easter. Any religious significance of that festival was of course anathema to the Jacobins. The theatre managers eagerly concurred, keen to reap the benefit of additional takings at such a favourable season.

Talma did however create one other part during this terrible year. Luce de Lancival came to his rescue with a rather moribund political thesis forced into the conventional rhyming five-act pattern. *Mutius Scévola*, even with Talma in the title rôle, need not detain us with its short life. The author we shall meet again however in circumstances slightly more memorable.

The Comédie-Française was continuing to operate somewhat uneasily at the Théâtre de la Nation, when misfortune again overwhelmed the *sociétaires*. On August 1st they had offered an apparently innocent comedy by François de Neufchâteau, entitled *Paméla ou la Vertu récompensée*, with Mlle Lange, a renegade from Talma's company, in the title rôle.[1] The Richardson story of the maidservant who married a lord had long been popular on the continent, and Voltaire had used it for his comedy *Nanine* away back in 1749. The trouble about Neufchâteau's play was that Paméla, when she is about to marry her aristocratic master, Mylord Bonfil, learns that she is really the daughter of Count Oxpen. Although this fairy story pleased the older members of the audience, its implications aroused resentment in younger minds. The next day the *Gazette Nationale* reminded readers that 'neither the English author nor Voltaire made his heroine a Count's daughter. There lies the whole difficulty.' *La Feuille du Salut public* went further with: 'Equality does not triumph at all. Paméla would not have got married if she had not been the daughter of an aristocrat.'

From that day the *sociétaires* faced threats and angry demon-

[1] A. Pougin, *La Comédie-Française et la Révolution*, pp. 99–116.

strations. On August 21st *La Feuille du Salut public* returned to the
attack. The Comédie-Française was infected with a large number
of royalists who eagerly seized upon or even imagined allusions
with which they agreed. On August 29th, one hour before curtain-
rise, the Committee of Public Safety forbade that night's announced performance of *Paméla*. The author readily agreed to
revise his text, leaving Paméla a simple serving maid. 'So you
would make her a commoner,' they leered. These extremists had
not forgotten the blistering effects of *L'Ami des lois*. They were
convinced that the *talons rouges* were at it again. Had not the
poignard that laid Marat low been sharpened in their theatre?
This and much more did the editor of *La Feuille du Salut public*
write in his edition of September 3rd, making the point that 'all
the actors of the Théâtre de la Nation deserved by their behaviour
to be regarded as very suspect individuals and as such should be
arrested. . . . As for their theatre, let this polluted seraglio be
closed for ever.' Yet on the previous night *Paméla* had been performed for the ninth time. In Act IV, Fleury had to speak the
following lines:

> *Ah! les persécuteurs sont les seuls condamnables,*
> *Et les plus tolérants sont les plus raisonnables!* [1]

A patriot interrupted him: 'No political toleration. That is a
crime.' At these words pandemonium broke loose. With great
difficulty some semblance of order was restored and the patriot
ejected. He turned out to be a certain Jullien de Carenton, a
provincial officer on a mission to the Committee of Public
Safety. Straightaway he went to the Jacobin Club where Robespierre held court and denounced as traitors to the Republic the
actors of the Comédie-Française and the author of *Paméla*,
François de Neufchâteau.

On September 3rd the National Convention ratified the decree
passed by the Committee of Public Safety on the previous day.
That document ordered that the Théâtre-Français should be
closed and that the actors together with the author of *Pamela*
should be put under arrest in a place of safety. Seals must be
affixed to their private papers.

The blow fell on the night of September 3rd–4th, 1793. The
thirty-three players who made up the company of the Comédie-

---

[1] Ah! only persecutors are worthy of condemnation,
And the most tolerant people are the most reasonable!

Française were arrested. The fourteen actresses, among whom were Mmes Lachassaigne, Suin, Raucourt, Louise Contat, Thénard, Joly, Émilie Contat, Petit-Vanhove, Lange and Mézeray, were carried off to La Pélagie prison; the men included Dazincourt, Fleury, Bellemont, Vanhove, Florence, Saint-Fal, Saint-Prix, Dunant, Champville, Dupont, La Rochelle, Marsy, Gérard, Alexandre Duval, all of whom were incarcerated in the most insalubrious of all revolutionary prisons, Les Madelonnettes. In the general proscription Molé appeared to have been forgotten; Naudet the fire-eater was in Switzerland; the news of his colleagues' arrest hastened the death of Desessarts who had been taking the waters at Barège. Larive, though no longer a member of the Comédie-Française, returned from Bordeaux and, on September 13th, shared the captivity with his old friends.

Well might the awful Collot d'Herbois, a really despicable member of the Committee of Public Safety, shout in the streets of Paris: 'The leaders of the Comédie-Française will be guillotined, the remainder deported.' Parisians were dumbfounded to learn that such a fate was to befall their admired, nay adored, favourites, players of the supreme quality of Dazincourt, Fleury, and Louise Contat. The *Journal de Paris* of September 7th merely listed the names of the captives, adding laconically that their arrest was for reasons unspecified (*point de causes expliquées*). The *Feuille du Salut public* did not display the same dignity. It exulted, it laughed, it leered. The fops and dandies had been caught unawares. The aristocratic elegance of their feeble puns had given way to wholesome fear. What a problem too to know whether Mlle Raucourt should be grouped with the men prisoners or the women . . . and so on. Bad taste could go no further. It was plain to all that the actors and actresses of that great national theatre stood in jeopardy of their lives. Although the details of their hardships lie outside this study, it will suffice to say that seven men, Dazincourt, Bellemont, Florence, Marsy, Gérard, Duval, Jules Fleury, and seven women, Mmes Raucourt, Louise and Émilie Contat, Thénard, Mézeray, Montgautier, Ribaut, had to wait until the fall of Robespierre on July 27th, 1794, before they regained their freedom. [1]

[1] A. Pougin, *La Comédie-Française et la Révolution*, pp. 118–133. A. Copin, *Talma et la Révolution*, pp. 141–146.

CHAPTER 14

The Reign of Terror

A burning question of the day was as to the part Talma played in the arrest of his former colleagues. He was of course a revolutionary, but his and his wife's political friends came from the Girondin party, whose enlarged views and political idealism, as the thinning groups at Julie Talma's salon revealed, were rapidly losing ground before the tyranny of Robespierre's Jacobins. Certainly the Théâtre de la République stood to profit by the liquidation of a rival establishment. All French writers on Talma take the line that the tragedian had no part in the imprisonment of the actors of the Comédie-Française. His own sense of camaraderie, they urge, coupled with his innate hatred of the Jacobins, would alone have prevented him from working against his old colleagues. Besides, was he not himself denounced before the Revolutionary Tribunal on October 26th with twenty-one Girondin deputies and charged with being their accomplice in an attempt to form a federal republic? [1] Were there not at those fateful interrogations many references to the Dumouriez visit to Talma's house in the rue Chantereine? The actor's Girondin friends perished and it looked as if he himself escaped the guillotine only by a miracle. Of course he had one great advantage. He was the idol of the revolutionary crowds. His friendship with David, *le farouche conventionnel*, in no small way helped him to walk the political tight-rope. David, the official painter of the Revolution, the Jacobins' pageant-master and designer of uniforms, proved at that time an all powerful protector. David, an enthusiastic supporter, was ever ready to pick a bone with Talma's rivals at the Théâtre de la Nation, where, in the comparatively moderate days of 1792, he had refused to design costumes for *Lucrèce* because its author, Arnault, sported a waistcoat patterned with fleurs de lys.

Talma had no desire to fish in these troubled waters. Besides

[1] A. Copin, *Talma et la Révolution*, pp. 159–161.

there is too much evidence on the other side. We know how, at considerable financial cost to himself, he suppressed a most dangerous piece of evidence against his old teacher Fleury. A blackmailer had got hold of a genealogy of Charlotte Corday in the handwriting of Fleury, who had been intrigued to note Charlotte's descent from the dramatist Corneille. With Marat idolized in the Panthéon such a document, identifying however remotely the actor with the murderer of the Ami du Peuple, might well have meant death. Talma paid the knave 600 livres for the paper with these words: 'And remember to be discreet. If I have paid, you have sold.'[1] Fleury remained unaware of this generosity until the abbé Aubert forced Talma to reveal his part in the transaction. A great reconciliation took place in Louise Contat's dressing-room on August 16th, 1794, when Talma had called to congratulate the actress upon her return to the Théâtre de la Nation where she was supported by Fleury and Dazincourt in *La Métromanie* and *Les fausses confidences*. The 198 charges raked up against the actors by the insatiable Collot d'Herbois could carry no greater stigma in the eyes of the extremists than this matter of Charlotte Corday's pedigree.

Undoubtedly Talma, on this charge of complicity, endured much from evil tongues and suspicious minds. Time is a good devil and with its passing came his complete vindication. That public-spirited woman, Louise Contat, sent the following letter to the newspapers which they published on March 25th, 1795.

It was at the very time of our persecution that I received from Talma, whom I had not seen for a long time, marks of real kindness. I considered them so sincere that they removed the slight differences that had clouded our horizon and brought us together again. I hasten to pay homage to truth. Can it be possible to wipe out a charge that I did not know even existed? I will never allow that an artist should coldly speculate upon the ruin of his own kind and Talma was at that time no more disposed to profit at our expense than we would be today to take advantage of him. I say 'we' without having consulted my colleagues, but I say so in the certainty of not being contradicted. L. Contat.[2]

In the *Républicain français* on March 25th, Larive[3] showed himself equally emphatic 'to do justice to one of my former comrades. Far from having contributed to the arrest of the actors of the

---

[1] Fleury, *Mémoires*, pp. 255–263. A. Copin, *Talma et la Révolution*, p. 153.
[2] A. Copin, *Talma et la Révolution*, p. 143.   [3] Ibid, p. 144.

Comédie-Française, Talma quite voluntarily forestalled a blow intended for me; thanks to his care and action I owed the salutary warning that saved me from the attention of four of Henriot's henchmen when they came into the country to outlaw me and order the firing squad.' Finally a Monsieur Trouvé,[1] a member of the literary staff of *Le Moniteur*, wrote to his paper on March 27th, urging it his duty, as a friend and a lover of the arts and truth, to declare that Talma was no persecuting informant. The dates of these letters prove that the charge against the tragedian had been widely and persistently made. After such evidence he stood acquitted.

What was happening at the Théâtre de la République during the imprisonment of the members of the Comédie-Française? Like most places of entertainment it found itself regarded by the National Convention as an instrument of propaganda. On August 2nd, 1793, that body had promulgated two decrees. The first stated that in Paris theatres, indicated by the Municipality, there should be performed weekly from August 4th to September 1st the tragedies of *Brutus*, *Guillaume Tell* and, wonder of wonders, Chénier's *Caius Gracchus*, as well as other dramatic plays which would recall the glories of the Revolution and the courage of its defenders. One of these performances would be given each week as a free treat for the populace at the Republic's expense. The second decreed that any theatre where plays would be performed that tended to deprave the public mind and to awaken the shameful superstition of royalty would be closed and their managers punished with all the rigour of the law. The Municipality of Paris was responsible for the execution of this decree. Both decrees appeared over the signature of J.–C. Battellier, Inspecteur.

With the trial of the Girondins in the forefront of events, Talma was not anxious to appear in public. In 1793 his supporting casts were not brilliant and before that uncontrollable parterre some performances sank to a very low level. Actors had first to be citizens and their revolutionary duties took precedence over stage obligations.[2] Often they had not time to dress and played their rôles in uniform. There was also a disastrous mutilation of text. No play, ancient or modern, dared to make use of titles such as *duc*, *marquis*, *comte*, *seigneur*. The only permissible form of address was *citoyen*. Such changes disturbed the balance of the

---

[1] Ibid, p. 145.   [2] Germain Bapst, *Histoire du Théâtre*, p. 500.

alexandrine and upset its rhythm. Dialogue was altered, revolutionary tirades were inserted. An actor playing chess on the stage had to say: 'Checkmate to the tyrant.'

Evenings memorable for artistic success there certainly were. Such a one occurred on February 3rd, 1794, when Talma reached sublime heights in Gabriel Legouvé's tragedy *Épicharis et Néron*.[1] To Talma fell the rôle of Néron, a character that would fascinate him all his life, and in Legouvé's powerful fifth act, where he dared to enter the underground chamber barefooted, he gave a masterly portrayal of abject fear and of a hysteria bordering on madness. This emperor feared to commit suicide.

> *Esclave, aide ma main à m'arracher la vie!*
> *Phaon, guide ce fer!*[2]

Here was a particularly Talmaesque moment. But drama lurked also in the audience. On that first night Robespierre, prominent in a stage box, and Danton, surrounded by friends in the orchestre, surveyed the painted scene. According to eyewitness Lemercier, when the expression 'Death to the tyrant' was uttered on the stage, Danton and his friends with raised clenched fists turned towards Robespierre's box. The sea-green incorruptible's head with its pinched white face darted forward, then retreated like a goaded serpent. At curtain fall, actors and friends besought Legouvé to take flight. 'You are lost. Robespierre will never forgive you for that awful curse.' Legouvé stayed in Paris. It was Danton who paid.

Épicharis et Néron, an obstinate success, remained long in the bill and at a performance after the fall of Robespierre, on that blessed Sunday, July 27th, Talma on his entrance was hissed by the parterre and roundly accused of supporting the dethroned Jacobins. The actor paused. With complete calm he addressed the audience. 'Citizens, I confess that I have loved and that I still love liberty, but ever have I hated crime and murderers; the Reign of Terror cost me many tears; most of my friends died on the scaffold. I crave the public's pardon for this brief interruption; I will now strive to make the audience forget it by the zeal of my efforts.' The play went forward to a triumphant conclusion. This par-

---

[1] E. Legouvé, *Soixante ans de souvenirs*, pp. 189–193.

[2] Slave, help my hand to pluck out my life!
Phaon, guide this sword!

ticular cabal against Talma had been broken. Arnault, a rival dramatist, neatly summed up the occasion. 'Even the judges of the King of France hesitated to strike a tragedy king.'[1]

The January and the February of 1794 saw the release of certain members of the Comédie-Française. Some of them regained their liberty on condition that they would accept service in the rue de Richelieu. The ranks of Talma's company now comprised such first-rate liberated players as Mlle Joly, Mme Petit-Vanhove, her father old Vanhove, Dupont and La Rochelle. This accession of strength meant better performances and some ease for those faithful, sorely tried adherents, Monvel, Dugazon, Mme Vestris and Mlle Simon. These new arrivals increased the range of plays, particularly on the side of comedy: Mlle Joly opened as Finette in *Le Dissipateur*, Dupont and Mme Petit-Vanhove shared honours in *Le Père de Famille*: old Vanhove lent Talma thunderous support in *Brutus*. Mme Petit-Vanhove particularly made an impression, and not only on the public. This brilliant all-round actress after her astonishing débuts had married, at the age of fifteen, in 1786, Louis Petit, a drunken musician from the theatre orchestra, but within three months of her appearance on the stage of the République she obtained a divorce, on April 26th, 1794. Caroline Petit-Vanhove, then only twenty-three, had become more than a little attracted to François-Joseph Talma. Her attentions did not go unrequited.

If rather more than half of the imprisoned actors of the Comédie-Française had managed to regain their freedom, those seven men and seven women already indicted found themselves in a parlous plight. With Collot d'Herbois constantly pressing for their trial, their escape from the guillotine reads like some fantastic fairy-tale. A certain Charles-Hippolyte Labussière,[2] the second son of an impoverished chevalier de Saint-Louis, after a rather worthless career as a soldier and actor, sought to save his neck by taking a clerical post, on April 24th, 1794, in the offices of the Committee of Public Safety, the very headquarters of the Terrorists. There it became his job to sort out the dossiers of prisoners and to pass on evidence (*les pièces accusatives*) to the Revolutionary Tribunal, which then summarily dealt with the accused. Labussière, guided no doubt by the light of his own

---

[1] E. de Manne, *La Troupe de Talma*, p. 103. A. Copin, *Talma et la Révolution*, p. 173.
[2] A. Pougin, *La Comédie-Française et la Révolution*, pp. 134–186.

aristocratic origins, and by his actor's spirit of camaraderie, conceived the plan of abstracting from the files incriminating documents of persons he wanted to save. Steeping the tell-tale dossiers in a pail of water at dead of night, he pulped them into papier-mâché. This substance he made into little balls and carried them away in his pocket. The next morning early, when he was taking his bath in an establishment moored on the banks of the Seine, he gently dropped them, reduced to pellets, down the current of the stream. Meanwhile Collot d'Herbois stormed and demanded the trial of the players. Despite the most rigorous searches in the offices, their *pièces accusatives* could not be found. Well might Fouquier-Tinville, the *accusateur public*, the man who held the key position at the Tribunal, write on July 2nd (5 Thermidor) to the citizen representatives of the people responsible for the general police: 'For some two months there has been total disorder in the Committee's records; out of thirty individuals set down to be tried, nearly always half or two-thirds of them are without papers; more recently still, all Paris awaited the trial of the actors from the Comédie-Française and I have received nothing with reference to that business; Couton and Collot (d'Herbois), representatives, had however reminded me of it and I am still waiting for orders on the matter. It is impossible for me to bring to trial any prisoner without papers that indicate at least the prisoner's name and place of detention; in such disorder. . . .' and so on.

For the Jacobins the sands of time were fast running out. The actors' papers could not be produced on July 22nd. On July 29th France breathed a sweeter, cleaner air. The Terror was at an end. Labussière, in heroic stealth, had performed a great deed for his fellow creatures. Apart from the actors, some of the bearers of the greatest names of France owed their lives to his efforts. Liénart, his biographer, named 1,153 persons his hero saved from the guillotine. No name in that impressive list was ever disputed. Among them was Joséphine de Beauharnais. It seems strange that this man, ever miserably poor, had to wait until April 5th, 1803, for that benefit performance at the Porte Saint-Martin Theatre which the sociétaires of the Comédie-Française organized as an expression of their gratitude. On that occasion, when the substantial sum of 14,000 francs was realized, Talma and Mlle Raucourt, as Hamlet and Gertrude, appeared before the first Consul in a special revival of Ducis' version of the Shakespearean play. For Labussière the rest was poverty, ill-health, madness and death. [1]

If Thermidor gave some semblance of order to the life of the average Parisian, it brought in its train upheaval, discord and difficulty for the released and apparently reunited members of the Comédie-Française. Talma and his troupe of course remained at the Théâtre de la République in the rue de la Loi, the name for the rue de Richelieu. Their popularity throughout the Terror had been almost notorious, but gradually it became evident that the public was not prepared to bestow its wholehearted patronage upon a theatre that had paid too overt a tribute to the Jacobins. It has been noted how Talma himself was hissed in *Épicharis et Néron* and had to appease a hostile audience by a speech from the stage.

The *sociétaires*, now at liberty, returned to their old home in the Marais, the Théâtre de la Nation, renamed through an excess of revolutionary zeal the Théâtre de l'Égalité. Unfortunately, during their incarceration, their stage had been seized by an operatic company, displaced from the Théâtre National de la rue de la Loi, a group which asserted its right to perform on particular evenings, leaving the rightful proprietors only two nights per week to present the extensive répertoire of the Comédie-Française. The *sociétaires* soon found themselves in dispute with the singers over the burning question of box-office returns and, after a stormy season which lasted from June 27th to December 23rd, they migrated to Citizen Sageret's vast Théâtre Feydeau, situated in the very centre of the Parisian pleasure ground and only a stone's throw from the Théâtre de la République. On January 27th, 1795, by an arrangement with Sageret, the Doyen Molé, Mlle Contat, Dazincourt, Saint-Prix and Mlle Devienne inaugurated a season which would allow the émigrés from the Théâtre de la Nation to appear every other night, alternating with musical productions provided by another company. Paris flocked to the new venture. The revival of Laya's *L'Ami des lois* played to packed audiences, thankful to applaud those who had endured imprisonment for having expressed, in days of tyranny, the author's plea for toleration.

The success of the Feydeau reorganization dealt a heavy blow at its near neighbour, the Théâtre de la République. There, for

[1] The date of his death is unknown. The last reference to him alive is in Fabien Pillet's 'Revue des Comédiens', Paris 1808.

some time, things had not been going too well. Chénier had writ-ten supposedly his last lifeless tragedy, *Timoléon*, in which Talma appeared on September 11th, 1794 as yet another usurper oppres-sing sorely tried citizens. Its disastrous first night killed the play. The Robespierre adherents did not, for political reasons, welcome the hatred Talma aroused by his performance of the tyrant, Timoléon, a character too close to their dethroned master. The anti-Jacobins were there too and, when the public called for the author's name, a voice from the parterre shouted: 'His name is Cain'. [1] The dramatist was never allowed to forget that he made no effort to save from the guillotine his poet-brother André Chénier.

Paris seemed no longer in the mood for *La Mort de César*, *Brutus* and *Guillaume Tell*, those unfailing stand-bys during the Terror. With the departure of Chénier, a new playwright, A-.V. Arnault, whose contemporary success Talma would sustain, swam into the literary firmament. His *Quintus Cincinnatus*, which saw the light on December 31st, 1794, provided the actor with the highly effective rôle of Servilius. Although fairly well re-ceived and honourably treated by the critics, the tragedy followed in all respects—subject matter, treatment and pedestrian verse— the conventional recipe of the day. Only Talma could give it a semblance of fleeting life. More important to us is the memory of this association of author and actor, which Arnault recorded in his *Souvenirs d'un Sexagénaire*. He says: 'The studies for *Cincinnatus* brought me into frequent contact with Talma; not for long were these limited to theatrical matters. It was difficult to make contact with Talma without becoming keenly attached to a man endowed with such rare qualities. The simplicity of his mind, the goodness of his nature soon exercised over me a sway which time has only strengthened and which earned for him friends among admirers attracted by his talent. This talent everyone knows. A product of the happiest planning, of the quickest intelligence, of the keenest sensibility, it appeared in all its superiority from the very moment Talma made his entrance on the stage.' These are not the flattered and flattering effusions of a young author fortunate enough to get his play produced by a star actor. Arnault was destined to write several successes for Talma and these observa-tions represent the sum-product of his associations with the actor.

[1] Germain Bapst, *Histoire du Théâtre*, p. 506.

Arnault's friendship with Talma gave him the entrée to the house in the rue Chantereine, where Julie's salon in 1795 had lost to the executioner so many of its brilliant habitués. True, a few of the faithful remained like Allard, Lenoir, Roederer.[1] Gone were the Girondins, Vergniaud, Gaudet, Gensonné. Apart from this terrible liquidation, poor Julie nursed other cares. Talma's ever growing passion for Madame Petit-Vanhove disturbed his friends, but Arnault speaks of many happy evenings *chez* Talma and pays great tribute to his charming hostess. 'She would discuss with equal clarity the most difficult political and philosophical questions but in terms suitable to her sex, steering a middle course between pedantry and frivolity, yet never in a masculine way, uniting the strength of her charm with the statesman, the man of the world and the philosopher just as Aspasia did in time past with Alcibiades, Pericles and Socrates.'

If Talma and his wife appeared to Arnault to live together in harmony, their marriage nevertheless was beginning to show the strain of many stresses. Julie, with a husband seven years her junior, was nearing forty. Talma, handsome, successful and attractive to women, had for some time been unfaithful to his wife. Louise Fusil, devoted to Julie, was deeply distressed by his filching a mistress from his colleague Michot, and hoped that her friend might be spared the gossip, all too true, that centred around Talma and Caroline Vanhove. The children of their marriage could give little comfort. Castor and Pollux were weakly little boys, each destined to a consumptive's early grave. A third child, christened Tell, died in infancy on April 3rd, 1794. And of course there were the inevitable money troubles. Both parties were wildly extravagant and generous to a fault. Accounts were never kept and Julie failed to supervise her servants. With open house, lavish meals and those beautiful but uncomfortable classical Greek beds available to all and sundry, is there any wonder that creditors knocked persistently at the door?

In the theatre Ducis had come forward with a play expressly written for his *cher filleul*, a tragedy of some scenic novelty entitled *Abufar ou la famille arabe*. The play had a Bedouin setting among the tents of the tribe of Samaël. Ducis first communicated

---

[1] Allard: wealthy business man in love with the theatre. Mlle Desgarcins was his mistress. Alexandre Lenoir (1762–1839): eminent archaeologist and founder of the Musée des Monuments Français. Pierre-Louis Roederer (1754–1835): one of the editors of the *Journal de Paris* who dared to defend Louis XVI. Held office under Napoleon.

his stage directions to Talma in a letter dated August 16th, 1794, and they would indeed have delighted Beerbohm Tree. 'The spectator beholds pastures with camels, horses and sheep grazing untethered; flowers, beehives, date-palms, incense-bearing trees and other productions of the country.' Beside such fertility must appear the sterile desert, conspicuous wells and everywhere a burning sun; 'in the distance some cedar trees, interlacing palms, ruins barely glimpsed and, on the horizon, a sky shades into sand'. Here was local colour with a vengeance. The tragic plot relied upon that ever successful situation, the son returning from his travels who falls in love with one he believes to be his sister. Voltaire as we know had used this device in *Mahomet* and Talma's mind must have flashed back to his début as Séïde when, in the part of Faran, he spoke Ducis' lines:

> *De quel front ai-je pu rentrer dans ma famille?*
> *Je suis fils d'Abufar et j'ose aimer sa fille!* [1]

Monvel acted the rigid, patriarchal Abufar; Mlle Simon played his ill-starred ward. The sub-plot, the love affair between Pharasmin and Onéïde, fell to Baptiste *aîné* and Mme Petit-Vanhove.

Abufar was presented at the Théâtre de la République on April 12th, 1795. The colourful background of the elaborately designed Arabian desert, the patriarchal mode of life and the picturesque Bedouin costumes of the actors made a welcome change from classical peristyle, togas and imperial posturings. We are told that 'neither the talent of Talma, nor the grace of Mlle Simon, nor even the ability and charm of Mme Petit-Vanhove could save the play from public indifference'. A rather surprising judgment. Ducis, in writing to his *cher* Faran from Versailles on October 21st, 1800, made it clear that *Abufar* was still in the repertory. Madame de Staël, even later on February 15th, 1810, writing from Geneva, made a most flattering reference to Talma's performance in *Abufar*. If Ducis' Arabian tragedy failed at that time to fill the coffers, on July 31st, 1795 prosperity awaited Legouvé's three act tragedy *Quintus Fabius*, a play remarkable not only for Talma's own contribution as Quintus but also for the acting success of that fine trouper Baptiste *aîné* in the rôle of Cominius. Strange as it may seem, this rather remote tragedy, dealing with the life of one of Rome's earliest historians, provided

---

[1] How have I been able so boldly to return home?
I am Abufar's son and I dare to love his daughter!

a much needed box-office retort to the overweening success of the Théâtre Feydeau.

In the world of the theatre fortune so often proves capricious. The year 1796, with the exception of an ungrateful part in *Les Artistes*, a rather feeble comedy by Collin-Harleville which never appears in the lists of Talma's creations, offered the actor no new experience. True, the classical repertory of Corneille and Racine provided him with ground for ample thought, especially in the interpretation of Néron in *Britannicus*, a rôle he was destined to make peculiarly his own. Alongside the comparatively rare performances of these masterpieces, all too frequently occurred such facile patriotic stuff as *Guillaume Tell*, *Le Siège de Calais* and *Gaston et Bayard*. There were personal difficulties too. That excellent actor, Monvel, Talma's greatest support at the Théâtre de la République, began to show signs of age. Only his consummate art enabled him to overthrow the physical disability of a stooping frame and an enunciation handicapped by a loss of teeth. More and more, kings and *pères nobles* became his lot, but his brilliant rendering of Auguste in *Cinna* with Talma's striking portrayal of the name part continued to give Parisians a memorable theatrical experience. Madame Vestris too was getting no younger and Ducis, writing to Talma in 1798, showed more than a little anxiety about her ability to memorize his revised lines for Lady Macbeth. Truth to tell, the leading players at the Théâtre de la République, having weathered the revolutionary storms and having found in them an elevation of spirit, which often lent an excess of nervous force to their acting, were beginning to feel something akin to exhaustion. Although the Terror was over, audiences still had to be politically placated by the orchestra playing '*les airs patriotiques*' like *La Marseillaise* and *Ça ira*; also, during the interval between two plays, all present had to sing *La Marseillaise*, an interlude hardly calculated to enhance the atmosphere of the performance.[1] The decree authorizing this, dated January 4th, 1796, at least forbade any public rendering of 'that homicidal song', *Le Réveil du Peuple*. Actors still had to walk warily, and woe betide the management if an *ouvreuse* chanced to address a spectator as '*Monsieur*' instead of '*Citoyen*'!

Yet in these drab days a sudden and most welcome success came to the 'République'. A young dramatist barely twenty-five years old, one Népomucène Lemercier, who as a boy poet had

[1] Germain Bapst, *Histoire du Théatre*, pp. 504, 505.

formerly won the patronage of Marie Antoinette, wrote a tragedy *Agamemnon*. The son of the playwright Legouvé tells us in his *Soixante ans de souvenirs*[1] how his father and Lemercier had both chosen at the same time to write a tragedy on this very subject. Legouvé *père*, anxious to follow in the wake of Euripides, wanted to portray Cassandra as a royal captive, condemned by servitude to share the bed of her master. 'You are wrong,' retorted Lemercier. 'Aeschylus, not Euripides, is the source for that terrible tragedy. Hands off Cassandra! Don't defile Cassandra! Cassandra is the solitary lamp burning in the shadow of the sanctuary.' Legouvé, impressed by the young man's fervour, left the subject alone. Assuredly something of Lemercier's fire gave warmth and life to *Agamemnon*. In performance, it was more than a success, it was a triumph. Étienne and Martainville, two contemporary historians of the French theatre, tell us that *Agamemnon* is 'in our opinion the finest tragedy that has been produced for thirty years'. As the most repulsive Égisthe, Talma was above all praise, and dulcet-toned Mme Petit-Vanhove lent a mystical quality to Cassandra that satisfied the most fastidious. On this night of April 25th, 1797, Talma leapt back to his brilliant best and, by the general acclaim he received on all sides, the tragedian looked upon this creation as an important milestone in his career.

No longer was he the lover living his hour on the stage with tender vows and passionate declaration, no longer was he even the unbalanced, terror-racked Charles IX, acting on his nerves often at the expense of subtlety and, through sheer physical exhaustion, lapsing occasionally into a monotonous delivery. No, by 1797 Talma had found himself as an artist with a perfected technique, sure of producing his effects. Had he not earlier in the year in *Junius*, a feeble tragedy by Monvel *fils*, electrified his audience when he raised his dagger against his daughter Tullie, played by Mme Petit-Vanhove. At that moment Talma was so terrible that from the whole theatre came a cry of fear. The brothers Goncourt wrote half a century later of his acting at this very period in the following terms. 'On his wan face, so beautiful in its outline, on his face lit up by his expressive eyes, rolls all the tumult of human passions. An ample gesture, simple, noble, epic withal, a gesture in marble, beautiful movements, conceal the man in the actor. . . . Then, above everything else, an intense concentrated playing in which there is no squandering of soul,

[1] E. Legouvé, *Soixante ans de souvenirs*, p. 62.

acting directed to mimetic perfection, a playing restrained, controlled, stressing with sudden lightning flashes the poet's thought and with everything unleashed for the vital lines. Talma, it is he who incarnates the high intelligence of strong, dark, awful tragedy. It is his work, his care, his sense of continuity in the part, his genius won by dint of talent, his art soaring often to the sublime.'

Before we leave the world of the theatre for more pregnant events, a word is due about that other Comédie-Française troupe at the Feydeau. As was to be expected, such highly charged, individual personalities, accustomed to rule in their own theatre, would not easily endure, despite the rewards of their initial success, the restrictions imposed by a frankly commercial management. The success of the association, which opened so auspiciously in January 1794, was compromised by internal jealousies and quarrels to such an extent that Mlle. Raucourt formed a splinter group of dissidents and on Christmas Day reopened the vacant Théâtre Louvois with Larive, Saint-Prix, Saint-Fal, Mlles Jolys and Mézeray and subsequently, the doyen himself, Molé. Thus there were three troupes of actors appearing in three different theatres, each claiming to be the Comédie-Française. This fantastic state of affairs caused Mlle Raucourt to write a very sensible letter to all her colleagues, urging them to re-form their ranks and restore the old Comédie-Française. The artists of the Théâtre Feydeau and of the Théâtre de la République were deaf to her appeal. She herself struggled on at the Louvois until an unfortunate incident occurred, arising from a play called *Les Trois frères rivaux*, in which a valet named Merlin had to be told 'M. Merlin you are a knave.' Merlin was the name of the Minister of Justice under the Directory. The laughter of the audience so riled him that, abusing his official functions, he secured the closure of the Théâtre Louvois. Mlle Raucourt and her colleagues were theatrically homeless.

CHAPTER 15

Talma Meets Bonaparte

No biographer of Talma can afford to underestimate the importance of his friendship with Napoleon Bonaparte, an enduring association that exerted no small influence upon the actor's art as well as upon his fortunes. When did Talma first meet Napoleon? Various dates have been assigned to this occasion. M. Moreau in his *Mémoires historiques et littéraires sur Talma* places the meeting between the two men towards the end of 1790. In that year Bonaparte was garrisoned at Auxonne and his official leave was spent in Ajaccio. Guy de la Batut[1] pinpoints the occasion more precisely and more convincingly. He claims they met on June 18th, 1792, after a performance of Champion's *Les Trois cousines* at the Théâtre de la République, where Talma was of course fully established as leading player. We are told they talked about the theatre far into the night and, two days later at a revolutionary gathering, Bonaparte is supposed to have outlined to Talma his political ideas. Napoleon was undoubtedly in Paris at this time to give an account of the Corsican campaign. Even M. Moreau waits until after the fall of Robespierre before allowing cordial relations to exist between them. The young impecunious artillery captain of 1792 was a keen theatregoer and Talma certainly provided complimentary tickets for the play, lent books and opened for the Corsican many Parisian doors. The persistent accusation that Napoleon sponged on Talma, borrowing money and writing at least one ignoble, piteous letter, begging a few crowns and assuring his friend that he was down to his last sou, must be rejected as a restored Bourbon forgery in a malicious attempt to denigrate the memory of a great man. Indeed many interests united the soldier and the actor. There was a love of antiquity, a very passion for all that pertained to ancient Greece and Rome. In the theatre Napoleon, like most of the revolutionary generation, preferred tragedy to comedy, Corneille

[1] In his *Talma: Correspondance avec Mme de Staël*, p. 121.

to Racine.[1] Corneille, he would say, was political in *Cinna*, military in *Les Horaces* and the gospel of the Cornelian superman in government and war he embraced without reserve. This friendship with Talma helps to explain why, during his heyday, Napoleon was hailed as 'the friend of artists and protector of the arts'.

With the fall of Robespierre the face of Parisian society assumed a relaxed, relieved smile. Mme Tallien, '*Notre-Dame de Thermidor*', that exquisite aristocrat of dazzling beauty and yet married to one of the organizers of the September massacres, held court in her picturesque residence La Chaumière, situated near the Cours-la-Reine in the Allée des Veuves. Here Talma was a frequent visitor and Napoleon, when in Paris, often found himself in that interior which was modelled like a Greek temple and where three graces, Thérésa Tallien, Jeanne-Françoise Récamier and Joséphine Beauharnais posed and pirouetted to music and song made by such distinguished habitués as Cherubini, Méhul, Garat the darling of the Opéra, and Rhodes with his violin. Madame Tallien knew how to adapt her salon to changing times. A spirit of toleration that came near to licence prevailed. Through her friendship with Barras she had a finger in many pies and, like many beautiful women, she loved to exert her influence and distribute her favours. She knew how to plead the cause of the little Corsican. With the revision of grades in the republican army, Napoleon at twenty-five became a general and the duchesse d'Abrantès,[2] writing of him in May 1795, gives a vigorous portrait of the thin, sickly-looking, olive-skinned officer, badly dressed, wearing ill-fitting riding boots that had not been cleaned. No one, she says, could have divined a future emperor in this ill-clad, emaciated soldier. Mme Tallien, on learning that '*il n'avait pas de culottes*', saw that from a government issue of cloth he was at once provided with a suitable uniform at the Directory's expense.

While it is not the purpose of this study to follow Napoleon's rise to fortune, reference must however be made to those appearances in Paris after his brilliant success against the English at Toulon. These visits of the Corsican to the capital brought him into close association with Talma. It was due to Barras and quite

---

[1] Duchesse d'Abrantès, *Mémoires*, Vol. X, pp. 211, 212. Lanzac de Laborie, *Paris sous Napoléon. Le Théâtre-Français*, p. 45.

[2] Duchesse d'Abrantès, *Mémoires*, Vol. I, pp. 254, 255.

possibly to the intervention of their mutual friend Mme
Tallien, that Napoleon made his spectacular success when, on
the 13th vendémiaire (October 4th 1795, as second in command
to Barras, the self-styled *général en chef*, he quelled in a matter of
hours an insurrection of the revolutionary sections which
threatened the very existence of the Convention. Bonaparte's
prompt dispatch of Murat to bring into Paris the government's
artillery from the Camp de Sablons saved the day. It is not without
interest to note that on the morrow in the Salle des Tuileries,
when Napoleon listened to the citation naming him a divisional
general, he was wearing a pair of buckskin breeches that Talma
had lent him the previous evening. [1] Napoleon was now the man
of the hour. Any kindnesses he had received from Talma were
amply repaid in his moment of power. He saw that, during the
dislocation of supplies the revolt had occasioned in Paris, bread
was delivered daily at the house in the rue Chantereine.

Possibly these last days of 1795, perhaps the beginning of
1796, saw the break-up of Talma's marriage. At the Théâtre de la
République, Caroline Petit-Vanhove was installed as queen.
Her intrinsic worth as an actress coupled with the notoriety
she enjoyed as Talma's mistress, could be relied upon to fill the
theatre even when her lover was not in the bill. Julie on the other
hand saw her own social life dwindle to a few friends, although
she did counter to some extent her husband's flagitious infidelity by a serene though intermittent friendship with Benjamin
Constant. To him we owe a most touching account of Julie
Talma's last years. [2] The house in the rue Chantereine she abandoned and in November 1796 sold it to Josephine, now married
to Napoleon Bonaparte. It was a sad day for Julie when she sent
to Talma's new lodging in the rue de la Loi all those stage
costumes and properties that had adorned a very large room in her
house. She herself with the twins repaired to Number 2, rue
Matignon, where Condorcet's widow was installed. The sale of
the house proved to be a long drawn out business, for negotiations
were finally completed only on May 31st, 1798, and in the name
of 'Napoleone Buonaparte, President of the French Delegation
at the Congress of Rastadt, the aforesaid house the property of
Citoyenne Talma.' Lefeuve in his history *Paris, rue par rue* tells
us that the purchase price was 180,000 francs. Michaud in his

[1] Roger de Parnes, *Le Directoire, portefeuille d'un incroyable*, p. 108.
[2] Benjamin Constant, *Mélanges de littérature et de politique*, 1829.

Biographie universelle put the price at 40,000 francs for the house, adding 120,000 francs for the furniture. Thus the home that had meant so much in Talma's life passed to his friend. It was here that Napoleon and Josephine, during those Parisian interludes so brief for the general, flushed with the triumphs of his Italian campaign and already dreaming of Egyptian conquests, spent their passionate early married life. No wonder Marmont called it the Temple of Love. Paris, when it acclaimed the general on his return from Italy on December 5th, 1797, renamed the street rue de la Victoire.

Napoleon and Josephine lost no time in making Talma's old home something of a centre in the midst of that all too tolerant, lax, immoral society that the Directoire had encouraged. Their dinners brought together not only political and military personalities like Talleyrand and Murat, but scientists like Berthollet, Laplace and Monge, writers like Bernardin de Saint-Pierre, dramatists like Legouvé, Lemercier, Arnault, Ducis, that inevitable painter David, a composer like Méhul and of course Talma. After the meal came lively talk and individual performances. Ducis would oblige with excerpts from his Shakespearean concoctions; Legouvé once read a dreary poem entitled *Sépultures* and Bernardin set the company ayawn with his overlong Socratic Dialogue. Arnault tells us how one evening they wanted to hear his tragedy *Les Vénitiens*. The author, who was having trouble with the censorship over this very play, excused himself on the grounds that not only was he suffering from loss of voice, but that he was without his manuscript. Napoleon gave immediate orders to an aide to bring the play from Arnault's house and, if necessary, to read the tragedy. Before that distinguished group the author read his work which elicited warm praise for its local colour, for its fidelity to Venetian politics, and for its representation of Italian character. When the bouquets had been presented, Napoleon had a reproach for Arnault's first act. 'What reproach, general?' asked the bewildered author. 'You don't make the Venetian Senate sufficiently hateful.' 'But I have not falsified the severity of its institutions.' 'You justify that severity by the goal the Senate sought, the maintenance of independence.' Furthermore, Napoleon learnt that Arnault, in deference to requests received from ladies, had changed his tragic ending. Napoleon insisted upon the original dénouement with its poignant death scene. Arnault was not a man to refuse a request from so powerful a personality. With Napoleon's approval, he could put an end to censors' quibbles. When *Les Vénitiens* eventually saw the foot-lights, despite Josephine's plea for a pardoned hero, Talma and his colleagues played the final act in accordance with Napoleon's wishes. In the course of this narrative we shall note many instances of Bonaparte's intervention in the theatre.

While the victor of Arcoli and Lodi entertained the actor so royally in what had once been Julie's salon, some account of the closing years of the first Madame Talma's life may not prove irrelevant. In a correspondence with her old friend of the Théâtre-Français, Louise Fusil, she poured out all her agonized jealousy and disillusion.[1] She was now well over forty and had the mortification of seeing her husband make nightly, in public, by no means mimic love to a young rival still in her twenties. The situation could not go on. After years of humiliation Julie Careau divorced Talma on February 6th, 1801. As we already know, her father recognized her legally in the following August. To Louise Fusil she gave the following account of the dissolution of her marriage. 'We drove to the Town Hall in the same carriage, chatting all the time of matters of no particular importance, just like people who might be going for a country drive. My husband handed me out of the carriage; we sat side by side in the waiting-room; we signed the paper as if it had been the most common-place of legal documents. When I rose to go, he accompanied me to the carriage door. "I hope," I said, "I am not to be deprived of your society altogether. That would be too cruel. You will come and see me from time to time, won't you?" "Of course I will. It will give me the greatest pleasure to do so," he replied, with a touch of embarrassment. I was pale and my voice betrayed my emotion in spite of all my efforts to control myself. At last, however, I got home and was free to give way and cry. Pity me for I am very unhappy.'

Poor Julie, she had not long to live. Upon her last surviving son she heaped a mother's frantic devotion. The boy had always suffered from a weak chest and it was in Switzerland, where his mother had taken him in a desperate search for a cure, that he died. When Julie returned to Paris, it was evident that she had contracted her son's complaint. Constant tells us how she faded visibly, with an ineffably sweet resignation. Talma, it is true, saw her from time to time. To him she made one of her last

[1] Louise Fusil, *Souvenirs d'une actrice*, Vol. II, p. 109 et seq.

requests. 'Will you come and dine with me on Thursday next?' 'I can't manage Thursday, but Monday for certain,' he replied. 'Very well then, till Monday.' Talma, true to his promise, came on that Monday, but Julie had already died in the interval, on May 5th, 1805.

Posterity has rightly censured Talma for his cruel treatment of Julie Careau. According to the brothers Goncourt she first of all divined the actor's gifts, encouraged his efforts, gave him a home and children. Even today their bitter reproaches sting. 'And Talma deserts you! Neither the fortune you brought to the penniless actor, nor the gentle love of your nature, nor the sweetness of your discourse, nor your imagination artistically nurtured and alive, nor even the silly misunderstandings amid the joys of your life together were able to keep him beside you, to whom he owed his success. . . . Ungrateful wretch!'

Julie had loved and lost. *Sunt lacrimae rerum.* It is useless to find excuse for Talma by stressing contemporary immorality and the popularity of easy divorce. He ought not to be absolved from such shabby treatment of a woman who, despite her dubious origins, had impressed by the sweetness of her nature and the strength of her mind some of the great personalities of her generation. Her deep, devoted love for Talma and for the children she bore him ought to stand heavily on the credit side when any final reckoning is made of Julie Careau and her deeds. Meanwhile, Talma rejoiced in the friendship of Napoleon Bonaparte and found amorous consolation in the favours of Caroline Petit-Vanhove.

CHAPTER 16

Talma Plays Macbeth

A more difficult and complicated piece of history than the wanderings, the groupings, the separations and the reunions of the actors and actresses who claimed to be legitimate members of the Maison de Molière would be hard to imagine. A volume indeed could be written about that strange odyssey. At the risk of over-simplification but with a desire to spare the reader, we will try, in order to make Talma's part reasonably clear during these disturbed years, to limit our references to three main groups.

Driven from the Théâtre Louvois, Mlle Raucourt, with a very powerful junta which included Saint-Prix, Saint-Fal, Naudet, Vanhove, Florence, Picard (the brilliant actor-author of that enchanting comedy *La Petite Ville*), Mmes Fleury, Simon, and later that great favourite Joly, knocked at many doors before coming to rest in their old home in the Place de l'Odéon. Here for five months (October 31st, 1798, to March 17th, 1799) and with varying fortunes they kept the flag flying until the old Théâtre de la Nation, the *ci-devant* Théâtre-Français, for some unascertained reason went up in flames. Talma, Monvel, Dugazon, Baptiste *aîné*, Damas, Mmes Vestris and Petit-Vanhove continued at the République, but it became increasingly clear that the favourite theatre of the Jacobins offered no great attraction for the wildly pleasure-loving Paris of the Directory. When the République was finally forced to close its doors on January 26th, 1799, Sageret, the remarkable impresario who ran both opera and plays at the Théâtre Feydeau, promptly engaged Talma and his colleagues to augment his dramatic company led by Fleury and Mlle Contat.

Sageret must have been a great diplomatist. He succeeded in overcoming the jealousies, the rancours, the political animosities and the professional amour-propre that racked these two groups of *sociétaires* and it is no small tribute to his powers that Talma and his friends with one exception were made welcome at the Feydeau. The exception was Dugazon whose revolutionary eccentricities Fleury and Mlle Contat could never pardon.[1] This reunion of two groups must engage our attention because on May 3rd, 1798, immediately prior to his departure for Egypt, Napoleon, accompanied by Josephine, after dining *chez* Barras, saw Talma in the new Ducis version of Shakespeare's *Macbeth*.

Ducis had offered his first *Macbeth* in 1790, when Larive as *chef d'emploi* for all major tragic rôles played the guilty thane with Mlle Raucourt as his ambitious spouse. It is important that English readers should have some idea of a French dramatist's treatment of one of the greatest tragedies in their literature. Ducis tells us in his Preface: 'First of all I applied myself to the task of eliminating the ever revolting expression of horror which certainly would have ruined my play; I then tried to lead the soul of my spectator to the first stages of tragic terror (note, we proceed by carefully graded emotions!), by artistically mingling it with what would render it tolerable.' The sleep-walking scene worried him, 'that strange scene risked for the first time on our stage'. The effort required for this absurdly executed innovation drained away any life-blood he might have given to the play. The Palace of Inverness was the general scene and he sited his first act nearby, 'in the most remote spot in an ancient forest, rocks, caves, precipices, a frightful haunt. The sky is threatening and gloomy.'

The plot of Shakespeare's *Macbeth* in Ducis' adaptation underwent considerable change. King Duncan is at war with Cador, a rebel. His son Malcolm is secretly brought up under the name of Loclin by a faithful retainer Sévar. Loclin is quite unaware of his royal lineage. The King's allies are Macbeth, Menteth and Herifort, and when the play opens Menteth is about to be executed for treachery. Macbeth fears Glamis, a prince of the blood whom he and Lady Macbeth, supplied with the euphonious name of Frédégonde—oh! those rhyming alexandrines!—have marked down as their enemy. Frédégonde goes so far as to accuse Glamis of having organized an attack by brigands upon their castle, during which her son narrowly escaped being burnt alive. With this terrible charge she plays upon her husband's love and fears. Macbeth has seen a supernatural creature, Yphyctone, bearing

---

[1] 'I would rather be guillotined from head to foot than appear on the stage with that Jacobin of a Dugazon'—Louise Contat. Legouvé, *Soixante ans de s.* II. p. 258.

a sceptre and a diadem. Again, in a horrible nightmare, inter-
polated by Ducis as a conventional classical *récit*, he sees three
hags bending over a newly slain child and as they disappear
in their flight towards the castle they prophesy Macbeth will be
king. Frédégonde, encouraged by such omens, urges her husband
to kill both Duncan and Glamis. Immediately afterwards Macbeth,
in another long set speech, proclaims his remorse and, tortured
by the corpse of Duncan ever before his eyes, reproaches his wife
as the instigator of the crime. The people offer the crown to
Macbeth who, modestly in 1790 fashion, agrees to become '*le
premier citoyen*'. However Sévar arrives with all the necessary
proof to press the claims of Malcolm as the rightful heir of Duncan
Despite the fierce and murderous opposition of Frédégonde,
prepared to do anything to retain her husband's power, Macbeth
urges Malcolm to accept the throne. Frédégonde walking in her
sleep is overheard by Sévar and Malcolm as she plans to murder
them both. With the dawn—neat and merciful unity of time!—
Macbeth makes public confession of his guilt just at the moment
when Frédégonde rushes in, distraught, to tell how she has killed
her own son instead of Malcolm.

In this far-fetched farrago of plot even Ducis felt his ending
was unconvincing. For the Talma production of 1798 he arranged
for Frédégonde to murder her son in her sleep and by such disaster
he assumed the fates would be appeased. It is really very difficult
to find any justification for this French distortion of Shakespeare's tragedy. Of course Ducis tried to crib, cabin and confine
the spacious play within the narrow prison of the classical unities
and to soften its barbaric horror to suit the requirements of contemporary, decaying French tragedy. That complex character
Macbeth shrinks to the proportions of a mere tool of a vicious
wife. That oft quoted slogan of French classicism, '*Aimez donc
la raison*', required of Frédégonde some sort of explanation for
her senselessly violent thoughts and deeds. This Ducis tried to
find by endowing her with an abnormal mother-love. Surely the
perversion of Shakespeare's intensely human and dramatic
sleepwalking scene could go no further.

It was to this jumble of nonsense, tricked out in threadbare
rhyme, that Talma and Madame Vestris were called upon to
direct their talents. If the critics disliked the play, its interpreters
reaped a harvest of adulation. The general comment was that only
Talma's acting made the performance endurable. During re-

hearsals in 1798, Ducis could write to Talma [1] 'Tragedy breathed upon you in your cradle. You have the authentic tones for remorse and love, for crime and virtue. The part of Macbeth fits you like a glove'. The philosophical *Décade*, ever ready to uphold the dying traditions of French tragedy, assured its readers that only the art of Talma would enable them to endure the 'raving madness of the English drama'.[2] Later, when *Macbeth* had become firmly established in the repertory as a Talma part, the critic Geoffroy in *Le Journal des Débats*[3] never failed to chronicle his displeasure. 'Talma renders in a terrifying manner everything that belongs to Shakespeare, everything that is natural and true; but he gets bogged down in the soliloquies, in Ducis' padding, and makes all this nonsense heavier still by a drawling delivery. To sorrow and remorse he lends a lamentable note. However, his acting makes the play bearable.' Again a little later[4] he lashes out. 'This kind of tragedy, good enough in the past to horrify London's rabble, is in no way suitable for the people of Paris. Since our return to reason and sanity, the French nation is affronted by this foreign and grossly savage conception of tragedy, intended for Northern hordes.' Another critic[5], though prepared to praise Talma's acting, saw in Ducis' versification the play's sole merit.

To return to its first night in May 1798, the play, thanks to the stirring performances of Talma and his leading lady, appeared to be a money-maker. Sageret their manager desperately needed a financial success. This extraordinary impresario entered the theatre business with the idea of giving in one theatre performances of every kind, comedy, tragedy, opera and even the lighter forms of musical entertainment. Assured eventually of some government support, largely through his friend Merlin, the Minister of Justice, Sageret, before his career ended so disastrously, succeeded in getting control of three theatres, the Feydeau, the République and for a short lease the Odéon. Of these only the Feydeau with its operatic and dramatic attractions achieved a measure of success. The promise of a government subsidy of 360,000 livres did not, alas!, materialize. He had redecorated the Feydeau from floor to ceiling and, with his heavy salary list for the artists he had so prodigally engaged, acute financial embarrass-

---

[1] Guy de la Batut. *Correspondance*, p. 67.   [2] An XI. Tome III. p. 244.
[3] An XII. 15ᵉ prairial.
[4] *Journal des Débats*. An XIII. Ier nivôse (feuilleton).
[5] *Mémorial dramatique*, 1810. p. 37.

ment awaited him. In a desperate effort Sageret tried to found at the Feydeau a subscription theatre based on an annual payment of 200 francs from each of the members of the *Conseil des Cinq Cents* and of the *Conseil des Anciens*. Here again he failed to interest his political friends. *Le citoyen* Sageret had offered and paid inflated salaries for those days to artists, whose chances of restoring his fortunes by the comparatively few opportunities they had to appear on a stage, mainly occupied by their operatic colleagues, were slight indeed. In his desperate plight he reduced Louise Contat's 30,000 livres per annum to 18,000; Molé fell from 24,000 to 18,000; Dazincourt had to accept 12,000 instead of 19,500; Mlle Raucourt, also on his books, received 18,000 instead of the 24,000 livres agreed upon. Old Vanhove learned to his spluttering indignation that his *pères nobles* netted only 10,000 livres and he had contracted for 15,000. Only one artist suffered no diminution of salary. Talma's 18,000 livres were respected, an indication of Sageret's faith in the actor's ability to draw the public. [1]

[1] A. Copin, *Talma et la Révolution*, pp. 283, 284.

Part 2

Napoleon's Tragedian

CHAPTER 17

Reconstitution of the Comédie-Française

M*acbeth* unfortunately proved a mere lightning flash in the dark, stormy sky. Yet Sageret, despite liabilities and dwindling assets, still pegged away. He decided to abandon his cherished idea of presenting in the same theatre every type of play and to reopen the République with an exclusively dramatic policy. In the world of the theatre the optimist thrives. He would put on Arnault's tragedy *Les Vénitiens*.

We already know that Arnault had had trouble with the censorship but Napoleon's approval, won at a reading of the tragedy, would surely, thought Sageret, ensure its production, especially if the General's suggestion for a tragic ending were met. But Arnault's difficulties were not yet over. The Censorship—Napoleon was somewhere in Egypt in October 1798—demanded the excision of the following turgid lines:

> *Malheur à tout pouvoir qui croit par l'injustice*
> *De sa grandeur sanglante assurer l'édifice!*
> *Il croulera bientôt avec son faible appui,*
> *Et le sang innocent retombera sur lui.*[1]

In the scene where the priest came to bless the marriage of Blanche and de Capello some budding censor had written in the margin: 'No priests! No priests! They are still among us, tormenting us! No priests!'

Even after the *'répétition générale' Les Vénitiens* was not allowed to be performed. Only the powerful intervention of Treilhard, a member of the Directory, secured its production on October 15th, 1798. *Les Vénitiens* with its spectacular novelty of a water display

---

[1] Woe to any power which through injustice strives
To base its structure on bloodshed's might!
Soon will it crumble with its feeble prop,
And the blood of the innocent will engulf it.

and four distinct scenes whetted the jaded appetite of the Parisian playgoer. The exactitude of costume demanded by the author in his elaborate stage directions must have delighted Talma. In Act V, scene 3, the dialogue between Montcassin, played by Talma, and his judges broke up the alexandrine line in order to provide some semblance of the cut and thrust of the law court. The play received a tumultuous reception. On all sides we are told that Talma was perfect. Caroline Petit-Vanhove as Blanche came in for her share of praise. The delighted Arnault wrote: 'Glowing with all the fire of youth, Talma played his part opposite a woman he loved and whose talents fitted marvellously the character of the rôle I had entrusted to her. The illusion in scenes where they played together was complete; these were feelings no longer simulated, they were real.'[1]

Even the success of *Les Vénitiens* could not disentangle Sageret from the ever tightening bonds of financial doom. Arnault lost almost his entire royalties in Sageret's impending bankruptcy. On December 22nd, 1798, with Lemercier's *Ophis* the impresario played his last card and lost. *Ophis* was a dire failure, that even Caroline in the name part and Talma as Thaulus could not save. The Théâtre de la République lingered on for thirty-two nights with *Macbeth*, *Othello*, *Abufar* and *Les Vénitiens* to eke out the classical repertory of *Iphigénie*, *Cinna*, *Britannicus*. The fickle Parisians were at this time crowding to the Odéon to see Mme Molé's translation of Kotzebue's *Misanthropie et repentir*, in which piece of sentimental twaddle Saint-Fal by his pathos as Meinau scored a signal triumph. This success was short lived. The République finally closed its doors on January 24th, 1799. We already know that the Odéon was burned down during the night of March 17–18th of the same year. Disaster followed disaster. The insatiable Sageret, unable to keep his creditors any longer at bay, was imprisoned for debt. The Feydeau, his last enterprise, which for some weeks continued to offer operatic programmes, closed its doors on May 3rd, 1799.

The Maison de Molière seemed to be no more. The great organization that Louis XIV had established and encouraged more than a century before had no longer any theatrical home and was dissolving fast. Talma, free after the closure of the République, set out for Bordeaux with Mme Petit-Vanhove and, for the first time in his career, acted in the south, enjoying there a financial

[1] *Les Souvenirs d'un sexagénaire*, Vol. IV, pp. 269–370.

and artistic success that would in later life tempt him from time to time to abandon Paris for the laurels more generously accorded in the provinces. We must not run on. Let us retrace our steps to the theatrical Paris of May 1799.

If the actors, a prey to their own selfish interests, showed little initiative to save the Comédie-Française from the extinction which threatened it, the contemporary dramatists worked to better purpose. By a stroke of good fortune, our old friend François de Neufchâteau, the author of that *Paméla* which sent the *sociétaires* to prison back in 1793, had become Minister of the Interior and, aided by the citoyen Mahérault, an ex-schoolmaster with a deep love of the theatre and now a *commissaire du gouvernement*, vigorously set about to reconstitute the Comédie-Française. How could any man remove so many obstacles, satisfy the vanity of so many temperamental personalities, wipe out rivalries and jealousies, obliterate political hatreds, reconcile so many opposing interests? Only by a miracle could these quarrelsome children of Thespis be made to see reason. Mahérault performed this miracle. François de Neufchâteau gave him carte blanche, although at a later date Mahérault would find his powers very ill-defined when he had to deal with difficult players. In these early stages of re-establishment all the work fell upon him. Powerful opposition was voiced curiously enough by Beaumarchais, who showed himself a staunch upholder of commercial competition, and the author of *Le Mariage de Figaro* made every effort to kill any resurgence of a nationally subsidized theatre. He had even won over Ducis, Legouvé and Arnault to his ideas. However, his sudden death on May 18th, 1799, put an end to his protest and allowed Mahérault to proceed with his uneasy assignment. Well might the actor Saint-Prix make to him his prophetic remark.[1] 'You are undertaking an impossible task. You don't know what actors are like. They will kill you with their pin-pricks.' 'I shall make them live again,' replied Mahérault. 'I want the Théâtre-Francais to be a national institution. I want the actors to act in their own home and their house to be called the House of Molière, of Corneille and of Racine.' He was as good as his word. On 30th May, 1799, the walls of Paris carried this announcement. 'Re-opening of the Théâtre-Français: *Le Cid* and *L'École des maris*. The Théâtre-Français, reintegrated and reconstituted, opened its doors on the exact site it occupies today. The Théâtre de la

[1] Legouvé, *Soixante ans de souvenirs*, t. II, p. 259.

République, so closely identified with Talma, Monvel and Mme
Vestris during the violent days of the Revolution, was chosen as
the *sociétaires'* new home. Thanks to the care and taste of the
unfortunate Sageret, the theatre was in a beautiful state of decora-
tion. Its handsome interior could hold an audience of 1,600. The
boxes were formed by a circular row of Ionic columns and above
these but beyond them a lesser range of Corinthian pillars. The
body of the house was lighted by a double crown of argand lamps, [1]
a system of illumination making the auditorium more brilliant
than the comparative penumbra of the stage which, at that time,
relied only on footlights. This relative gloom that enveloped the
stage is important for its effect on the acting of the day. To draw
attention to himself the actor had to resort to emphasis; some even
stamped on the boards to inform the audience that a purple
passage was about to begin. Gas did not come to the Théâtre-
Français until 1832. Meanwhile the *incroyables* and the *merveil-
leuses* of the Directory and the Consulate could flaunt their jewels
and their elaborate toilettes before an admiring audience, often
more interested in fashion than in the play. In 1799 the Théâtre-
Français started its performances at six o'clock and usually dismissed its patrons by ten at the latest.

Mahérault had found an appropriate theatre from which to
launch the revived Comédie-Française. What of the actors?
Let us cast a glance at the official list he drew up. The dates
opposite the names of the *sociétaires* are those of their acceptance
of such status at the Théâtre-Français when it was controlled by
the Gentlemen of the King's Bedchamber.

State of the Personnel of the Comédie-Française
on the 31st May 1799

Commissaire du gouvernement: Mahérault

MM Molé, doyen	1761	
Monvel	1772	
Dugazon	1772	
Dazincourt	1778	
Fleury	1778	
Vanhove	1779	Ex-sociétaires
Florence	1779	of the former
Saint-Prix	1784	Théâtre-Français

[1] These were lamps with cylindrical wicks invented in 1782 by Argand, the Swiss
chemist and physician.

Saint-Fal	1784
Naudet	1786
Larochelle	1787
Talma	1789
Grandménil	1791

The ladies are listed as follows:

Mmes Lachassaigne	1769	
Vestris	1769	
Raucourt	1773	Ex-sociétaires
Suin	1776	of the former
Louise Contat	1777	Théâtre-Français
Thénard	1781	
Devienne	1785	
Petit-Vanhove	1785	
Fleury	1791	
Mézeray	1791	

To these lists were added the names of certain artists who had acted with the *sociétaires* during the revolutionary dispersal and who were deemed worthy of inclusion in the reconstituted national theatre. They are Talma's old colleagues at the République, Duval, Michot, Damas, Baptiste *aîné*, and his brother Baptiste *cadet*. From the Feydeau came Caumont. A great artist in the person of Mlle Mars, the illegitimate daughter of Monvel, earned, through her services at the Théâtre Montansier, a place alongside the *sociétaires*. The *pensionnaires*, always lesser fry, were represented by Desprez, Lacave, Dublin, Marchand, and by Mmes Gros, Desrosiers and Patrat. These were the talents and the tempestuous personalities that Mahérault, at a salary of 6,000 francs per month, was called upon to control. It will be readily understood that Talma and Mme Petit-Vanhove lost no time in returning to Paris to take their rightful place at the Théâtre-Français.

In the light of the earth-shaking political events which marked the end of the year 1799, this re-opening of the Théâtre-Français must be viewed as a somewhat tentative enterprise. The Directory as a government, by its own corruption and the general lack of confidence it inspired, was losing ground. Its days were clearly numbered. When Mahérault presented his early programmes, Napoleon, that most powerful patron of arts and letters, was still in Egypt, and Paris had to wait until the morning of October 16th before he returned. Napoleon, in close collaboration with Sieyès, saw the time had come to overthrow the five members of the Directory and, by a very determined and forceful persuasion, in which Talleyrand, Fouché and brother Lucien played significant parts, the *Conseil des Anciens* and the *Conseil des Cinq Cents*, artfully transferred to Saint-Cloud, committed hara-kiri and voted for a change of constitution. The Coup d'État of the 18th brumaire (November 9th, 1799) produced the Consulate with Napoleon, Cambacérès and Lebrun elected as Consuls for ten years. In 1802, after the Treaties of Lunéville and Amiens, Napoleon was to become Consul for the term of his natural life.

During those pregnant twenty-five days, between Napoleon's arrival at his house in the rue de la Victoire and the evening of the 19th brumaire,[1] when he emerged from the Orangerie at Saint-Cloud as virtual master of France, he even found time for a visit to the Comédie-Française, where he saw his admired Talma in his current success, Arnault's *Les Vénitiens*. We shall see before long Napoleon exercise his newly acquired power in all government departments and his friendship with Talma helping him to an understanding of some of the problems that face a national theatre.

Some attempt, however inadequate at this stage, must be made to review Talma's contribution to the French theatre from the time of his début in November 1787 until his return to Paris in the summer of 1799 when, aged 36, he rejoined his old colleagues at the newly reconstituted Théâtre-Français, rue de Richelieu. We have noted how from his early appearances he was ever at pains to achieve historical accuracy of costume and décor, firm in the belief that the theatre had a duty to hand on to youth a faithful evocation of a living past. Throughout this early period the habitués of the parterre applied only one standard to the male tragedian, the memory of the impersonations of Lekain, that great actor who, under the tuition of Voltaire, had created the Sage of Ferney's heroes in dramas still acted in the repertory of the Théâtre-Français at this time. To play Séïde in *Mahomet*, Brutus in the tragedy of that name, Orosmane in *Zaïre* and César in *La Mort de César* as Talma had done, was to challenge comparison with their creator and to run the gauntlet of summary criticism. Lekain had all the pompous delivery, the slow-motion

[1] 10th November 1799.

gestures, the conscious 'nobility', the stereotyped declamation of the rolling alexandrine. Let it not be forgotten that such characteristics were deemed desirable qualities, accepted by the literary pundits of the day as the only method of playing a tragic part. Talma's crime—and the criminal charge endured until the death of the last critic to use Lekain as a yardstick—was to pour an impetuous, often an unrestrained emotion into his parts, to break up the alexandrine under tension, to base his by-play and gestures upon 'nature and truth', in short to infuse his rôle with a warm, pulsating humanity. Unlike Lekain, he had no physical handicaps to overcome. Contemporary drawings and paintings reveal him as an unusually handsome man who could lend to classical heroes his own sombre beauty. He had too the great gift of dominating the stage. The moment he appeared he commanded attention and his sonorous voice, which he cultivated assiduously, could lend a semblance of poetry even to the pedestrian verse of a Legouvé or a Ducis.[1] So different was his attack and his timing from the slow, stylized performances of Lekain that there is little wonder that those who in their youth had worshipped at such a formal, symmetrical shrine found the incense of a new altar somewhat overpowering.

At this point it is fruitless to try to analyse Talma's readings of the great rôles of Corneille and Racine. To these challenging parts he gave relentless study, applied a cast-iron discipline and submitted himself to the most rigorous self-examination. So many of his colleagues were content to repeat a performance, even in a revival, that had become rigidly patterned after a few nights. For Talma, the imagination of the actor, his sensitivity, his intelligence and of course his spontaneity must have full play. In his *Quelques Réflexions sur Lekain et sur l'Art théâtral* he makes no bones about his own feelings on acting. 'I confess I prefer the sublime interpretation to the technically perfect performance.' During these prentice years his Oreste, Cinna, Néron were but preliminary sketches of those fully grasped and brilliantly executed renderings that were to send Napoleon, Madame de Staël, Chateaubriand and Stendhal, to name only four great minds of that fertile generation, into ecstasies of homage and praise. We are dealing with an actor who studied his art as long as breath was in his body. Was there anything he lacked? Yes. The highborn chivalry of a Rodrigue in *Le Cid* or of a Tancrède, Voltaire's

[1] Chateaubriand, *Mémoires d'outre-tombe*, Vol. II, p. 275.

preux chevalier, seemed to escape him although, let it be understood, he could give an adequate performance of these aristocratic gentlemen. But they were not Talma's parts. One wonders if Chateaubriand[1] was right in ascribing to Talma's jacobinism his inability to convince, at the highest level, in such chivalrous rôles.

As one looks over these years, Charles IX and Henri VIII stand out pre-eminently as successes where Talma displayed violence, intolerance, nervous tension and overweening power with great effect before audiences impatient of kings and their tyranny. Alas! So many of the contemporary tragedies he appeared in were corpses embalmed in the rotting bands of outworn theatrical tradition. To us today their heroes remain mere petrified abstractions, consigned to a frosty limbo, lacking even a spark of fire to help an actor to breathe life into their dead monologues. Authors seemed determined to freeze their actors in pseudo-classical poses on a bleak, draughty stage where inevitably the solitary confidant with hero or heroine maintained a semblance of speech and action. A thaw was long overdue, and Talma's sun was rising. Is there any wonder that he hailed the Shakespearean adaptations of Ducis as a means of escape to a less anaemic drama? After all, Ducis could not rob Othello entirely of the agony of his jealousy nor Macbeth of his haunting fears and remorse. Here was stuff to act, to bring to life, and had he not in London and in the English tongue made contact with the real Shakespeare? It is significant that, of parts provided by dramatists of the Revolution, only Othello and Macbeth found a permanent place in Talma's own *répertoire*. The time is not far distant when he is to add Hamlet to his Shakespearean creations. All his critics, even the grudging Voltairians, agreed that in the portrayal of strong emotions, murder, hatred, madness, fear, Talma was without a rival.

The actor's father, disappointed at seeing his son turn from dentistry to the stage, can be numbered among his sternest critics. In a letter from London, dated July 12th, 1796, he wrote: 'These last days I have seen high praise for young Talma and I suppose you are the person they are talking about. I note with pleasure you are making progress; I hope that with a little work you will make even more. I see that you are keen to render nature as she really is, as much by your acting as by your costumes; one cannot

[1] *Mémoires d'outre-tombe*. II, p. 274.

do better when one is fortunate enough to be gifted with the power to portray her really well.'

A less personal estimate deserves quotation from *La Lorgnette des Spectacles* or *La Revue des Acteurs* by Fabien Pillet, which appeared in 1798. The author assures us that it is his intention to steer between those old playgoers who express horror at Talma's audacious innovations and the young members of the audience who accept his acting without reserve. His appeal is to that body of enlightened spectators who can be trusted to bring a purely objective judgment to Talma's acting. Let us see what he has to say:

Citizen Talma possesses, among his theatrical qualities, a dark, expressive face, whose striking character is admirably suited to tragedy, a resonant voice, penetrating and with a rather fine middle register, an easy gait, poise, a warm delivery of his lines, great accuracy in the matter of costume and a scrupulous observance of good taste, etc. etc. He collaborates perfectly with his authors, is careful about his diction and clearly varies his gestures, he prepares and carries off with skill declamatory effects and any dramatic situation, he knows the art of filling the stage, he is eloquent even in his silence; in a word, he reveals himself in many parts as an artist, knowledgeable and profound.

Yet, according to this critic, Talma in his early thirties had not yet found himself. Let him continue:

That sonorous, penetrating voice ceases to be beautiful when it becomes noisy. An unpleasant roughness takes over in moments of anger and despair. In grief, it seems throaty and trails off into a harsh plaintive monotone which ends by tiring the least perceptive ear. Talma's face, though expressive and notable for good features, lacks that dignity suitable to noble-minded, chivalrous rôles; it is right only for those parts where gloom, unbridled passion, a kind of madness, heart-rending remorse, I might almost say, conspiratorial fervour, have a place. His constitution is not sufficiently robust to carry conviction in certain tragedies where the hero must display physical strength and a martial appearance. His diction, usually competent, is not always sufficiently varied. He sometimes errs as to the degree of pride he should impart to a particular rôle; finally, if he often succeeds in moving the soul of the spectator, he hardly ever ennobles it.

These are by no means laudatory comments. The perfecting of his voice was Talma's constant care and we already know that from Dorival, a poor actor but a brilliant exponent of voice production, he learned the great art of breath control. One could take a breath after the subject of a sentence but never between a verb and its object, never between noun and adjective. Dorival had worked out with meticulous care when and how the deep breath might fill the lungs and, as the tirade progressed, when the half and the quarter respirations could be permitted. All these vocal defects received attention. Whether one should ennoble the mind or stir the heart left Talma in no doubt whatever. 'Nobility', 'pomposity', 'good taste' were in his opinion stifling French dramatic writing and acting. He subjected every moment of his playing to the most earnest examination. Even on his death bed he regretted not being able to live sufficiently long to perfect still further the art to which he had given his whole life.

Talma now enters upon a new and vital phase of his career. In the reconstituted Théâtre-Français great acting opportunities were to await him. No longer would he have to tear his passion to tatters in order to flatter the fanatical, politically minded audiences of the Théâtre de la République: in those days the cart of Thespis had to compete with the tragedy of the tumbril. All that was now changed. From an ordered society was to come, thanks to Napoleon's government, an audience thoughtful and knowledgeable, to inspire the actor, to place him firmly on that pedestal where posterity still pays its tribute to a tragedy king.

A playbill of the Revolutionary era

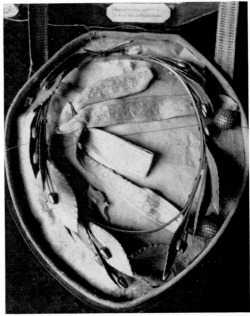

Talma's property sword and crown

CHAPTER 18

A Rival and a Hostile Critic

It was not long before Mahérault began to find the directing of the newly constituted Comédie-Française an almost impossible task. Talma was by no means an easy actor to work with and his popularity in those close Consulate circles made him difficult to control. Josephine, who had bought out of her dowry the pleasant property of the Malmaison, sought to beguile the tedium of Napoleon's absence in Egypt by inviting Talma and Michot to coach her guests for the amateur theatricals that took place there.[1] It was no consolation to Parisian playgoers to learn that their favourite actor had extracted from Hortense and Eugène de Beauharnais, from Bourrienne and Junot, performances worthy of the professional stage. Again, the tentative basis upon which François de Neufchâteau had opened the theatre allowed all too soon a resurgence of old jealousies and rancours. The lack of money was a pressing difficulty. In a word, there was no discipline and little loyalty. In the spring of 1800 the newspapers were rightly shocked that the small female part of Panope in a very rough and ready revival of *Phèdre* had to be played by a man. No actress was available. Indisposition was invoked on the flimsiest pretexts and Mlle Mézeray's foot and Dugazon's sciatica became Parisian jokes. More difficult to control was a malaise known as fatigue, and Mahérault, to the intense annoyance of the public, frequently had to cancel at the very last moment performances already billed.

The archives of the Comédie-Française reveal an extreme case of closure which occurred on 'the 30 prairial, year X' (June 19th, 1802). 'We were to give *Le Mariage de Figaro*. The play was changed on the 29th at eleven o'clock at night because citizen Dugazon had to appear on the 30th in a performance of *Alzire* at Lucien Bonaparte's house at Neuilly. At midnight *Wenceslas* was substituted. Citizen Monvel at one o'clock after midnight

[1] Bourrienne, *Mémoires sur Napoléon*, Vol V, pp. 25, 26.

I

wrote to say that he could not play. *Tancrède* was put in its place. Citizen Talma intimated during the morning that he was ill; we sought for citizen Lafon to play in his place but he was not to be found. The theatre was closed.' This bald statement shows the prickliness of poor Mahérault's task. Then, as tiresome as Talma's withdrawals to the Malmaison, there were the *congés*, periods of official leave to appear outside Paris. Quite often, without any official authorization, a *sociétaire* would sally forth to the provinces where, supported by the local theatre company, he could command a substantial salary. While he reaped the laurels of easy adulation, an understudy in Paris would face disappointed audiences. In those days of difficult transport, an actor had only his costumes and personal properties to take to the beckoning stages of Amiens, Rouen or Orléans, where a few profitable, surreptitious performances could always be arranged.

If Mahérault had succeeded in getting his players acting under one roof, he had failed to establish anything like discipline and order in the rue de Richelieu. Napoleon, ever sensitive to anything of national importance, immediately interested himself on his return from Egypt in the affairs of the Comédie-Française. From Talma he could learn everything and the tragedian was a conspicuous member of that illustrious band of savants and artists that Napoleon received at least once a week during his *déjeuner* either at St. Cloud or at the Tuileries. The direction of that theatre required strengthening. For this delicate and thankless task Napoleon selected Auguste-Laurent de Rémusat, an eminent lawyer from Aix-en-Provence with considerable financial experience. The *sieur* Rémusat was created a prefect of the palace with a clear mandate to supervise the Théâtre-Français. When other duties compelled him to accompany the First Consul on his European travels, his responsibilities devolved upon Charles-Maurice de Talleyrand who, with characteristic adroitness, permitted Madame de Rémusat, the lady of voluminous memoirs, to queen it in her husband's unquiet realm.

Rémusat with Napoleon's support applied himself to tackling the quite fantastic financial problems of the Comédie-Française. On July 2nd, 1802, the First Consul endowed the theatre with an annual income of 100,000 francs. 'By means of the afore-mentioned subsidy the actors will pay: firstly, the rental of their theatre; secondly, pensions upon retirement which will be granted with the government's approval; thirdly, the annual sum of compensa-

tion promised to a few artists at the time of their return to the
Théâtre de la République and which hitherto has been borne by
the Ministry of the Interior.'[1] The daily takings were to be used
paying the shares of the *sociétaires*, the salaries of the pensionnaires and for running expenses. 'No actor shall receive any sup-
plementary payment or indemnity from the funds of the Ministry
of the Interior or of Police.' The vexed question of the fractional
part to be allocated to newly accepted sociétaires he solved.
The promoted pensionnaire should begin by drawing a quarter
share; after two years' service he had a right to three-eighths. After
that, only by a decision of the Comité could come a further
increase in his share.[2]

Mahérault, confirmed in his appointment as Director, was
given as deputy the very dynamic but tactful Bernard, who knew
how upon occasion to buttress the crumbling authority of his
superior. Rémusat saw at once that an indiscriminate distribution
of complimentary tickets to the value of 100,000 francs per month
played havoc with the revenue. He also regularized the Poor Tax
at a ten per cent levy on all theatre seats. A burning question, as
we already know, was the treatment meted out to dramatists. At
the Comédie-Française an author would henceforth receive for
a four or five act play one-eighth of the takings, for three acts one
twelfth and one sixteenth for a shorter piece.

Such financial power enabled Rémusat, who tended to interpret
his functions very much in the spirit of the old time *Gentilhomme
de la Chambre du Roi*, to interfere on the artistic side of the theatre's
direction. To curb the laziness of a Mlle Raucourt, who appeared
when she thought she would, or the excessive zeal of a mediocre
actress like Mlle Fleury, who always wanted to play and, alas!
to empty houses, Rémusat brought a wholesome discipline. The
abuse of the *congé*, if not entirely checked, suffered some diminution. He instituted fines and another reform affected the grumbling
understudies. He decided on June 11th, 1802, that, after the first
five nights of any play revived from the repertory, the understudy
had the right to play the leading part once in every three subsequent performances. To help the contemporary author, to whom
the classical répertoire seemed a frustrating monopoly of acting
opportunity, it was decided that the Théâtre-Français must stage
every week at least one modern comedy and one modern tragedy.

[1] Laugier, *Documents historiques sur la Comédie-Française*, pp. 64–66.
[2] Laugier, pp. 29–42.

Enough has been written to show that the stimulus of Napoleon's interest produced some sense of order in the Comédie-Française, at least on the administrative side. The acting quality of the company on the male side remained very much what it was. With Larive's retirement in 1800 Talma virtually became *chef d'emploi* for all major tragic rôles, which he was tactful enough to share upon occasion with the brilliant but ageing Monvel. Saint-Prix, whose name either by accident or design had been omitted from the list of the reunited *sociétaires*, owed his position to Napoleon who, remembering the actor's fine performance as Caïn in Legouvé's play of that name around 1791, insisted upon his inclusion in the reorganized company. Both he and Saint-Fal were two worthy 'seconds', capable of giving reliable support to any star. Damas, Baptiste *aîné* and Baptiste *cadet* tasted their first successes with Talma at the Théâtre de la République but, versatile performers as they were, they tended to prefer comedy to tragedy. The new enterprise had barely run its first year when the male contingent of the Comédie received an accession of acting strength, destined to upset many established reputations and Talma's not the least of them.

On a memorable Thursday, May 8th, 1800, Pierre Lafon, a pupil of Dugazon and with his *ordre de début* signed by Lucien Bonaparte, then Minister of the Interior, appeared as Achille in Racine's *Iphigénie*. This recruit, ten years younger than Talma, had received for those days a really first-class education at Bordeaux under the famous Benedictine teacher, François Ferlus, who encouraged his pupil to pursue obvious gifts of poetic feeling and declamation. Lafon's father, a surgeon practising in Périgord, intended his son for medicine and to that end Pierre studied, first at Bordeaux and later at the famous medical school at Montpelier. Here the desire to act upon a stage drove him to Marseilles, where he subsequently fell in with a band of strolling players, then touring the Mediterranean hinterland. In Draguignan Lafon had the good fortune to meet the dramatist Raynouard. So impressed was Raynouard by this handsome, well-graced young barnstormer that he advised him to go to Paris, giving him a letter of introduction to the then all powerful Barras. Once in Paris and free from financial cares, thanks to a pension Barras had provided, Lafon after a few months' study sought the suffrages of the parterre. His success as Achille was immediate. This triumph he followed with Tancrède and finally with Orosmane in *Zaïre*.

The reader will have noticed that the parts Lafon chose for his débuts were precisely those in which Talma had to overcome temperamental and physical handicaps. Yet he welcomed the southerner and Charles Maurice[1] tells us he supported the *débutant* in *Zaïre*, taking the comparatively minor rôle of Nérestan. At one point in the play Talma's part called for the following lines:

> *Seigneur, c'est trop vanter un service vulgaire,*
> *J'ai fait ce qu'à ma place on vous aurait vu faire.*[2]

The audience rewarded him with 'a triple salvo of bravos', and in rightly acclaiming Lafon they could not forget the senior player's graceful compliments to a beginner.

Despite the attraction of Lafon's lovely voice with its rich southern quality, his virile beauty and above all the Gascon touch of panache he lent to these young heroes, his personal gifts were variously appreciated. 'Lafon's face suffers no loss of nobility; his figure is sufficiently tall; his appearance is good. He has the tragic gait, he lacks neither poise nor ease. His eyes are expressive; he carries his head well but he has some unfortunate gestures and too often raises his hands aloft, which is ungraceful.' According to another, 'the newcomer's face was wholly without expression and, in an effort to bring animation to his features, he had recourse too often to writhing and grimaces.'[3] Whatever one may make of these contradictory opinions, Lafon became an idol overnight and the darling of the ladies.

For many who regarded themselves as Talma's rivals, Lafon seemed a gift from the gods. Here at last was someone who could stand up to him. Yet Talma himself had been particularly kind to the *débutant*, who had received tuition from his own beloved master, Dugazon. To the envious, the way to intrigue, even to cabals, now lay open.

Unfortunately for Talma, more sinister than any backstage influence was the attitude of a dramatic critic, newly installed at the *Journal des Débats*. When Bertin reorganized this famous newspaper, he persuaded Julien-Louis Geoffroy, a Breton, born in 1743, often called 'l'abbé Geoffroy' because of his jesuitical education at Rennes, to leave *L'Année littéraire*, where he had made

---

[1] C. Maurice, *Histoire anecdotique de Théâtre*, p. 70.
[2] My lord, you praise too much a simple duty,
   I have done what in my place we would have seen you do.
[3] E. de Manne, *La Troupe de Talma*, p. 234.

a name for himself by his bitter attacks upon anything new and remotely savouring of revolutionary thought. The *philosophes* and the *novateurs* Geoffroy loathed. In this new post Bertin expected from him a *feuilleton dramatique* to appear every other day. His first article was published on March 2nd, 1800, and these continued until his death on February 27th, 1814. This rigid classical scholar, so ultra-conservative that he invoked the taste of a vanished epoch, certainly loved the theatre but showed himself merciless to any actor who dared to depart from the traditions of the French classical stage. Caustic to the point of insolence, severe to the point of injustice, he forced Larive to premature retirement and hurried Molé to his grave. He never scrupled to discourage the beginner nor to flatter his favourites. It was for Talma that this ex-pedant of the Collège Mazarin reserved the vials of his wrath. Here was an actor who had dared to breathe a new spirit into French acting and stage production, who had had the impertinence to shock susceptibilities with those Shakespearean farragos of nonsense and, alas! in the absence of informed and academic criticism, had actually got away with such monstrosities. This *laudator temporis acti*, whose acting yardstick was Lekain, would lose no time in pricking the Talma bubble.

Now Oreste in Racine's *Andromaque* counted by common consent as one of Talma's finest parts and, until Geoffroy saw him in it, had earned for the actor universal praise. Here is the Breton critic's first notice of Talma's interpretation.

It seems to me that M. Talma has misunderstood the character of Oreste; this son of Agamemnon should be gloomy, melancholy, consumed with a passion all the more violent because he has to stifle it; but his tone should be firm, noble and proud; his accents should express deep impassioned feeling. I do not know why he has chosen to rant on a pitiful, whining and lamentable note, to present the character as a languid, paralysed lover uttering his wails. His gestures match the tone and we see him frequently stretch forth his arms as if in crucifixion which, allied to a declamation unbearably slow and stultifying in its monotony, does not help to bring vivacity and interest to the part. However, this actor appears to have rendered the madness of Oreste to the public's satisfaction. For myself, I think he has represented not so much madness caused by despair arising from violent passion, as a state of actual dementia. These were not the transports of Oreste but the extravagances of an inmate of a lunatic asylum. Moreover, for an actor who is never natural the finest moment must be when his part compels him to leave the stage.

Lafon's success brought honeyed words from Geoffroy,[1] who lost no opportunity to praise him at Talma's expense. However much some of the *sociétaires* took umbrage at the newcomer's lack of modesty, the *Comité*, with a watchful eye on the box-office, promoted Lafon to the rank of *sociétaire* less than five months after his début. As there was no share vacant, he received a salary of 3,600 francs, which the Comité doubled in 1801; so rapid was Lafon's rise that in 1807 he drew seven-eighths of a share.[2]

This baleful conjunction of Geoffroy and Lafon boded ill for Talma's star. Lafon's head was completely turned and he felt affronted as Talma's understudy. Overweening ambition would lead him to ruse and intrigue, planned by older, jealous and unscrupulous players. Geoffroy, by his vivid, partisan pen, soon established himself as the arbiter of the French stage. His *feuilletons dramatiques* were everywhere read and everywhere discussed. Even Stendhal later in life declared that the kidneys of the Café Hardy lost their flavour when there appeared in the *Débats* no article by Geoffroy.

[1] Duchesse d'Abrantès, *Mémoires*, Vol. XVII, p. 247.
[2] *Archives of the Comédie-Française.*

CHAPTER 19

Mlle Duchesnois and Mlle George

There could be no doubt about Lafon's acting success nor about the malignant criticism that poured from Geoffroy's pen. Neither actor nor critic could challenge Talma's rightful position as tragic lead, but each lost no opportunity to belittle a favourite who, to the knowledge of all Paris, was the only member of his profession to enjoy the intimacy of Napoleon's intellectual reunions. Talma's popularity remained unimpaired during these early years of the reformed Comédie-Française, where Caroline Petit-Vanhove brought to him the consolations of love and the highly competent support of a leading lady. Their joint appearances were anathema to Geoffroy who under no circumstances would accept the new style of acting and lashed out in fury after Talma's resumption of Othello. The following article is dated November 9th, 1800.

Talma belongs to the new school of acting, created by a few people who had more presumption than experience and taste. These innovators disregard declamation and the good practice of reciting verse; their delivery is drawling, emphatic and monotonous. Under pretence of getting close to nature, they demean tragedy by an everyday, common-place manner, by comic gestures; often they aspire to a sensitive quality and often they carry it to the point of burlesque and the ridiculous. Then they flatter themselves they have attained the sublimity of pathos. Without any care for established rule and tradition they claim to act by instinct and sudden inspiration; they are the quakers of dramatic art; whence it follows that for the sake of a few happy moments one has to endure much flatness.

It seems that parts calling for extreme and awful passion Talma has made his own. His triumph is the painting of emotions carried to frenzy and folly. He heads the company of the friends of macabre drama. Just as Ducis is his father, so Voltaire was Lekain's. As between the two actors, so is the difference the same between the two authors. The school of horror is intrinsically bad because horrifying plays do not suit the French; they must be left for the citizens of London.

Moreover, it is too severe a limitation of talent to display it only in madness. Such moments on the stage should be merely lightning flashes; when passion is pushed to mental derangement it no longer finds a place in the sphere of dramatic art. It is true that Talma, thrown out of normal behaviour in these moments of delirium, sometimes finds beyond the natural gamut extraordinary tones which chill one's spine; but these good moments are so rare and brief that he would do well to keep within the confines of art; instead of astounding occasionally he should please us more often. Talma had fine moments in the fourth act and especially in the fifth. When the action is lively and the dialogue is broken up, his declamatory faults disappear completely. Moreover his diction is very clear, a great merit, but in his delivery there is a monotone and an emphasis which are wearisome and also some odd tones which are very disagreeable to those not used to them. On the whole he lacks dignity and nobility but he is a natural and sensitive player when he does not declaim and when he has only a few words to say.

This criticism reveals for us today not only the prejudices of Geoffroy—his hatred of any tampering with the incantatory alexandrine and his inability to accept any tragic part played outside the classical conventions—but also Talma's ever upward efforts to give emotion its full value and to make those heroes speak and act like human beings. We who are English know that Othello's jealousy bordered on the insane. The feelings of the Moor could not be confined within rhyming alexandrines; they would burst such bonds. Talma saved the part by making more flexible, i.e. by breaking up the twelve-syllable line and avoiding the classical pause on the rhyme. The hide-bound Geoffroy failed to comprehend that tragic feeling could not be adequately expressed by the stylized playing of a bygone age.

After Ducis, the reader may well ask what about Racine? A few months later, after Talma had delighted a crowded house with a brilliant portrayal of Néron in *Britannicus*, Geoffroy criticized him in the following terms. 'Talma played Néron; at times heavy, at others extravagant, hardly ever noble; good in a few incidents; he lacks especially taste and intelligence. Although his most common fault is a languid declamation, sometimes he quickens his delivery with a startling volubility. For example, when he enters in the second act,

Je le veux, je l'ordonne[1]

---

[1] 'I want it, I order it.'

the brusque manner in which he whips out this hemistich seemed to me common-place; I mention it because, bad as he was at that point, the audience overwhelmed him with applause. This actor's zeal, his efforts to please the public, deserve the highest praise; but his principles are wrong and a defective method mars the gifts nature has heaped upon him.' Poor Geoffroy! He sought nobility even in Néron; he objected because a dramatic command did not flow harmoniously along the Racinian line.

Talma continued to survive. His need to turn his back on Paris from time to time and to seek the peace of the countryside led him to Brunoy, where on the banks of the pleasant Hières he had built a charming house, for which his father sent over from London a number of trees. [1] As in Paris he entertained bountifully and Ducis, a frequent guest, commemorated in verse those rustic pleasures:

> *Où cet Othello terrible*
> *Se perdait dans l'herbe et les fleurs*[2]

Unfortunately, Talma could never be prudent over money. Brunoy's expensive furniture and decorations, its costly building extensions, its lavish hospitality, made severe demands upon his resources. True, his earnings were substantial. He drew at the Comédie-Française the coveted *part entière* and he could count upon command performances at 1,600 francs a time, Napoleon's own gratifications and, most profitable of all, provincial tours. Yet all his life Talma lived oppressed by debt. At the turn of the century, when Brunoy played havoc with his finances, his separation from Julie had deprived him of any credit that might have come from her fortune. A growing passion for the gaming table complicated still further his constant insolvency.

All pointers indicate Talma's happiness at this time. With his divorce from Julie now ratified the way lay open to regularize his union with Caroline Petit-Vanhove. He had had his share of mistresses and at thirty-nine wanted to settle down. Before their civil marriage, performed by the Mayor of the Xe Arrondissement on July 16th, 1802, Napoleon in the January of that year ordered Talma and Caroline to join Mlle Raucourt at Lyons, where, on

[1] Guy de la Batut. *Talma. Correspondance*, p. 61.
[2] 'Where that terrible Othello
    Lost himself in the flowery meads.'

the occasion of the First Consul's convening the State Council of the Italian Republic, they were to appear at the Grand Théâtre in four tragedies, *Oedipe*, *Andromaque*, *Sémiramis* and *Rhadamiste et Zénobie*. The visit proved a triumph for all concerned. This diet of Racine, Crébillon and Voltaire seemed so much to the taste of the Italian delegates that Napoleon perceived in the leading players of the Comédie-Française a means of lending a cultural significance to his political and military triumphs. This summons to Lyons was the first instance of what was soon to become an established policy.

Back in Paris, Talma and Caroline set up house as man and wife in the rue de la Seine, not far from the former dwelling of their friend David, the painter, now by Bonaparte's favour accorded apartments at the Louvre. Charles Maurice[1] offers a fleeting glimpse of the couple in those early days of their married life. 'Still very young at the time of his second marriage with Mlle Vanhove, Talma gave full play to his domestic inclinations. The policy of the Comédie-Française, whose programme invariably consisted of two plays, was to begin with the longer play so that actors performing in this piece were free fairly early. Talma, who lived in the Faubourg Saint-Germain, rue de Seine, went home very often on foot, his wife on his arm and the old-fashioned cotton bonnet pulled down over his ears to keep out the night air.' This is a delightful touch. One can well believe, as Henri d'Alméras assures us, that to Caroline her contemporaries applied the epithet '*matrimoniale*'.[2] Certainly the new ménage started well.

In the theatre, however, life was becoming more difficult for Caroline Talma. *La Lorgnette des Spectacles* at the end of 1798 had saluted her as an artist of the first rank. Its anonymous critic went so far as to say that '*dans le drame*' she was superior to all rivals and that only in comedy did she yield the palm to Mlle Contat. She herself was conscious of holding a position won by her own competence and versatility. The year 1801 saw the débuts of two *tragédiennes*, whose mediocre talents would be used unfairly against her. On March 1st appeared Mlle. Bourgoin as Chimène in *Le Cid*. This shoemaker's daughter, more courtesan than actress, was at once hailed by Geoffroy as an artist destined to add lustre to the tarnished glories of the Comédie-Française.

[1] Charles Maurice. *Histoire anecdotique*, Vol. I., p. 21.
[2] H. d'Alméras, *Mémoires sur Talma*, p. 318.

A little later Geoffroy, sated by the lady's beauty and her alcove successes, saw fit to revise his early glowing opinions. On May 2nd Mlle Volnais faced the parterre for the first time as Zaïre and found immediate favour with the critic of the *Journal des Débats*. By her discreet visits to the rue Matignon, where Geoffroy lived, and by bearing gifts to his coarse, common wife, Mlle Volnais contrived always to receive excellent notices.[1] The two newcomers quickly showed themselves uncompromising rivals, but any chance to humiliate Madame Talma they grasped as the firmest of friends. Geoffroy never scrupled to mention Mlles Bourgoin and Volnais as worthier substitutes for Caroline in the rôle she happened to be playing.

Much more serious competition came the following year. There arrived at the Comédie-Française two actresses who would make history in totally different ways and whose rivalry would split the Parisian playgoers into two opposing camps. The first of these was a humble peasant, Cathérine-Joseph Rafuin, born of miserably poor parents who kept a lowly inn near Valenciennes. Cathérine, who took the stage name of Mlle Duchesnois, was so ugly of countenance as to be almost repulsive. Legouvé[2], to whom she had been sent, gasped when he noted her hideous mouth and her dark, gipsy-like complexion. Her only physical assets were her expressive eyes, a voice that was sheer music and a willowy figure that would carry the peplum *à merveille*. This aspirant had seen a company of strolling players perform *Phèdre* and, fired by their example, she saw herself as Racine's heroine. In 1797 she left her sewing to appear with success in tragic parts at the local theatre. Later she came to Paris where she took lessons in declamation from Florence the actor, who found her abysmally ignorant. She believed that Troyes in Champagne was Priam's capital and convinced herself that, but for an assassin's hand, the France of her day would have found its saviour in Henri IV. On July 4th, 1802, at the age of twenty-five, Mlle Duchesnois made her début as *Phèdre*. Sémiramis, Didon and Hermione followed and older playgoers saw in her acting a spontaneity and a fidelity to nature that had characterized the great Mlle Dumesnil's interpretations. Geoffroy and the critic of the *Petites Affiches* tore her to shreds; the *Journal de Paris* and *Le Publiciste* proved luke warm; but

---

[1] A. Copin, *Talma et l'Empire*, p. 75. Duchesse d'Abrantès, *Mémoires*, Vol. V, p. 150, Vol. XVII, p. 247. Mlle Flore, *Mémoires*, p. 285.
[2] *Soixante ans de souvenirs*. I. pp. 195, 196.

Salgues in the *Observateur* and Le Pan in *Le Courrier des Spectacles* espoused her cause, hailing her as the great actress she would show herself to be. Here indeed was a leading lady for Talma, one whose fire and sensitivity would one day transcend even the very competent dramatic support that Caroline had never failed to give him.

And what of the other? Mlle Raucourt during a tour had paid a visit to the Amiens theatre and, with her predatory eye for a beautiful girl, had seen in the fourteen year old daughter of the chef d'orchestre, Georges Weimer, *'un bel oiseau de tragédie'*.[1] With such distinguished support, the parents raised no difficulties about their daughter going to Paris with a government pension in order to receive a stage training which Mlle Raucourt herself would direct. Thus did Marguerite-Joséphine Weimer, a strapping, well-made girl, already Junoesque in her imposing carriage, become Mlle George. The night of November 19th, 1802, Racine's *Iphigénie* was performed with this child of fifteen making her début as Clytemnestre. On her entry her dazzling beauty caused a gasp of admiration to run through the house and she proceeded to give a rendering in which the studied manner and mannerisms of Mlle Raucourt were all too evident. This faithful copy of her mistress's art delighted Geoffroy, who saluted this youthful Brunhilde as an ideal exponent of those noble qualities inseparable from French tragedy.

It is not the purpose of this study to go into the details of the bitter jealousy that divided Mlle Duchesnois and Mlle George, nor of their insane rivalry to which Parisian playgoers subscribed. Two major *tragédiennes* of opposite acting schools had arrived. Mlle George, as we all know, became Napoleon's mistress in a rather slaphappy, rough and tumble way; Mlle Duchesnois received encouragement, professional support and even gifts from Josephine. Mlle George in her lazy way was content to display her opulent charms to the soldiers enjoying brief leave in the capital; Mlle Duchesnois, heedless of the acrid Geoffroy, slaved to perfect her playing. She was incomparably the greater artist, who could conjure her very soul by sheer imagination and supreme sensitivity into those ill-starred queens and princesses of the French classical répertoire. Intelligent audiences paid their homage to her.

For the Talmas the theatrical swings did not offer the same

[1] E. de Manne et C. Ménétrier, *Galerie historique de la Comédie-Française*, p. 2.

happiness as the domestic roundabouts. While both husband and wife ran the gauntlet of Geoffroy's acrimonious comment, the new plays in which they appeared together between the years 1799 and 1803 failed signally to attract. Although Legouvé, Carrion de Nisas, Ducis, Arnault and Lemercier came forward with variations on old tragic themes, these vehicles for the Talmas collapsed after a few nights. It might seem a novelty to hear Talma declaim on the icy Siberian steppe[1] or Caroline as a Druid priestess bewail a hapless love.[2] Such deadness need not detain us. One new play performed during this period deserves mention. Lemercier, who had given Talma an enduring success with *Agamemnon*, had produced on March 22nd, 1800 *Pinto ou la Journée d'une conspiration*, described as *une comédie historique* and, sure enough, the author dared to mingle both comic and tragic interest. Such an innovation, irrespective of any intrinsic merit, sufficed to make the play notable. Talma's brilliant comic acting of Pinto, the lively secretary to a Portuguese tyrannical politician, Vasconcellos, brought this mixture of the genres very near to outstanding success. Lemercier's *Pinto* certainly gave Victor Hugo more than a hint for his great comic character, Don César de Bazan, in *Ruy Blas*. Although the author made hay of historical fact, adhering to the essential truth of background and manners he brought to life a bygone Portugal. The play moved lightly and, unusual for those days, displayed a vein of humour, fancy and wit wholly pleasing. Le Pan, the dramatic critic of *Le Courrier des Spectacles*, praised Talma and his wife, who appeared as the Duchesse, to the skies. Geoffroy frowned on this *mélange des genres*. The almost frothy lightness of the playing he failed to see, castigating the actors for performing much too slowly a play that he felt never achieved momentum.[3] The play gave every indication of being a resounding success when Napoleon intervened. Too many people, he feared, identified him with Vasconcellos, so, by the rather underhand means of multiplying authorizations to the actors for provincial tours, he succeeded in disrupting the cast and thus securing the withdrawal of *Pinto*.[4]

This dearth of good plays sent Talma back to the classics, to those great tragic rôles upon which he poured endless study in a

[1] Ducis, *Fédor et Vladimir*, April 24th, 1801.
[2] Lemercier, *Ysole et Orovèze*, December 23rd, 1802.
[3] *Journal des Débats*, March 27th, 1800.
[4] John Charpentier, *Napoléon et les hommes de lettres*, p. 66.

quest for perfection. So many of his colleagues at the Théâtre-Français found their stimulus only in the creation of new parts. Not so Talma. For him a major rôle from the repertory always excited self-criticism and never failed to offer scope for experience, for improvement. Throughout 1803 he appeared in no modern play. At Napoleon's behest he read *Polyeucte*. This great play with its theme of Christian martyrdom had been literally stifled by the combined efforts of the atheistic *philosophes* and the ultra-classicists, who would have none of its Christian message. The converted Polyeucte's love for the Christian God transcends his affection for his wife Pauline, a situation out of keeping with revolutionary thought. Pauline, too, sees in the Roman knight, Sévère, a man she has admired, a worldliness quite foreign to the spirituality of her husband who, by his noble example and martyrdom, helps Pauline to a higher conception of love. Bonaparte, who had signed with the Pope the famous Concordat and had hailed Chateaubriand's *Le Génie du Christianisme* as a great Christian apologia, saw in the neglected *Polyeucte* a play of positive religious, propagandist value. He ordered the play's revival for the spring of 1803.

Talma like most actors of his day failed to see the full import of *Polyeucte*. He allowed the mediocre Saint-Fal to play the Christian martyr and contented himself with the rôle of Sévère, whose sentimental disappointments, zeal for freedom of thought and outbursts of generous feeling would, he thought, be interpreted by post-revolutionary audiences as more sympathetic and more Roman. As it turned out, Talma had judged accurately. The parterre wildly applauded the scenes between Sévère and Pauline who, impersonated at first by Mlle Fleury, received before long a deeply moving and magnificent portrayal from Mlle Duchesnois. Geoffroy, glad to see this Cornelian masterpiece revived, still found fault with Talma. For the *Débats* of May 4th, 1803, he wrote: 'This tragedy was poorly performed. It belongs to a type to which the actors are entirely unaccustomed; this admirable dialogue requires naturalness, truth, warmth, a delivery of lines perfectly understood. Sévère is a part little suited to Talma's talents: however, this actor delivered with energy and strength some long argumentative speeches. Saint-Fal is a little cold in the part of Polyeucte.'

Actors today escape usually with but one set of criticisms of a particular part. In a repertory theatre of the standard of the

Comédie-Française players may endure the slings and arrows of many attacks. To show how Geoffroy harried Talma, this is his comment of the actor's performance in the same play nine years later, in 1812.

Talma is not suited to the part of Sévère. It calls for great nobility, an unimpeded, natural, animated delivery. As the character lives only by the strength and beauty of his feelings, because of a lack of action and of flamboyance, the actor must rely upon his own personality and draw from his own soul any effects he may create; the manner Talma assumed does not give him that something with which to enhance and carry off, in an incisive way, the scenes of love and tenderness which degenerate into the mawkish. In dialogue with his confidant, Talma is simple and natural, but his naturalness is too simple and his simplicity too commonplace. Tragedy requires everywhere, even in its minutest detail, simplicity and naturalness without any trace of familiarity.

Poor Talma! Actors will sympathize. At his feet the great ones of his generation were prepared to sit and applaud. Only the disgruntled die-hard Geoffroy, whose bitter pen had become a source of literary excitement for the Parisians of his day, heaped reproaches upon a player who sweated blood in order to lead French acting and play production towards 'nature and truth'.

CHAPTER 20

British Tourists in Paris

The Peace of Amiens was finally signed after protracted negotiations on March 22nd, 1802. It ended the war between England and France and restored to the English people the long denied pleasures of foreign travel. This settlement with Napoleon, although not destined to be of long duration, permitted crowds of our compatriots to cross the Channel, anxious to see for themselves the effects of the French Revolution, whose horrors they had learned only from the partisan lips of an expatriated nobility. The British visitor generally held in detestation the Revolution and all its works. The eloquent Mr. Burke had made it so clear that when a separation occurs between liberty and law neither is safe. It was therefore with a very critical and pro-British eye that these first travellers viewed the French scene. Comparisons of course they made and usually to the advantage of their own land.

These visitors sampled the pleasures of Paris, particularly the theatrical entertainment it offered. Maria Edgeworth[1] did not even wait until she got to the capital. 'We saw at Brussels,' she wrote on October 29th, 1802, 'two of the best Paris actors, M. and Mme Talma. The play was Racine's *Andromaque* (imitated in England as *The Distressed Mother*). Mme Talma played Andromaque and her husband Oreste, both exquisitely well. I had no idea of fine acting till I saw them, and my father, who had seen Garrick and Mrs. Siddons, Yates and Lekain, says he never saw anything superior to Mme Talma.' After a visit to Paris she confided her misgivings. 'We have been to the Théâtre-Français and to the Théâtre Feydeau, both fine houses; decorations etc. superior to the English; acting much superior in comedy; in tragedy they bully and rant and throw themselves into academic attitudes too much.'

Bertie Greatheed, a Warwickshire squire, accompanied his artist son to Paris in order to inspect the pictures of the Louvre and

[1] *Life and Letters of Maria Edgeworth* (A. J. C. Hare) pp. 91, 99.

to meet the great David. The Greatheeds, friends of John Philip Kemble, showed considerable interest in Talma, whom they saw both on and off the stage. On January 19th, 1803, Squire Greatheed and his son went to the Comédie-Française. [1]

We dined rather early and all went to *Sémiramis*. The wooden columns hinder the view very much and are cut in a very ugly manner by the upper tier of boxes. There was no orchestra but all laid in seats. Three stamps gave notice to raise the curtain. Mlle George and Talma acted. She has a fine person but not much expression of countenance. As in their painting, so in their acting, they are quite over antique. Talma was constantly etruscanizing himself. As to the grand air, the strutting bloated pomp, the bombast, gesticulation and declamation, the trembling body and the quivering hands, I cannot bear them and should be inclined to laugh were it not prevented by disgust. In the more impassioned parts they would have acted well if the corruptness of the dramatic school had not prevented them. The death was most correctly grouped. The audience were delighted and Talma and George called for. The curtain was raised and they made a hurried, half-dressed appearance at the back of the theatre where they saluted the spectators and hastily retired.

On March 5th the Greatheeds paid a private visit. 'I called with Bertie upon Kemble with whom we went to visit Talma. He is not a handsome man and is a conceited actor, throwing himself into antique postures, but seems a very good humoured, pleasant person.' Again, on March 14th 'Kemble and I went to see Talma, who was very pleasant and animated. His picture of Paris when it was threatened by the Prussians was very good and animated. . . .'

The Greatheeds imprudently stayed on in Paris after the resumption of hostilities. On October 7th, 1802, Talma and Michot with other company came to dine with them. [2] 'We had a very pleasant day. Talma who often sees Bonaparte had an hour's talk with him a day or two ago. It was soon after his playing *La Mort de Pompée*. Bonaparte said: "You made César too much a soldier. Recollect he passed all his youth as an intriguing tribune and senator and when he refuses the crown you make him do it too pompously, too much as if he meant it. Now a man like César never says what he means, and in this refusal before his attendants it was not worth his while to simulate very well; he only meant that the talk of it should get abroad." "Then," said he, "the actor

[1] Bury and Barry, *An Englishman in Paris*, 1803. pp. 31, 32.
[2] Bury and Barry, ibid. p. 184.

who played Ptolomée bent too much and was too humble in his gestures. Servile language was all that a king in his situation could be expected to give; in a letter he might have sunk still lower." He says: "Take away great names and put common men in the place of your heroes, and I feel no more".' Talma's hearers must have been intrigued, not only by the interest Napoleon showed in acting but also by the machiavellian diplomacy he seemed to advocate.

Francis Blagdon, a London journalist who had been well acquainted with Paris before the Revolution, arrived in the city just after the ratification of the treaty preliminary to the Peace of Amiens, that is to say during the last week of October 1801. During a stay which lasted until the following April, he formed a most unfavourable opinion of Talma. [1] 'He is small in stature, thin in person and rather ill-made, his arms and legs being bowed, which he takes care to conceal by the fullness of his garments. . . . As an actor he has no nobleness of manner and not unfrequently his gestures are awkward. His deportment is always ungraceful, though he often endeavours to imitate the postures of antique statues; but even then he only presents a caricature. His countenance has little or no expression except in moments of rage or terror. His utterance is slow, minced and split into syllables. His voice is hollow; but in moments of rage it is strong yet without being of considerable volume. He is generally reproached with being deficient in sensibility. I think however that by dint of labour he might paint feeling; for I have heard him render passages happily enough. He is accused here for having adopted the English style of acting though, as far as my opinion goes, with little or no foundation.' Could condescension go further? If Talma had been bowlegged, Geoffroy would never have accorded him 'every gift of nature'.

As Albert Babeau has pointed out in his *Les Anglais en France après la Paix d'Amiens*, English visitors to the French theatre preferred comedy to tragedy and tended to express their disapproval of the extravagant tragic diction, the swashbuckling tone and the wearisome academic poses. 'However, Talma, whose talent is beyond dispute, excels as Oreste. Talma, brought up in England, "half English" some say, seems to have taken Kemble as his model but to have given to his faults a French character.'[2]

[1] C. Maxwell, *The English Traveller in France*, pp. 233, 234.
[2] Op. cit., p. 48.

Talma seems to have impressed the visitors, sometimes very badly. In this context we shall do well to bear in mind that English acting, compared with French, has a restraint that for continental performers comes near to underplaying. On the stage French actors may appear to us a little larger than life, rather more emphatic in the effects they so consciously create, and our native reticence may shrink before the bravura performances that Talma and his colleagues undoubtedly gave. We must also remember that Talma in his later years developed amazingly. No better evidence of his improvement as an actor can be shown than John Scott's [1] account of seeing Talma in 1814, the next point in time at which British tourists could go to France. 'Talma's principal power is shewn in the representation of the terrible; his features, his voice, his figure, his conceptions unite to assist him in this respect. I saw him, among other parts, in *Oedipe* and his acting in the scene where the horrible truths of his situation, after affrighting the wretched prince by indistinct shadows of misery and guilt, burst upon his knowledge as intolerable realities, was the most awful exhibition I ever witnessed in public. We certainly have not an actor on the English stage that could have produced so prodigious effect.'

Perhaps a German judgment may not come amiss. Kotzebue, in his *Travels from Berlin to Paris in the year 1804*, judged the French tragic scene in these terms:

I have already, on other occasions, set forth my opinion on the manner in which tragedy is performed in France. I cannot endure it because it is so mannered. All French heroes are made in the same mould, all express in the same way their feelings and their passions. Who has seen one tragedy has seen them all. Talma alone deserves to be excepted; he admits himself that he strives to combine the German with the French manner. His envious rivals censure him but the great effect he produces nightly proves incontestably that his method is the best because he knows how to touch the heart. Talma is a handsome man; his face bears the stamp of a gentle sadness but is yet capable of giving energetic expression to every passion. He discourses thoughtfully about nature and art, to which by turns he gives priority. Also he rightly thinks one must try everything and retain only the good.

[1] Scott. *A Visit to Paris*, 1814.

CHAPTER 21

The Raucourt-Lafon Cabal

The success of *Polyeucte* made memorable for Talma the summer of 1803. Not only did Napoleon attend the first night on May 3rd, but even returned eleven days later to applaud his favourite as Sévère. Backstage, beneath a very deceptive surface of artistic endeavour and patriotic fervour, lurked personal rancours and jealousies. Mlle Raucourt resented the admiration the First Consul bestowed upon Talma and saw in Lafon's growing popularity a possible weapon to use against her adversary. We know that she helped to foster the ignoble strife between her pupil Mlle George and the physically less favoured Mlle Duchesnois. Remembering old scores, she did not scruple to pay a section of the parterre to hiss Talma and his wife and to call for Lafon and Mlle Volnais in their places. She had convinced herself, and not herself alone, that Talma had found at last a dangerous rival in Lafon, perhaps even a master. Lafon of course played into her hands. The Gascon had little modesty and already saw himself supplanting Talma, to whom he disparagingly referred as 'the other'. A more willing and manageable tool Mlle Raucourt could not have found. In 1803 Talma could shrug off this underhanded opposition. The persistent, masterful Raucourt would see that throughout 1804 and 1805 the cabal would grow in power.

The resumption of the war with England filled the public mind. On June 4th the *Assemblée Générale des Sociétaires*, 'guided by its love for the country and its unswerving devotion to the august leader of the government', made a gift of 2,500 francs towards the cost of the struggle with England.[1] The First Consul was deeply touched. Having built a new theatre behind the Orangerie at Saint-Cloud, he commanded for June 12th a performance of *Esther* with a starry cast to include Talma, Monvel, Lafon, Mmes Duchesnois and Volnais. This solemn rendering of

[1] *Archives de la Comédie-Française.*

149

Esther marked the first of those dramatic occasions which appear in the records of the Comédie-Française as '*service de la cour*'. Napoleon had insisted not only upon the inclusion of the choruses but also that Talma should play Assuérus, Monvel Mardochée, Lafon Aman, Mlle Duchesnois Esther and Mlle Volnais Zarès. Determined to revive the etiquette of the court of Versailles, he summoned the diplomatic corps, ministers and all members of his personal suite as well as Josephine's ladies to attend this awesome function at which, in accordance with Bourbon tradition, no applause could be vouchsafed until the First Consul, at the play's end, should by his own example permit such recognition. The actors, unaware of the royal protocol and somewhat embarrassed by such unresponsive spectators, played doggedly to a stiff, silent audience. After the performance Lafon read a patriotic cantata composed by M. Fontanes, a member of the First Consul's entourage. M. Fontanes was a dyed-in-the-wool classic, a partisan of Geoffroy. When Napoleon used to ask him for his opinion of Talma's playing, his invariable reply was: 'I saw Lekain.'[1] A secret agent of Louis XVIII present on this occasion described Lafon's ranting and the bombastic effect he and Fontanes produced upon the diplomatic corps as 'deplorable'.[2]

The First Consul had planned a state visit to Belgium and, mindful of the propagandist value of the Comédie-Française, ordered Talma, his wife, Monvel and Mlle Raucourt to proceed to Brussels, where they arrived on June 24th, ready to perform with the help of Belgian actors such tragedies as *Mérope*, *Cinna*, *Esther* and *Britannicus* and certain comedies, notably Bouilly's *L'Abbé de l'épée*, in which Mme Talma had scored a resounding success as the deaf and dumb boy Jules, Marivaux's *Le Legs* and Monvel's own *L'Amour bourru*. Of the fourteen performances the French actors gave in Brussels, the annals of the Belgian theatre speak in terms of rapturous praise. The tumultuous welcomes and the gala atmosphere began on July 4th with Talma's and Mlle Raucourt's success in Voltaire's *Mérope*, which had to be repeated on July 8th and 10th, so great was the public demand to see these distinguished artists.

The great anniversary of the Fall of the Bastille Napoleon and Josephine celebrated in Ghent, where our actors had to give a special performance of *Cinna* with Mlle Raucourt as Émilie,

[1] Sainte-Beuve. *Portraits littéraires*, II, p. 272.
[2] Remacle. *Relations secrètes des agents de Louis XVIII*, p. 333.

Monvel unsurpassed and unsurpassable as Auguste and Talma as
the conspirator Cinna. Madame Talma too in the after-piece,
Le Legs, won golden opinions for her comic verse. We get a
more intimate glimpse of Josephine at *Cinna* again, this time in
Brussels on July 22nd. Arriving late as usual, she entered the
consular box, a wondrous affair 'hung with sky-blue draperies
fringed with silver, and with a background of stars as well'.
Talma as Cinna was declaiming:

> *Romains contre Romains, parents contre parents,*
> *Combattaient seulement pour le choix des tyrans.* [1]

'Loud and prolonged applause broke forth from every corner of
the house and interrupted M. Talma in the midst of the fine
passage he was reciting, a passage that made the great Condé
weep. We will say nothing of the perfection of the artists; merely
to mention Mlle Raucourt, MM. Monvel and Talma is to praise
them in few words.'[2] These fifteen performances in Belgium
fully confirmed Napoleon in his view that actors such as these
could play a valuable part in the dissemination of French culture
throughout the Europe of his conquests.

During Talma's stay in Brussels the sad news of the death of his
father-in-law, Charles-Joseph Vanhove, reached him. The old
trouper had died of an affection of the liver at Brunoy, in Talma's
own bed on June 27th, 1803. Paris mourned a worthy *père noble*
who, but for this last illness, would have played Félix in the
exciting revival of *Polyeucte*. His reputation suffered much from
the censure of Arnault, strictures that his daughter Caroline
Talma contested all her life, and in her *Études sur l'art théâtral*[3]
she left on record a moving tribute to an actor who, utterly devoid
of vanity, deemed it a duty to give always of his best in any rôle,
however unrewarding, for which he had been cast. He was interred
beneath a walnut tree in Talma's garden. Geoffroy in a notice
before the old man's death wrote: 'Useful and diligent Vanhove,
although held of little account, is ever ready to sacrifice himself
to the pleasure of a thankless public. He has height, lungs and at
times character and he extracts with great difficulty applause that
has been too easily lavished upon others.' Other critics proved
more generous and remembered with gratitude and pleasure the

---

[1] Roman against Roman, kinsman against kinsman,
    Were fighting only for the choice of a tyrant.
[2] *L'Oracle*, July 24th, 1803.   [3] Pp. 273–277.

noble indignation Vanhove communicated to Géronte in Corneille's *Le Menteur*.

After ovations that seemed unending the artists of the Comédie-
Française took coach for Paris on July 28th. Bonaparte and Josephine were back at Saint-Cloud by August 12th. During the ensuing weeks Bonaparte's interest in the Théâtre-Français took on
an added zest. Mlle George, '*ce superbe morceau de chair*', had
stirred Napoleon's passions to the point of her being necessary
to his waking and sleeping hours. Just as the First Consul upset
the *semainier*'s arrangements by selecting his own cast for *Esther*,
so for a performance of *Andromaque* to be given on October 8th
did he insist that those two implacable rivals should fight it out,
George as Hermione, Duchesnois as Andromaque. Talma would
of course electrify the dull assembly by his Oreste and with Lafon
as Pyrrhus, would no doubt be well upon his toes. After this visit
of Mlle George to Saint-Cloud Napoleon's infatuation for the
young actress became the *on dit* of Paris. Anxious, unsure Josephine began to interest herself in the career of Mlle Duchesnois. [1]

The generous fees that Napoleon out of his own purse paid
to the *sociétaires* summoned to act at the consular court hardly
compensated them for their diminishing share of profits from a
theatre attracting such poor audiences. With actors and actresses
suddenly withdrawn at the First Consul's behest, playgoers were
not content with understudies. The year 1804 might be described
as a year of failure for the Comédie-Française. It opened with
Alexandre Duval's comedy *Shakespeare amoureux*, with Talma as
the Bard and Caroline, in a breeches part, as Clarence. The joke
proved a damp squib and fizzled out after twelve performances.
More was expected from Aignan's classical exercise in three acts,
Polyxène, given on January 14th in the presence of Napoleon.
Talma appeared as Ulysse, supported by Saint-Prix as Agamemnon, Mlle Volnais as Priam's hapless daughter and Mlle Duchesnois as her mother Hécube. Because of the awful din this mediocre
piece excited, notwithstanding the presence of the First Consul,
the third act could only be mimed. *Polyxène* achieved only four
performances.

On February 4th worse was to follow. Popular imagination had
been stirred by Napoleon's boastful threat to invade England.
Alexandre Duval had concocted a *pièce de circonstance*, *Guillaume le
Conquérant*, a prose drama in five acts that ought to draw the

[1] Mme de Rémusat, *Mémoires*, Vol. I, p. 208.

crowds. In the more emancipated form of the drama, Duval dispensed with the unities of time and place and gave free rein to scenic innovations. The production was exceptionally costly, requiring not only heavy machinery to launch the Norman ships but an army of supers as well. Talma was a noble Harold and Mlle George a bonny Mathilde. The classicists murmured at the breach of the unities and the monkish processions in two scenes raised objections from the anti-clericals. [1] The public however cheered to the echo any reference to perfidious Albion, but reserved its wildest applause for the couplets, set to music by Méhul and sung by Michot, which celebrated the exploits of Roland.

> *Soldats français! chantez Roland;*
> *Son destin est digne d'envie*
> *Heureux qui peut, en combattant,*
> *Vaincre et mourir pour sa patrie!* [2]

To the surprise of all who had participated in this chauvinistic orgy, the play was withdrawn after a single performance. Rumour blamed the censorship, but many thought the real explanation of the play's demise lay in Napoleon's own superstitious nature. In that wily Corsican head plans were taking shape: the liquidation of the Duc d'Enghien, the proclamation of the Empire, the invasion of England. Why tempt fate? This wildly applauded reference to the disaster of Roncevaux dismayed the First Consul. Could it be an evil omen? The risk was too great to take. Duval's play disappeared.

To retrieve the conspicuous failure of *Guillaume le Conquérant* the *sociétaires* had placed high hopes upon a work by Carrion Nisas who, in a rather time-serving spirit, had conceived a tragedy founded on the regeneration of the Russian Empire by a man of genius, Peter the Great, who in order to attain his ends had to triumph first over a base conspiracy. The incidents in the play, as well as the tendentious way in which they were expressed, offered an exciting parallel with Bonaparte's establishment of a hereditary Empire and his victory over the partisans of General Moreau. Unfortunately for the *sociétaires* Carrion Nisas had many enemies. The dramatic critics remembered his venomous comments on

[1] Lanzac de Laborie, *Paris sous Napoléon. Le Théâtre-Français*, pp. 189–191.
[2] Soldiers of France, sing the glory of Roland,
His fate deserves our envy.
Happy is he who can in battle
Conquer and die for his country!

their reception of his *Montmorency*. With Cambacérès, an uncle by marriage, behind him, this son of Languedoc, true to his boastful, combative spirit, had been at considerable pains to advertise his play as a masterpiece and, in enlarging upon its theme, lost no opportunity to curry political favour by stressing the rightness of the Napoleonic principle of heredity, a principle based solely upon the democratic criteria of worth and achievement. Many Frenchmen saw in such a conception a betrayal of the revolutionary cause. The play, *Pierre le Grand*, was produced on May 19th[1] on the very morrow of the proclamation of the Empire. Literary rivals, political adversaries and the supporters of Moreau filled the theatre to overflowing. Outside the doors in the street, an undisciplined crowd seethed. To Talma fell the thankless task of playing the title rôle and, despite the perfervid eloquence he brought to Carrion Nisas' platitudes, he had several times to appeal to the audience for silence. The uproar increased to such an extent that the curtain fell before the end of the play. Disorder reigned inside and outside the theatre. The angry mob in the street enjoyed itself by shouting '*A bas le Carillon*', an obvious pun on the author's name, and made virtually impossible any action inside the theatre by the police, who did however intervene during the play's second performance. On that occasion arrests and evictions half emptied the theatre. The rowdiest sections of both audiences proved to be the students, especially the young men from the *École polytechnique*, whose misconduct caused an embarrassed principal in a letter to the press to deny their presence in the theatre! *Pierre le Grand* revealed so much opposition to Napoleon's imperial project that the *sociétaires*, prodded by the censorship, at once withdrew the piece.

After four such spectacular failures, Talma's one desire was to return to the great parts of the classical repertory. Lafon, officially still his understudy, proved unco-operative and aired his grievances in the green room. The Raucourt faction, ever ready to advance Lafon at Talma's expense, encouraged such odious comparisons between the two men's playing of the same part that Talma was goaded to challenge his rival not to a duel but to the critical verdict of the playgoers. Lafon openly boasted that in chivalrous parts he was superior to Larive and of course to 'the other'. Talma thereupon informed his colleagues that he would

---

[1] I am indebted to Mme Sylvie Chevalley, bibliothécaire-archiviste de la Comédie-Française, for this information. Lists of Talma's creations strangely omit this play.

play alternately with Lafon those disputed heroic rôles, Achille, Orosmane, Tancrède. Mlle Raucourt and her cabal desired nothing better; she saw that her friends in the parterre received their well paid instructions. Let us quote Alfred Copin. 'Talma was hissed in these parts at almost every performance; at one of them he endured the humiliation of hearing the public demand that the part of Tancrède he had just performed should be acted by Lafon the following day.'[1]

The cabal's joy knew no bounds. It really looked as if Talma's star was on the wane. Unfortunately Napoleon still believed in '*l'autre*', and had he not granted him a pension of 1,200 francs on February 1st, 1804? The First Consul was always well informed by M. and Mme de Rémusat as to what happened at the Français and he took care not to involve himself in this dispute between Lafon and his favourite. Apparently he contented himself with a single observation to Talma. 'He is waking you up. You were sleeping.'[2]

[1] A. Copin, *Talma et l'Empire*, p. 72.　　　[2] Mlle George, *Mémoires*, p. 17.

CHAPTER 22

Talma Revives 'Hamlet'

The year 1804 proved a difficult period professionally for Talma and his wife. Caroline shared with her husband a hostility that, born in the jealousies of the green room, quickly extended to the venal journalists of that day. The *Opinion du Parterre*, a theatrical organ upon which the Talmas had always counted for sympathetic, even flattering, comment, quite suddenly discovered in Caroline's playing 'a wearisome monotony, an everlasting tearful note, and these two defects, the only ones of which we complain, are unfortunately major faults and increase from day to day.' Bitter words for one who had been led to believe that Legouvé's judgment, 'every word she utters is a sigh from the soul', was universally accepted. Husband and wife shared a mutual misfortune in close affection.

Caroline Talma had all the qualities, save inches, of the brilliant actress. She could play comedy and tragedy with equal success, a versatility rare in those days. We know how after a performance of the exacting part of Zaïre, Talma rushed into her dressing-room his eyes shining with tears, 'You were admirable. See how moved I am.' Years later, when he found himself rehearsing a novice as Monime in Racine's *Mithridate*, he referred to Caroline's rendering. 'I know of only one woman who could play this difficult part in an admirable manner. She is my wife. What a fine actress!'[1] Caroline really deserved that tribute. Her misfortune in life was to be eclipsed by a greater artist, her husband.

Nor in this critical year of the Raucourt-Lafon cabal did Talma enjoy the thrill of playing before Napoleon at the Comédie-Française. Until the proclamation of the Empire on May 18th, 1804, Napoleon fought shy of public appearances in a theatre. The murder of the Duc d'Enghien had shocked many people and, with a war on his hands, he would run no risks of hostile demonstrations. At this bitter-sweet time Lafon, the darling of

[1] M. G. T. Villenave, *Études sur l'art théâtral, préface*, p. XXIII.

the parterre, had succeeded in obtaining a six months' leave of absence to gather the laurels and the financial harvest the French provinces so readily provided. For Talma this temporary absence of an overweening rival meant a much-needed respite. No more struttings as Achille, Orosmane and Tancrède for a little while, God be praised! What about bringing into the bill the Ducis version of *Hamlet* that went so well at Labussière's benefit in 1803? Mlle Raucourt might even be persuaded to reappear as Gertrude, although about this Ducis expressed his doubts.[1]

Of all Talma's 'Shakespearean' creations Hamlet brought him the greatest success. It became a part that remained in his own *répertoire* all his life. Before we can hazard any estimate of his interpretation, we must have some idea of Ducis' treatment of our greatest tragedy. To quote Ducis again, we are told that on April 10th he had revised the text, had rewritten the '*mourir dormir*' soliloquy and had supplied an entirely new fifth act.[2] The letter ends on a note of ecstatic admiration for his interpreter. 'I adore your talent. I love your person. My glory, if glory there be, will be to have been your poet.'

Ducis, ever mindful of the canons of French 'taste', strayed far from Shakespeare's original. He himself confessed that his version was an amalgam of Shakespeare and Dante. By setting his scene in the palace of the Kings of Denmark, he preserved the unity of place and cut out the 'grotesque' graveyard antics. Again, in the manner of Corneille, Hamlet must be supplied with an inner conflict between love and filial duty. In the Frenchman's play the Prince is in love with Claudius's daughter Ophelia. The Ghost, visible only in Hamlet's imagination—a spectral presentation to the audience was unthinkable—warns him of Claudius's guilt and bids him avenge a murdered father by killing Gertrude and her paramour. Hamlet's friend Norceste, really our Horatio, returns from England where an evil queen has murdered her royal husband and, by his graphic account of the English regicide in front of Hamlet, Claudius and Gertrude, Ducis contrives a situation akin to the original Play Scene. Hamlet thereupon renounces his love for Ophelia. The Ghost renews his murderous demands. As a concession to French susceptibilities Gertrude is not married to Claudius and, although filial duty boggles at matricide, this

---

[1] Guy de la Batut. *Talma. Correspondance.* October 24th 1803. Ducis to Talma October 24th, 1803, p. 71.
[2] Ibid. Ducis to Talma., April 10th, 1804, pp. 71, 72.

Hamlet extracts from Gertrude a confession that, at the instigation of Claudius, she had placed a cup of poison by her husband's bedside, which her conscience subsequently directed her to retrieve but unfortunately too late. Altogether this Gertrude is less 'revolting' than Shakespeare's Queen, a fact which robs the Closet Scene of its bitter tang. In a desire to atone for her guilt, Gertrude joins forces with Hamlet against Claudius. Even in the emasculated Ducis version Talma and Mlle Raucourt could grip their audience, especially at the moment where Hamlet forces his mother to swear upon his father's ashes. Distraught at the inner promptings of the Ghost, Hamlet dismisses his mother. Meanwhile Norceste, having aroused the populace in his friend's cause, defends him from Claudius and his minions. Hamlet then kills Claudius, Gertrude makes a public confession of her share in the late King's murder and then commits suicide. The play ends with Hamlet proclaimed King, determined to bring liberal ideas to his realm and dedicated to the welfare of his subjects.

Here if ever was a Talma part, exactly suited to his own gloomy melancholy, to his preoccupation with death and to his febrile, nervous intensity. Geoffroy, dealing with this literary 'outrage', did not pull his punches. 'What does one go to see in *Hamlet*?' he asks. 'Well drawn characters? No, because the play has no character except a madman and a visionary. Situations well contrived and really pathetic? No, because the only situation in the play is the scene between Hamlet and his mother, as improbable as it is horrible. Then it must be Talma's miming that draws the curious; his distorted features, his wild eye, his quivering voice, his gloomy, sepulchral tone, his taut, muscular frame, his tremblings, his convulsive passion. If to please an audience one must indulge in fits of frenzy, what actor, however noble, natural and restrained, will not appear insipid and cold? True tragic declamation, all the fine shades of feeling and passion, all the technique of an actor's expression will no longer be felt and will no longer delight. What is merely well said and well thought, what is reasonable and right, eloquent and pathetic will simply remain ineffective. One will admire only what terrifies, what outrages, what pales the cheek and chills the spine; and what is so tiresome, people will get blasé about the most frightful happenings, even to the point of laughing at them; and that will be the end of tragedy.'[1] To Geoffroy it seemed that Talma's complete

[1] *Journal des Débats*, March 19th, 1804.

surrender to the emotions of the Prince of Denmark was but a case of out-heroding Herod.

Moreau[1] who saw our tragedian many times in *Hamlet* writes in a different vein. We must remember that Moreau belongs to a younger generation and lived to see the flowering of the Romantic Theatre in France. Of Talma he writes:

Hamlet is his triumph among tragedies imported from abroad; the spectators do not see the shade of Hamlet's father on the French stage; the apparition moves wholly in Talma's mind and, of a truth, it is no less terrifying. When in the midst of calm, melancholy dialogue he suddenly perceives the spectre, one follows every glance in the eyes which behold it and, on the evidence of such a look, the presence of the Ghost is not to be doubted. When Hamlet enters alone in the third act and when he says in beautiful French verse the famous soliloquy, 'To be or not to be'. . . .

> *La mort, c'est le sommeil. . . . C'est un réveil peut-être.*
> *Pêut-être!—Ah! c'est le mot qui glace, épouvanté.*
> *L'homme au bord du cercueil, par le doute arrêté;*
> *Devant ce vaste abîme il se jette en arrière,*
> *Ressaisit l'existence et s'attache à la terre.*[2]

Talma would make no gesture, only occasionally would he shake his head as if to question earth and sky as to what is death! Motionless, dignified contemplation absorbed his whole being; we saw a man in the midst of two thousand silent men question thought on the fate of mortals. In a few years everything that is there will exist no longer; but other men in their turn will become a prey to the same uncertainties and will also plunge into that same abyss, ignorant of its depths.

When Hamlet wants to make his mother swear on the urn containing her husband's ashes that she had no part in the murder, she hesitates, becomes confused and ends up by confessing her share in the crime. Then Hamlet draws the dagger which his father bids him bury in his mother's bosom; but just before he strikes, tenderness and pity overwhelm him and, turning towards his father's shade, he cries out, 'Forgiveness, forgiveness, father' his words charged with all his heart's feelings and, throwing himself at the feet of his unconscious mother, he says in a tone of infinite pity these two lines:

---

[1] *Mémoires historiques et litteraires sur J. F. Talma*, pp. 36, 37.
[2] Death is a sleep. . . . Perhaps an awakening.
   Perhaps!—Ah! that is the word that chills, appalling word.
   Man on the brink of the tomb halted by doubt;
   Before that vast abyss he recoils
   Grasps life again and clings to the earth.

Votre crime est horrible, exécrable, odieux;
Mais il n'est pas plus grand que la bonté des cieux.[1]

M. Tissot[2] claimed that he saw Talma as Hamlet in what the biographer regarded as three distinct readings. He convinces his readers that Talma was superior to Larive who, some fifteen years previously, had essayed the part, and he alleges that 'all the startling theatricality, all the glamorous posing [of Larive] had disappeared before nature and truth. There was grief, deep and sincerely felt, ever present like some guardian spirit; there was melancholy, at once gloomy and tender, which love could momentarily illumine but not wholly efface.' As the years went by, the actor by relentless study plumbed the depths of the rôle, explored its every emotion, echoed its very overtones. Well might Tissot say: 'He had attained perfection and, more natural than ever, he corrected both Ducis and Shakespeare, pouring truth into protracted grief. . . . Finally, he was by turn a son, a lover and a king; in this last aspect of the character how terrible he appeared when he revealed himself in all his power to Polonius.'

However inadequate posterity has judged Ducis' attempt to confine Shakespeare's tragedy to the rules of the French theatre, its historical value should not be understimated. Ducis certainly made plain the desperate need for a freer conception of French tragedy which, in rather a dim and hesitant way, he saw could come from an infusion of English ideas. Here we note the stirrings of the Romantic revolt and Ducis, to his credit, had pushed subject matter and local colour far beyond greco-roman frontiers. Perhaps unaware of the full implications of his efforts he had strained the unities to breaking point, even to ridicule. Talma, thanks to such a vehicle as this *Hamlet*, revealed the true spirit of Romanticism while Victor Hugo was still whimpering in his cradle. It required *'le moi superbe et sans crainte'* of François-Joseph Talma, magnificently displayed in this Ducis adaptation, to reinvigorate French acting with intelligence and imagination and to banish its formal mouthings and frozen postures. The timid innovations of Ducis, but for the imaginative courage of Talma, might well have counted for very little.

Hamlet brought success to the Comédie-Française in what was

---

[1] Your crime is awful, abominable, heinous;
But it does not exceed heaven's mercy.
[2] Tissot. *Souvenirs historiques de F. Talma.* pp. 25, 26.

to prove a financially lean year. With its actors now officially ranked as '*Les Comédiens ordinaires de l'Empereur*', Talma felt that the old, easy reunions of men of letters and science that the First Consul had convened at Saint-Cloud would, in view of the pomp and circumstance that now surrounded him, become a thing of the past. He would not presume; he kept away. Had not Dugazon overstepped the mark when, in response to Napoleon's gay remark about the comedian's increasing girth, he had dared to tap the great man's incipient paunch and assured '*petit papa*'[1] that he himself was putting on weight? Napoleon was not amused. Dugazon no longer enlivened the intimate circle at Saint-Cloud. However, to Talma's great joy, he himself received a cordial invitation, sent by M. de Rémusat, to visit the Emperor who had regretfully noticed his absence. With characteristic thoroughness Talma appeared before His Majesty at the Tuileries wearing court dress!

Such social success did not altogether compensate for what must have proved for Talma a great disappointment. The Emperor again went off on his triumphal progress and September was to find him at Cologne, Coblenz and Mayence, where the Princess of Hesse, the Duke and Duchess of Bavaria and the Elector of Baden would swell his train like the sycophantic vassals they were. The prescribed dose of French tragedy, which had proved so efficacious at Lyons, and Brussels, would be administered this time by Saint-Prix, Lafon, Damas, Desprez and Lacave with the support of Mmes Raucourt, Thénard, Bourgoin, Duchesnois and Gros. Indeed a goodly company. Furthermore, the great Talma parts in *Cinna*, *Andromaque*, *Horace* and *Bajazet* would fall mainly to Lafon, who with his colleagues returned to Paris on October 11th, proud of their success and of the imperial largesse they had received. And Talma was not included. Why? The Raucourt cabal might well be deemed a contributory cause. Talma's success in *Hamlet* had aroused jealousy to such a pitch that enemies were prepared to cast doubt upon his whole-hearted devotion to French art. M. de Rémusat may of course have insisted that, in the interests of French playgoers, the Talmas and Mlle George should stay in Paris. If such an idea lay behind the arrangement, it did not fructify. With the Emperor out of Paris, Talma and his wife betook themselves to Lyons and Mlle George went touring elsewhere. During this period the Comédie-

[1] Lanzac de Laborie, *Le Théâtre-Français*, p. 110.

Française had to be closed on several occasions, so many of its actors were absent. Still, the fact remains that Talma had no part in the imperial gala performances in Germany. His vanity must have suffered a severe blow.

Everything now centred on the Emperor's coronation by Pope Pius VII, arranged to take place in Notre-Dame on December 2nd, 1804. On the eve of that great event a free performance of *Le Festin de Pierre* and *Sganarelle* was given at the Français to a wildly enthusiastic audience. Napoleon had commissioned Chénier to write a tragedy that would commemorate worthily his crowning. Chénier, who had been critical of near dictatorship under the Consulate, seemed a strange choice for such a delicate task. The dramatist of *Charles IX* and *Henri VIII* had treated kingly power with the scantest respect. Rumour breathed a return to imperial favour and the promise of a seat in the Senate for a reformed author. Chénier chose Cyrus and his accession to the Persian throne as his theme and Talma for the title rôle. The play was performed on December 8th before an expectant audience that included the newly crowned Emperor and Empress. Madame de Rémusat recorded in her *Mémoires*: 'Chénier had taken Cyrus as his subject and the fifth act of his play represented quite faithfully the coronation of this prince as well as the ceremony at Notre-Dame. . . . The play was a mediocre affair, revealing all too clearly its propagandist quality. The Parisian parterre, ever independent, booed the piece and even permitted itself to laugh at the enthronement. The Emperor was displeased; he sulked and held my husband responsible for what took place, as if he were answerable for the public's judgment.'[1] She does not tell us that the brand new Emperor took particular exception to the promises of liberal government to the Persian people, which Chénier had put into the mouth of this Cyrus. The old republican which was ever in Chénier peeped out in the praise he bestowed on royal power, a praise amounting to advice.[2] For all the efforts of Talma, so conscious of the solemnity of the occasion, and of his colleagues, Saint-Prix, Baptiste *aîné*, Lafon and Mlle Duchesnois, *Cyrus* died after this single performance.

The authoritarian Emperor brooked no opposition, no opinion other than his own. The censorship increased its vigilance. The four recently established censors, Brousse-Desfaucherets, Lemontey,

---

[1] Mme de Rémusat, *Mémoires 1802–1808*, Vol. II, pp. 79, 80.
[2] John Charpentier, *Napoléon et les hommes de lettres*, p. 85.

Lacretelle *jeune* and Esménard took their duties very seriously, often at Fouché's behest. They made no bones about forbidding, withdrawing or altering any play thought to be critical, however slightly, of the imperial régime. Esménard had the audacity to write into Corneille's *Héraclius* a speech of thirty lines stressing Napoleon's right to the throne, which Talma in the title rôle had to recite. When accused of this enormity, Fouché replied: 'Are not Esménard's verses as good as Corneille's?'[1]

The Comédie-Française, with the resounding failures of four consecutive new plays, all involving Talma, and which together accounted for but eighteen performances, could hardly expect an encouraging statement of accounts for the year 1804. Gross receipts totalled 559,671 francs,[2] from which Talma as sociétaire with a full share drew a sum in the neighbourhood of 25,000 francs.

[1] Mme de Chastenay, *Mémoires*, Vol. II, p. 45.
[2] A. Copin, *Talma et l'Empire*, p. 86.

CHAPTER 23

'Athalie', 'Nicomède', 'Les Templiers'

Talma's coach often rattled out to Saint-Cloud or more
sedately entered the courtyard of the Tuileries, carrying
the actor to those informal discussions which prolonged
the imperial *déjeuner*. Napoleon at this time showed a particularly
keen interest in French tragedy, and Talma enjoyed many talks
on this theme with the Emperor, whose criticisms of his performances the actor found both stimulating and profitable. On
one of these occasions Napoleon kept waiting an important
deputation, come to congratulate him upon his coronation,
while he propounded his views on the art of tragedy. Talma in the
circumstances making a move to withdraw, was told to remain.
Turning to his chamberlain, the Emperor said: 'Let them wait
in the Throne Room'; to Talma: 'Let us continue.' Then and
there Napoleon discussed with remarkable insight the actor's
playing of Néron, which did not altogether satisfy him:

I should like to see more clearly in your acting the struggle between
an evil nature and a good upbringing; I should also like to see you make
fewer gestures; such natures do not give themselves away; they are
too close, too self-contained. Moreover I cannot praise too highly
the simple and natural outlines you have restored to tragedy; indeed,
when persons duly constituted in authority, whether they owe that
elevation to birth or to ability, are stirred by passions or caught up in
serious thought, they no doubt speak in louder tones; but then
language should be no less true, no less natural.' Just then he interrupted his train of thought to say: 'For example, at this moment we
are talking in a conversational manner, very well then, we are making
history.'[1]

To Tissot[2] Napoleon's observations on Talma's Néron,
interesting and shrewd as they were, did not appear altogether
valid. 'When Néron, who was no less impetuous than cruel,

---

[1] Regnault-Warin, *Mémoires historiques sur Talma*, pp. 497–499.
[2] Tissot, *Souvenirs historiques*, p. 35.

gives way to blind fury, it is plain that his character, and conse-
quently the actor's rendering of it, cannot be self-contained. The
mind of this emotional monster, passing violently from one
crisis to another, must reflect the most contrary thoughts and
feelings, because the very nature of passion is to be inconsistent.
Moreover that is what Talma perfectly realized and to his admirable playing of the part for over twenty years he added new per-
fections. . . . Tacitus and Racine imagined nothing deeper,
nothing more tragic; and in the unique way he conceived and
expressed the intentions of both historian and poet the great
actor takes his place as their equal.'

Talma never lightly dismissed Napoleon's advice. We have
already heard how he told Bertie Greatheed the great man's
criticism of his playing of César in *La Mort de Pompée*. What at
that time he could not add was how Napoleon on a later occasion,
doubtless flattered to see that Talma had responded to his
suggestion to take the line '*Pour moi qui tiens le trône l'égal à
l'infamie*' in a more off-hand way, complimented the actor after
a performance at Fontainebleau with these words: 'For the first
time I have seen César.'[1]

Not only did the Emperor interest himself in the acting of
Corneille and Racine. As a reader he paid scrupulous attention
to their texts. It annoyed him to find that l'Infante had to be cut
out of *Le Cid* and he demanded the restoration of the character
to the acting version of the play. Another alteration due to respect
for an integral text was the return of Junie to Racine's *Britannicus*.
Both these two parts had been excised for reasons of length.
The reappearance of Junie created difficulties, for its new interpreter, Mlle Bourgoin, an actress notorious for her scabrous
wit and her light virtue, playing opposite Talma in the great
scene in Act III had to say:

'*Seigneur, j'irai remplir les rangs des vestales.*'[2]

So outrageous was the mocking laughter that greeted her line, the
poor woman fled to the wings only to return a few moments
later, her eyes filled with tears. The parterre, a little ashamed
of its ungallant mirth, offered its excuse by warm applause and
the tragedy proceeded.[3]

---

[1] Regnault-Warin, *Mémoires historiques sur Talma*, pp. 481, 482.
[2] My lord, I will go to swell the ranks of the vestal virgins.
[3] Lanzac de Laborie, *Paris sous Napoléon. Le Théâtre-Français*, p. 77.

The Emperor had also noted that because of its religious fervour *Athalie* had not been performed since the Revolution. Permission to revive the play he readily gave provided Luce de Lancival scrutinized the text, expunging any uncomfortable lines such as:

'Si du sang de nos rois quelque goutte échappée' [1]

where a possible allusion to Louis XVII might be construed. On March 24th, 1805, *Athalie* was performed publicly by order of the Emperor. Saint-Prix proved an admirable choice for Joad, a part Talma declined in favour of the brisk, efficient Abner, a character more in keeping with the military spirit of the times and one which would not embroil the actor with the atheistical *philosophes*. Mlle Raucourt as Athalie thundered in the grand manner and Mlle Duchesnois brought a tender sweetness to Josabeth. New music for the Choirs had been composed by Marc. So pleased was the Emperor with the reception of *Athalie* that he commanded its performance three days later at Saint-Cloud as part of the festivities arranged for the christening by Pope Pius VII of Queen Hortense's son. Geoffroy damned Talma's acting in defiance of all other contemporary opinion. The play of course he saluted as the masterpiece it is and praised its rescue from an ill-judged neglect. Then came his customary rancour for Abner. 'Talma from the first scenes fell into a heavy, gloomy, monotonous delivery and one could recognize the superior talent of this artist only in a few places in the last acts where the dramatic situation helped him. Talma seems to have forgotten that Abner is a warrior, outspoken, generous, full of zeal and courage; these attributes should be established right from the first scene; the character requires a simpler, more open treatment; it calls for more candour and liveliness in the playing.' Geoffroy would never never accept Talma's way of declaiming the alexandrine. He would never allow any new reading of a part but even in his censure he could scarce forbear that muted note of praise *'le talent supérieur de cet artiste'*.

During that late spring yet another production the Parisian public owed to the Emperor's intervention, this time Corneille's *Nicomède*, with Talma in the title rôle. The actor revelled in this part, where he had to fight for his rights as heir to the kingdom

---

[1] If from the blood of our kings escaped some drop. John Charpentier, *Napoléon et les hommes de lettres*, p. 118.

of Bithynia, first against his father Prusias, now a doting adorer of a second wife who pressed the claims of her own son Attale, then against the machinations of Rome, ever ready to depress an allied state to subjection. The domestic intrigue and the external situation that Corneille had·exploited in *Nicomède* chimed with contemporary events, the crowned Emperor and the discredited Bourbons, France against Europe. The *Opinion du Parterre* wrote as follows. 'We owe Napoleon the pleasure of admiring Talma in *Nicomède*; and the reward[1] he deigned to accord him in this rôle proves sufficiently how satisfied he was with this so justly celebrated actor. . . . After having imitated Caesar, he has seen that unto Corneille is rendered ancient tribute, suspended all too long.' Geoffroy of course had something to say in the *Journal des Débats*, March 23rd, 1805. 'Talma as Nicomède shows all the pride, all the irony, the arrogance and the bitterness suitable to the part; but he lacks sufficient nobility in tone and bearing, sufficient light and shade in his delivery, sufficient power and lightness in his voice.' Again his strictures are directed against Talma's delivery of the verse.

The Emperor, after such signal homage to the theatre of Corneille and Racine, departed in the early days of April for Milan, there to be crowned King of Italy. Barely had he gone when a new play went into rehearsal at the Comédie-Française, a play that would bring money to its sorely depleted coffers. François-Juste-Marie Raynouard, *député* for the department of Var, the same theatre-loving politician who had discovered Lafon at Draguignan, had drawn from French history the subject for his play *Les Templiers*. Since the December of 1803, the newspapers had talked of Raynouard's play as being 'so rich in scenes of pathos, that the actors shed tears as they read it'.[2] Public curiosity was suitably whetted but frustrating delays ensued, due mainly to a certain amount of rewriting at the behest of the censor, Esménard. Madame de Rémusat, privileged to be present at the dress rehearsal, wrote of *Les Templiers* in high terms. 'I found great beauty in this work, great and noble characters, a fine sustained style, taut appropriate dialogue, well defined parts.'[3] The public on May 14th, 1805, fully endorsed this verdict. At last the run of bad luck had come to an end. The success of *Les*

---

[1] A public reference to the many gifts Talma received from Napoleon.
[2] *Journal des Débats*, December 11th, 1803.
[3] *Lettres*, Vol. I, p. 126.

Templiers for those days was quite fantastic. For the second performance there were no fewer than eleven applications for Madame Junot's box. [1] Seats had to be reserved days in advance. Before the month end Raynouard had received 5,000 francs in royalties, and for a similar sum had sold his manuscript to a bookseller.

Its cast dazzled. Let us look at the distribution.

Philippe le Bel	Lafon
Enguerrand de Marigny	Baptiste *aîné*
Guillaume de Nogaret	Desprez
Jacques de Molay	Saint-Prix
Gaucher de Châtillon	Damas
Marigny fils	Talma
Jeanne de Navarre	Mlle George
Laigneville	Lacave
Un Officier	Varennes

The play dealt with Philip IV's persecution, spoliation and final destruction of the powerful military and religious order of the Templars. Within the twenty hours permitted by the unity of time, the dramatist had to accuse, judge, condemn and burn his protagonists, a precipitation that shocked even Geoffroy. He pointed out that Raynouard waits until his third act before even arresting the Templars and liquidates them in the fifth act 'with incredible speed'. 'This great trial is for him [the dramatist] merely the matter of a few hours.'[2] The critic suggested changing the play's title to *Le Procès impromptu*.[3] Philippe le Bel, one of history's enigmas, oscillates like a mere puppet between feelings of mercy inspired by the Queen and cruel oppression, a policy advocated off stage by the Grand Inquisitor. Against this background of court intrigue, the young Marigny (Talma) wavers in his loyalty to the Order to which he belongs, but finally in an ill-prepared scene of renunciation decides upon sharing the tortures of his brother Templars. The Grand Master (Jacques de Molay), a mouthpiece of Voltairian platitudes, shows himself a crashing bore. Although Raynouard made great play of his own historical erudition, his tragedy nevertheless is a tissue of anachronisms, largely because his characters are conceived as eighteenth century creations, spouting the slogans of the encyclopaedists.

[1] Duchesse d'Abrantès, *Mémoires*, Vol. V, p. 42.
[2] and [3] *Journal des Débats*, May 22nd, 1805.

If the play by its framework offered a touch of novelty, it reads today as stilted and highflown. The alexandrines were linked by the flattest and most conventional of rhymes; prosaic periphrase masqueraded as verse. When young Marigny had to say that the certificate of his vows had been burnt, the author served him as follows.

> *La flamme a dévoré les sacrés caractères*
> *De mes serments écrits, témoins dépositaires.* [1]

One naturally asks how such fustian could be passed off as cloth of gold. The answer lies in the superb acting the play received. Lafon, in his slapdash way, made a handsome Philippe, but Alfred Copin insists that he failed to outshine Talma. Valleran, the critic of the *Opinion du Parterre*, praised Saint-Prix as Jacques de Molay to the skies, declaring his stock had never been so high, admiring his noble resignation as the Grand Master, affirming 'he completely realized the Christian hero whose only goal is the glory of martyrdom'. To Damas fell the great *récit* of the fifth act, with its description of the burning of the Templars. The same critic opined that 'no ordinary confidant would have sufficed. Damas took care of the speech and rendered it with prodigious success'. Beginning with '*Un immense bûcher, dressé pour leur supplice*'[2] in the awesome tones reserved for such an occasion, he made his audience see the Templars, caught up in the fiery flames, and hear their defiant chanting; then on a note of hopeless despair he ended, '*Mais il était trop tard; les chants avaient cessé*'.[3]

For Mlle George and Talma that evening spelt triumph. The flowing period gown and the becoming head-dress enhanced the lady's beauty and even the partisans of Mlle Duchesnois had to admit that she played the Queen 'passably well'.[4] As for Talma, posterity is assured that 'he decorated with colours so touching the portrait of young Marigny' and 'proved himself the energetic, sublime tragedian'. 'I saw Lekain in his last years,' wrote an enthusiastic admirer, 'and am neither his fanatical admirer nor his impassioned detractor; it is with moderation that I merely say, in my opinion, he has been replaced by Talma, just as Brizard

---

[1] The flames devoured the sacred script,
   Legal witness of my written vows.
[2] 'A mighty pyre erected for their torture'.
[3] 'But it was too late; their songs had ceased'.
[4] Copin, *Talma et l'Empire*, p. 96.

was and advantageously by Monvel.' Of course the croakers croaked. Some reproached him for his haggard eye, his sunken cheek, his terror-stricken voice; on the other hand, admirers recalled his expressive eyes 'which conveyed every emotion and in which were reflected by turns love, hatred, scorn, pride and vengeance'.

All the acting in the world failed to convince Geoffroy that *Les Templiers* was a good play. He devoted no fewer than four *feuilletons* to his reflections on the performances he attended and a further six when the play was published by Giguet and Michaud. All ten articles, each getting steadily worse, attacked the poverty of Raynouard's invention, his threadbare 'poetic' treatment, and pronounced the critic's own growing belief in the utter falsity of the play. Particularly did he lash out at the audiences who acclaimed such rubbish. 'Some of them weep as if they were present at the Crucifixion; others are numbed by a stupid admiration; all of them give way to the most violent transports of emotion.'[1]

Geoffroy was not alone in his denigration of the play. Napoleon in Italy, hearing of its sensational success, confided in a letter to Fouché,[2] Minister of Police, his doubts about the suitability of the subject and the author's handling of kingly power. When, on his return to Saint-Cloud, he saw the play, he formed a very poor opinion of the vacillating Philippe le Bel and wanted Raynouard to make alterations in his text. To the Emperor's chagrin, Raynouard refused to accept his suggestions. Strangely enough, Napoleon got angry with Geoffroy who, he felt, by persistently unfavourable comment, had merely served to confirm an obstinate public in its admiration of the play.

Triumphantly the play ran on, defying the summer's heat. After the thirteenth performance Talma fell out of the cast through illness we would describe today as extreme nervous prostration. The incident claims our attention. Ducis, writing to Lemercier on October 28th, 1805, expressed deep concern over Talma's extreme lassitude, his tendency to drop asleep, his melancholia, and his hints that the strain of playing Oreste was a contributory cause. Happily Talma soon returned to carry *Les Templiers* to its thirty-fifth packed performance. Nor was that the end. *Les Templiers* would be revived at the Français time and time again

[1] *Journal des Débats*, May 21st, 1805.
[2] *Correspondance*, 8821, 1st June, 1805.

and would reap rich rewards in the provinces. It proved the money spinner of its day.

The Emperor's return to Saint-Cloud meant a resumption of those informal discussions with the eminent personalities of his day. With the projected Boulogne operations against England and a contemplated dash against Russia and Austria, Napoleon had much on his mind. No wonder that M. de Talleyrand described him at this time as *'inamusable'*. Mme de Rémusat has neatly summed up the situation as far as Talma was concerned. 'The Emperor loved Talma's acting, or rather the man himself, with whom he had been friendly during the years of his early obscurity. He gave him generous gifts of money and received him as an intimate; but Talma himself, more than any other, succeeded in interesting him.' He was sufficiently interested to command *Les Templiers* with its stellar cast for performance at his private theatre. However, Raynouard's conception of the monkish knights as innocent victims annoyed him. He took umbrage at the dramatist's robust independence and said somewhat irritably to M. de Fontanes, after having discussed *Les Templiers* with its author, 'Very well, let him keep his independence, but he is a man we must keep our eye on.'[1] Into this overcharged atmosphere Mme Talma and Fleury brought the release of laughter. On July 19th they played together in Corneille's *Le Menteur*, a lighthearted affair that earned for Fleury a substantial *douceur*, bestowed from Strasbourg a few days later for having made the Emperor laugh!

Once again war gripped all France. On October 10th the Emperor took the field at the head of his troops. On November 26th the playbill of the Comédie-Française proudly proclaimed *'spectacle gratis'* to celebrate the entry of the French army into Vienna. All this despite Nelson's destruction of the French and Spanish fleets at Trafalgar. However Trafalgar's gloom was to vanish on December 2nd before the sun of Austerlitz. Paris, so long anxious and tense, could now bask in a new security, in the glory of Napoleon's greatest and most desperately needed victory.

[1] Lanzac de Laborie, *Paris sous Napoléon. Le Théâtre-Français*, pp. 203, 204.

CHAPTER 24

The Triumph of 'Manlius'

With so gigantic a tragedy holding the European stage, it seems almost ludicrous to turn to the petty posturings of the theatre's puny world. Prosperity had returned to the Comédie-Française, a prosperity created by wartime audiences, never remarkable in any age for discernment and taste. Under such circumstances '*le beau Lafon*' stirred easy raptures. So insufferably arrogant had he become that he went out of his way to belittle Talma on each and every occasion. His spiteful comments on '*l'autre*' so irritated the Duc de Lauraguais that the annoyed nobleman turned on him. 'M. Lafon, I find you are too often the one and not sufficiently the other.'[1] Into the green room often strayed the aged Marquis de Ximenès, a playgoer who carried the studied grace and the social experience of the *ancien régime*. One evening, Lafon, having just played Orosmane, was still in his dressing-room surrounded by his admirers, when he learned that the distinguished playgoer had been in front. 'I hope our Marquis has been pleased with me,' he commented. Thereupon he hastened to the green room and to his delight saw the Marquis coming towards him. Interpreting this as a good sign, he prepared himself to receive the old gentleman's praise with studied modesty. 'M. Lafon,' said the malicious aristocrat, 'you have played Orosmane as Lekain never played him.' 'Ah! Monsieur le Marquis!' 'No, Lekain did not play him like that; he would have taken care not to do so.' Unfortunately, Lafon's reaction to such acid comment went unrecorded.[2]

Védel, a later director of the Comédie-Française, saw Talma very often during those difficult days when the Raucourt cabal plotted against him. He tells us that the actor became desperate, suffering acutely from persistent pinpricks and even overt demonstrations in favour of Lafon. Talma, with tears in his eyes, told Védel of his decision to leave the Comédie-Française and return

[1] Copin. *Talma et l'Empire*, p. 74.
[2] E. D. de Manne, *La Troupe de Talma*, p. 237.

to London, where he would play in English. Védel did his best
to dissuade him from such an ignominious retreat. One day on
Talma's table he noticed three play books *Thomas-Kouli-Khan*,
Manlius by Lafosse and Piron's *Gustave*. As the plays were
unknown to him, he asked the actor what he proposed to do
with them.

'With no new part, I am looking for a few plays to revive
from the old repertory. I have just read these but have found nothing to encourage the hope of a possible success,' replied Talma.

Védel asked for the loan of the plays and a few days later told
Talma that only *Manlius* was worth revival.

Talma replied: 'That is also my opinion, but that tragedy has
only one scene, no climax and the leading character disappears
miserably in the fourth act. You understand, my friend, that it
offers scant opportunity for an actor.'

'I grant that,' answered Védel, 'but you will allow that, if there
is only one scene, it is a very fine one.'

'Yes, I am going to do it and I also know what I ought to get
out of it. But afterwards, what then?'

'You cannot act the play other than it is. At least, take a chance.'

'I believe you are right,' Talma replied after a moment's reflection, 'especially if the piece can be really well mounted. The
playing will carry off the weak last act.'[1]

Manlius Capitolinus, to give the play its full title, was the work
of one of Racine's earliest imitators. Lafosse, as far back as January
18th, 1698, when the author of *Phèdre* was still alive, had got his
play produced. In plot and characterization it was an exact copy
of Otway's *Venice Preserved* transposed of course to a Roman
setting. Manlius conspires against the Roman Senate and confides
his secret to his friend Servilius, whom he had loved as a brother
for fifteen years. In so doing he runs counter to the advice of his
fellow conspirators, who mistrust Servilius because of his love
for his wife, daughter of the Consul they seek to overthrow.
What they fear, happens. Servilius cannot conceal from his wife
the danger which threatens her father. At once she warns the
Consul. Manlius is arrested, his plans are revealed and the Senate
condemns him to be hurled from the Tarpeian rock. So much for
the outline of the plot. This rather weakly written play had not
been performed for more than twenty years. Talma, throughout
his service as *pensionnaire* and *sociétaire*, had never seen it acted.

---

[1] E. D. de Manne, *La Troupe de Talma*, pp. 235, 236.

He grasped at once the possibilities of the great moment in Act IV, where a letter from a fellow conspirator Rutile, informs Manlius of the betrayal by his passionately loved Servilius, already a prey to remorse. Manlius confronts him with the incriminating letter. 'You know Rutile's hand? Read on. What have you to say?' That '*Qu'en dis-tu?*' from Talma's lips brought forth all the pent-up fury which, by the alchemy of his art, he contrived to soften to an indignation in which still lurked the agony of a friendship betrayed. As Manlius draws his dagger to strike Servilius, the memory of those years of devotion comes like a mist of tears between his vengeance and his love for his friend.

Moreau, much influenced by the opinions of Mme de Staël, saw the play many times and thought Talma even more admirable in the fifth act. Servilius risked everything to expiate his crime and to save Manlius. If his dear friend perished, he would share his fate. The grief of Manlius is softened by Servilius's remorse; nevertheless he dare not tell him that he has pardoned his frightful treachery. Stealthily, he takes Servilius's hand and draws it to his heart. Talma's almost involuntary movements so clearly groped for the guilty friend he wanted to embrace before leaving him for ever. Here of course are Pierre and Jaffier in *Venice Preserved*. Such imagination, such intelligence and such sensitivity did the actor bring to this mediocre play that he raised Lafosse's creaking structure to heights where passion and crime could not obliterate the secret understanding of the heart.

On January 11th, 1806, Talma played Manlius for the first time with the faithful Damas, old friend from the Théâtre de la République, and trusty companion of many provincial tours, in the vitally important part of Servilius. Saint-Prix, Naudet, Desprez and Mmes Fleury and Thénard figured in the supporting cast. The success of the revival was immediate and emphatic. Just listen to Geoffroy, Talma's mortal enemy and prejudiced detractor:

It was a glorious achievement for Talma to have got at once into the skin of Manlius, a part absolutely new to him; nothing can give greater proof of the depth of his dramatic studies. This actor, who often leaves much to be desired, but who is endowed with qualities sufficiently outstanding that he may be reproached for defects without offence or injury to his reputation, has shown himself immediately pre-eminent in the part of Manlius and by the excellence of his playing has put himself above criticism. His delivery shows firmness and strength without heaviness; his voice suffices for all the feelings he wishes to express without recourse to shouts and screams; his depth and concentration serve to increase his energetic grasp. I venture to affirm that, in these great characters of gloomy and proud conspirators, he is better and shows himself a greater actor than in the portrayal of madmen and demented creatures. In Manlius's scenes with his friend he even rendered very naturally and truthfully that kind of sensitive grief which, far from being weakness, is on the contrary, especially in a man as inflexible as Manlius, the very sublime of generosity and friendship. One might perhaps wish that Talma were a little taller, that he had had a more dignified bearing, a more imposing manner; but when this actor gives us everything that art can give, we can excuse him for not having all that nature might provide.[1]

Talma must have rubbed his eyes incredulously when he read Geoffroy's *feuilleton*. Of course Lafosse and his play belonged to a period that, to an ultra-classic like Geoffroy, represented a golden age. Obviously the critic had been bowled over by the romantic Talma's ability to play with complete success a part that required before everything classical restraint and yet a display of emotional feeling. For the actor the real measure of his success was taken a few days later. On January 29th Napoleon, flushed with triumph, attended a performance of *Manlius* at the Comédie-Française, where he received an ovation. The Emperor entered his box at the end of the first scene, but the audience, transported by its own acclamation of the hero, interrupted the play so much that it had to be started again from the beginning. Napoleon listened, we are told, right to the very end.[2]

There really was no holding Geoffroy. Again he took up his pen in praise.

Talma's success increases from day to day. This actor arouses a lively curiosity and draws an extraordinary crowd. The energy, the depth and the truth of his acting are really remarkable. This part of Manlius accords perfectly with his resources and with the quality of his talent. It is worth noting that Talma, whom we had long thought limited to madness, to nervous spasms, to English horror, has achieved true glory only in tragic characters, restrained and reasonable. Nico-mède and Manlius have done him more credit than all the Hamlets and Othellos. Of a truth, the actor finds greater scope in turning good plays to profitable account and in realizing that genuine ability lies within the boundaries of art and nature.[3]

[1] *Journal de l'Empire*, January 13th, 1806.
[2] Copin, *Talma et l'Empire*, p. 105.
[3] *Journal de l'Empire*, January 27th, 1806.

Talma's triumph in *Manlius* from his own professional stand-point cannot be exaggerated. Not only did the old tragedy serve to show Parisian playgoers that his acting range embraced both Hamlet and Manlius, but also to remind his grudging colleagues that they had a successor to Lekain. *Athalie, Nicomède, Les Templiers* had all provided varied rôles, which allowed him to communicate his own intense, imaginative readings to a public whose loyalty a squalid cabal had tried so persistently to undermine. The Emperor's favour, the unanimous praise of the critics, the plaudits of the parterre, dispelled any doubt about Talma's place as leading tragedian at the Comédie-Française. In his new unassailable position Manlius would take its place alongside Oreste, Néron, Hamlet, as a major creation. Just as our own great Irving found in *The Bells* a fustian play that would fill his theatre anywhere and at any time because of his unforgettable Mathias, so this poor effort of Lafosse, under the magic of Talma's art, became, throughout his career, an unfailing money maker. Every year he played it in Paris. He toured it extensively and often chose it for an opening night on his return to the Comédie-Française. On one such occasion, March 28th, 1810, Talma with *Manlius* broke all records with a house worth 5,376 francs. [1]

As evidence of the perennial popularity of *Manlius* we must quote again from Geoffroy, his notice written more than three and a half years after the revival under review.

Talma gave a well-judged, ripe and penetrating performance. Manlius is perhaps the part that shows his talents to greatest advantage, although it seems to exact less effort from him. Perhaps it is more difficult to depict the torment of a strong, courageous mind than to imitate excess of passion and grief bordering on madness. We declare that Talma's genius, ablaze with every tribute of public admiration, has leapt to a great height and that he has never put more feeling into the part of Manlius, unless perhaps on the first occasion he essayed that rôle. Judges of acting all agree that on that night he had an almost divine inspiration, an especial favour accorded by Melpomene, which he has not since repeated to the same degree. He had just created the part and perhaps in that moment of creation he had put forth in a miraculous way all his tragic resources. That first rapture exceeded anything Talma has revealed in later performances, where he has never ceased however to show us an actor deeply thoughtful, energetic and consummate in his art. [2]

[1] Archives. Comédie-Française.
[2] *Journal de l'Empire* August 31st, 1809.

With the war going so well the Emperor found time for theatre going. True, M. de Rémusat received orders to stimulate patriotic fervour and occasionally, after the sublimity of Manlius, Talma found himself playing Bayard in Debelloy's old-fashioned exercise on mediaeval chivalry *Gaston et Bayard* (1771). The ever vigilant censorship required that the line '*Et suivre les Bourbons, c'est marcher à la gloire*' should be emended to '*Et suivre les Français*' out of compliment to the victorious Napoleon. On February 24th the Emperor sent a note to Talma from his box, bidding him announce from the stage the news of the entry of French troops into Naples. Mme de Rémusat affirms that the play was immediately interrupted; M. Laugier puts the bulletin between the first and second acts. At any rate Talma, in the costume of Abner, boomed the good tidings from the stage and a frenzied audience acclaimed a very happy Napoleon.

Public demand had reinstated Talma and had set him on a pinnacle that Lafon and his acrid supporters could no longer assail. A still greater tribute would be paid to him by the Imperial Court. From April 13th to September 18th Napoleon commanded the company of the Comédie-Française to give no fewer than thirty-one performances on the stage of his private theatre at Saint-Cloud. For one moment let us consider the immensity of the task thrown upon the management of the national theatre. There were twenty tragedies and twenty-seven comedies (some of these short pieces), in all one hundred and seventy acts of plays that were mounted with the utmost care and performed with that polish and sense of occasion inseparable from the traditions of the Théâtre-Français. Furthermore, Napoleon often delayed issuing his demands for a particular play until the eve of the required performance; more difficult still, he always had clear ideas about the players he wanted to see. To meet such exacting, inconsiderate requests the *semainiers* must have endured agonies. They had also to satisfy a clamorous Parisian parterre, ever ready to disapprove of hastily summoned understudies who were not always prepared for major rôles. Never in the rue de Richelieu was the prompter more audible than during this summer. Never were baggage-men, wig-makers, dressers more harassed as they bumped over the cobbles on the road to Saint-Cloud, to wait upon highly strung and often quite unpredictable *sociétaires*. Napoleon brooked no complaint, condoned no falling from his ideals of perfection. The man who commanded armies scorned to consider difficulties in a company of players. And what a galaxy! These *Comédiens ordinaires de l'Empereur*, an imperial service, included Talma, Monvel, Damas, Dazincourt, Dugazon, the brothers Baptiste, Lafon, Mmes Raucourt, Contat, Mars, Duchesnois, George. English troupers of the old school would say that only the 'wines and spirits' were left. Their French counterparts would substitute '*le fromage*'. Here is a list of the tragedies that were performed:

Athalie	April 13th	Talma
La Mort de Pompée	May 1st	Talma
Polyeucte	May 15th	Talma
Coriolan	May 18th	Talma
La Mort de César	May 25th	Talma
Cinna	May 29th	Talma
Le Cid	June 1st	Talma
Sertorius	June 8th	Talma
Andromaque	June 22nd	Lafon
La Mort de Henri IV	June 29th	Talma
Britannicus	July 3rd	Talma
Zaïre	July 10th	Lafon
Rhadamiste et Zénobie	July 13th	Talma
Oedipe	July 20th	Talma
Mahomet	July 22nd	Lafon
Nicomède	July 31st	Talma
Héraclius	August 7th	Talma
Bajazet	August 10th	Saint-Prix
Iphigénie en Aulide	August 28th	Talma
Omasis	September 18th	Talma

In these twenty tragedies performed, the Emperor's expressed wish demanded no less than sixteen performances from Talma. Lafon received three commands, Saint-Prix only one. The rôle of Achille in *Iphigénie en Aulide* had become a bone of contention because of Lafon-Talma rivalries, likewise that of Rodrigue in *Le Cid*, and it is therefore of interest to note that Napoleon called for Talma in both of these parts. After such a choice for these Saint-Cloud performances, all Paris could have no possible doubt as to who was the Emperor's favourite actor. Lafon had been put in his place.

Napoleon, ever anxious to stimulate theatrical tragedy, made every effort by offering prizes, gifts of money or even personal praise, to encourage the dramatist, provided of course he conformed to the canons of taste governing the genre and offered no criticism of the imperial régime. At Saint-Cloud two new tragedies rubbed shoulders with the tried favourites from the classical repertory. Legouvé had written *La Mort de Henri IV* of which Napoleon had heard during his Italian peregrinations. In a letter dated June 1st, 1805, he informed Fouché that in his opinion a play dealing with events so recent might stir old rancours and passions. 'The stage requires a touch of antiquity and, without upsetting matters too much, I think you ought to prevent it and not let your intervention appear too obvious.'[1] Fouché took the hint but he had reckoned without Mme Legouvé, the dramatist's intriguing wife who, by ways known only to a French woman, determined to give *'un coup de piston à son petit mari'*, succeeded in reversing the decision of the Chief of Police. The play had been read in small, influential social groups who delighted in its novelty. Just think of it, a hero who swore! A hero who could talk about the chicken in the pot! Mme Legouvé triumphed. The Emperor, hearing of all this excitement, asked for a reading of the play at Saint-Cloud. Excellent reader as Legouvé was, he had the forethought to take Talma with him for the actual reading while he himself watched the Emperor. Napoleon gave every sign of pleasure, murmuring his sympathy, repeating frequently, 'Poor man, poor man.' Only to one line did he take exception. When, in a scene with Sully, Henri says: *'je tremble, je ne sais quel noir pressentiment. . . .'* Napoleon interrupted to say: 'That word "tremble" M. Legouvé is impossible. You must cut it out.' 'Sire,' replied the poet, 'Henri IV's fears are part of history.' 'No matter, you must cut out the word. A sovereign may be afraid, but he must never say so.'[2] That was the only change.

With Napoleon's approval the play went into rehearsal. Although Legouvé wanted Talma for Henri IV, the actor had to fight for the part. Admittedly as *chef d'emploi*, Talma could pick and choose, but his colleagues made it clear that in their opinion odious, gloomy characters fitted him admirably, but that a good natured, hearty fellow like Henri IV was outside his range. 'That is exactly why I want this part,' replied Talma. 'For a long time I have been playing monsters and would like to play a decent fellow. I shall be all the better in the part because I have been accustomed to playing the other types and I shall return to them all the stronger having acted a good man. Only by renewing ourselves do we make progress in our art. To limit

[1] *Correspondance*, 8821, June 1st, 1805.
[2] Legouvé, *Soixante ans de souvenirs*, Vol. I, p. 195.

oneself to one range of parts is to be condemned to exaggeration and mannerisms. My dear Legouvé, trust your Néron to play Henri IV really well.'[1]

Events proved Talma right. On the night of June 25th, 1806, we are told by Legouvé's son, his father rejoiced in the actor's interpretation. By gesture and tone of voice he infused a hearty bonhomie into the character of the King, with which the sustained elegance of the author's alexandrines was so often at variance. The penetrating sadness of his voice endowed such lines as:

> *Il est, il est des jours de sinistre présage*
> *Où l'homme dans son coeur cherche en vain son courage!*
> *Ils me tueront Sully.*[2]

with a rare poignancy. How Talma pounced on every line that carried even a hint of feeling! How he must have jibbed at saying, in place of Henri's forthright 'a pullet in the pot for every peasant', the quite awful periphrasis so rightly lampooned years later by Victor Hugo in the *Préface de Cromwell*:

> *Oui, je veux que le peuple ait par ma bienfaisance,*
> *Quelques-uns de ces mets réservés à l'aisance!*[3]

Of a truth something ailed French tragedy. Yet, thanks to his brilliant playing, Talma could stir its dying embers into a fitful blaze. The play was voted a success and Damas brought to the part of Sully all the incisive astringency of his talent. Lafon, 'by dint of his nobility and handsome appearance' helped the play along in the difficult rôle of Épernon. Mlle Duchesnois, Legouvé's ever grateful protégée, raised the roof as Marie de Médicis. *La Mort de Henri IV*, despite the anxiety of the police, the fervour of Bourbon partisans and the leers of the Voltairians, achieved fourteen performances. The parterre accepted all references to Henri's popularity as a tribute to their own Emperor. Geoffroy loathed the play. To him the squalid assassination of a king lacked the essential pathos and dignity of pure tragedy.[4] A merely

---

[1] Legouvé, *Soixante ans de souvenirs*, Vol. I, pp. 197, 198.
[2] 'There are, there are days of dark foreboding
When a man vainly seeks courage in his heart.
They will kill me, Sully.'
[3] 'Yes, I want the people, through my beneficent rule, to have
A few of those dishes reserved for the affluent.'
[4] *Journal de l'Empire* July 8th, 1806.

deplorable event provided no ground for the conflict of passions —in short, a play unworthy of the Comédie-Française.

There were of course other opinions. The play before production had excited great interest. On the first night the takings amounted to the record sum of 5,600 francs. So great was the press at the doors that Talma's carriage was caught in a dangerous traffic jam. The *Opinion du Parterre* exclaimed: 'What tears have been shed over the performances of 'Henri IV'! Yes, such must have been this man whose subjects were unworthy of him and who died from the daggers of fanaticism. His pathetic kindness, his sincere friendship for a minister whose name will live for ever, his magnanimity, his noble resignation, Talma gave us them all.'

The second new tragedy of that year was *Omasis ou Joseph en Égypte* by Baour-Lormian, a young poet from Languedoc, making for the first time his bow in the theatre on September 13th. This biblical idyll, we are told, had a few sonorous alexandrines and won great applause for Talma as Joseph, a success he shared with Mlle Mars as the boy Benjamin. So perverted by neo-classical prejudice was the public that there were sensible men ready to damn the love intrigue which made Joseph the lover of Pharaoh's daughter Almaïs, played by Mlle Volnais, and the rival of his brother Siméon (Damas). Geoffroy, forthright as ever, decided that 'Joseph should have neither wife nor mistress; he should have only a father and brothers.' He did however admit that if 'Talma did not appear to be suited to the part of Joseph, he nevertheless caught the appropriate tone of goodness and candour.'[1] It is interesting to set beside such grudging praise the almost ecstatic eulogies the *Opinion du Parterre* heaped upon Baour-Lormian and Talma. 'Eloquent painter of *Joseph*, hope of the French stage, you whose faithful brush has limned the enchanting features of Jacob, of Benjamin and of Joseph, recognize with us that the sublime talent of Talma and the ancient patriarchal colour he has imparted to your *Omasis* have increased your success and surpassed your hopes. How wonderful to submit, as you have done, to numerous irksome corrections when the public's tears witness at every performance to the success of your tragedy; but how fortunate to find a man like Talma to play that admirable scene, the purpose of which is made so clear by that beautiful opening line:

[1] *Journal de l'Empire* September 15th, 1806.

Je voulais un remords, je n'ai pu l'obtenir. [1]

Pursue your brilliant career, sublime Talma, you truly astonishing man! Perhaps you have done enough to assure your glory; but, if you can add to it, think how at this moment you make us enjoy the fruits of your labours. We shall regret neither Baron, nor Dufresne, nor Lekain.'[2] *Omasis* achieved the respectable run of twenty-one performances.

Talma the actor walked on air. Effective parts, a devoted public and an admiring Emperor all conspired to make this year of *Manlius* a truly memorable milestone in his career. The cabal had been utterly routed, discomfited and brought to nought. In June Talma had been appointed to a professorship at the Conservatoire together with Fleury, Monvel, Dazincourt, Dugazon and Lafon. This office he took most seriously to the end of his life. A spirit of toleration, if not of friendship, now reigned in the green room. Even Mlle George and Mlle Duchesnois made up their differences, if only temporarily. An astounded parterre saw these two ladies, after playing together in *Horace*, take a curtain hand in hand and then fall into each other's arms, clasped in sisterly embrace. Geoffroy reserved judgment. 'It was a fairly good comic scene played by two tragic actresses.'[3]

[1] 'I wished for remorse, I could not find it.'
[2] *Opinion du Parterre.* Quatrième année. Février 1807.
[3] *Journal de l'Empire* December 2nd, 1806.

Qu'en dis-tu? Manlius Act IV, with Talma as Manlius and Damas as Rutule.
Sketch by David Angers

CHAPTER 25

Talma in Debt

If ever a marriage appeared to be solidly based on deep love, professional interests and social success, it surely was Talma's union with Caroline Petit-Vanhove. So often had they delighted Parisian playgoers by their shared triumphs in plays both new and old, that in the eyes of the public and certainly in the opinion of writers like Arnault they seemed an ideally matched couple. Clouds unfortunately began to gather on a hitherto untroubled horizon and before long cast their shadows over the Talma ménage. Money again was the primal cause of their early disputes. Talma as we have seen quickly acquired the extravagant tastes of Julie Careau and no effort of his second wife could lead him to a more prudent expenditure. For some time now he had led the life of a man about town, his friendship with Napoleon had opened up for him new social perspectives, his lavish entertainments both in Paris and in his country house at Brunoy, all contrived to swallow up his substantial earnings and to increase his debts. It is doubtful if Talma, at any time in his career as an actor, had ever been solvent. Apart from his own generous nature which, when he toured Belgium, compelled him to break his journey at Poix to heap gifts upon his needy kinsfolk, and apart from an almost seigneurial attitude towards the peasants of Brunoy and Les Bosserons, who hailed him as their *boulanger*, there were the expenses of magnificent theatrical costumes and properties to be met. The artist in the man forbade the pinchbeck. The constant building projects to extend both house and gardens at Brunoy bit deeply into his resources. The more practical Caroline would remonstrate with her husband. 'Suppose I had extravagant tastes like yours, suppose I wanted diamonds, boxes at all theatres, suppose I had whims and fancies. . . .'[1] Talma, unperturbed, simply replied: 'Well, we should have more debts.'[2]

[1] C. Talma, *Études sur l'art théâtral*, p. 301.
[2] C. Talma, *Quelques Particularités*, p. 299.

On another occasion, she tells us how she proposed to make herself responsible for all their accounts. 'All right,' agreed Talma, 'I will hand them over to you if you can make head or tail of them.' Indeed, poor Caroline's self-imposed task proved impossible. He handed over a small notebook, beautifully bound in green morocco, in which his minute, spidery handwriting had recorded every item of his expenditure, but so illegible were the entries that no one could possibly read them![1] Caroline goes on to tell us that the Emperor's favour had made ordinary life impossible for her husband. Luxury, notoriety and, she adds a little menacingly, emotional experience became necessities. 'He sought happiness but in ways destined to be the cause of all his troubles.'

Sharp as was this disagreement, the marriage still stood firm. Money oddly enough seemed to pursue them. Late in 1806, Napoleon offered Talma a heavy subsidy, the sum of 160,000 francs was mentioned, to organize a company of French actors and present the masterpieces of the French stage in the subjugated Italian cities. Talma declined the Emperor's offer, suggesting Mlle Raucourt for the task, who gladly accepted such a propagandist piece of work. In the midst of her preliminary arrangements she found time to appear with Talma on February 27th, 1807, in Le Hoc's *Pyrrhus*. For a sixty year old diplomat, Le Hoc seems to have ignored the most elementary tact in writing this formal exercise in tragedy. The action dealt with a usurper Alcétas, who had occupied the throne of Pyrrhus, the rightful heir, and who was eventually expelled with ignominy. Geoffroy liked the play, Napoleon detested it, and it was stopped by order of the imperial government. The Bourbon partisans cheered references all too obvious to the restoration of a rightful king. 'An honourable success'[2] and 'a meagre *succès d'estime*'[3] must be regarded as rather conflicting epitaphs.

The Italian venture proved so profitable to Mlle Raucourt that Talma may well have regretted an ill-considered refusal. Madame de Rémusat makes it very clear that at this time the Emperor was spending huge sums, not only on the direction of the four State Theatres, the Opéra, the Comédie-Française, the Théâtre Feydeau (Opéra-Comique) and the Théâtre de l'Impératrice (Odéon), but was lavishing something like 600,000 francs annually in pen-

[1] Ibid. p 300.
[2] Lanzac de Laborie, *Le Théâtre-Français*, p. 211.
[3] Copin, *Talma et l'Empire*, p. 145. Desgranges. *Geoffroy*, p. 381.

sions and in money gifts to players and authors. In a footnote
to her general statement of such expenditure, she draws special
attention to some interesting details. 'His [the Emperor's]
capricious admiration for certain actors decided as a rule these
money gifts. Several times did he pay Talma's debts, an actor
whom he had known and liked, and at the same time he gave him
sums of money amounting to 20, 30 or 40,000 francs.'[1] Well
might Caroline worry over her husband's lavish way of life in
which she herself was beginning to play a more and more
secondary rôle.

The arrival on June 10th, 1807, of a promising débutant,
Joanny, the leading tragedian from the Grand Théâtre at Lyons,
bringing a répertoire that included Cinna, Coriolan, Rodrigue,
Oreste and Ninias, gave Talma an opportunity to tour the Midi,
not only to make a little money but also to benefit his own and
Caroline's health. This time Talma did not go alone. He engaged a troupe of actors with his wife as his leading lady. Talma
was to play Faran in *Abufar*, Bayard in *Gaston et Bayard*, Oreste
opposite Caroline's Andromaque in Racine's play of that name
and Achille in *Iphigénie en Aulide*. Caroline whose versatility enabled her to play classical comedy insisted on Marivaux' *Le Legs*
being carried because her performance as the Marquise had been
highly praised. She also acted Saléma in *Abufar*.

On August 4th Talma, writing from Tarbes to a friend entrusted with his finances in Paris, one Jallu, bitterly complained
that just as he was preparing to make some money at Toulouse,
where he had arived on July 24th, a letter from Bernard,
Mahérault's deputy at the Comédie, informed him that he must
return forthwith to Paris to be in readiness for the arrival of the
Emperor. Talma grumbled that all the money he had brought
from Paris as well as the Limoges takings had been spent and that
only 2,000 francs remained. His stay at Toulouse had been limited
to a few hours because Caroline's health had dictated a cure at
Cauterets whither he had taken her. Here he expressed his
gratitude to the Queen of Holland, who had received the Talmas
with great affability, and the five days the tragedian spent at
Cauterets proved beneficial to his own health. The letter goes on to
say that Talma reached Tarbes on August 1st and since then he
had played in *Andromaque* and *Omasis*. He would spare M. Jallu
the laurel wreaths and the verses; more to the point the takings

[1] Mme de Rémusat. *Mémoires*, Vol. I. p. 371.

pleased him. Then followed details of loan payments and manipu-
lations. Two more performances at Tarbes should improve his
position and a few appearances at Toulouse do even more.
Caroline's nervous complaint appeared to have been aggravated
by this enforced separation from her husband, although the presence of Mlle Mars at Cauterets beguiled the tedium of her loneli-
ness. Then came details about debt payments falling due with the
comfortable assurance that Jallu would know how to come to
terms with the creditors. A postscript added: 'I have not yet
recovered my health. I should have to spend a month taking the
waters.' [1]

This letter to Jallu throws a rather harsh light on Talma's
monetary troubles. Caroline's breakdown and withdrawal to
Cauterets interrupted what might have proved a very profitable
tour. M. de Rémusat did not succeed in getting the actor back to
Paris at once and one must surmise that the Toulouse performances during a torrid August gave Talma sufficient funds to
bring himself and his wife back to the capital in September. We
find him playing *Héraclius* for the Emperor at Saint-Cloud on
September 17th. For the general public Talma elected to return
on September 19th, 1807, in *Cinna*, an occasion honoured by the
presence of the Emperor and Empress. At this performance
Napoleon faced a Parisian audience for the first time after that
bloody February day when the terrible battle of Eylau was fought.
The parterre, which for some months had had to be content with
the mannered, over-emphatic acting of Joanny, greeted both the
victorious Napoleon and their idol Talma with all the enthusiasm
the occasion demanded.

Two days later the Emperor and Empress repaired to Fon-
tainebleau where they were to hold court for the next two months.
A quite formidable programme of festivities had been arranged
to celebrate the marriage of Catherine of Württemberg with the
Emperor's youngest brother, Jérôme Bonaparte, created by the
Treaty of Tilsitt King of Westphalia. The actors of the Comédie-
Française were once again pressed into service and in deference
to the Emperor's wishes chose for their inaugural production
Corneille's *Horace*, in which Talma played the young Horace,
supported by Mlle Duchesnois as Sabine and Mlle George as
Camille. Mlle Raucourt, now back from her Italian progresses,
rejoined Talma for *Iphigénie*, *Oedipe* and *Rodogune*. Among the

[1] Copin, *Talma et l'Empire*, pp. 151, 2, 3.

plays in which Talma appeared to very great advantage should be mentioned *Rhadamiste et Zénobie, Le Cid, Les Vénitiens* (Arnault), *La Mort de Pompée, Iphigénie en Tauride* (de la Touche), *Manlius* and finally, to conclude the celebrations, on November 13th, 1807, *Nicomède*. Here surely is quite a formidable list. Only an actor of the greatest accomplishment and with an unusually wide range could have performed under conditions so exacting this challenging repertory. Again, only an actor completely acceptable to Napoleon would have been asked to play with such frequency and prominence.

It must be remembered that the actors played before a captive audience, and a not too happy one at that. There sat the Bonaparte clan. Madame Mère grimly garbed in black, the Princesse Borghèse a selfconscious beauty and leader of fashion but already the hypochondriac, Madame Murat restless for a crown, the Queen of Holland in the throes of a difficult pregnancy, alarming all and sundry by spitting blood and sighing for the seclusion of a convent, the Queen of Naples thankful to be in France and with no regrets for Vesuvius, Josephine just a little tearful and beginning to wonder how long she would remain at Napoleon's side. Jérôme the bridegroom had had to repudiate his Baltimore bride, Elizabeth Patterson and their little son, in order to marry a German princess, this Catherine of Württemberg, to further his brother's social and political ambition by becoming King of Westphalia. He must have found Melpomene a harsh commentator on his unenviable lot as he sat ill at ease amid the gold lace of his brand new entourage. Nor could much gaiety be expected from the German princes. The Grand Duke of Würzburg (Prince Primate of the Confederation of the Rhine), Prince William of Prussia, representative of a king who had bitten the dust at Jéna, the Duke of Mecklenburg-Strelitz, the Prince of Baden, sycophants all, knew only too well on which side their bread was buttered and fawned discreetly. Diplomacy too produced its minions, the suave M. de Metternich and, suaver still, the Prince of Benevento, our old friend Talleyrand.

In holding court, Napoleon had enregimented pleasure itself to provide an appropriate imperial background. M. de Rémusat and his henchmen had worked out to the last detail *les menus plaisirs*; banquets, hunts, balls, plays and concerts. There really was no escape. Napoleon complained of his guests' long faces and felt ill-requited for all his efforts by their lack of enthusiasm.

He would come to the play preoccupied and often irritated by some article in an English newspaper. Even Talma, playing his favourite tragedies, did not always succeed in keeping him awake. Then there weighed the problem of Josephine's sterility. He had created an empire and wanted an heir of his own flesh and blood to succeed him. Of course there was also that tricky situation in Spain, a country he must deal with. Altogether, light-hearted gaiety could hardly be said to have reigned at Fontainebleau. With utter thankfulness the guests departed after the final edification supplied by that example of Cornelian heroism, *Nicomède*. Tragedy, forsooth, had they not their own?

For all these lugubrious junketings M. de Rémusat presented the Emperor with a bill for 150,000 francs. For the actors of the Comédie-Française Napoleon paid out of his private purse the sum of 24,300 francs.

Fontainebleau must have provided an opportunity for Talma and the Emperor to discuss the actor's private affairs. A jubilant Talma sent off to his financial adviser, Jallu, a letter from Brunoy that merits quotation in full:

This Thursday.

My friend, I have my own best news to tell you. I have seen the Emperor. He sent away everybody present at his déjeuner and remained an hour with me alone. He went into all the details of my financial position, spoke to me about my debts, my country house. He told me I was not earning enough at the Comédie, that my share was too small. In short, my friend, never has he received me with such affability and kindness; he asked me when I should be free from debts, whether I was still contracting them; he promised that he would look after me. Finally, from all he said to me, never before have I had so much hope of surmounting my difficulties. I am writing all this to you in haste because I know it will give you pleasure.

I get back to Paris on Saturday and return here on Monday. Try to come to my house on Sunday, early in the morning, and I will give you all details.

Farewell, my friend. I am delighted.

TALMA.[1]

Such a letter could not fail to tranquillize the anxious, sore tried M. Jallu. For Talma it gave a respite to extend his credit for still further extravagances at Brunoy and in Paris.

[1] A. Copin, *Talma et l'Empire*, p. 164.

CHAPTER 26

'A Parterre of Kings', Erfurt, 1808

More and more was the Emperor using the theatre, not only to impress the foreign notabilities that found themselves at the upstart imperial court, but also to distract the French from too close a preoccupation with the war. On November 25th, the Imperial Guard returned to Paris and great were the festivities in honour of the heroes of Iéna, Eylau and Friedland. The playhouses offered free entertainment. The Opéra gave *Le Triomphe de Trajan*, the Comédie-Française *Gaston et Bayard* with Talma as Bayard, *le chevalier sans peur et sans reproche*; the Vaudeville put on a triple bill, *'Ils arrivent!'*, *Les Pages* and *La Colonne de Rosbach*, all redolent of an aggressive patriotism; the Variétés staged *Les Bateliers du Niémen* and from the Gaîté came the most terrific spectacle of all, *Le Retour de la Grande Armée*. The veterans had certainly arrived. Paris went mad with joy and sought a momentary relief in frenzied fervour from the persistently gnawing anxieties of war.

Napoleon's construction of a private theatre in the Tuileries reached completion in the December days of 1807. He intended to use the new stage for both French and Italian plays, for opera and for ballet. His obedient courtiers would attend these gala performances; he would distribute seats in the upper galleries to worthy citizens who, no doubt, would be more interested in a bird's eye view of the court than in the entertainment provided on the stage. The opening night was January 16th, 1808, with Talma in *Cinna* as the attraction. For the actor the occasion must have held a touch of sadness, because Monvel, that stalwart of the tragic team, had retired the previous year, leaving Talma unchallenged as the new senior exponent. Monvel's reading of Auguste in this very play can be reckoned among the outstanding performances of the age, and no longer would Talma hear the famous *'Soyons amis, Cinna'* from the lips of an actor whose imagination and intelligence overcame many physical handicaps. Saint-Prix, a competent substitute, played the magnanimous

Auguste on this tremendously formal occasion, with Mlle George and trusty Damas lending a more than adequate support. Unfortunately, on that first performance, the auditorium proved glacially cold. The audience froze. The Emperor and Empress withdrew and the comedy *Brueis et Palaprat*, arranged to follow *Cinna*, could not be given. All went well with six later performances, January 23rd, February 6th, 13th, 20th and March 5th and 12th, when Talma appeared in turn as Titus in Voltaire's *Brutus*, as Sévère in *Polyeucte*, as le Comte d'Essex in the play of that name, as Ladislas in Rotrou's *Venceslas*, as Achille in Racine's *Iphigénie* and finally as Oedipe. At the Comédie-Française the lot of Talma's understudy, compelled to appear before disappointed audiences, was hard indeed.

In 1808, Talma had only one new part, and strangely enough a comic one at that. Lafon, whose conceit since *Manlius* had been somewhat deflated, had turned to comedy, hoping to find there a possible vehicle for his own rehabilitation. On September 20th, 1806, he appeared with moderate success as Clitandre in *Les Femmes savantes*. Geoffroy was most encouraging and gently hinted in his stilted way that Melpomene's darling, in paying homage to Thalia, had yet to receive from that lady love's full reward. Of course at that time comedy and tragedy were rigidly separated and only a quite exceptional versatility could permit an actor to essay principal parts in both genres. Lafon would not fail to turn such a qualification to his own advantage in the green room. A nice question might be asked. Did Talma undertake to play the name part in Lemercier's *Plaute ou la Comédie latine* in order to keep up sides with Lafon? We do not know. The announcement of Talma's appearance in this comedy read as follows: 'He does not limit himself to the speeches of Melpomene; Thalia also at times receives his allegiance and is no less proud of it than her sister.'

During the Empire, contemporary comedy was an exceedingly ticklish form of art, both for dramatist and player. Napoleon of course counted it a waste of time and not even Molière's immortal laughter did he export to his vassal states or exploit for formal functions in his private theatres. The brand new imperial court, uncertain of its own protocol, offered an all too easy target for ridicule. M. de Pourceaugnac would never do! Innocuous laughter at the expense of some pre-Revolutionary period might be risked; country manners as depicted in Picard's *La Petite Ville* might amuse; satire might come too near home. It is therefore not surprising that Lemercier chose Plautus and the classic jest of the loss and recovery of his crock containing his manuscripts and his money as a really safe subject which, by its very antiquity, could give no possible offence.

On January 20th, 1808, the parterre was anything but impressed by Lemercier's comedy. The author's imagination and style won praise from the more discerning, but they felt that too great a liberty had been taken with classical history, and further condemned the play for the exaggeration of its characters. 'Talma, entrusted with the part of Plaute,' said the *Opinion du Parterre*, 'showed himself a great actor who embraces and endows with character all the personae he represents; nothing could excel the warmth and comic verve by which he brought to life his part; and those who have seen performances of this comedy, in which M. Lemercier took us back to the very beginnings of art, will never forget Talma's energetic and astonishing pantomime in the great scene where Plaute finds the casket containing his gold and manuscripts. The other parts in this play were well acted, a matter for no surprise since they had been entrusted to Grandmesnil, Michot, Baptiste *aîné*, Armand and Mlle Mars; but we run no risk of contradiction when we say that Talma alone saved the piece from immediate failure and won for it the performances it achieved.'

The tragedian's services were soon required by the Emperor who, after holding court at the Tuileries, passed on to Saint-Cloud. Talma and Mlle Raucourt, whose sexual aberrations had always intrigued Napoleon, appeared together there on March 31st in Crébillon's one hundred year old play, Électre, which at least gave the actor another nerve-racked Oreste and the actress a majestic, deep-toned Clytemnestre. Then, to the surprise of all Paris, off went the Emperor to Bordeaux and Bayonne, where he could study at close quarters the Spanish question.

Sensation of quite another kind awaited the *sociétaires*. Mlle George, who for four performances had graced the rôle of Mandane in Delrieu's *Artaxerce*, could not be found in Paris for the fifth on May 11th. To the great alarm of her pressing creditors, she had run off to St. Petersburg with a charming dancer from the Opéra, Louis Laport disguised as a woman. On the journey, the first stage of which led to Vienna, Mlle George was known as Julie, the *femme de chambre* of her 'mistress'. The reason for this sensational flight from duty transpired to be a promise of marriage, made by the Russian ambassador, Count Tolstoy, on behalf of Count Benckendorff, then resident in St. Petersburg. When Mlle George eventually reached the Russian capital, she discovered Benckendorff had no intention of marrying her. His real aim was to use the actress to wean Alexander from the affection of Mme de Narishkin, a dangerously powerful woman who all too long had wielded the influence of *maîtresse en titre*. Mlle George, despite her amorous successes with Napoleon, Talleyrand, Metternich and the banker Ouvrard, made but little headway with the Czar. Her failure was due to no lack of experience as she quickly found compensation in more than one profitable quarter. At the Théâtre-Français she was at first fined, then finally the authorities removed her name from the list of *sociétaires*. Mlle Duchesnois sighed with relief. A hated rival had left her in undisputed possession of all the queens and young princesses in the tragic *répertoire*.

August and September saw Talma back at Saint-Cloud in what even for those days were three old-fashioned tragedies, Laharpe's *Philoctète*, Voltaire's *Oreste* and once more Crébillon's *Électre*. These need not detain us. The Emperor was meditating great things in the world's theatre as well as in the theatre's world. He had decided that Russia must become his ally. With such an alliance he could hold Austria and Prussia in utter subjection. In due time England would be humbled. Alexander, the strange, mystical, unpredictable Alexander, even after Tilsitt's preferential treatment, must be wooed still further. Talma, you shall play before a parterre of kings! The meeting between the two Emperors, ready to divide Europe between them, would take place that autumn at Erfurt in Saxony. Napoleon was considering the need to divorce Josephine and to make a marriage that would not only provide an heir to his Empire but would also confer high social prestige upon a court that all Europe had stigmatized as parvenu. Such portentous transactions must have in little Erfurt an appropriate and culturally French background and, what Metternich later called *la levée en masse de tragédie*, Napoleon with characteristic thoroughness conscripted from the Comédie-Française. He therefore instructed M. de Rémusat to send his best actors to Erfurt with a particular request that Talma should play there in *Cinna*, *Andromaque*, *Mahomet* and *Oedipe*. Comedy he rigorously excluded, not because he underestimated the genius of Molière but because he believed such wit to be beyond Teutonic comprehension. 'We must show the Germans the beauty and the grandeur of our tragic stage; they are more able to appreciate them than to penetrate the depths of Molière.[1]'

On the morning of September 19th, a specially chosen band of players left their theatre in Paris for the small Saxon town of Erfurt. They were, aligned in their order of seniority, MM Saint-Prix, Talma, Damas, Lafon, Desprez, Lacave, Varennes, Mmes Raucourt, Talma, Duchesnois, Bourgoin, Gros, Patrat and a débutante Rose Dupuis. That well-graced comedy actor, Dazincourt, had been appointed as Director of the Imperial Theatre and to his unenviable lot fell the task of directing plays and players. Direction of course in those days meant the mere assembling of casts and of the scenery required for the plays. Dazincourt was miserably ill at the time, suffering from an intermittent fever, but like a true trouper he put the theatre's demands before his personal ailments. We must not think that his caravan numbered only seven actors and seven actresses. Damas and Lafon took their wives, Mlles Duchesnois and Bourgoin each a sister, Mlles Gros and Dupuis their mothers and four ladies required the services of their own personal maids. A prompter, a scene-shifter, a call-boy and a commissionaire completed the convoy. After such a withdrawal of talent from the Comédie-Française, one wonders how the needs of Parisian playgoers were served.

When Dazincourt saw what passed for a theatre in Erfurt, his horror knew no bounds. Mme Talma in her memoirs described the small, dirty building as a 'barn'. Thanks to the Director's superhuman efforts, which occupied him for seventy-two hours, broken only by snatched meals, the theatre after his redecorating and refurbishing assumed, at least, on a first glance, an elegance appropriate to the great occasion. Alexander's deafness, discovered by Napoleon on the first night, made their ceremonial box at the rear of the auditorium quite untenable, so the Emperor gave orders that, on a platform placed immediately before the stage, two gilded, throne-like chairs should be provided, a favoured position which allowed the two sovereigns to be visible to this most aristocratic audience. Behind this slightly raised platform, upholstered chairs accommodated crowned heads and behind them in nice gradation were the benches for sovereign princes, grand dukes, electors, ambassadors and other notabilities.

[1] Sainte-Beuve, *Causeries du Lundi*, Vol. I, p. 151.

The box vacated by the two Emperors was subsequently occupied by princesses. Napoleon could congratulate himself upon having brought together so goodly a company, the Kings of Bavaria, Saxony, Württemberg, Westphalia, the Prince Primate, Prince William of Prussia, the Prince of Baden, the Prince of Neufchâtel, the Grand Duke Constantine of Russia, the Duke of Oldenburg, the Duke of Saxe-Weimar, the Duke of Mecklenburg-Strelitz, the marshals and generals in their glittering uniforms and the corps diplomatique with an especial eye on Talleyrand, the limping Prince of Benevento.

So much has been written about these sixteen gala performances given by the cream of French acting talent and about the effects of particular plays, even of particular lines upon the two Emperors and their subjugated audiences. Napoleon saw himself as another Caesar and woe to the tributary kings who withheld their homage! The first play, performed on September 28th, was *Cinna*, with Talma rising to great heights as the conspirator against the all-powerful Auguste. Saint-Prix had the line of the evening: '*Soyons amis, Cinna, c'est moi qui t'en convie.*'[1] If only Alexander heard it! Here was victorious Augustus, magnanimity itself, ready to pardon his enemy and giving still valid reasons for such a noble act. *Mutatis mutandis* the situation had its parallel here in Erfurt. What nobility Talma infused into that ecstatic couplet:

> *O vertu sans exemple! ô clémence qui rend*
> *Votre pouvoir plus juste et mon crime plus grand!*[2]

as he seemed to acknowledge the generosity and the imperial power of the master of the world! The following day came *Andromaque*, and Talma's terrific rendering of the *fureurs d'Oreste* in Act IV elicited the inevitable, overwhelming applause. On September 30th, the great Goethe came over from Weimar to admire Talma as Néron in *Britannicus* and to extol the genius of Racine. The next three days saw *Zaïre*, *Mithridate* and *Oedipe* performed and, during the course of the last-named play when Philoctète says to his confidant Dimas in Act I Sc. i,

> *L'amitié d'un grand homme est un bienfait des dieux*[3]

something like a sensation occurred when Alexander turned

---

[1] 'Let us be friends, Cinna, it is I who bid you.'
[2] 'Oh unparalleled virtue, oh clemency which makes
Your power more just and my crime the greater.'
[3] 'The friendship of a great man is a gift of the gods.'

conspicuously to Napoleon and grasped his hand, appearing to say, 'I count on yours.' How reassured Napoleon must have felt at that moment with such a sign that the carefully planned scheme of a close alliance with Alexander showed promise of fruition. Here indeed was a charm to dispel the gloom caused by those luckless operations at Baylen and Cintra. Even the kings, somnolent in their padded armchairs, and the princes, drowsy on their joyless benches, came out of their coma to gaze with astonishment at Alexander's gesture. M. de Talleyrand could not have agreed more with the Czar. The trouble of course was that Europe had so many great men and, more tiresome still, they were in opposing camps.

On went the plays, inevitably unfolding in strict conformity with French design, the doom of kings and princes. To this politically and socially imprisoned audience no concession was made in the way of lighter entertainment. *Iphigénie en Aulide* on October 4th gave way to *Phèdre* on the following night. Then came a slight diversion. On October 6th, the Grand Duke of Saxe-Weimar had arranged, in honour of the two Emperors, a hunting party in the Ettersburg forest with a banquet to follow at the ducal palace. Replete with Teutonic fare, the distinguished company repaired to the local theatre, where the French actors, having come over from Erfurt, performed *La Mort de César* preparatory to the state ball, which was to crown the Weimar festivities. Here indeed was a strange choice of play. Voltaire's tragedy seemed to abound in lines that could be applied to the current European situation. Was Napoleon surrounded by hypocritical conspirators as Caesar was in ancient Rome? Constraint laid such a hand upon this assembly of potentates that none dared scarcely breathe lest any involuntary gesture be interpreted amiss by Napoleon and his vigilant henchmen. Of the actual performance Alfred Copin wrote:[1] 'Let us add that the part of Brutus, interpreted by Talma, a part he had never ceased to study for sixteen years, was one in which he seemed to excel himself; a deep knowledge of classical history, generous emotion, unflinching stoicism, a simplicity hitherto unknown even in the play's most tragic moments, all these aspects he communicated with an art so marvellous, with such compelling truth, that the spectators were at the same time terrified and fascinated.' It was during this short visit to Weimar, which included an inspection of the battlefield of Iéna, that the

[1] A. Copin, *Talma et l'Empire*, p. 183.

Emperor found time for a long conversation with Goethe on the beauties of French tragedy and on the rôle of fatality in the ancient Greek drama, adding by way of farewell a final 'Go thou and do likewise' counsel to the author of *Werther*.

Back to Erfurt went the distinguished band to endure the last courses of this truly Napoleonic banquet of French tragedy. The remaining masterpieces to be performed give some idea of the herculean labours wrought by Dazincourt and his fourteen acting colleagues.

October 7th	*Les Horaces*
October 8th	*Rodogune*
October 9th	*Mahomet*
October 10th	*Rhadamiste et Zénobie*
October 11th	*Le Cid*
October 12th	*Manlius*
October 13th	*Bajazet*, the last play to be acted.

Talma emerged from this ordeal with the greatest credit. Throughout, he enjoyed the privilege of being admitted to the Emperor's private apartments at all hours and savoured the exquisite pleasure of being addressed by his sovereign in terms of intimate friendship in the presence of the Czar of All the Russias. Praise, laurel wreaths, gifts of a more substantial kind, were poured upon him. Such immediate recognition from princes who vied with each other in bestowing their favours, can never have fallen to the lot of any other actor. By his art he had conquered them, a parterre of kings. In the hot-house of adulation that Erfurt had become for the members of the Comédie-Française the ladies of the company, by their manoeuvring and intrigues, contrived to stimulate no little gossip. Mlle Bourgoin, a hussy if ever there was one, not content with acting on the stage, decided, when she was not required in the play, to make herself conspicuous in the auditorium by a display of opulent jewels upon an ultra-smart gown, that provoked gasps of admiration and continuous interest so that her colleagues on the stage received somewhat scant attention, to the lady's great joy. Napoleon, from the eminence of his dais, observed with a show of anger this exhibitionism and ordered Dazincourt at once to forbid Mlle Bourgoin ever to be seen in the theatre except upon the stage. She had however caught Alexander's roving eye and he contemplated amorous adventure in that quarter. Napoleon's sinister advice to his brother sovereign that any business done with Mlle Bourgoin would certainly result in all Paris knowing its most intimate details and—here the friendly Bonaparte spoke in earnest solicitude—there was of course the Emperor's health to consider . . . . The Czar's meaningful glances, which had encouraged the actress to hope for high rewards, suddenly stopped. Some time later, when Mlle Bourgoin acted in St. Petersburg, Alexander, as a mark of his favour, presented her with a funerary urn dug up in Herculaneum, which finally graced the actress's tomb in Père-Lachaise. Napoleon, if he ever knew of this macabre gift, must have smiled.

Luckily for the ladies, there were other noblemen not so infirm of purpose and any account of Erfurt would be incomplete if references were not made to the private parties given by the Grand-Duke Constantine, who had found in Murat a knowledgeable guide where accommodating beauties were concerned. From these merrymakings the women guests emerged bedecked with furs and diamonds. The Emperor of Russia, in lavish mood, made costly presents to all the actors and actresses whose art he had admired. Every petty prince deemed it his duty to follow suit. Napoleon, ever a realist, made gifts of money. Talma received from him 10,000 francs; there were smaller sums for the others. Even the youthful Rose Dupuis, a mere débutante who had made but one appearance at Erfurt as Palmyre in *Mahomet*, received a gratuity of 3,000 francs.

Over these outward felicitations and visible signs of triumphant success one shadow fell. Alone of the company Caroline Talma failed to win the Emperor's approval. Before the conclusion of the performances at Erfurt, Napoleon called Talma aside to tell him very bluntly: 'I am pleased with you, but your wife offends me; tell her not to go on acting in tragedy.'[1] For Caroline this was a bitter blow to her professional pride. Before Erfurt, Talma had found in his wife a true partner, a talented actress who could hold the stage opposite him in Cornelian and Racinian masterpieces. True, her beautiful voice, once so touching in its tragic entreaty, had somewhat deteriorated, a disability which Mlles Volnais and Bourgoin, as well as their servile journalists, took care to underline. Talma, shaken by the Emperor's dictum, did not leap to his wife's defence. So great was his vanity, alas! that sufficient unto the Erfurt day was the success thereof. The

[1] E. D. de Manne, *La Troupe de Talma*, p. 81.

Emperor's dislike of Caroline Talma did not help to bind husband and wife together.

When Napoleon's purse-bearers had worked out the cost of transporting the actors from Paris to Erfurt and back, a memorandum dated October 27th, 1808, was duly presented to His Imperial Majesty. It informed him that the following sums had been paid to the artists mentioned.

Received by Mmes	Outward Journey	Subsistence	Return
Raucourt	1,500 frs.	500 frs.	1,000 frs.
Talma	1,500	500	1,000
Duchesnois	1,500	500	1,000
Bourgoin	1,200	500	800
Rose Dupuis	1,200	500	800
Gros	1,200	500	800
Patrat	1,200	500	800
MM			
Saint-Prix	1,500	500	1,000
Talma	1,500	500	1,000
Lafon	1,500	500	1,000
Damas	1,500	500	1,000
Desprez	1,200	500	800
Lecave	1,200	500	800
Varennes	1,200	500	800
	18,700 frs.	7,000 frs.	12,600 frs.

When the actors' professional fees and other expenses were added, the total bill which faced Napoleon amounted to 71,284 francs 12 sols. The individual presents of money, Talma's 10,000 francs and Rose Dupuis' 3,000, came out of the Emperor's privy purse.

A weary aristocratic assembly greeted October 14th, 1808 with feelings approaching thankfulness. Even the most spectacular ceremonies must come to an end. Napoleon himself was already beginning to get preoccupied with the Spanish business, which looked ugly. He too must get away, back to Saint-Cloud. Two carriages awaited the departing Emperors at the palace door, each to journey in opposite directions. During the hypocritical leave-takings, M. de Talleyrand found a moment to whisper to Alexander: 'If only you could get into the wrong carriage.'[1]

---

[1] Charles de Rémusat. Appendix to *Mémoires de Mme de Rémusat*. Édition Paul de Rémusat, p. 512.

Napoleon arrived at Saint-Cloud on October 18th. The follow
ing day, at eleven o'clock in the morning, M. de Rémusat received
a command to the effect that His Imperial Majesty wanted a performance of *Tartuffe* and *Les Héritiers* for the night of October
20th with Fleury and Mlle Mars in the cast. Talma and his colleagues had not yet arrived in Paris. In the light of later events,
Tartuffe seemed an almost divinely inspired choice after the
intrigues of Erfurt. On October 29th, Napoleon took the road
for Spain.

CHAPTER 27

Talma and Madame de Staël

Talma returned to Paris with the laurels of Erfurt upon his brow. In the enclosed order of the Comédie-Française he stood supreme, both as an artist and a personality. Fleury might become Doyen in 1809, through the mere count of years, and he could still show himself to be a brilliant actor in the field of polished comedy; but that genre had suffered a serious eclipse because of Napoleon's almost unique preoccupation with tragedy. For all the respect he commanded, Fleury could not hold the candle of his reputation to the dazzling star of Talma. With his debts paid, the tragedian had every inducement to contract new obligations and to plunge once more into the extravagant life that flowed around the imperial court. Only one trouble beset him. There was a dearth of new plays, a real hardship for the creative actor. Rather than fall back upon the somewhat stereotyped repertory, he decided to revive *Macbeth*, *Hamlet* and *Othello*, plays that he passionately loved and that still carried a touch of novelty for the Parisian playgoers. Geoffroy wrote of *Macbeth* in his *feuilleton* dated January 9th, 1809: 'Talma excels in depicting madness and the remorse of Macbeth, Mlle Raucourt makes one shudder in the rôle of Frédégonde; her by-play is awe-inspiring and of a terrible truth. In paying tribute to these two artists, let us hope that their talent will be expended upon nobler objects in better plays. *Macbeth* is a thoroughly bad play. . . .'; and the critic in wearisome fashion proceeded to air his ingrained prejudices against Shakespeare and the English theatre.

Then came on January 18th the benefit performance for Naudet, Talma's old adversary during the *Charles IX* run. Talma, happily, was not vindictive by nature. A childlike generosity informed so many of his deeds, provided of course that his own vanity could be flattered by such benevolence. To assure maximum takings for the not too popular Naudet, he put on *Hamlet*, this time supported by Mlle Volnais as Gertrude. Geoffroy noted with a show of annoyance that only half of those who besieged the doors of the theatre found a place inside. The following quotation from a notice that would be Naudet's last gives a fair idea of Geoffroy's lack of generosity. 'Naudet, a poor actor, never aroused any keen interest. When they gave *Hamlet* for his farewell, one knew that *Hamlet* would enrich Naudet and that Naudet would not contribute anything to *Hamlet*. Talma was undoubtedly one of the chief reasons for all this curiosity and certainly the real cause of this great concourse of people, to whom any other motive would be difficult to assign. It is unfortunate for dramatic art that actors can make a play. Mlle Volnais showed great ability in the scene where Hamlet confides to Gertrude all his plans. Everything considered, the essential weakness of the play is that it carried only one part.'

The greatest of all benefit performances was yet to come. That adored, witty and brilliant *comédienne*, Louise Contat, the original Suzanne in *Le Mariage de Figaro*, decided after thirty-three years of service to take her final curtain on March 6th, 1809. A recent marriage to a dashing cavalry officer may have prompted her to retire. So beloved and admired was this superb artist that her colleagues determined to make her farewell a truly memorable occasion. Seats in boxes, in the orchestra and in the balcony fetched twenty-four francs, an unheard of price for those days; even places in the parterre cost nine francs. The Emperor and the Empress graciously signified their intention to be present. The programme for this quite exceptional event opened with Talma and his wife in a revival of *Othello*, Mme Talma playing Hédelmone, a tragic rôle for the first time since Erfurt. Her husband used for his turban an oriental scarf, the gift of Josephine, who had been so deeply moved by the actor's performance on a previous occasion that she sent through Napoleon the cashmere stole that draped her shoulders.[1] After *Othello* followed Manteufel's *Les Deux Pages*, a comedy adapted by Dezède, which had the sole merit of providing Contat herself with a favourite part, the coquettish hostess Mme Philips. In this adaptation from the German she was supported by her old colleagues, Fleury, Michot, Mlle Mars and even Mlle Raucourt muting her sonorities to the trivial humours of a major's widow. The remaining members of the comedy team accounted it an honour to walk on.

[1] A. Copin, *Talma et l'Empire*, p. 125.

At the conclusion of *Les Deux Pages* Louise Contat was duly garlanded on a stage filled with her male colleagues in the uniform of generals of the Grande Armée, and her actress friends, sumptuously apparelled and bejewelled, as Ladies of the Court. No queen could have commanded greater or more sincere homage. Then, to conclude these impressive proceedings, the dancers from the Opéra, led by Vestris, *le dieu de la danse*, and Mlle Gardel, performed a ballet. Even Geoffroy was moved to admit that Mlle Contat's setting sun preserved the brilliant freshness of her dawn. More acceptable still, the takings amounted to 24,000 francs.

In the life of Talma, Mlle Contat's benefit signifies much. After *Othello* Caroline's appearances with her husband at the Comédie-Française became rare indeed. Their joint efforts on that auspicious occasion could hardly justify future appearances together, for it must be acknowledged that their rendering of *Othello* fell below their usual standards. Talma, ill at ease in the knowledge that the Emperor objected to his wife in tragic parts, rose to great heights only when alone on the stage and seemed almost flat and ineffective in dialogue with Hédelmone. Mme Talma's voice waxed more and more monotonous in its cloying sweetness. The parterre, which had clamoured for this revival, added their ribald laughter to an already hazardous situation. The English play was deemed inferior to *Zaïre* and, although *Macbeth* and *Hamlet* never invited obvious comparisons with particular French masterpieces, it was the fate of *Othello* to be chastized by the Voltaire yardstick. Nor could tittle-tattle of the Talmas' private life be discounted. For years they had made passionate and utterly convincing love on the stage in a wide range of parts and as a happily married couple. Everyone now knew that all was not well with the Talma ménage.

The only new part Talma essayed in 1809 was the much vaunted *Hector* of Luce de Lancival, a middle-aged professor of literature, who, inspired by the beauties of Homer, had constructed a rather static play around events that Racine had treated so magnificently in *Andromaque*. On February 1st, Talma in the title rôle and Mlle Duchesnois as Andromaque carried everything before them, but Geoffroy, firm on his Homeric ground, quibbled over a presentation of Greek manners which allowed Andromaque to mingle freely with Hector's soldiery. He found the play totally denuded of tragic pathos and denounced the conventional use of dreams and oracles as poor substitutes for the interplay of passions and dramatic situations.[1] Luce de Lancival could not abide criticism of any kind and showed his resentment by a blistering lampoon. On this occasion he could have afforded to be generous. The Emperor's admiration earned for him a pension of 6,000 francs, enjoyed alas! all too briefly. Luce de Lancival died the following year.

Time wrought inexorably its changes at the Comédie-Française. Dazincourt, who never recovered from the strain of Erfurt, died on March 28th. In April Dugazon, the inimitable valet, played for the last time. Mlle Bourgoin had wheedled out of Rémusat a six months' *congé* to display wily charms if not acting talent at the Russian court. The conscientious but somewhat limited Mlle Fleury took her benefit on May 1st, when Talma, ever ready to help an old comrade, appeared in the title rôle of a worthless old play *Le Comte de Warwick* with such success that old playgoers who had seen Lekain in this creaking vehicle agreed that Talma had surpassed his predecessor. Only Mlle Raucourt's departure from the cast on extended leave in Italy cut short the very profitable run the old play looked like enjoying.

Talma too heard the call of the provinces and, with debts again beginning to pile up, he could not resist the lure of financial gain that a season at Lyons would surely provide. As events will show, this visit to the Grand-Théâtre in that city would confer immortality on the actor not only in the impassioned pages of Mme de Staël's *De l'Allemagne* but also in the admiring even affectionate letters she penned to the tragedian. Just as Lekain had found his champion in Voltaire, so Talma would owe to Neckar's daughter an appreciation that would preserve the quality of his acting for generations to come.

Mme de Staël, whom Napoleon loathed and had exiled because of her politically independent opinions, lived conveniently near the French border at Coppet, on the shores of Lac Léman in Switzerland. She got wind of Talma's approaching visit to Lyons and, through the influence of Queen Hortense, managed to secure a permit from the imperial police to enter France on the strict understanding that her activities would be limited to play-going. With Mme de Staël came Benjamin Constant and his newly wedded wife, Charlotte de Hardenberg, who must have been a little piqued to see her husband interrupt their honeymoon at Sécheron and so easily fall under the spell of his old mistress.

---

[1] Marc Desgranges, *Geoffroy et la Critique dramatique*, pp. 373, 383, 384.

In their party at Lyons was another exile, the beautiful Mme Récamier. This little group of notabilities so interested in his performances certainly flattered Talma who, accompanied by Caroline, could not fail to remember Benjamin Constant's friendship with his first wife Julie. However, the really important thing to bear in mind is that Mme de Staël was putting the finishing touches to *De l'Allemagne* (due for publication in 1810), a work which dealt mainly with the romantic quality of German poetry and drama, but because of this visit to Lyons it would eventually include pages of panegyric on a French actor.

Maillocheau, the Lyons police superintendent, reported the arrival of Mme de Staël with her son Auguste, '*quelques aides de camp et toute sa maison*' on June 7th, 1809.[1] The Talmas were of course already installed, playing their season with the members of the local company. It would be a simple matter for a fanciful biographer to conjure up imaginary scenes in which the authoress of *Corinne* and her friends attended the play and, after such exquisite exertion, relaxed in social ease to discuss the triumphs of their adored tragedian. Let us rather stick to fact. Before quoting two letters that Mme de Staël addressed to Talma on the subject of his Lyons performances, some reference however brief should be made to the quite extraordinary influence that Talma could exert upon women. In his early years as an actor and the friend of David, he was essentially the student, busied with history, costume and all the arts and artifices of the theatre. By 1809 he had become the philanderer, the womanizer, all too conscious of his powers, which then could affect even a robust, overpowering bluestocking like Mme de Staël, at that time forty-three years old. One other point. The reference in the first letter to Mme Mylord is to the distinguished leading lady of the Lyons company, who crowned Talma on the stage after a performance of *Hamlet*. Now for the first breathless letter.

Lyons, July 4th, 1809.

Have no fear that I shall crown you with a laurel wreath as Mme Mylord did at the most moving moment; but as I can compare you only to yourself, I must tell you, Talma, that yesterday you surpassed perfection, even imagination. There is in that play, faulty as it is, a remnant of tragedy stronger than our own and your talent in the rôle of Hamlet appeared to me like the genius of Shakespeare, but without his lapses and homely touches, which of a sudden became what is noblest on

[1] Henri Welschinger, *La Censure sous le premier Empire*, p. 231.

earth. That depth of human feeling, those questions about the ultimate fate of us all posed before that crowd of people all doomed to die and who seemed to listen to you as to the oracle of fate itself; that ghostly apparition more terrible seen through your eyes than if it had taken a most fearsome shape; that deep melancholy, that voice, those glances revealing great emotion, a character beyond all human reckoning, all that is admirable, thrice admirable; and my friendship for you does not count in this emotional experience, the deepest I have ever felt on an artistic plane. I admire you socially, I admire you in stage parts where you are within our range; but in this rôle of Hamlet you fire me with such enthusiasm that transcends both our personalities: it was a poetry of glances, of voice, of gesture, which no other writer has yet achieved. Farewell, pardon me for writing to you when I expect you this morning at one o'clock and this evening at eight; but if social etiquette did not forbid such things, I am not sure whether yesterday I would not have gloried in giving you myself that laurel wreath which is the due of a talent such as yours rather than according it to any other; for you are not only an actor you are a man who uplifts human nature by giving us a new conception of life. Goodbye till one o'clock. Do not answer this but love me for my admiration.

The second letter, equally enthusiastic, is a little more controlled.

Lyons, July 8th, 1809.

You went away yesterday, *mon cher Oreste*, and you saw how that separation caused me pain. This sadness will remain with me a long time because the admiration you inspire in me cannot be effaced. In your career as an actor you are quite unique and no one before you has ever attained that degree of perfection where art unites with inspiration, premeditation with spontananeity, genius with reason. You have caused me pain, the pain of making me realise more bitterly my exile and the power of the Emperor who, independently of this little Europe, is master of the ideal world of poetry. Hardly had you gone when Senator Roederer arrived on his way from Spain to Strassburg. We talked for three hours and often mentioned your name in our discussion of the world's affairs. He saw *Hamlet* on Sunday and you delighted him. We argued over the merits of the play itself and to me he seemed very conventional in his outlook and claims that Napoleon is also. I expounded to him my ideas about your acting, that astounding combination of French restraint and foreign energy; he claimed that there were French classical plays in which you did not shine and when I asked him what they were he could not name them. But in Paris you must play Tancrède and Orosmane entrancingly; you can do it if you want to. You must treat these two parts naturally. Both are susceptible to such an interpretation and as we have got used to a certain style in their playing an infusion of truth in the acting would make them seem new parts. But I ought not to take upon myself the task of telling you what you know a thousand times better than I. In very truth, your reputation means so much to me. You must become a writer; you must master thought as well as emotion; you can do it if you wish. I saw Mme Talma after your last visit. I was deeply touched by her gracious attitude towards me. Do tell her so, I beg of you. She is a wife worthy of you and in saying that I know I am praising highly. When shall I see you both again? Ah! that question wrings my heart and I cannot raise it without grievous emotion. God bless you and me also![1] I am going to write about dramatic art and half my ideas will come from you. Adrien de Montmorency, who is the arbiter of all that pertains to good taste and dignity of manners, says that you and Mme Talma are perfect in these matters. All my friends are devoted to you both. Everywhere in town people are talking of my hymns of praise about your talent and I really found them quite pindaric when Camille Jordan passed them on to me; but I am not Corinne for nothing and you must pardon this display of feeling. The theatre manager came to see me after your departure to talk to me about you. I was grateful to him for coming to the right person. His conversation was amusing but I was in no mood for laughter and I allowed him to go on saying all he wanted in order to give me a good opinion of himself. So does everyone strive to succeed; only genius triumphs and almost unawares. Goodbye, drop me a few lines about your health, your successes and also about the chance of my seeing you again. My address is Coppet (Switzerland). Goodbye, goodbye; my warm regards to Mme Talma. P.S. I leave in an hour's time; *Les Templiers* has been translated into Spanish and is being played in Madrid.

To this gushing effusion Talma made an actor's reply. He was shrewd enough to realize that support from a literary personality of Mme de Staël's standing would help more than anything to enshrine his fame for posterity. He had not forgotten Voltaire's panegyric of Lekain and how that actor's playing achieved a kind of permanence through those lapidary phrases. Mme de Staël must be cultivated but not at the risk of the Emperor's displeasure. This ample literary Brunhilde could offer no amorous excitement to an actor who had the women of Paris at his feet. Yes, in the circumstances, even Caroline had her uses; their presence together in Lyons could be explained on professional grounds but hardly on any other. Mme Talma's gracious behaviour had made such an impression on Mme de Staël and her circle that the temperature of the blue-stocking's ardours dropped slightly in the equable atmosphere of what she imagined, quite wrongly, to be a

[1] In English in the original text.

happy, well-assorted marriage. There still remained this book, *De l'Allemagne*, that the literary world awaited. It was well worth keeping her in play until those epoch-making pages appeared which would set forth the glories of those interpretations of Shakespearean and French tragedy by one François-Joseph Talma.

His undated letter began by an apology for a delayed reply. He wrote from Paris, assuring his *chère Iphigénie* that her letter had reached him only on the 25th and, in view of the contents of his answer, the month may well have been August rather than July. He and Caroline had not proceeded directly to Bordeaux, but had tarried at Montpelier, where the medical pundits of Rabelais' old university advised the nerve-racked Mme Talma to take a cure of sea-bathing. The couple proceeded to the Atlantic coast where at Bayonne Talma redeemed a long standing promise to act. His account of the theatre at Bayonne is not without a touch of humour. The local leading lady, entrusted with the rôle of Hermione, threatened his face with clenched fists and at one moment looked like pulling his hair. The actors seemed to play as in a trance and to deliver their lines in muted tones. 'They were good fellows, very quiet and haters of noise', especially the noise that came from loud braying donkeys stalled against the theatre walls. The poor Bayonnais had to strain their ears to catch a word. He gave seven performances to a public that even crowded the passages inside the theatre. With a characteristic touch of vanity he added that the dignitaries of the town received him with military honours befitting *'une puissance'*. About his own health he wrote: 'I cannot tell you if I am well or ill. I am in the middle state which is neither one nor the other.' Caroline, we learn, profited from her salt water baths.

Continuing with his letter, Talma showed that Roederer's comments had touched him on the raw. He really liked acting Tancrède, which he found quite easy to play. Orosmane, he thought, was so smothered by a tradition of mannered chanting that innovations would be resisted. However he would do his best and he trusted his dear friend to help him by her criticism. 'Your exquisite taste, your lively imagination will teach me more than all the reasoning in the world.' Her suggestion that he should write does not commend itself to him. Certainly he has ideas to put on paper but they would require for their expression the stimulus of her alert mind. 'The few happy moments I spent beside you clearly showed me that with you I really know more than I imagined. My lute is a good instrument but you must tune it and play upon it. When shall we meet again? That thought distresses me too. But as I have always been fairly fortunate in my life, I cannot think that my good star will desert me over what I desire most in this world. *Adieu, ma chère Iphigénie!* Why am I not with you in the Coppet woods? Accursed chain, which holds us tethered a hundred and fifty leagues apart from one another! Farewell, my dear Iphigénie, your Oreste throws himself at your feet and says to you, a hundred times over, *ma chère Iphigénie*, in the tenderest tones the heart can find.'[1]

Talma, on his return from this provincial tour, reopened at the Comédie-Française on August 29th, 1809, in *Manlius*. His reappearance in this now famous part attracted a bumper audience, so prodigal of its demonstrative affection that Geoffroy had to recall an ancient Greek occasion when, one summer's day, the spectators of Euripides' *Andromeda*, fired by their excessive admiration for a favourite actor, were stricken with madness. He rejoiced that Talma, in order to avert such a catastrophe, had chosen to play a reasonable, reflective and satisfying part for the occasion. 'We affirm that the genius of Talma, taking fire from the popular acclaim, has risen to great heights and that never has he put more feeling into the rôle of Manlius.'[2] For his second play Talma chose Guimond de la Touche's *Iphigénie en Tauride*, in which the actor could pull out every stop of his dramatic organ for *les fureurs d'Oreste*. The public flocked in even greater numbers to see this amazing flamboyant performance, where a great actor brought Promethean fire to ignite the dead wood of what then passed for a French tragedy written in accordance with the rules.

[1] Guy de la Batut, *Talma. Correspondance avec Mme de Staël*, pp. 22–29.
[2] *Journal de l'Empire*, August 31st, 1809.

Talma in his maturity

CHAPTER 28

Nervous Breakdown

The trouble with Promethean fire is that it can be all-consuming. Talma had barely returned to Paris when a severe nervous disorder struck him down and compelled him to withdraw from the stage for five months. During this period his life was despaired of and the newspapers of the time reflect the anxiety felt for the health of an actor who had earned the love and admiration of their readers.

What was the nature of Talma's complaint? Corvisart, Napoleon's own doctor, who attended the tragedian at this time, considered the nature and progress of his illness as quite outside the normal range of human ailments, and Alibert, another eminent physician interested in his case, reached the same conclusion. We must remember that maladies of the mind and nerves were but little understood by the medical faculty of the period, who were more concerned with the amputation of limbs, the efficacy of violent purges and the application of leeches as sovereign remedies for suffering mankind. We must also bear in mind that, for more than twenty years, Talma had poured out on a public stage the tense, heightened emotions inseparable from the great tragic heroes of the French *répertoire*. The terrifying reality of frenzied love, deep melancholy, murderous desire, deranged passion, even madness itself he had simulated with such authenticity, with such absolute conviction, that, in his own actor's mind, ever seeking for 'nature and truth', the intensity of his performances often obliterated for him that finely drawn line which divided the boards of a theatre from the ordinary ways of life. The most alarming situations for him took on absolute reality. Earlier in his career, it was possible at curtain fall to throw off the dread feelings his playing evoked. His stature as an actor grew with the years; as his studies deepened so did his parts acquire a greater substance. Let us not forget that his acting was addressed to his contemporaries, a generation that had had its finer susceptibilities blunted by the excesses of the French Revolution and, at a later date, by the tales of hideous carnage that seeped through from the Napoleonic battlefields. No gentle portrayal of tragic nobility would suffice for such audiences. They expected an explosion of human emotions, a bravura tearing of the heartstrings, in a word, a performance with no holds barred. Talma, by a sheer miracle of acting power, yet controlled within the limits of an art he had developed from French traditions and to which he had added something acquired from the English stage, gave these insatiable Parisians unsparingly what they so exigently demanded. But at what a cost of relentless study, of nervous energy, of vocal cords, of health itself!

This nervous and bodily collapse did not show itself without warning. We know how in 1804 he suffered from fits of melancholia, haunted by the thought of the skull beneath the hair, the decay to which man is doomed. We know how worried Ducis was about the actor's health in 1807, when Népomucène Lemercier took it upon himself in his *Épître à Talma* to warn the tragedian of the ill effects of over-work.

> *Ces fiers ressentiments, ces transports que tu feins*
> *Produisent, Talma, les maux dont tu te plains*

adding, as a final word of advice

> *De tes travaux, Talma, ne te rends pas victime* [1]

Unfortunately, Lemercier's well-intentioned words were as wind along the waste. In this autumn of 1809, hallucinations and terrors possessed the actor. He thought he would go blind: all his life he had been shortsighted. He feared he might fall down dead in the street. The dread of paralysis conjured up another nightmare. Referring to his acting, just before his breakdown, he told his friend Audibert that, when he played *Cinna*, he saw all around him dark, bottomless pits. 'To make you shudder, I begin by shuddering myself,' he would say, a method that sooner or later was bound to make inroads on his health. In his over-excited state, the mere reading of a crime in the newspaper would send him wandering around Paris, a severed head before his eyes. He would enter a church, lost in melancholic gloom, and then, in a

---

[1] 'Those proud feelings, those raptures that you feign
Are the cause, Talma, of the ills of which you complain.'
'Talma, do not make yourself a slave to work.'

sudden lucid moment, remember that he had to play *Hamlet* that same night. 'That evening when I raised my dagger against my mother I frightened myself.' Pathetically he added: 'I needed compassion. I received only applause.'[1]

To these heavy demands made upon his energies the continual pinpricks of Geoffroy must be added. The critic, quite rightly, enjoyed a prestige that placed him high above the theatre scribblers of his day. Unfortunately, where Talma and his wife were concerned, Geoffroy could never bring himself to be objective. That the tragedian had really suffered from the critic's bitter comments a subsequent event will show. No one can acquit Talma of conceit, but he undoubtedly was, on the stage, a dedicated perfectionist. To such a man, those *feuilletons* must have played havoc with his sensibilities and deeply wounded his vanity. The effects of the Raucourt-Lafon cabal also left their mark. Those terrible nights when he played in direct competition with Lafon, before a hostile, paid parterre, would not calm frayed nerves or bring tranquillity to an unquiet mind. By a strange whirligig of fate, now that Talma was out of the bill, Lafon had to bear the burden of playing tragic leads, a burden under which he collapsed and which sent him in his turn to a sick man's bed.[2]

After his comparative recovery, if one may anticipate a little, Talma wrote on May 27th, 1810, to Mme de Staël as follows: 'For a week, madame, I have endured such nervous prostration that the slightest concentration, even for a few moments only, has caused me a discomfort which the longest and most intensive study would (normally) not have given me. . . . I realize, *ma chère Iphigénie*, that one does not play Oreste or Oedipe with impunity. Contacts with such folk cost one dearly.'[3]

To return to the actual five months of illness, Geoffroy's comments in the *Journal de l'Empire*, October 29th, 1809, are noteworthy. 'Alas! Talma very nearly went to join the shades of Baron and Lekain and to tell them about the changes in our theatre. His loss would no doubt have been a blow to tragedy, which indeed would have been sorely tried to don its buskin. This artist, creator of a new style of acting, endowed with most vigorous qualities, possessing public support which borders on enthusiasm, would have certainly left an immense gap, impossible

[1] Audibert, *Indiscrétions et Confidences.* p. 72.
[2] *Archives de la Comédie-Française.*
[3] Guy de la Batut, *Correspondance avec Mme de Staël*, p. 32.

to fill at a period when the lowliest losses are irreparable. But our fears have proved groundless. Talma is not lost; we have only to wait for his return; and we can now discuss calmly the causes of a danger that no longer exists.'

The early days of January saw Talma out of danger and Caroline, who had nursed her husband during the worst period of his terrible illness, felt that she could return to the stage. At Napoleon's court serious events were casting dark shadows. The Emperor, in his desire for an heir, had decided to divorce Josephine, who no longer graced the entertainments he commanded at the Tuileries. It was on one of these occasions, on February 1st, 1810, that Talma acted for the first time after his illness. The play was *Polyeucte*, a wise choice for him because his part as Sévère, in its studied dignity, had nothing of the cat-tearing rages that stamped so many of his other interpretations. The general public had however to wait until March 28th, when he returned to the Comédie-Française in his beloved *Manlius*. Let us quote the *Opinion du Parterre*.[1] 'One might fear that an illness as long as Talma's might have caused some deterioration in his physical powers; he recovered them all when he trod that stage which had witnessed so often his triumphs and the public's enthusiasm. The reception he got on the day of his return and at all subsequent performances must have proved to him how dear he was to the public and how rightly a talent as rare as his influenced the fortunes of his theatre.'

The day before Talma's return as Manlius, an ardent Napoleon awaited, as he sheltered from the pouring rain in the church porch at Courcelles, his new bride, Marie-Louise, daughter of the Emperor of Austria. The bridal couple's arrival at Compiègne was the signal for the start of festivities that seemed to have no end. On March 31st, the Emperor and his new Empress left Compiègne for Saint-Cloud where, on the following day, in the Galerie d'Apollon, beneath the frescoes of Mignard, Napoleon and Marie-Louise went through the civil formalities of their marriage. That evening, reckoned among the most memorable of the First Empire, the Court, after a quite Sardanapalian dinner, crossed the brilliantly illuminated Orangerie to the private theatre, where Agamemnon (Saint-Prix), Clytemnestre (Mlle Raucourt), Achille (Talma) and Iphigénie (Mlle Duchesnois) unfolded Racine's tragic tale of events at Aulis. The actors gave

[1] March 30th, 1810.

a performance worthy of those glittering surroundings, but eyebrows were raised at the choice of the play. In classical mythology, Iphigenia takes her place conspicuously as the symbol of sacrifice. Europe had seen all too readily the sacrifice of a Habsburg princess to the overweening ambition of a Corsican ogre. Clearly, more care would have to be exercised over the choice of play to be performed before the new Empress. On the night in question, *Iphigénie* was followed by *Le Legs*, the delightful Marivaux comedy which gave Fleury and Mme Talma an opportunity to amuse the young Empress who, although her knowledge of French enabled her to enjoy to the full the players' efforts, nevertheless showed unmistakeable signs of boredom during the long tragic recitals.

For April 9th, in the midst of this continuous merrymaking, once more back at Compiègne, the Emperor without any qualms commanded *Britannicus*. In Act II Sc. ii, Talma, as Néron, endured agonies as he declaimed:

> *Trop heureux si bientôt la faveur d'un divorce*
> *Me soulageait d'un joug qu'on m'imposa par force!*
> *Le Ciel même en secret semble la condamner:*
> *Ses voeux depuis quatre ans ont beau l'importuner.*
> *Les Dieux ne montrent point que sa vertu les touche:*
> *D'aucun gage, Narcisse, ils n'honorent sa couche;*
> *L'Empire vainement demande un héritier.*

> Narcisse.

> *Que tardez-vous, Seigneur, à la répudier?*[1]

In the circumstances no greater gaffe could be imagined. No one had foreseen those lines, neither Napoleon, nor Rémusat, nor Talma. The Emperor feigned slumber, the assembled courtiers knew not where to look. Well might Mme de Rémusat write to her husband: 'I am not astonished that they slept or pretended to sleep at *Britannicus*. A fine idea to have come into

---

[1] Only too happy would I be if the favour of a divorce
Relieved me of a yoke, laid upon me by force!
Heaven itself in secret seems to condemn her:
For four years her prayers must have wearied it.
The Gods give no sign that her virtue moves them:
And with no pledge honour her marriage bed:
In vain the Empire asks for an heir.

Narcisse.

Why do you delay, Sire, to cast her off?

your mind and a good excuse for a witty man to say "They asked for it".[1]

All manner of festivities marked this stay at Compiègne, where the Emperor and Empress took up residence on April 5th. Banquets, balls, playgoing, fireworks. Let joy be unconfined. Amid such splendours, the Empire seemed stable enough. Prussia and Russia were impotently quiescent. Austria was now an ally. *Nube, felix Austria*! If only that Spanish business could be disposed of. There must be a limit to English gold. No matter. On April 6th Talma obliged with Rodrigue in *Le Cid*, on the 8th with Oreste in *Andromaque* and, on the following night, as we have seen, with a rather embarrassed Néron in *Britannicus*. At this point in the revels, tragedy gave place to comedy and, where Talma and Mlle Duchesnois had wrung the heart at the Emperor's bidding, Fleury and Mlle Mars now brought their infectious laughter to the relief and delight of sonsy Marie-Louise. To her wishes, so naïvely sincere, her indulgent husband yielded. Molière and Marivaux replaced Corneille and Racine.

The Empress, accompanied by the Emperor, paid her first visit to the Comédie-Française on June 20th, 1810, when the playbill announced Talma, terrific as Cinna, and a comedy *Les Fausses infidélités*. Napoleon had heard that the *sociétaires* were about to launch a somewhat controversial play, *Les États de Blois*, by Raynouard, author of *Les Templiers*. The central theme was the assassination of Henri de Guise, ordered by the King of France, Henri III. The King of Navarre, the future Henri IV, had been presented in a most favourable light as an apostle of peace and religious concord. The big scene in Act V, where Crillon refuses to carry out the murder of the Duc de Guise, declaring vehemently that no crime committed for reasons of state could ever be justified, recalled all too vividly the assassination of the Duc d'Enghien. As we already know, the Emperor considered any play about Henri IV far too modern for tragic treatment and quite likely to stir up rancorous quarrels. Curious however to see the play, he commanded '*ses comédiens*' to perform it at Saint-Cloud. The *sociétaires*, not unmindful of the great success of *Les Templiers*, had assembled a most distinguished cast.

Cathérine de Médicis	Mlle Raucourt
Le roi de Navarre	MM Lafon
Le duc de Guise	Talma

[1] Mme de Rémusat, *Lettres*, Vol. II, p. 295.

Le duc de Mayenne	Damas
Bussy le Clerc	Saint-Prix
Crillon	Baptiste *aîné*

Unfortunately in Raynouard there lurked an unrepentant liberal. His praise of Henri de Navarre could not fail to awaken Bourbon loyalties; his diatribes against revolutionary excess would offend political extremists. Apart from the dramatist's wholesale condemnation of political murder, such lines as:

> *Souvent par un terrible et rapide retour*
> *Le Héros de la veille est le tyran du jour* [1]

were not exactly enjoyed by Napoleon. No wonder he said of Raynouard: 'His politics are dangerous and possibly harmful.'[2] He demolished the play for what he deemed a falsification of history, condemned root and branch its characterization and refused to allow it to be performed publicly. The censorship came forward with the feeble excuse that, as the Empress was related to the House of Lorraine, such a play about a member of that distinguished family, the Duc de Guise, would give grave offence.[3] So *Les États de Blois* after that single performance before a displeased Napoleon, had to wait until the return of the Bourbons for its first public showing, on May 31st, 1814. Napoleon's censure, even in those 'white days', proved no recommendation. The play was hissed and Raynouard left the theatre, never to return. He found consolation in Romance philology and in editing texts of Provençal troubadours.

With his one new play so disastrously received, Talma had to fall back on old favourites for the remainder of 1810. We know he kept alive *Hector*, the hateful Égisthe in Lemercier's obstinately successful *Agamemnon* and Marigny in the ever popular *Les Templiers*. From the classical repertory he selected Sévère, Manlius and Nicomède, parts played with the head rather than with a pulsating, nerve-racked body. So great however was the public's demand for '*les fureurs d'Oreste*' that he was constrained to yield. With returning health and strength, he added Cinna, also Ladislas in Rotrou's old play *Venceslas*, which had contrived to hold the stage from 1647 by the sheer beauty of its subject, the relationship

---

[1] Often by a dire and sudden change,
   Yesterday's hero becomes today's tyrant.
[2] Las Cases, *Le Mémorial*, Vol. I, p. 520.
[3] Laugier, *Documents historiques sur la Comédie-Française*, p. 137.

between an old king and a young and energetic prince. Even the grudging Geoffroy had to accord Talma a modicum of praise as far back as February 8th, 1803, for his handling of this dynamic rôle. 'If there is a part,' he wrote in the *Journal des Débats*, 'which suits Talma, it is Ladislas, whose fiery nature seems to coincide with the actor's impulsive and jerky manner. It would be difficult to control the sudden outbursts of Ladislas by any system of declamation. Talma's wild impetuosity, his excessive warmth, his shouting, his energy, almost always unrestrained, achieve their greatest effect in parts of this kind. Perhaps in them there is a great deal of art, precisely because they appear to have none.' The prejudiced classic surrendered little to the creative romantic artist. Nevertheless, Ladislas can take an honourable place in that gallery of portraits alongside Oreste, Oedipe, Cinna and Néron, studies that over a period of twenty years had contributed to the tragedian's breakdown. The actor, while not forgetful of the public's wishes, husbanded his returning strength by fewer appearances. Copin hinted at backstage unpleasantness as a cause of Talma's regretted absence from the casts. [1]

There were however other reasons. The claims of the Emperor upon Talma and his colleagues, as he progressed with Marie-Louise from one imperial residence to another, account for some absence from Paris. The following list gives some idea of the contributions which the actors of the Théâtre-Français made at Fontainebleau.

September 28th, 1810.
    La Mort de Pompée, Talma (*César*), Mlle Duchesnois (*Cornélie*)
October 10th
    Oedipe, Talma (*Oedipe*), Mlle Raucourt (*Jocaste*)
October 15th
    Esther, Talma (*Assuérus*), Mlle Duchesnois (*Esther*)
October 20th
    Polyeucte, Talma (*Sévère*), Mlle Duchesnois (*Pauline*)
October 27th
    Les Horaces, Talma (*le jeune Horace*), Mlle Duchesnois (*Sabine*)
November 2nd
    Rodogune, Talma (*Antiochus*), Mlle Raucourt (*Cléopâtre*) (For this night *Les Templiers* had been chosen but, Mlle Duchesnois being ill, the whole company of tragedians went to Fontainebleau, prepared to play any piece His Imperial Majesty might select. The Emperor chose *Rodogune*.)

    A. Copin, *Talma et l'Empire*, p. 218.

November 10th
    Les Templiers, Talma (*Marigny*), Mlle Duchesnois (*Jeanne de Navarre*).

Talma certainly had recovered from his breakdown! His responsibilities during the Emperor's sojourn at Fontainebleau would have been much greater had not the more frivolously inclined Marie-Louise insisted upon nine evenings being devoted to the acting of comedies.

CHAPTER 29

Caroline in Eclipse

Caroline Talma, ten years after the death of her husband, set down her recollections of their life together in a maddeningly evasive book she called *Études sur l'Art théâtral*. A section, sub-titled *Quelques particularités sur la vie de Talma*, occupies pages 276–316 of this rather rare volume and one could wish she had not drawn such a thick veil over those interesting years that she, more than anyone, could have illumined by intimate comment. We have already quoted the lady on the ménage's rocky finances. We must quote her again, making use of a rather vague but sinister paragraph tucked away in her rag-bag of recollection. Without any precise reference to persons or places, she wrote, in 1836: 'Talma suddenly became the affluent man about town. Pursued, pestered by women in the highest society, he fell for this kind of notoriety, so detrimental to domestic happiness. His wife, who easily forgave his extravagant tastes, was not so lenient when she saw infidelity added to his disordered finances.'[1] And that is all! The years may have softened Caroline's unhappy memories, but the sharp precision of her criticisms of poor Julie Careau, whose marital happiness she did not scruple to undermine, prompt the thought that quite possibly, out of wifely amour-propre, Caroline preferred to conceal much interesting information.

Let us return to the realities of 1810. Mme Talma certainly showed herself attentive to the needs of her ailing husband. She returned to the stage only when he was out of danger. This professional self-denial carried its own element of sacrifice. We know Louise Contat had retired in 1809 and her wonderful range of comedy parts now fell to Caroline, who could not have enjoyed Geoffroy's boosting of Mlle Volnais in those very rôles where Caroline herself knew she could have acted her hated rival

[1] C. Talma, *Quelques Particularités*, p. 299.

off the stage. When she did play the name part in *Madame de Sévigné*, reckoned one of Louise Contat's greatest successes, she scored a personal triumph. Napoleon's hatred of her as a woman[1] and an actress had, after Erfurt, driven her out of the ranks of tragediennes, a matter that Fabien Pillet in his *Revue des Comédiens* (1808) regarded as a calamity. Caroline Talma, except in Geoffroy's acrid pages, was generally esteemed as a brilliant actress by her fellow artists as well as by an unprejudiced public. 'Born for the arts, this cultivated woman, endowed with distinction of mind, knew how to combine with the study of dramatic art other interests. She practised drawing, even painting and writing. She wrote with an engaging facility her most interesting memoirs and composed a manual of stage elocution, where the excellent precepts she had so long followed are set forth in a remarkable manner.'[2] Aged thirty-nine, Caroline Talma was at the height of her powers, yet, to the surprise and dismay of friends inside and outside the theatre, she intimated her wish to retire from the Comédie-Française after a quarter of a century's service there.

Mlle Flore, that luminary of the lighter stage, in her dateless chronicle expressed amazement at such a premature withdrawal. Her *Mémoires* tell us that, when she was financially embarrassed, the Talmas played *Othello* at a benefit performance for her, apparently arranged at Rouen, where the couple were appearing at the Théâtre des Arts. If Mlle Flore is vague as to time and place, her impressions could not be clearer. Talma surpassed himself and Caroline '*fut ravissante dans Hédelmone*'. She continues: 'That excellent actress, who had left the Théâtre-Français in 1811, well deserved the regrets her withdrawal provoked among true lovers of acting. Nothing was more moving, more true than the sound of her voice; nothing more delightful or more restrained than her posture. The gentlest sensitivity lit up her glance and the features of her distinguished face. Her diction, her gestures, her very bearing had a touch of the languid, that made her adorable in a serious play. I shall never forget the tears she caused to flow as Madame Michelin in *La Jeunesse de Richelieu* and the heart-rending effort of her '*Mère coupable*', in which good judges preferred her to Mlle Contat. In Hédelmone she sang in the last act that exquisite Willow Song, which Ducis had inserted in his tragedy and which no one since has dared to sing at the Théâtre-

[1] Constant, *Mémoires*, p. 155.
[2] E. D. de Manne, *La Troupe de Talma*, p. 83.

Français.'[1] From Mlle Flore, queen of the Variétés, this is a bouquet indeed.

There were of course reasons other than the Emperor's displeasure and Geoffroy's persecution for Caroline's action. Commentators on her retirement, which became effective on April 1st, 1811, make much of her laryngitis. In June, 1810, her superlative acting in Marivaux' *La Mère confidente* gave no indication of waning vocal powers. No doubt, that almost too beautiful voice of hers, with its melting cadences, had been prodigally used, even abused, for her own treatise on declamation set almost excessive store by an actor's voice and even claimed that in many poetic rôles sound took precedence over sense. Her voice may have suffered fatigue, but in those days at the Théâtre-Français no actress need overwork her vocal cords. Laryngitis as the deciding factor in Caroline's retirement can be discounted.

Talma had become very much the man about town. The brittle Empire society with its moral laxity, its crude hedonism and its get-rich-quick philosophy went to the vain actor's head like raw spirit. The Emperor's favour had taken him into a widening court circle, where in its parade of wealth, ambitious men and beautiful women flaunted their attractions. In that amoral society the mistress displaced the wife. Vain, recklessly generous Talma, ever mindful of his kingship in the theatre and posing as the rich landed proprietor, must have astonished and delighted these supplicating beauties. This study is not an account of the amours of Talma. It will suffice to say that, in the Paris farmyard of 1810, Talma crowed on many squalid dunghills. Caroline, when she eventually sought divorce in 1815, referred in her statement to *le sieur* Talma living in concubinage with several women upon whom he had heaped gifts quite beyond his resources. Beauvois, her lawyer, affirmed that, when she had complained of such conduct to her husband, he reacted by throwing discretion to the winds and appeared ostentatiously with his mistresses in public places, even according them unrestricted use of his house both in Paris and at Brunoy.

Only one woman did Caroline name, a Madeleine-Jacqueline Bazire, whose surname is sometimes given as Basile. Bazire is so unusual a name that one is inclined to wonder whether Talma's mistress had any connection with that Mlle Florine Bazire who, making her début as Phèdre at the Comédie-Française in August,

[1] *Mémoires de Mlle Flore*, pp. 302, 303.

Caroline Vanhove, Talma's second wife

1808, was not accepted as a pensionnaire. Madeleine-Jacqueline emerges from a half-world in a half-light. So little is known about her before her association with Talma that one is almost inclined to clutch at any straw that might explain her position in the bohemian circles where the actor moved. A more shadowy creature nowhere confronts any biographer of Talma. That she entered his life around 1810, introduced by Damas, there seems little doubt. That he installed her in his home, No. 6 rue de la Seine, and there shared with her his bed and board alongside his legal wife, still under the same roof but relegated to another part of the house, is an established fact. This state of affairs continued with a show of amiability for some time: in the quarter his neighbours spoke of M. Talma and his two wives.[1] Caroline, like Julie Careau on a previous occasion, felt that such a situation could not go on. She and Talma separated with every sign of friendliness: 'However the rupture between the two parties does not stem from the passionate storms of this liaison. No doubt they live on quite good terms but they have separated their lives.'[2] Could the comparative ease and the apparently sweet reasonableness of this break about 1810 owe something to Caroline's knowledge of her own marital shortcomings? Had she lovers? The two authors already quoted resuscitate from the columns of *L'Opinion du Parterre* the following sinister paragraph: 'Mme Talma is yet young and already her appearance is deteriorating, even showing signs of exhaustion. The abuse of pleasure, no doubt, is making her pay dearly and it is a salutary lesson for those young *débutantes* who take up so passionately this brilliant career where they imagine only flowers are gathered.'[3] If she erred, she had great provocation. Talma and Caroline's outward show of domestic felicity had deceived even a shrewd observer like Mme de Staël as late as 1809. After Erfurt, their acting lives in Paris became separate; he worked exclusively with the tragedians, she with the comedians, and such diversity of professional interests did not contribute to private happiness.

While Caroline's association with the Comédie-Française was drawing to its honourable close, Talma created a new part on March 9th in Baour-Lormian's *Mahomet II*, a conventional tragedy centred around the dilemma of a fierce sultan faced either with the

[1] A. Augustin Thierry, *Le Tragédien de Napoléon*, Le Temps, June 3rd, 1938.
[2] Fleischmann and Bart, *Lettres d'Amour de Talma*. Intro. p. 10.
[3] Fleischmann and Bart, *Lettres d'Amour de Talma*, p. 104.

execution of his favourite odalisque or the disloyalty of his janissaries. Only by the gruesome sacrifice of the former could he regain the fanatical support of the latter. Mahomet for Talma was just another monster. One member of the first-night audience earned expulsion by his solitary hisses. Geoffroy deemed the play a failure but considered that it improved on subsequent perform-ances.[1] The *Opinion du Parterre* contented itself with the following lukewarm comment. 'The character of Mahomet II, at least such as M. Baour-Lormian has imagined it, has been well grasped by Talma.' This '*demi-succès*' was withdrawn by its author after the seventh performance, an unusual course of action explained in a letter to the press. 'I thought I must withdraw this play. My intention is to bring it back one day to the stage in a form less unworthy of the public's kindness.'[2]

Throughout 1811, *Mahomet II* was Talma's only new play. He found himself back on his own *répertoire*, but the tittle-tattle caused by Caroline's premature retirement tended to reduce the frequency of his public appearances. Happily for Talma, interest switched to the Empress who, on March 20th, gave birth to a son, Napoleon's long desired heir, the King of Rome. On that night Mlle Mars and Mlle Thénard, after the play, sang three couplets specially written to celebrate the great occasion. Public rejoicings at the Emperor's command found expression in free theatrical entertainments, in firework displays and in the illumination of public buildings. Pleasure seemed unending. Perhaps the climax was reached on August 25th, when the lavish birthday party for Marie-Louise took place at the Grand Trianon, specially restored to its former glories, where six hundred ladies of the Court, the brand new duchesses, comtesses, baronnes, superbly dressed and bedecked with diamonds, waited upon their Empress to escort her in triumph to the little jewel casket of a theatre at the Petit Trianon, where she would enjoy comedy and ballet performed by artistes from the two principal State Theatres. Talma and his col-leagues were not invited. The shades of Marie-Antoinette surely sufficed to supply the tragedy that obsequious mummers had excised.

Shortly after all this Trianon splendour, Talma obtained leave of absence to play in the Netherlands. He knew Brussels would receive him *en prince* and Amsterdam, where he had long promised

[1] *Journal de l'Empire*, March 14th, 1811.
[2] Lanzac de Laborie, *Le Théâtre-Français sous Napoléon*, p. 217.

to appear, renewed its pressing invitation. By a strange coincidence, Napoleon had decided to take Marie-Louise on an official tour of these two countries, now virtually departments of France. As on all such occasions, the Emperor called for the help of the Comédie-Française, so the capitals Talma had intended to visit at his own expense would now receive him as an imperial envoy. Marshal Duroc instructed Talma, together with such trusty colleagues as Mlle Duchesnois, Mlle Bourgoin and Damas, to be ready to play before the Empress at Brussels, which they did on September 25th.[1] Five days later she rejoined the Emperor at Antwerp, where the Belgians showed their divided feelings. Marie-Louise, the aristocrat sacrificed to a tyrant, they cheered to the echo; Napoleon's own reception was coldly formal. On the other hand, in Holland, which they entered on October 9th, they were both wildly acclaimed. The phlegmatic citizens of Amsterdam almost carried the Emperor and his horse to the palace doors, so great was the cheering press about him; Marie-Louise, processing in a gilded glass coach, won all Dutch hearts. After the chilly Belgian climate, Holland's enthusiasm warmed the heart.

The efforts of Talma and his friends matched the occasion. Talma carried everything before him as Oreste, Bayard, Hamlet and Orosmane, in the particular plays chosen for this Netherlands tour. His acting revealed beauties unsuspected by the Dutch, whose native actors had clung to the outmoded tradition of an incantatory delivery. Mlle Duchesnois had a more difficult task because a local tragedienne, Mme Wattier-Ziegenis, by an outstanding performance as Phèdre had earned a pension of 2,000 francs, which the Emperor bestowed with becoming grace. During this visit to Amsterdam there arose some malicious gossip about a supposed liaison between the Emperor and Mlle Bourgoin. On every count this ill-natured chatter can be ignored. Napoleon's views as regards the lady had been plainly expressed to the Czar at Erfurt. Constant, his valet, refutes the whole affair in his memoirs and adds that the Emperor was discretion itself at this time when Marie-Louise was the apple of his eye.

On his way back to Paris, Talma tarried in his beloved Brussels. The Belgians could never have enough of Oreste, of Néron, of Cinna, of Oedipe, of Manlius. To them, during this visit, he entrusted himself in a new rôle, yet to be seen in Paris. When that

---

[1] F. Faber, *Histoire du Théâtre-Français en Belgique*, Vol. II, p. 263 et seq. *L'Oracle*, September 27th 1811.

cast-iron success, *Les Templiers,* found its way into the Brussels playbill, Talma, instead of playing young Marigny the juvenile lead, took over the part of Jacques de Molay, the Grand Master, in which Saint-Prix had made the greatest success of his career. At forty-eight the youthful ardours of Marigny might well yield to the statesman-like protagonist, Molay. His success in the new rôle at Brussels was such a triumph that in all future revivals Talma cast himself for the more mature part.[1]

He returned to the Comédie-Française on December 4th as Oedipe in Voltaire's play. The new practice of adding an actor's name to every playbill, inaugurated on November 19th, 1810, allowed the public to know that it would surely assist on this occasion at the triumphant return of its favourite. The Emperor and the Empress were both present to welcome Talma in what had come to be regarded as one of his major tragic creations. A few days later, December 19th to be precise, Talma, in Luce de Lancival's *Hector,* moved his sovereign to tears. When in vibrant tones he prayed for his son:

D'un Hector au berceau, Dieux, protégez l'enfance[2]

all thoughts flew to the baby King of Rome, all eyes turned to the box where a father wept. When the audience saw the Emperor's emotion, its applause knew no bounds.

At this point in Talma's career all nineteenth-century biographers agreed that a drab monotony coloured the immediately succeeding years. Apart from chronicling the 1812 performances at the Tuileries where, out of fourteen performances, Talma was required only for two, *Hector* and *Andromaque,* the writers pad out the story with the European background, Napoleon's suspicions of Alexander, the Czar's flirtations with the Poles and with the Prussians, English gold, available for another coalition and already paying handsome dividends in Spain. Behind all the pomp and circumstance of Saint-Cloud and the Tuileries lurked great anxiety. With Madame Mère's *'pourvu que ça dure'* chimed Napoleon's *'tout rentre en problème'.*[3]

In the world of the theatre the year 1812 brought into the open the disastrous finances of the Théâtre-Français. Napoleon's demands upon the *sociétaires* to send their stars to perform at

---

[1] A. Copin, *Talma et l'Empire,* p. 245.
[2] 'Oh Gods, protect the childhood of a Hector in his cradle.'
[3] J. Bainville, *Napoléon,* p. 359.

court, often at a few hours' notice, had played havoc with their playbills. The theatre somehow had to be kept open. Mahérault, to whom the actual management of the theatre had been entrusted, had struggled despite his failing health to maintain some semblance of continuous dramatic fare. His position was made no easier by an energetic subaltern, Bernard, who in one way or another seemed able to straighten out quarrels and exercise a usurped authority. The public, now apprised by the playbill of the actual cast, obstinately stayed away from understudy performances.[1] Takings fell and their fall resulted in diminished shares for the *sociétaires*. To bring up their incomes to a reasonable level, the actors went out to the provinces, where they would appear with the local company either at a nightly fee or on sharing terms with the proprietors. So great was the abuse of the *congé* that, in this very year of 1812, no new play could be produced because the stars were shining elsewhere, and in August Voltaire's *Adélaïde du Guesclin* had to be put on with a cast entirely composed of *pensionnaires*, not a single *sociétaire* being available.[2]

Interesting as these details are, they do not lead us to Talma. What was he doing? Where was he? To answer these questions, it required the discovery of a dusty file of papers in the Bibliothèque Mazarine, deposited there in 1838 by Madame Lebrun, the wife of a dramatist who, as we shall see, had served Talma well. This portfolio of manuscripts, Talma's private papers written in his own hand, eluded both his biographers and the social historians of the Empire, until two scholars, Hector Fleischmann and Pierre Bart, no doubt intrigued by the superscription in Mme Lebrun's hand: 'Ought not these to be preserved? That remains to be seen. Letters to the Psse P . . .', examined the Papiers du Fonds Lebrun, Carton 29, and lost no time in communicating to the literary world their sensational contents. These were no less than Talma's unpublished love letters to Princess Pauline Bonaparte, which, with other documents in Carton 29, they brought out in 1911. The following year an English writer, mainly interested in the romances of the French theatre, included in his theatrical love stories[3] the tale of Pauline Borghèse and Talma. The French editors of these remarkable drafts evinced understandable surprise that the liaison, or at very least a passionate correspondence between the actor and

[1] Mme de Rémusat, *Lettres*, Vol. I, p. 27.
[2] A. Copin, *Talma et l'Empire*, pp. 254, 255.
[3] Francis Gribble, *Romances of the French Theatre*, pp. 267–273.

the Emperor's sister, should have escaped the vigilance of the imperial police. With the circumstances surrounding these letters we must now deal. Talma, true to the bargain he had made with the Princess, had destroyed all her replies. No letters from Pauline to Talma exist; only copies in Talma's own hand of the letters he wrote to this highly placed lady provide the evidence of their intimate friendship.

CHAPTER 30

Talma and the Princesse Borghèse

In July of 1812, Talma left Paris with the immediate aim of giving performances of *Manlius* and *Hamlet* at Chambéry. His doctors had advised that he should stay awhile at Aix-les-Bains and take the waters there. After his cure arrangements had been made for a season at Lyons, with a possibility of performances at Marseilles and Bordeaux to follow. Chambéry accorded the actor its adulation and also provided him with the ready money which enabled him to cut a figure at the very fashionable Aix-les-Bains, where royalty and the quality abounded. During these summer days, before Talma descended upon the resort, there had arrived on the slopes above the Lac du Bourget, at the Maison Chevaley, Princesse Pauline Borghèse with her impressively numerous household. To Talma, taking the waters lower down the slope in the elegant pump-room, the presence of the Emperor's sister in the immediate neighbourhood afforded no little interest. The waters apparently disagreed with the actor but, if their curative powers proved of no avail, a more potent stimulus of another kind set his blood pulsing and restored the virile swagger. The Princesse required him to come and read to her.

Pauline, then aged thirty-two and married to the complacent Prince de Borghèse, was at the height of her languorous and arrogant beauty. Already a hypochondriac, she spent all her time in royal progress from spa to spa, enjoying all too obviously her nebulous maladies, which never denied her sufficient energy for her intense and short-lived amorous intrigues. She had just said farewell to the brilliant Jules de Canouville, a dashing hussar who had had to forsake dalliance for the rigours of the camp. She was at a loose end when Talma appeared at the Maison Chevaley. The actor, ever vain, snobbish and, where women were concerned, incurably romantic, fell an easy prey to Pauline's charms. In lovely Aix, so close to those shores that Lamartine was later to make immortal in the stanzas of *Le Lac*, Talma found the perfect background for a love affair that amazes, not so much by the passion it aroused as by the secrecy which surrounded it.

The Duchesse d'Abrantès in her *Mémoirse*[1] makes more than passing mention of this season in Aix, where she found herself taking the waters with so many distinguished persons. Not without malice, she relates how Talma was condemned every evening to read Molière to Princesse Pauline and her friends, who desired above everything to laugh. Poor Talma! A tragedy king compelled by the Emperor's sister to coach her as Agnès in *L'École des femmes* and later as Angélique in *Les Femmes savantes*! The Duchesse, who doubtless saw through the ruse, discreetly pitied Talma. What a bore, all those private rehearsals, she thought. Pauline's interest in amateur theatricals, however, had a purpose not exclusively dramatic.

During that August and until September 13th, when Talma left Aix to play at Geneva, he and Pauline were unquestionably lovers. His subsequent passionate letters could hardly have been written merely on a basis of platonic friendship. He lost his head completely and, as will be seen, cuts a rather ridiculous figure in their ensuing correspondence. The all too experienced Pauline kept her feelings well under control. For her, in the midst of that royal and debilitated society which had congregated at Aix, Talma proved a heaven sent distraction, a virile and handsome lover even at forty-nine, who brought with him the mystery of the theatre and the glories of Paris. As was her wont, she would take all and give little in return. He would delude himself, seizing upon this new part with every fibre of his actor's being: his surrender to Pauline he imagined complete. Vanity played its part too. He was already the Emperor's friend and to become his sister's lover would confer a social cachet beyond his most sanguine expectations.

Before Talma left Aix, the prudent Pauline consented under certain conditions to a correspondence with the actor. As has been said, anything she wrote to him must be destroyed. His letters were to be addressed to a Mlle Sophie *poste restante* at Aix, where they would be collected by Ferrand, the Princesse's *maître d'hôtel*, who throughout this affair behaved with almost superhuman discretion. By this neat subterfuge Pauline deceived the efficient imperial police who in that area, as was seen on the occasion of Mme de Staël's visit to Lyons, showed exceptional vigilance.

[1] Vol. XIV, pp. 292, 293, 346–348.

In the Lebrun papers are to be found the drafts of twenty-one letters Talma wrote to Pauline from September 16th, 1812, to July 31st, 1813. These copies he treasured no doubt to give reality to a dream. What pains he took over the writing of his letters to the Princesse! Of the epistle dated October 25th from Lyons he wrote four different drafts before he allowed the last one to be posted. His very first letter begins: '*Mon amie je t'ai donc quittée*'; his last one '*Mon amie, je reçois à l'instant votre lettre*'. The intimate '*tu*' of most of the letters, a bold usage when Pauline's rank is remembered, and the final formal '*vous*' tell their own tale of waning affection.

The first two communications at the Bibliothèque Mazarine stand outside the Talma-Pauline exchange. They are letters addressed to Louis Ducis, the painter, Talma's brother-in-law, and reflect the actor's anxiety over what people might be saying in Paris about his doings at Aix. 'I assure you, I received no one except a solitary lady and I received her in such a manner that none of her neighbours knew anything about it. I tell you this in strict confidence for you will understand the trouble that might arise if people knew. What are they saying about it in Paris? Are they gossiping? For my own part I like to believe they are not and that the absence of the two persons involved will put an end to the scandal mongering. I have heard from my wife on the subject. She tells me people are talking but I do not think that can be true.' This cryptic letter at least helps to explain Caroline's reference in her recollections to Talma being pestered by '*des femmes de la plus haute société*'.

Geneva turned out in strength to welcome Talma, who seized an eager pen to write to Pauline. 'So I have left you, dearest! I am separated from you and for such a long time. You wished it; my absence was necessary for your peace of mind; I had no choice but to obey. But what a sacrifice you have imposed upon me! Your kindness, the tears I saw you shed and the balm of consolation you poured upon my heart have failed to soften the bitterness of my regrets, though they have left me a ray of hope that you will not altogether forget me.' The enthusiasm of the Swiss crowds impels him to add: 'If the homage of their interest has any value in my eyes, it is only because I feel it may make me worthier of your love.' The answer to that first letter came from Ferrand, the butler, a rather galling experience for Talma. The Princesse had been ill, but not too ill to write other letters, as her collected correspondence reveals. At once came Talma's reply on September 18th: 'Poor little dear! How I sympathize with you! How it distresses me to hear you are so ill.' In the midst of his protestations of love he spoke of his Genevan triumphs. 'During the four days I have been here, I have been overwhelmed by calls and invitations.' Such comparatively mundane details gave place to ecstatic outbursts on September 21st. His '*cher bien de ma vie, chère bien aimée*' had deigned to write to him and his gratitude, like his love, knew no bounds. Yet he never forgets his success as an actor. 'Ah! dearest, if only you could have seen my success here—the amazing admiration accorded me by a whole town, an entire nation. I cannot doubt that the homage I have received would have made me dearer to you . . . I have refused all their invitations. I wish to visit only those places that we planned to visit together.'

When the curtain fell at Geneva, he burned to return to her. 'Dearest, there are moments when my sufferings are so intense that I can no longer endure them and I am on the point of hurrying back to Aix to throw myself at your feet and to see you once again. Alas! I know that would only disturb your peace of mind and invite fresh trouble. Say the word and I will come to you for a last good-bye. I can return to Paris by way of Aix and Lyons. The route is the same, but why should I ask such a favour? I fear I expose myself to a refusal; and a refusal would be hard to bear.' It is almost amusing to note the cold douche Pauline never fails to pour on Talma's ardour. His letter from Geneva, dated September 23rd, began: '*Oh mon trésor, l'unique bien de ma vie.*' To this possessive invocation the trusty Ferrand made suitable reply. Talma's remaining days in Geneva were haunted by his '*horrible inquiétude*' (September 30th) into which Ferrand's account of the Princesse's diplomatic illness had plunged him.

After Geneva the actor was due to play for three weeks at Lyons. His *répertoire* consisted of *Oedipe, Manlius, Abufar*—Ducis' Arabian tragedy still held the stage—Raynouard's *Les Templiers* and, by popular demand, *Hamlet*. The *Journal de Lyon*, quoted by the *Gazette de France*, October 17th, 1812, stated that Talma's performances were 'vastly greater' than those he gave in June 1809, and that of all his efforts *Hamlet* produced '*sa plus vive sensation*'. Clearly, during these three weeks in Lyons, the actor had his hands full and the frequency of the Geneva letters, eight in a fortnight, diminished considerably. The theatre's demands must explain only one draft for October 2nd and four rough copies for October 25th, when his Lyons engagement terminated. Another factor that might have contributed to this falling off in the correspondence could have been the uncertainty of Pauline's movements. Ever about to leave Aix, she finally made the journey by an invalid's easy stages to Marseilles, which she reached on November 9th. Her stay at Lyons on October 29th in the archiepiscopal palace of her uncle, Cardinal Fesch, was surely planned to exclude any possibility of meeting with the urgent Talma.

Back in Paris on November 4th the actor resumed his passionate advances with renewed vigour. He addressed the Princesse as the only asset in his life, his guardian angel. His undying love sought opportunity for her service. Could he go out to Neuilly and report upon the alterations that were proceeding in her house there? He would love to have one of the small boats from her lake to sail on the little stream at Brunoy. 'And your bust, dearest, do not forget to have it sent to me. Arrange the matter with Ferrand. I want this bust above everything in the world. I must have it. I shall leave you no peace until you send it to me.'

Of course the bust never came. The wily Pauline was running no risks and her ability to keep Talma dangling depended solely on his agreement that, at all costs, public scandal must be avoided. In vain did he point out that, during a visit to his doctor, Corvisart, he beheld the coveted bust of the Princesse; she remained deaf to his entreaties. The tone of the Paris letters may be judged by the following extracts: 'My sufferings, dearest, are the same whether I am near you or far away; I implore you on my knees to grant me just one moment of your society. Alas! dearest, it is my misfortune to fail to obtain this favour. . . . Grant me this moment of happiness. . . . My treasure, while I am waiting to have the lock of hair you gave me made into a bracelet, I have attached it to the tresses you gave me before. I have wrapped them in the handkerchief you gave me and I wear them next my heart. And your bracelet with it, the one you bade me take from your arm on the day of our terrible parting.' The grim reality of his current financial difficulties prompts: 'My affairs are in considerable disorder and compel me to make a journey to Bordeaux and Toullouse.' Pauline was at Nice and he wondered if she could hold out any hope of a meeting. Rather pathetically he tells her: 'Dearest, I am still busied about a little ring I want to send you. Unfortunately it will not be ready for Ferrand to take it.'

The shrewd Pauline, just a little concerned that Talma's vanity might betray him into some unguarded reference to their meeting at Aix, sent the faithful Ferrand to call upon the actor at his house, rue de la Seine. Ferrand could be trusted to impose discretion, if not silence, upon his mistress's ardent lover. 'Oh, my beloved,' he wrote from Paris on March 25th, 1813, 'can I possibly tell you what happiness, what joy were mine when I saw Ferrand enter my house. I hardly knew if I was awake. What intense feelings were mine! How my heart palpitated! What memories his presence so suddenly evoked! It seemed I was back in Aix, in those happy days spent at your side. . . . That you should remember me in the midst of all your sufferings moved me to tears. Oh, how I recognize your good, tender, loving heart which sent him here to see me. And you wear my ring. You even showed it to Ferrand in the presence of other people when he left you, as a reminder to execute your orders. My beloved, so many touching expressions of your perfect kindness quite go to my head. You are indeed the truly beloved of my heart, the adored of every moment, of all my life; what unchanging limitless devotion have I vowed to you. Never, beloved, can time destroy or weaken within me this deep, ineffaceable feeling, whose passion has survived hope itself. Guardian angel! . . .' And his violent protestations proceed *ad nauseam*. The actor is wringing emotion to its very last drop. Ferrand no doubt had let fall hints, not only on the need for absolute discretion, but also on the score of the Princesse's exalted position, for after the butler's visit a more circumspect form of address becomes evident in the letters. Little did the actor know that Pauline had now found a new attraction in Commander Duchand. By the time Talma played for the Emperor at Dresden, the cosy '*tu*' of the letters had finally disappeared and friendship had usurped the place of passion. Yet there remained one still more humiliating anti-climax. As the correspondence came to its end, Talma made a request, ostensibly on behalf of a friend, that Pauline should use her influence with the *Ministre du Commerce et des Manufactures* to secure a licence to export merchandise to England, an authorization rendered necessary by the Continental Blockade. Love, art, trade. What a conclusion!

It comes as something of a shock to learn that, during this protracted and passionate correspondence with Napoleon's sister, Talma maintained at the same time an exchange of letters with Madeleine-Jacqueline Bazire, who was established in his own house, which his lawful wife, Caroline, still shared. Almost coincident with his last letter to Pauline, written from Dresden on July 31st, must be noted a very revealing communication to Mlle Bazire. He asks her with a show of earnestness to let him know her wants and to deal with him as she would with a father, a friend and a lover, from whom nothing need be hid. Only his own French can convey adequately the intensity of his conclusion. '*Je t'adore, je suis fou de toi; adieu, ange trésor, je te couvre, je t'inonde, je t'abîme de baisers, et le petit nez et une bonne partie de tout cela.*'[1]

Talma has surely been caught off his guard. The uninhibited sensuality of these phrases tells its tale. That he could be completely frank about himself the Lebrun papers show. There exists a note in his own hand: 'I live in the moon and I cast my chamberpot upon the earth.' Where his art was concerned he could rise to the very heights; passion could consign him to the depths. His relations with women did not always redound to his credit. In a knowing sentence Regnault-Warin sums him up as a lover. 'Ask the women whose love sometimes delighted his leisure hours or possessed his heart, ask them if he knew how to make love!'[2]

---

[1] André Antoine, *La Vie amoureuse de Talma*, pp. 152, 153. I adore you, I am mad about you; farewell, treasured angel, I enfold you, I overwhelm you with my love, I engulf you in my kisses, both your little nose and. . . .

[2] Regnault-Warin, *Mémoires sur Talma*, 1827, p. 4.

CHAPTER 31

Geoffroy Assaulted

In following the course of Talma's futile love affair with Pauline Borghèse we have made no mention of some very important matters. Napoleon had embarked upon his disastrous invasion of Russia and had entered Moscow during the night of September 15th, 1812. Almost immediately, fire broke out in the city where, despite its ruinous and charred condition, Napoleon determined to remain in the hope of coming to terms with Alexander. Napoleon's valet, Constant, tells in his *Mémoires* how his master spent those crucial weeks. 'I saw the Emperor spend three evenings in drawing up rules for the Comédie-Française in Paris. It is difficult to understand this care for administrative problems when the future was heavy with foreboding.'[1] Bourrienne[2] saw in this preoccupation with a national theatre a way to deceive the Parisians about the true state of the Grande Armée's desperate position. If the Emperor could find time to make rules for fractious actors, all must be well in Moscow. The signing of this famous Moscow Decree on October 15th amounted to a complete redrafting of the theatre's constitution by Napoleon, although Bernard, Mahérault's deputy, had undertaken much of the preliminary work.

Rules and regulations of any organization make wearisome reading. A few may be mentioned and those briefly. The Moscow Decree defined precisely the somewhat extravagant powers of the *surintendant de nos spectacles*, affirming his right to arrange the débuts of stage aspirants, not only from the Conservatoire, but also from private teachers, and he could summon to such an ordeal 'actors from other theatres in our Empire whose engagements there would be concluded in the event of their success at this test'. (Article 63.) To this official also fell the delicate task of drawing up a list of players, in strict precedence, for each rôle in

---

[1] Constant, *Mémoires*, p. 300.
[2] Bourrienne, *Mémoires sur Napoléon*, Vol. IX, p. 122.

any play performed at the Comédie-Française. On this list would stand the names of actors and actresses who must play *'en premier, en double et en troisième'* parts in every play 'according to their genre, comic or tragic, and to their seniority, in order that there may be no further disputes about this matter'. (Article 46.) Such a regulation might look impressively final on paper, but experience soon showed that it could never be more than tentative. Nothing was more productive of internal strife than this list. The financial arrangements for shares and pensions, the duties of the *sociétaires*, the procedure affecting retirements and farewell performances, the reading of new plays, the necessity for fixing the *répertoire* a fortnight in advance, official sanction for provincial tours, breach of contract, the imposition of fines, all these nice details found a place in this vast and comprehensive document. Alfred Copin states that on the evening the Emperor appended his signature 'in the suite he occupied in the Kremlin, beneath the Czar's apartments, he spoke of the Comédie-Française in gracious terms, seeking thus to distract his mind from the agony of his own soul. Then, with long strides, he walked up and down the room, talking volubly about art, Corneille and Talma'.[1]

Unfortunately no decree from Moscow or from anywhere else could put a stop to the squabbles between *sociétaires* and *pensionnaires*, nor to the lack of *esprit de corps* shown by many prominent players who acted together for certain nights of the week and let the rest go hang. The new decree had been in force only a few months when Geoffroy observed: 'There is no longer any medium between crowded and empty houses. Each week the stars play to three packed houses; the remaining performances are handed over to *pensionnaires*, who appear only in unsuccessful or commonplace plays. Total receipts for the month are poor and show that the bad days eat up the good.'[2]

Perhaps the immediate cause of the Moscow Decree lay in the abuse of congés by the *sociétaires*, who nearly brought their theatre to the point of closure during the summer of 1812. At one and the same time, Fleury, Saint-Prix, Talma, Baptiste *aîné*, Mmes Raucourt, Devienne, Mars and Duchesnois were making money in the provinces. Small wonder that the Parisians grumbled, extending their complaints even to *'décorations lamentables'*, to ill-dressed supernumeraries and to an inadequate orchestra.[3] Talma's

[1] Copin, *Talma et l'Empire*, p. 266.   [2] *Journal de l'Empire*, June 6th, 1813.
[3] *Opinion du Parterre*, 10e Année, p. 48.

reappearance on November 16th promised a return to better performances and the crowds which besieged the doors to greet his Oreste in *Iphigénie en Tauride* required barricades in the rue de Richelieu and a doubled cordon of police. Paris would turn out for its favourites, but rumour had buzzed that Talma would shortly leave the Comédie-Française and with such persistence that the actor felt it necessary to issue a denial that same day for inclusion in Geoffroy's newspaper. Geoffroy, ever critical of Talma, may well have spread the rumour.

In his letter to the press Talma wanted to make known to the public, ever indulgent to him and to whom he owed his feeble talents, that it was his intention to serve it as long as it found pleasure in his art and that, despite particular disappointments, he would never be ungrateful to it. So much for the rebuttal of the retirement rumour. Passing to more personal issues he added:

Those who have spread abroad that I have been touring for six months are in error; my absence has lasted only four months and two of them I have taken to undergo a treatment indispensable for my health. I thank them however for having given me this opportunity to express to the public my gratitude for its favours and my thanks to artists and men of letters whose advice has influenced me in my theatrical career. I am, etc. Talma.[1]

These words were but the first raindrops that precede the storm. Geoffroy's notice on Talma's performance that night showed unusual restraint.

Talma's return was very brilliant. Barricades, a double police guard barely sufficed to contain the crowd which rushed to the doors, so keen was the curiosity of the public to see this actor after a long absence. This Oreste in *Iphigénie en Tauride* is for him a brilliant part, his favourite part; for a special occasion he could not make a better choice. His byplay is excellent, his face tragic and if at times the energy of his delivery exceeds reasonable limits, it is the author's fault and not the actor's. An unrestrained author throws the actor off balance. Damas played Pylade with much warmth and sensitivity and Mlle Duchesnois supported both Talma and Damas to the utmost. All three, loudly called for, appeared at the end of the performance.

So far, so good. Unfortunately, after this triumph at the Français, an admirer of Talma's had written a letter to Geoffroy's newspaper lauding the actor to the skies. From the citadel of his column Geoffroy felt constrained to make malevolent reply.

[1] *Journal de l'Empire*, November 16th, 1812.

I leave the writer to flounder in his own calculations to prove that
Talma brings more money to the Comédie than all the other artists
put together and that the theatre owes him handsome compensation,
even when he draws a full share, without appearing for months on end.
These stupid calculations are farcical rather than mathematical. For
my own part I prefer facts to such estimates and I will merely add that
recently Fleury and Mlle Mars in *Le Misanthrope* and *La Jeunesse de
Henri V* have drawn a more brilliant house than Talma on his return,
barricades and a doubled police force notwithstanding. In an effort
to justify the long and continual financial forays Talma makes in the
provinces, the writer by his flattery has merely called attention to this
queer abuse. My own opinion is that leave of absence ought, in the
interests of art, to be regarded as it was formerly, a very rare and brief
concession; even Lekain was granted a congé only with difficulty
and if he returned to duty a day beyond the stated period, he went to
prison; and yet Lekain is the greatest tragic actor ever to have appeared
upon a stage. Discipline produces a Lekain, but such fatal indulgence
would spoil and even ruin a Lekain if we had the good fortune to have
one. . . .

Great actors sometimes make money and always deteriorate by
too long a sojourn in the provinces; too certain of praise from un-
sophisticated audiences and too sure of the loyal efforts of his boosters,
the Parisian prince of tragedy gets careless, yields to bad habits, becomes exaggerated and absurd. Art's two greatest enemies, pride and
luxury, together beset him. The laurels he has solicited rain upon his
head, the extravagant eulogies of the journalists overpower him in
their embrace, the river of gold flows into his coffers, all these tributes
seem to deny him a mere mortal status; he returns to Paris half as rich
again and with less than half his talent; now he is merely a bad actor
who fancies himself a god. [1]

For Talma this was indeed a knock-out blow. Geoffroy, rarely
anything but bitter in his comments on Talma's playing, had never
extended his strictures so far. All Paris talked; presently it would
shout. It so happened that a few days later, on December 9th,
Geoffroy, his wife and two friends occupied a ground floor box
at the Comédie-Française and were engrossed in a performance of
La Revanche when from the corridor outside came a thundering,
threatening voice demanding admission. Talma, blind with fury,
was banging on the door. He invaded the box and, seizing
Geoffroy by the collar, shook him like a rat, dragged him to the
door and bade him come out. The noise of the altercation—
Mlle Flore in a neighbouring box is the authority for this episode

[1] *Journal de l'Empire*, November 21st, 1812.

—stopped the play, while actors, musicians, members of the audience glued their eyes on the unseemly scuffle that the screams of Mme Geoffroy made more disturbing. Talma's repeated shouts of 'Come out!' brought his friends to the scene and they with great difficulty led the actor away.

This sensational assault upon the sixty-nine year old journalist filled the newspapers. *Les Fureurs d'Oreste* was but one of many caricatures and Luce de Lancival in a lampoon *Folliculus*, not unmindful of the critic's mauling of his own *Hector*, had added to Geoffroy's discomfiture. Many actors felt that a long-standing account had been settled. So exaggerated were the reports of this regrettable incident that Geoffroy felt compelled to issue his own version, '*l'exacte vérité*' of his encounter with 'the great Talma'. After discounting stories of his own abject fear, he continued:

Suddenly the door of the box opened. A man entered abruptly in a raging temper, wild-eyed like Hamlet pursued by a ghost or Oreste tormented by the Furies. 'You are the person I am looking for,' he said to me, grasping my hand more firmly than a friendly clasp warranted. The hand, I felt, which shook mine was armed with sharp claws such as poets provide for princely devils. A rather deep scratch is the only wound I received in this memorable encounter and I still carry its glorious scar. But my redoubtable adversary must be judged by his intentions rather than by his actual deeds. 'Come out!' he repeated in a tragic tone. 'Get out yourself.' Immediately we drove off the enemy.[1]

Geoffroy relates how Talma uttered threats to the consternation of the two ladies in the box, until his friends intervened. Then came his final resolution:

'This is my last word on this actor; henceforth I owe him complete silence; to me he has become a stranger; I know him no longer; I cannot as an honourable man speak well or ill of his talents. My praise would seem inspired by fear, my strictures would seem like hatred and revenge; such feelings are far from my heart.[2]

When he had recovered his temper, Talma suffered the agony of remorse, the tortures of the damned. On December 16th in the *Journal de Paris*, the *Gazette de France* and the *Journal de l'Empire*, his own expiatory letter appeared. He was not worried about replying to M. Geoffroy, but he felt he owed the public an explanation of his conduct. At some length he made the point

[1] Mlle Flore, *Mémoires*, pp. 286, 287, 288.
[2] *Journal de l'Empire*, December 15th, 1812.

that, having endured the critic's attacks for years, he could not suffer to see him ensconced in a box for which he had made no payment. He admits that his anger knew no bounds and pleads that he acted without reflection of any kind. As for the ill-treatment that M. Geoffroy complains of, if such exists, why does he not take the matter to the law courts? There, says Talma, I could explain my right to drive him from a box he had no business to occupy. 'I should welcome the opportunity to make public in a decisive way the motives that lie behind his praise or blame. I am not the only one[1] who longs to confound him and who has the means to do so.'

The following passage from Talma's account was suppressed in the *Journal de l'Empire*: 'Some persons, excusable perhaps because of their need of public acclaim and who have tried to buy their peace of mind, are ready to give evidence which will embarrass M. Geoffroy. Maybe these revelations will persuade many artists, whom he blackmails by fear, to join forces with me and finally rid themselves of the terror of his persecution. I openly challenge M. Geoffroy and am ready for him.'

All papers printed the concluding paragraph:

It is undoubtedly grievous for me to have to inform the public of such details. Moreover it is for the public to judge whether, as M. Geoffroy claims, I am spoiled by flatterers when, in a widely circulated newspaper, I see myself covered with insults and with loathing. At least M. Geoffroy will agree that he knew how to provide a terrible antidote to his pretended flatteries, by the bitterness of his strictures which I have endured patiently for twelve years; and if on this occasion I yielded to sudden temper, dictated by a deep feeling of great injustice, my one and sincere regret is that I forgot momentarily that I was in the presence of this same public, under whose eyes my poor talent has developed, who has always honoured me with great goodwill and to whom I owe all gratitude and respect. I have the honour, etc. Talma.

The tragedian's letter hardly exonerates him. True, Geoffroy had not paid for his seat, but Talma alone could not decide when and to whom the *Comité* might offer complimentary tickets. That the critic deserved some correction for his insolence and severity, not only to Talma, few will deny; that he was mercenary many actors and actresses could prove;[2] but his caustic pen must not

---

[1] Louise, Contat had flicked her fan in Geoffroy's face. Mlle Mars, Mémoires, Vol. I, pp. 168, 169.

[2] Mlle Flore, *Mémoires*, p. 285.

be accepted as a valid reason for this squalid incident of fisticuffs. It is after all the function of a critic to criticize and, let it not be forgotten, Geoffroy, in spite of his ingrained prejudices and deeply rooted classicism, brought a new dignity, a greater content and a more percipient judgment to dramatic criticism in France. One has only to read the perfunctory references to theatrical activity in the Paris newspapers previous to Geoffroy's *feuilletons* in the *Journal des Débats*, to realize how low was the level of what then passed for dramatic criticism.

Talma, on his appearance a few days later in *Rhadamiste et Zénobie*, received both applause and hisses, which broke out again at curtain fall. One spectator had shouted '*Talma en prison*', only to be quickly and forcibly expelled.

In that December Napoleon returned to a Paris totally unaware of the Russian disasters. Constant[1] gives the Emperor's reactions to the Talma-Geoffroy fight. 'His Majesty spoke to me of the quarrel Talma had had with Geoffroy a few days before his arrival. The Emperor, although he liked Talma, found him completely in the wrong. Several times he repeated: "He was an old man! An old man! There is no excuse. Goodness, do they not criticize me?" he added with a smile. "Have I not also my critics who do not spare me? He should not have been more thin-skinned than I!" This incident passed without any ill effects for Talma for, I repeat, the Emperor liked him and heaped on him pensions and presents.'[2]

Marc Desgranges in his masterly study of Geoffroy as France's first real dramatic critic makes the point that not all Geoffroy wrote was unfavourable to Talma. He therefore with considerable ingenuity constructed a synthetic appreciation of the actor derived from Geoffroy's comments on his acting. By a rigid exclusion of the bitter censure which annoyed Talma, he achieved this composite picture of the actor's talents.

Geoffroy in truth judges Talma as being altogether outstanding in parts in which passion, madness, confusion of mind, remorse, dementia, heartbreaking situations dominate. Oreste, Hamlet, Manlius, Othello, Cinna, Oedipe, Ladislas, Macbeth, Marigny, these are Talma's incontestable successes. As Oreste he deserved some criticism at the beginning, but he plays the last scene with a frightening truth. (June 23rd, 1804). He hypnotizes the public when he plays a Shakespearean

---

[1] Constant, *Mémoires*, p. 307.
[2] Marc Desgranges, *Geoffroy*, pp. 485, 486.

rôle. (June 22nd, 1807). In Manlius he soars beyond criticism by the excellence of his acting. (January 13th, 1805). In a word he alarms one by his truth and his naturalness; the field of madness belongs to him by right (March 8th, 1804); in all his parts he has sublime moments (November 3rd, 1804). Like Lekain, he has created in his time a new method, more heart-rending, more pathetic, a gloomy method he has brought from England (March 29th, 1806). Compared with Lafon he has the merit of being original and creative, a sure mark of genius (March 12th, 1807); he gets inside a tragic part long before he (Lafon) does and depicts with greater art and depth violent and terrible emotions (March 31st, 1806). One would like to see in Lafon more virility and more resolution; this actor is better at arousing pity rather than terror (August 1st, 1804). That is not all. Talma, when he wishes, has no need of convulsive fits and English horrors; he plays Pompée with great restraint and dignity (December 29th, 1804). He is subtle, dynamic, full of natural warmth as Nicomède (January 6th, 1805); it is a part he seems to have created a second time (September 8th, 1807).

Desgranges asks: 'Could one give Talma greater praise?' Ingenious as this mosaic of criticism may appear, in the interests of truth a statement from Geoffroy's own lips should be recorded as a pendant: 'It is possible that having been accustomed in my youth to another style of acting, to another manner of delivering lines, I may not have been as sensitive to Talma's playing as those who have known no other actor nor any other method.'[1] There lies the root of the trouble. Posterity has decreed that Talma was a greater actor than Geoffroy was a critic. Talma, the Romantic before his time, could make no real contact with the belated reactionary Classic that was Geoffroy.

The critic kept his word. Never in any article he wrote did he mention Talma by name or make the slightest reference to his acting. Unfortunately Geoffroy's death on February 27th, 1814, deprived him of seeing Talma at his unsurpassed best, in the memorably great and developed renderings of parts new and old that the actor's relentless study and quest for perfection would give to the Comédie-Française in the decade to come. Well might a contrite Talma regret his moment of temper and admit to his friends how helpful he had found Geoffroy's advice. There could be no reconciliation; in the confined world of the Paris theatre the two men remained strangers.

[1] Quoted by Desgranges as emanting from Geoffroy in 1807, p. 483.

CHAPTER 32

Dresden, 1813

The year 1813 gave early promise of being dramatically more fruitful than its barren predecessor which saw no new tragedy at the Comédie-Française. The Emperor made an early appearance at the theatre in the rue de Richelieu to see Talma play Hector once more, before a Paris still ignorant of the magnitude of the Russian disaster. An excited audience bestowed generous applause upon sovereign and actor. For January 7th was billed a new play, *Tippoo-Saïb*, by a new dramatist, Étienne de Jouy, who as a midshipman had fought against the English on the side of the tyrant of Mysore, destined to become the whitewashed hero of his first tragedy. Jouy had turned to this daringly modern subject, so far removed from greco-roman frontiers, because his first idea to write a tragedy to be called *Bélisaire* received no encouragement from the *Comité*, who regarded the subject as scabrously unsuitable.[1] No such complaints attended the production of *Tippoo-Saïb*. Politically the play exploited every anti-British sentiment. Much preliminary puff had assured Parisians that Talma had spent three whole days deciding the details of his costume for Tippoo. Ever eager to extend the range of his parts, Talma also saw in Jouy's play opportunities for scenic innovations. The opulence of Mysore and its palace would altogether eclipse the timid orientalism of *La Veuve du Malabar*. Again, the author had presented Tippoo as brave and generous, loathing the English and their perfidious ways, a noble defender of his wife and his young children.

As in the case of all great actors, certain moments of their playing so rivet the attention and, by deep penetration of the spectators' mind and heart, pass into legend. In *Tippoo-Saïb* Talma had such a moment. Constantly one reads in the memoirs of the period how Talma, with poignard raised, terrible to behold, his little brood sheltering behind him, defied the English adversary

[1] Lanzac de Laborie, *Paris sous Napoléon. Le Théâtre-Français*, p. 218.

as he uttered, 'Wait, traitor!'[1] and with those two simple words frightened a theatre full of people, chilling their very marrow. Everybody agreed that the rôle of Tippoo-Saïb fitted Talma like a glove, but a tragedy without a love interest, bogged down by constantly repeated political invective, had obvious drawbacks. In a one man play other actors fill in the corners. Mlle Bourgoin and Baptiste *aîné*, while giving all they could, hardly added to their reputations. Jouy came off well, earning praise for his courageous innovations, but the critics reserved their laurels for Talma. Geoffroy, mindful of his vow, found himself in a difficult situation. To praise the play could only mean praise for Talma. In any case some difference of opinion existed as to its ultimate success. Copin boldly states that the play was an enormous success.[2] Another authority writes it down as a near failure, which a prudent author withdrew in order to rewrite.[3] Copin is probably nearer the truth because on February 4th Napoleon commanded Talma to play *Tippoo-Saïb* at the Tuileries. Dire failures never achieved such imperial distinction. Another proof of the play's popularity comes from a burlesque, *Le Cimetière de Parnasse on Typoo malade*, put on at the Vaudeville. Here Geoffroy really let himself go, making the point that much more fun could be extracted from the burlesqued Tippoo if only the mimic would remember the coarse voice, the shouts, the jerky movements and the groans of the original performer!

The dramatic evenings that took place at the Tuileries were, in accordance with Marie-Louise's wishes, devoted to comedy. After *Tippoo-Saïb* Talma appeared but once, on March 25th, in the Emperor's favourite play, Corneille's *Cinna*, which gave the actor yet another opportunity to create a picturesque yet harrowing effect. In the scene where Cinna, having evoked the memory of his banishment, pronounced

> *Le fils tout dégouttant du meurtre de son père*
> *Et, sa tête à la main, demandant son salaire.*[4]

Talma would bring forward with a nervous shake his red-plumed helmet and, with his other hand outstretched, demand a murderer's fee. This suiting of the action to the word never failed to

---

[1] E. D. de Manne, *La Troupe de Talma*, p. 108.
[2] A. Copin, *Talma et l'Empire*, pp. 282, 283.
[3] Lanzac de Laborie, *Le Théâtre-Français*, p. 218.
[4] The son, dripping with the blood of a murdered sire
And, with severed head in hand, asking for his reward.

electrify the audiences of his day.[1] Women uttered cries of alarm, others turned their heads away or hid their faces in their hands. Talma's voice and flashing eye held the spectators in thrall at such a moment. On that particular night Talma must have been in form. A letter to Pauline, dated that very day, bears every mark of his joy and gratitude for her carefully regulated kindness. He walked on air.

Ninus II, Talma's second new play in 1813 and, as it proved, the last of the Napoleonic tragedies, saw the light on April 28th. Its author, Charles Brifaut, had conceived and half written his play, then entitled *Don Sanche*, on a Spanish theme, when the censorship made it very plain to the dramatist and the *sociétaires* that, in view of the Peninsular War, Spain must under no circumstances be brought to the public notice. The accommodating Brifaut took a step backwards in time, sought an Assyrian setting, changing Barcelone to Babylone for the sake of his alexandrines, and, by allowing his characters to grope in the dawn of history, made utter nonsense of his original plot. *Ninus II* provides the best example of the bankruptcy of French tragedy in Talma's day. This farrago of nonsense showed the tyrant Ninus contriving the murder of his brother in order to usurp his throne and to marry his widow, Elsire. This lady, having escaped the toils of Ninus, lived for ten years in hiding whilst her son Zarame was brought up in the usurper's care. Improbability was stretched still further when Elsire, at last discovered, stood trial for the murder of her husband before *le Mages*, the wise men. In the original draft *les Mages* had appeared as that more credible tribunal, the Cortes. Elsire, in the passionate tones of Mlle Duchesnois, proclaimed her innocence and proved Ninus the assassin. The latter, before taking his life, restored Zarame to his rightful kingdom. This ridiculous hotch-potch, devoid of any semblance of local colour and completely failing to achieve any trace of its generation's preoccupation with 'nature and truth', received good notices from the critics. The young author was praised for the ingenuity of his plot and the vigour of his style. Talma, Mlle Duchesnois and Baptiste *aîné* reaped easy rewards. After the second performance the play, which looked like drawing the town, was withdrawn on account of Baptiste's illness.

Paris had barely had time to take in the magnitude of the

---

[1] Duchesse d'Abrantès, *Mémoires*, Vol. V, p. 147. Lanzac de Laborie, *Paris sous Napoléon. Le Théâtre-Français*, p. 55.

Moscow defeat when bells were again ringing for that May Day victory over the Prussians and Russians at Lützen. National confidence seemed momentarily restored and Talma turned his attention to yet another provincial engagement. Although his love affair with Pauline was drawing to its unedifying conclusion, the south still beckoned and Bordeaux with its immense Grand-Théâtre promised great rewards. He opened his season there with *Iphigénie en Tauride*, Guimond de la Touche's play, which has the merit of introducing a most showy Oreste. The plaudits of the Bordelais had to cease abruptly. Napoleon summoned Talma to Dresden, where seventeen actors from the Comédie-Française, led by Fleury and Mlle Mars, were already assembled. The Emperor was in residence at the Marcolini Palace, where he had had constructed in the Orangerie a theatre for the performance of French comedies.

Napoleon after Lützen had made a truce with his enemies that would expire on August 15th, and he planned that this brilliant court he held in Dresden, with the connivance of his new ally the King of Saxony, should astonish and bewilder both France and the rest of Europe. The world might regard the Russian reverse as a mere setback that subsequent victories had redeemed. Wellington was indeed entrenched at the very gates of France—but one thing at a time. Dresden would prove another Erfurt, and certainly the players felt the same.

Fleury and his comedians were exultant. At long last tragedy seemed to be in total eclipse. Events however proved them wrong. Mlle George, it appears, during her stay in St. Petersburg had developed strongly patriotic feelings, and the disasters that had attended her countrymen in Russia decided her to leave an enemy country, heedless of the flattering inducements of the Czar to continue her services as an actress. She crossed to Stockholm, where she was rapturously received, not only by Swedish actors but by Mme de Staël and Bernadotte as well. Germany was Mlle George's goal. She sought out Jérôme, King of Westphalia, at Brunswick, where she learned of Napoleon's presence at Dresden. Here she returned to her old colleagues like some prodigal daughter, still able to frolic with the Emperor—his valet has moments of unpardonable indiscretion on this matter—and to win her complete reinstatement as *sociétaire* without any loss of service, seniority or status. Obviously with Mlle George at hand, more Junoesque than ever, tragedy must find a place on the

Dresden playbill. The primitive telegraph got busy and Talma was recalled to partner the lady, not in the little Orangerie band-box, but in the more spacious surroundings of Dresden's own theatre.

The arrival of the Emperor and Empress of Austria to swell the ranks of princelings from the Baltic and the Rhine recalled the splendours of Erfurt so vividly that Mlle George, without experience of the previous occasion, alluded to this array of crosses, decorations and diamonds as the 'Chamberlains of the Eagle'.[1] Before Napoleon and Marie-Louise, surrounded by these august notabilities, Mlle George and Talma played together in Voltaire's *Oedipe*, he in the title rôle, she as Jocaste. Then came a request for *Sémiramis*, perhaps Mlle George's finest part, in which she copied sedulously the tones and gestures of her preceptress, Mlle Raucourt. In this tragic Amazonian tale, Talma played Arsace, son of the powerful queen. To his brother-in-law, Louis Ducis, the actor confided in a letter, dated July 23rd, 1813, and bearing the stamp of the Grande Armée[2] that he had been twenty days in Dresden where he had played only twice. *Andromaque*, with Mlle George as Hermione and himself as Oreste, had been commanded for the following day, but he described his stay in this city as *fort triste*. Eager for news of Paris, he mentioned that Mlle Bazire had been his only correspondent, an interesting fact when one remembers the Pauline Borghèse letters. He outlined a plan to Louis Ducis to visit Lyons and to cut out Bordeaux, in order not to overrun his congé which expired on October 15th, but rather wistfully he added that without an extension of leave he did not see how he could make ends meet. Mlle George, he thought, played Jocaste and Sémiramis '*assez bien*', but she needed more control if she were to make a Paris success. As the friend of both Mlle George and Mlle Duchesnois, he gave sound advice to both ladies, who seemed likely to revive old feuds. 'I think Duchesnois is wrong to be alarmed. I found George quite reasonable about the arrangement they both came to.' If only the newspapers would keep out of it, he shrewdly added. On behalf of both ladies he offered to intercede with Bernard in order that peace might reign in the green room.

To the outside world the lavish entertainments of Dresden seemed yet further evidence of Napoleon's power. That glowing

[1] *Mémoires de Fleury*, Vol. II, pp. 405, 406.
[2] Guy de la Batut, *Talma. Correspondance*, pp. 134, 135.

tapestry ill concealed the cracks in the walls of the imperial edifice. The armistice, due to expire on August 15th, determined Napoleon to take time by the forelock and celebrate his birthday on the 10th, with appropriate festivities provided gratis for the populace. All the actors were hurried out of Dresden on the 12th, when the Emperor ordered M. de Rémusat to make individual gifts of money to eighteen players and to the utility gentlemen, the prompter and the wig-maker, concerned in the twenty-five performances. These presents amounted to 111,500 francs, to be taken from the '*caisse des théâtres*', and for once Thalia received a better remuneration than Melpomene. Fleury and Mlle Mars rewarded with 10,000 francs each, Talma and Mlle George, with but four performances to their credit, had each to be satisfied with a mere 8,000 francs. The total cost, when travel and subsistence charges were included, reached the substantial figure of 259,539 francs 38 centimes. On November 30th Bertrand, now promoted to the office of Grand Marshal, had the uncomfortable task of informing the Emperor that, as a result of Dresden, the '*caisse des théâtres*' showed a deficit of 209,803 francs, 98 centimes, which, at his suggestion, might be wiped out by a loan of 210,000 francs from the police funds, repayable on a basis of one-twelfth deduction from the theatre takings.[1] Napoleon gave the necessary approval.

Back in Paris on August 24th, Talma immediately set out for Bordeaux, where he resumed his interrupted engagement. Lyons he abandoned to Mlle Duchesnois. Had his '*aventure galante*' with Pauline Borghèse shown the slightest sign of renewal, he could no doubt have used Lyons as a base for further contacts with his valetudinarian inamorata, then enduring cures and diets along the Mediterranean shore. But all that was over and Bordeaux on September 7th offered substance for shadow. The *Gazette de France* with commendable brevity took notice of Talma's success in the wine city. On September 18th it stated: 'Talma has played at Bordeaux Oreste, Néron and Hamlet; this actor intends to play during his season *Ninus II* and *Tippoo Saïb*.' On September 23rd the same newspaper recorded: 'We learn from Bordeaux that Talma continues his performances with the greatest success. The ladies follow him madly; they have abandoned every other pleasure. Recently they have been packing the theatre for *Hamlet*. Talma with his terrifying byplay has stirred them to unimaginable

[1] Lanzac de Laborier *Le Théâtre-Français*, pp. 305, 306.

transports. He has also acted Manlius and Coriolan.' Although no financial accounts are available of Talma's performances in that huge theatre, he must have made a great deal of money. With some show of impatience, Paris awaited his return to resume the run of *Ninus II* with a restored Baptiste *aîné*. The actor's answer was to proceed to Nantes.

Bernard, who had rather shabbily jockeyed himself into Mahérault's post on February 3rd, 1813,[1] stormed in Paris, demanding Talma's return on October 15th. *The Gazette de France* for October 22nd announced: 'Talma has played Oreste and Hamlet at the Grand-Théâtre in Nantes. He has given proof of the greatest talent. The *Journal de Nantes* informs us that the great tragedian, having been recalled to Paris, will give only a few performances in Nantes.' Still Talma dallied by the Loire until October end, when he took a benefit performance which must have opened the eyes of the Nantais to the great actor's versatility and remarkable accomplishment. On this occasion he played the tragic rôle of Jacques de Molay in *Les Templiers*, which he followed by an interpretation of the Bard in *Shakespeare amoureux*, a comic part he had created ten years previously. Singers from the local Opera House performed a specially written cantata, extolling his virtues as an actor, but so deafening was the applause that greeted any reference to Talma that their vocal efforts went almost for nothing. The curtain fell on a reluctant Talma, surrounded by his colleagues and almost smothered by the garlands and laurel wreaths that his talents had conjured from the pockets of his admirers. Talma basked, Nantes applauded, Paris waited.

[1] Lanzac de Laborie, *Le Théâtre-Français*, pp. 8, 9.

Part 3

Under the White Cockade

CHAPTER 33

The Bourbons Return, 1814

Talma did not reach Paris until after the first week in November when, contrary to all expectations, he elected to appear, not in *Ninus II* but in Voltaire's *Oedipe*. Geoffroy paid his customary tribute to the author but refrained from mentioning Talma or Mlle Duchesnois who was a powerful Jocaste. Then, to appease Mlle George, Talma duly partnered her in *Sémiramis*, which led Martainville of the *Journal de Paris* to the unkind remark that Mlle George's fate seemed to consist in being carried along by Talma like a satellite by the planet it escorts. On December 5th, for the very last celebration of the Austerlitz anniversary, Napoleon ordered his *'comédiens ordinaires'* to play *Ninus II* at the Tuileries. Although the threatening European situation left scant room for hope, Parisians strangely enough crowded to the theatre during the months of January and February, when Talma, Fleury, Saint-Prix, Baptiste *aîné* and Mlles Raucourt, Mars, Duchesnois and George never failed to provide a desperately needed anodyne. *Ninus II* went back into the bill to rapturous receptions. Mlle Raucourt, whose stage appearances were becoming somewhat rarer, stirred the memories of older playgoers when she acted in her majestic way Cléopâtre in *Rodogune* with Talma and Mlle Duchesnois. For this revival the actors played to capacity. Yet nearer and nearer came the armies of the Russians and the Prussians. Gone were the days when a cry of *'la patrie est en danger'* sent every able-bodied man to the recruiting station. France was weary, utterly war-weary, and in no mood for heroic sacrifice. Why had not the Emperor made peace after Lützen? What madness led him to conclude a mere truce when the fruits of victory had been won? During that critical February destiny played fast and loose, showering upon Napoleon military successes in pitched battles, Champaubert, Montmirail, Château-Thierry, Vauchamps, but withholding from him every advantage of his brilliant feats of arms. Now in the very fields of France, on pressed the enemy ever nearer to Paris.

The Comédie-Française, in common with the other playhouses, tried to stir patriotic fires by putting on plays like Debelloy's *Le Siège de Calais*, with its too obvious appeal to a fighting resistant spirit, but, for all that Talma and Saint-Prix could do, it fell flat. Even the Voltairian catharsis of *Oedipe* failed to cleanse the national heart and mind. '*La France s'ennuyait*' and before her officially historical time. The little life that *Ninus II* could generate ceased on March 3rd, when Baptiste *aîné* again fell ill. As a substitute Talma played his trump card, Oreste, whose '*fureurs*' in his portrayal never failed to make *Andromaque* a profitable undertaking. With the courage of despair the *sociétaires*—and they must have been pretty desperate—decided to risk on March 17th a new effort by Arnault, *La Rançon de Duguesclin* which, described as 'an heroic comedy', aimed at mingling the two genres, comedy and tragedy, in an elaborately costumed fourteenth century play centred around the perfect knight. Talma as Duguesclin acted with Michot, a comic valet, Mlle Duchesnois joined forces with laughing Mlle Mars, and the two ladies had hoped to make theatrical history by singing a duet. *La Rançon de Duguesclin* came to grief. The plot proved dull, the writing lacked the sparkle of comedy on the one hand and the dignity of tragedy on the other; disappointment reigned and, as a crowning disaster, the two leading ladies sang so badly out of tune that the audience laughed derisively. A din of catcalls and hisses served as a requiem for Arnault's unfortunate attempt to extend the range of subject matter within the confines of the contemporary dramatic pattern.

After the death of Geoffroy, Talma had no better fortune with his successor, Grimod de la Reynière, a critic equally prejudiced as far as the actor was concerned, but without the journalistic skill of his predecessor. His first *feuilleton*[1] dealt with *Ninus II* and he made no bones about the annoyance he felt when Talma spoke rather than sang his lines, when he paused where sense dictated, when he committed the unpardonable crime of running his words from one line to the next forgetful of the pause on the alexandrine's rhyme. In a concessive moment he wrote: 'Let us hasten to add however that these faults spring less from the nature of Talma's own talent than from the false method he has followed and in which he persists, simply because the parterre encourages him in these false values. This method, we say it with grief, will

[1] *Journal de l'Empire*, March 5th, 1814.

mean the death of tragedy in France.' Poor Talma's luck was quite out with the *Journal de l'Empire*. He must have taken heart when the *Journal de Paris* chided the new critic for his unfair treatment of Talma.

With the war news getting steadily worse, the theatres raked up old favourites with a distinctly national flavour. Talma and Mlle Duchesnois resuscitated Debelloy's *Gabrielle de Vergy* which dated from 1777. A notice in the *Journal de Paris* for March 28th, 1814, gives a clue to Talma's performance. 'The part of Fayel is exactly suited to Talma's talent, I might almost say to his faults. The gloomy suspicions by which he is tormented, the efforts he makes to dissemble them, the sudden change from hope to fear, from love to anger, the planning of his horrible revenge and the heartbroken accents of his remorse which he utters as he dies; all these shades of feeling merge into the gloomy hue that Talma imparts to most of his rôles.' Truly a meaty performance, but one that on March 29th, when the Russian and Prussian cannon could be heard in the capital, netted only 345 francs 84 centimes.

The bivouac fires of the allied armies could be plainly seen on the heights of Montmartre. The Comédie-Française stood closed on March 30th and 31st. Paris capitulated. In a spurt of business as usual the Théâtre-Français resumed its performances on April 1st, when Fleury and Mlle Mars, each in a different comedy, attracted a house worth 1,639 francs 64 centimes. The theatre crowds, sporting the white Bourbon cockade, besieged the Opéra, where they wildly acclaimed Alexander, Emperor of Russia and William, King of Prussia as liberators, and during the ensuing *La Vestale*—although Napoleon's favourite opera *Le Triomphe de Trajan* had been billed—celebrated their warrior prowess in a haze of incense that flattery knows well how to burn. It was indeed strange to hear in this opera house, where Napoleon, Josephine and Marie-Louise had graced so many imperial occasions, the vociferous, thankful shouts of *Vive Alexandre! Vive Guillaume!* and, although his obese and gouty person had not yet arrived from Ghent, *Vive Louis XVIII! Vivent les Bourbons!*

Paris had changed its politics as if by magic. The *violettes impériales*, worn tenaciously and to their credit by Mlle George and Mlle Mars, gave place to the white Bourbon rosettes which Mlle Bourgoin affected in such unseemly haste. Henri IV had become the stage hero of the hour and no fewer than seven Paris theatres exploited him in one way or another as the founder of the Bourbon dynasty. The Théâtre-Français immediately put on Raynouard's *Les États de Blois* with Talma in his old part of the Duc de Guise and Lafon as a most engaging Henri IV.

What of Talma's feelings in this sudden, overwhelming change? As a *sociétaire* of the Comédie-Française he occupied an official position, the exercise of which transcended political change. How did this friend of Napoleon react to the impassioned fervour of the pro-Bourbon audience? Did he forsake his benefactor at this critical hour? It might be urged that he could have resigned from the Comédie-Française and renounced a career that had absorbed all his energies and to which he would dedicate his whole life. To leave the stage for political reasons seemed frankly illogical. On a professional issue he would always fight, as on the occasion of the Raucourt-Lafon cabal, which almost drove him to London. Even those powerful revolutionary influences in his early days, if they stirred within him democratic feelings, never drove him into the arms of a political party, not even as an active participant in the Girondist faction where perhaps his real sympathies lay. No, to Talma, as to any dedicated actor, the stage and the iron discipline it imposes, could never lightly be forsaken.

On this question of Talma's loyalty or disloyalty to Napoleon, two very conflicting pieces of evidence, which derive from a performance of *Iphigénie en Aulide* on April 2nd, should be examined. The first comes from the recollections of M. Régnier,[1] an actor who became 'Doyen de la Comédie-Française' during the years 1865–1871, after which he retired. He states that as a small boy he went with his grandmother to see Mme Régnier, his mother, as Ériphile acting with Talma in *Iphigénie* on this night of April 2nd. His impressions were vividly set down: the dark clothes of the few French members of the audience, the preponderance of Russian and Prussian soldiery, the absence of men in civilian dress. This child of seven claimed that he remembered all his life the deafening applause that greeted Talma's entrance and the enthusiasm the great actor communicated to every part of the house. After the performance a white packet was thrown on to the stage. Régnier's grandmother told him that it would be some verses. The parterre, not yet dispersed, shouted out, 'Read! Read! We want them read!' A commissionaire appeared, picked up the packet and withdrew. So insistent became the cries of

---

[1] Régnier's *Mémoires* first appeared in fragmentary form in *Le Temps* on December 27th, 1885, and were published in book form by Ollendorff in 1886.

the crowd that the man reappeared and, on hearing shouts of 'Talma!', retired to make hasty consultation with someone in the wings. After an interval Talma appeared in ordinary dress. The commissionaire handed him the packet which he opened, letting fall some coins which had weighted its flight to the stage. 'He came forward,' says Régnier, 'holding the scroll sideways towards the footlights. I saw him hold it away from him, bring it forward and, almost with his nose against the paper, read it with difficulty, stumbling frequently. What could he be reading? An extravagant eulogy, a plea for royalty. I was most astonished, I found Talma did not read fluently. Curious to check the accuracy of my impressions, I looked up the *Journal de Paris* for April 4th, 1814, and over Martainville's signature I saw the following lines: "At the Théâtre-Français, upon Talma devolved the task of reading some verses, more energetic than correct, and bearing upon the current situation. They were much more applauded than Racine's. Foreigners, to whom the masterpieces of our stage are not unknown, could not have formed a high opinion of the way in which they are interpreted at our first theatre, if they judge them by this performance of *Iphigénie*." Régnier adds: 'I must confess that I cannot, like the *Journal de Paris*, blame Talma, Saint-Prix and Mlle Duchesnois for being below their normal best.'

One ventures to think that the graphic details of Régnier's account coincide with the real facts of the situation. In childhood there are some things one never forgets. The boy saw his mother act on that memorable night. The throwing of the white packet of Brifaut's verses—for they were his—and the ensuing excitement would stamp themselves on a young memory. He recalled how Talma, like a shortsighted man, read the paper close to his face and it is well known that the actor's myopia was a lifelong handicap. Above all, the boy makes clear that Talma had been pressed into reading this precipitate plea for the Bourbon restoration. As an actor employed in a national theatre, Talma could hardly escape such obligations. That these verses came to him as a complete surprise, his halting perusal of them clearly indicated.

Charles Maurice in his *Histoire anecdotique de théâtre*[1] gives an entirely different slant to the incident. This is his story. 'The first verses that were written against the fallen Napoleon were by M. Brifaut, the academician. They were recited on the stage of the

[1] P. 186.

Théâtre-Français after a performance of *Iphigénie en Aulide*. It was Talma who read or rather recited them, because seldom did he cast his eyes upon them to create any doubt that he knew them by heart. He had just finished playing Achille and had taken only the time necessary to change into ordinary dress. He ended these verses with a slight gesture of his right hand, accompanied by the rather feebly uttered cry of, "Long live the King!"'

What is one to believe? Maurice, before everything a journalist of the gossip column order, though he would claim to be a dramatist, does not pretend to have been present on this occasion. He might well have obtained his 'story' from an actor who, possibly jealous of Talma's friendship with Napoleon, took pleasure in vilifying him in a wounding context. He insinuates that Talma knew Brifaut's lines by heart; little Régnier was almost shocked that Talma read them so badly. Even Maurice admits that it was a very feeble '*Vive le Roi!*' that came from Talma's lips.

Happily there is no room for doubt as to Talma's feelings. In those precious papers that Mme Lebrun confided to the care of the Bibliothèque Mazarine is a copy of the letter that Talma wrote and sent to his departed master after the Fontainebleau abdication. If the document contains here and there a touch of that egotism inseparable from the actor's nature, its sincere expression of loyalty cannot for one moment be held in doubt.

Sire,

Pardon me if I take this opportunity to write to you. My burdened heart must lighten its load, I needs must set down at your feet the tribute of my tears as well as my deep sorrow. I shall see you no more! that generosity, to me such a privilege, which allowed me at times to approach you, is indeed snatched away for ever. Ah Sire, I lack words to express my grief to you, I who had staked all my happiness on your love, on devoting to you my feeble talents and on the hope of ending my days near to you. For me everything has vanished. Sire, God is my witness, the good fortune now taken from me and which I used to enjoy through you, does not weigh with me. My regrets spring from motives more griefstricken and more pure. It is your person, it is you alone I mourn. Sire, your kindness and the gracious favour with which you have honoured me will ever remain in my heart. My memory will ever be faithful to you and never, no never, will I be numbered among the ungrateful who owe you their fortunes. The calamities and the fate that betrayed you have served only to increase my loyalty to your person and have made you greater in my eyes, if that is possible, and more worthy of veneration. I submit, since I must, to destiny and to the laws of my country but, Sire, only base, ungrateful hearts could blame me for making you the everlasting object of my gratitude and my sorrow. Sire, my heart goes with you; accept the wishes I offer for the peace of your days as well as the assurance of the deepest respect and of the sacred loyalty with which I have the honour to be, Sire, Your Majesty's most faithful and devoted servant.

TALMA.

Throughout his life Talma remained staunchly loyal to the Emperor, who was always for him '*le grand homme*'. When he wrote that letter who could have foreseen the Hundred Days? Who could have believed that Napoleon would again occupy a box at the Comédie-Française? After the Elban exile, which Pauline Borghèse nobly shared with her brother, Talma met once more his beloved benefactor and must have rejoiced to hear Napoleon thank him[1] for the letter just quoted. Retracing our steps for a moment to that summer of 1814, when Louis XVIII reigned in the Tuileries, Talma had the courage at that time to repair to Aix-les-Bains and beguile with poetry readings the tedium of the ex-Empress, now Archduchess Marie-Louise.

[1] Audibert, *Talma*: *quatrième entretien rapporté* Paris 1845.

CHAPTER 34

Charles Nodier on Talma

'*Notre père de Gand*', as the women of the Halles called Louis XVIII, did not enter his '*bonne ville de Paris*' until May 1st. All through the month of April the Czar and the King of Prussia, joined a little later by the Emperor of Austria, had been everywhere fêted and, by their visits to theatres, had made a close contact with the Parisian crowds only too eager to acclaim their foreign saviours. One such occasion deserves a passing mention. On April 3rd, when the Czar and the King of Prussia went to the Comédie-Française to witness a performance of *Les Fausses confidences* and *La Jeunesse de Henri V*, Fleury, who was then carrying out the duties of *semainier*, entered the royal box to present the Czar with the programme of plays. Charles Maurice[1] would have his readers believe that Talma, wearing court dress, hung about outside the royal box in the hope of attracting the Czar's notice. Why linger over such a spiteful remark? At Erfurt Talma had been presented to Alexander, had conversed with him in Napoleon's presence and had subsequently corresponded with Count Narishkin, the Emperor's first chamberlain, on matters affecting the Imperial Theatre at St. Petersburg.[2] Charles Maurice for his own journalistic ends, had from time to time to praise the actor's brilliance but he never neglected an opportunity to enjoy a thrust at Talma's expense.

If the restored King cut a rather grotesque figure beside his brother sovereigns, his genial, smiling good nature and gracious ways endeared him to his newly acquired subjects. Very quickly he showed himself a man of wide culture with a perceptive taste for the arts and, early in his reign, made it clear that he had no intention of discontinuing the pensions to actors and other artists which Napoleon had so lavishly dispensed. Such generosity assured to Talma his monthly 1,500 francs. An early indication of the new King's favours was the award of the Legion of Honour

[1] Charles Maurice, *Histoire anecdotique du Théâtre*, Vol. I, pp. 188, 189.
[2] Guy de la Batut *Talma: Correspondance*, pp. 141–146.

to old Ducis, whose verses Louis remembered to quote when the Duc de Duras, as on of the pre-revolutionary '*gentilhomme de la chambre du roi*' and now the royal intermediary on all matters affecting the Comédie-Française, arranged the dramatist's presentation at the Tuileries.[1]

Although many members of the royal family, notably the Duc de Berri, quickly availed themselves of the pleasures of the playhouse, the King himself did not appear at the Comédie-Française until May 23rd, when Corneille's *Héraclius* played by Saint-Prix, Damas and Lafon, filled the bill. Talma's absence is significant. As '*chef d'emploi*' he had first claim upon the part of Héraclius. One would like to think that his loyalty to Napoleon weighed with the actor. No doubt it irked him to read of Lafon's success in the title rôle and to note that the King, so delighted with the actor's diction, had made him a gift, the exact nature of which escaped the newspaper reporters. It must not be forgotten too that at this time Talma was caught up in the domestic toils of his complicated love life.

True also that he still smarted under the resounding failure of Lebrun's first play, *Ulysse*, produced on April 28th. This most conventional tragedy, quickly renamed *Le Retour d'Ulysse* for the sake of an appropriate pun, *Le Retour du lys*, cut little ice with the Parisians, hardly in a mood to speculate upon the fidelity of Penelope or the valour of Télémaque. Although some ink was spilt over this interesting recruit to the ranks of dramatists, and over rather perfunctory praise of Talma for his portrayal of a man who had endured misfortune for ten years, success did not crown the play. The author, writing of his maiden effort, felt that it contained one moment of magic when Talma electrified the audience with his cry of '*Je suis Ulysse!*'[2] Mlle George, now becoming alarmingly stout, more than filled the wifely rôle, and the slender grace of Mlle Duchesnois lent distinction to the boy. Lebrun had written his play in the comparatively stable days of the First Empire; in the fantastically changed times his lines were misconstrued and allusions were speciously sought to the play's final disaster.

In his domestic life Talma faced a crisis. That '*ménage à trois*' in the rue de Seine, where mistress and wife had worked out a *modus vivendi* that at least ensured a quiet household, came to a

[1] A. Copin, *Talma, et l'Empire*, pp. 333, 334.
[2] Lebrun. *Oeuvres*. '*Ulysse*', pp. 2, 3.

sudden end. The lively, dark-haired Mlle Bazire was pregnant and on May 18th gave birth to a son, Alphonse-Alexandre. Caroline Talma, still cordial in her relations with her husband, felt the time had come, not only to change her quarters but also to seek a divorce. Before the arrival of the baby, she had betaken herself to a little house with a garden on the confines of the Faubourg Saint-Germain, made there her own social life, in which a certain M. Moreau figured conspicuously, especially on Saturdays when the lady received. It was during this summer of 1814 that Caroline took counsel with her lawyer, Maître Beauvois, to institute proceedings for divorce. The precise grounds for her action have already been given. For years she had borne with complaisance Talma's notorious infidelities, both in Paris and at Brunoy. It was the birth of an illegitimate son that sent her to the courts, at a time when much confusion reigned in the French legislature. A further complication came from Talma himself, who made no effort to instruct a lawyer to watch his interests. As far as he was concerned the matter could drag on, and drag on it did. Caroline's petition for divorce was formally filed on May 17th, 1815, right in the midst of those bewildered and bewildering Hundred Days. André Antoine, in his *Vie amoureuse de Talma*, states categorically that Caroline obtained her divorce on that day, but all other writers on Talma, as well as evidence available in the Lebrun papers, declare that the case never came to a legal conclusion. Some assert that the papers were lost, others that the suit was adjourned never to be reopened. It is well to remember that, after Waterloo, divorce in France would not be lightly pronounced, with the reactionary 'Throne and Altar' party pursuing an ultra-Catholic policy of the most bigoted kind. If Talma had been free, he would have married Mlle Bazire, who on September 28th, 1816, gave him another son, Paul-Louis, named after the actor's pamphleteering friend, Paul-Louis Courier. The two little boys, whose civil status was later to cause some difficulty, bore their father's name and lived with their mother in his house like the united family they had become. Still more remarkable, Caroline Talma showed an affectionate interest in the boys' welfare, an interest she translated later into a practical and generous concern for them, which must always stand to her credit.

In the theatre, so royalist had playgoers become that any piece capable of stirring resurgent Bourbon sympathies seemed certain of success. To satisfy such royalist demands, the *sociétaires* revived

Les États de Blois which, it must be remembered, Napoleon allowed to be performed only once. Considerable curiosity about this forbidden fruit attended its revival on May 31st, but the hasty production of a tragedy almost devoid of action and overloaded with long political conversations, played havoc with Talma's memory as he worked upon the long-winded speeches of the duc de Guise. What lustre there was in the play was accorded to Lafon, sympathetic as Henri IV, and to Mlle Raucourt, unfailingly impressive as he worked upon the long-winded speeches of the Duc de Guise. new dramatic critic for the *Journal des Débats*—no longer called the *Journal de l'Empire*—opined that Talma 'was quite good in the rôle of Guise, apart from lapses of memory'. He considered that the character of Guise was wrongly keyed, a fault he laid squarely upon the playwright's shoulders. Success again eluded Talma and his colleagues. Disappointment followed the preliminary puffs and not even the plea of a newly found freedom could make *Les États de Blois* interesting.

Among his sure-fire successes Talma repeated during those summer months his now rightly famous reading of Néron in Racine's *Britannicus*. Charles Nodier, who later became one of the stalwarts of the emergent French Romantic movement, still clung to the conservative tenets of his newspaper employers. If his criticisms of Talma carried little of the bitter comment of a Geoffroy, he could upon occasion be vitriolic. On July 5th, 1814, Nodier attended a performance of *Britannicus*, in which Mlle Raucourt and Talma supported a promising débutante in the person of Mlle Stéphanie Lombard. Néron was one of Talma's great parts, the interpretation of which he completely revolutionized and to some extent set his seal upon for all time. He presented, as Napoleon wished, a man torn by the struggles that an educated, cultivated mind was called upon to endure when at war with an inherited cruel nature. Talma realized the terrible oscillations of such a character, the tigerish outbursts, the occasional contemplative moment of restraint. One piece of 'business' he introduced, an effect his successors still make. In that terrific Act IV, where Agrippine begins '*Approchez-vous, Néron, et prenez votre place*' and continues in a speech of 107 lines to explain all she has done to establish this ungrateful son upon the throne, the old actors, including Lekain, sat glum, listless, waiting for this terrible recital of a son's debts and duties to end. Talma astonished his audiences by showing his complete boredom and indifference to

Agrippine's diatribe with a nonchalant tracing of the pattern of his robe, arranging its folds and caressing with wearied fingers the arm of his chair. M. Robert Hirsch, in a brilliant portrayal of Néron seen at the Comédie-Française on October 15th, 1961, the 1,110th performance of *Britannicus*, listened to Agrippine's speech in the Talma way. What had Charles Nodier to say of this particular performance? 'Mlle Raucourt plays Agrippine as if she herself were Agrippine. It is one of the parts in which she shows her greatest fulfilment, since she does lack something. Talma, who has made, I know not where, a deep study of Néron and who acts Néron with exact costume, walk, gestures and a coin-like profile likely to deceive the most expert antiquarian, rises in this play, if not above his natural talent, at least above his customary talent which is much more slipshod. He brings to the part a firm outline, vigour, warmth of expression and above all a rapidity of diction that I feared I would never find again in the theatre and which has the happiest effect upon the actors around him.' Surely here is a critic who came to scoff but remained, even against his will, to praise. Talma's scrupulous accuracy over costume and movement, his '*physionomie numismatique*', his intensive study ('*je ne sais où*') were all sneered at, but this simply proclaims the small-minded theatre reactionary. Yet even he takes fire at the actor's playing. Talma's performances, like those of every other player, varied no doubt; memory at times, understandably in his vast repertory, might play an occasional trick, but never, never could the work of this dedicated disciple of Melpomene be dismissed as slipshod (*négligé*).

The call of summer—'*la belle saison*' in more senses than one—sent the stars of the Comédie-Française posting off to the provinces. Mme de Staël, in a letter dated July 19th, tells us: 'Talma is rather sad and depressed and literature shares in the weariness of everything and everybody.' Nodier on the same day fulminated against the iniquity of the actors' *congés*. 'Now is the time for travel,'[1] he declared, 'the time when our celebrated actors take from the provinces their annual tribute of gold, of laurels, of bad verses. Already Talma has relinquished his sceptre to his rivals without even indicating the destination of his distant flight; we merely know that this prince of the stage, fundamentally a thinker and happy to lay aside for the time being his royal grandeur, maintains a very strict incognito.'

[1] *Journal des Débats*, July 19th, 1814.

Talma went of course to Aix-les-Bains where the ex-Empress had taken up residence since July 17th. As has been said, he spent some time in reading to the lady, but it can be understood that the signal favours that the mother of the King of Rome lavished upon the Austrian general, Neipperg, would find scant approval from the faithful Talma. No wonder he escaped to the Swiss theatres.

Talma's return to Paris coincided with Mlle Raucourt's *rentrée* and, on October 16th, they appeared together in Voltaire's *Oedipe*. Charles Nodier made much of the occasion.[1]

The public always turns out for *Oedipe*, but the day before yesterday its curiosity was excited for reasons other than the merit of the play. Talma and Mlle Raucourt were the objects of this curiosity. A long absence had snatched them both from our pleasures; they reappear together. The theatre was much too small to contain their numerous admirers. The orchestra, stripped of its musicians, provided a few extra seats; but many were turned away lamenting. Talma and Mlle Raucourt made their entrance together and received unanimous applause. Even those who had been annoyed with Talma for his long absence forgot their displeasure when they saw him. The public treats the actors it loves as one treats one's sweetheart; at the least sign of their relenting it pardons their caprices and wrongs. . . .

. . . As it is the first time I am discussing Talma [here he is in error], before relating the effect he produced in *Oedipe*, I think I ought quite frankly to express my general opinion about this famous actor's talent. This opinion, once known, will serve to explain or, if one wishes, to excuse what I shall say about his talent when I have to write about him. I saw Talma make his début and, with few interruptions, I have followed his theatrical career. I discerned in him from the very start the seeds of these qualities he has since so profitably developed; they are intelligence, strength, and an expressive, mobile face; I knew he was passionately devoted to his art and at that time I predicted his success and events have justified my prophecy. One single defect appeared to me to counterbalance these brilliant qualities, a monotonous, heavy diction; but I hoped that this fault would disappear with time. On this score I have been cruelly disappointed. Being unable to correct this defect, he has apparently raised it to a system; somehow he has accustomed the public to it just as some singers do with their trills and their gurglings. We have been told quite categorically 'It is his manner', and, as he rightly pleases in other ways, one has had to accept this fault at the risk of losing his good qualities.

I confess that for my own part I have never shared the public's

[1] *Journal des Débats*, October 20th, 1814.

gracious indulgence. I would wish the public to be generous but severe and would like it to know how to set a value upon its applause, imparting through it useful lessons to actors. For example, while applauding Talma for those beautiful movements which are his alone, I would like the public to make the actor feel, at least by silence, its displeasure in the passages he delivers with such heavy and wearisome emphasis.

Talma confirmed in *Oedipe* the rightness of my estimate of his abilities. He had some fine flashes. He said remarkably well the last two verses in Act III:

> *. . . Suivez-moi*
> *Et venez dissiper ou combler mon effroi*

In the fine scenes in Act IV he took up with perfect correctness the line beginning '*Un seul homme. . . .*'

This long notice seems to run counter to all that has been written about Talma. Those who saw him at the beginning of his career noted this particular fault of a ponderous delivery, no doubt a young actor's assumption of the prevailing method of his senior colleagues. All of them, Tissot, Moreau, Regnault-Warin, make very clear that he corrected this defect and 'spoke' his lines in a natural tone that carried conviction. Geoffroy railed at Talma for his lack of dignity, for ignoring the classic pomp that had almost killed French acting. Nodier finds him too heavy and at a time when Talma, by infinite study, intense self-criticism and ripe experience, was about to come into the kingdom of his own perfection whose throne he would occupy unchallenged for the rest of his natural life. Mercifully Charles Nodier did not linger too long in the difficult art of dramatic criticism, where the objective mind, the emotional response and the fleeting nuance must play their receptive parts. Consolation he found in his charming fairy-tales, where hobgoblins and water-sprites lured him to a less factual, less complicated folklore.

For Talma the close of 1814 held yet a memorable experience. He had earned high praise from the Duc de Berri, a truly royal playgoer, but so far he had not appeared before the King. When the announcement went forth that His Majesty, accompanied by Monsieur and Madame, the Duc and the Duchesse d'Angoulême and the Duc de Berri, would honour a performance of *Britannicus*, '*par ordre*', public excitement knew no bounds. Popular interest can be measured by the payment of 120 francs for a seat in the parterre. With due pomp and ceremony and preceded by the

Duc de Duras, who announced to the crowded auditorium '*le Roi*', Louis and his party took their places in a specially contrived open box on the first gallery, to the frantic cries of '*Vive le Roi! Vive la Famille royale!*'

As the play progressed, every line that might offer an allusion to the current situation drew forth wild cheers, but at the moment when Burrhus tries to dissuade Néron from murdering Britannicus, his lines

> *Quel plaisir de penser et de dire en soi-même;*
> *Partout en ce moment, on me bénit, on m'aime*
> *On ne voit pas le peuple à mon nom s'alarmer;*[1]

caused the audience to rise as one man, bursting its lungs as it turned to the royal box where the King, moved to tears, stood up to bow his acknowledgements. The actors were exhorted to repeat the passage; minutes elapsed before the play could continue.

Two days later, Nodier's account of this performance almost flattered Talma, lauding to the skies the actor's intelligence and his complete grasp of a difficult rôle. Yet something had to be singled out for blame. The critic faulted '*certaines familiarités*', even though he admitted they were natural and historically correct. He dreaded to think that the sublimity of tragedy might sink to the mundane level of the '*drame*'. 'For example, in the great scene with Agrippine, Talma wants to convey the boredom and the fatigue he feels at the long enumeration of his mother's kindnesses. I really do not see that it is necessary for him to toy with his robe; Talma has enough power in his face to express by features alone the impatience which stirs him.' Even Charles Nodier should be consistent. If in the critic's general opinion Talma was too heavy and pompous, why should the actor be reproached for such light, familiar and human touches in his playing?

The King appeared to have been profoundly impressed by Talma's playing of Néron. Subsequently, when the tragedian had the privilege of being presented to Louis XVIII, the King is credited with saying:[2] 'I have indeed a right to be critical, M. Talma. I saw Lekain.'

---

[1] 'What a pleasure, within oneself to think and to say:
Everywhere at this moment I am blessed and loved;
The people are not at all affrighted at my name:'
[2] A. Copin, *Talma et l'Empire*, p. 334.

CHAPTER 35

Funeral of Mlle Raucourt.
The Hundred Days

If the year 1815 stands as a decisive landmark in European history, it must be numbered among the least illustrious in the annals of the Comédie-Française. Talma without a new play was once more thrown back on the repertory tragedies which, stimulated by occasional visits from the King and the constant patronage of the Duc de Berri, still served to reveal his mature powers. *Manlius, Iphigénie, Philoctète, Rhadamiste et Zénobie, Coriolan* and *Gabrielle de Vergy* took their unequal chances with Parisian playgoers. A literary journal of the day, *Le Nain jaune*, bitterly complained of such a reactionary policy and took up the cudgels on behalf of authors who suffered the handicap of being alive. It is therefore of some interest to quote its views on Talma's rendering of Laharpe's *Coriolan*, especially as it had so vehemently attacked the *sociétaires*' choice of plays which seemed especially designed to propagate the outmoded ideas of the '*philosophes*' and to reflect palely the tragic manner of Voltaire.[1] 'The revival of *Coriolan* has given Talma the opportunity to achieve a success that it would be unfair to conceal. Apart from a few touches of that gloomy shading he is wont to impart to all his rôles, it is impossible to portray more worthily the proud indignation of that illustrious exile, whose victories and death did not absolve him, in the eyes of posterity, from the crime of having borne arms against his own country. Talma, despite his faults which need not wearily be recalled, is the only tragedian our theatre possesses today; those who are in it do not know how to appreciate him.'

The return to Paris of Mlle Duchesnois made possible yet another series of performances of *Andromaque*. Talma at fifty-two made no bones about taking the very exhausting part of Oreste. With them appeared Mlle George, at the height of her substantial

[1] *Le Nain jaune*, No. 337, December 15th, 1814.

266

beauty, who made an excellent foil in the name part to her rival's Hermione. *Le Nain jaune* thought the occasion impressive.[1] 'Last Saturday they gave for Mlle Duchesnois' second appearance since her return one of the most brilliant performances of *Andromaque* that I have seen for a very long time. Talma, admirable as he always is in Oreste's madness, more triumphantly than ever, by the way he played the other scenes, confounded those who would limit his powers to the school of horror.' But there is no need to multiply quotations. Talma, the vivid, exciting, if somewhat unequal actor of the old days of the Théâtre de la République, by the exercise of his intelligence and his imagination, has moved steadily towards that perfection which will make the last decade of his career one of the imperishable glories of the French stage. This will be seen. Ripeness is all.

On January 9th, Mlle Desbrosses, Dazincourt's devoted, constant friend, retired from the Comédie-Française where for many years she had played *soubrettes*. Her farewell benefit is important because it brought a mature Talma back to *Hamlet* to tackle the Danish prince, a fully romantic part after a round of classical and pseudo-classical heroes. How did he come through what is, even in an emasculated Ducis version, a testing ordeal? The *Journal des Débats* had of course never loved him. On January 11th, all Paris, at least that part of it interested in the theatre, read:[2]

Never has this great actor shown himself so much above criticism and beyond praise; not for one moment was he at fault. Right from his entrance, his disordered appearance, his dull and inarticulate cries, the terror writ upon his face, seemed to make visible in the public's eye his father's apparition hovering over his head, then fast upon his heels. In the scene where Norceste, carrying out Hamlet's orders, tells the story of the murder of the English monarch in the presence of Gertrude and her accomplice, emphasizing the same circumstances as those which surrounded the death of the King of Denmark, Talma's piercing glance, lighting in turn upon his mother and Claudius, reflected in a wonderfully varied way the different impression that the story produced upon these two characters. One could read in those glances his contained indignation against the casual indifference of the greatest criminal and his despair at never being able wholly to dispel the doubt of his mother's complicity in his father's murder. With infinite art he brought light and shade to the long, too long and much too metaphysical, soliloquy that opens the fourth act. It seemed that terror could

[1] *Le Nain jaune*, No. 342, January 10th, 1815.
[2] *Journal des Débats*, January 11th, 1815.

be carried no farther. Yet Talma has found the secret of rendering it even more alarming, especially at the moment when, for the second time, his father's ghost appears to hand him the avenging dagger; then when the actor, recoiling before this awful gift, cries out in agonized, moving tones, 'I can never do it', heart strings were plucked and every eye was wet with tears. Scarcely had the curtain fallen when the actor was recalled with acclamation. Yielding to the public's insistence, he came forward to reap in the renewed, unanimous applause the well-merited reward of his inspired efforts.

The dramatic critics, commenting on that performance, brushed up their superlatives and gasped out their praise. *Le Journal de Paris* became rhapsodical. Martainville its critic had actually 'seen' *Hamlet*. *Le Nain jaune* reported that this performance of *Hamlet* proved worthy of the public's support. 'Talma is penetrating, dynamic, terrible in the part of Hamlet. Mlle Duchesnois triumphed with much art over all the difficulties that beset the ungrateful part of Gertrude. The urn scene,[1] played with convincing truth, was applauded by all those who were not trembling with emotion.' There can be little doubt that Talma gave his generation a masterly study of Hamlet.

While the actor wreathed his brow with Hamlet laurels, Paris on January 15th learned of the death of Marie-Antoinette Saucerotte, better known as that eccentric but powerful *tragédienne* Mlle Raucourt. At the age of fifty-nine she had died from an inflammation of the lungs at her home in the rue du Helder. This extraordinary creature lived in male attire and, in her later days, found her greatest happiness in her own home where she ruled as 'master', *'en redingote'*, with the *'amie'* of her choice. To complete the picture of her assumed masculinity she had added to the *ménage* a girl who addressed her as 'papa' and had for years excited pardonable curiosity which even Napoleon shared.[2] Mlle Raucourt, as can be well understood, was everywhere regarded as a character and, even when her stage appearances as in 1814 were few and far between, she was always a centre of Parisian gossip. After the storms of her youth she had turned her attention to good works and, at the time of her death, the Paris poor owed her much.

The funeral of this distinguished actress, who had served the Comédie-Française since 1773, had been arranged for January 17th. The hearse was to leave 2, rue du Helder, proceed to the church of Saint-Roch in the rue Saint-Honoré, where the rites of

---

[1] Shakespeare's 'Closet Scene', *Hamlet*, Act III, Sc. 4.

[2] A. V. Arnault, *Souvenirs d'un sexagénaire*, Vol. I, p. 319.

Christian burial were to be performed and afterwards make its way to Père-Lachaise, where final inhumation would take place. To the utter surprise and distress of the deceased's relatives, the curé of Saint-Roch made it known before the start of the funeral procession that under no circumstances would he permit the entry of Mlle Raucourt's remains into his church. For two hours they tried vainly to persuade this rigid exemplar of the Roman faith to change his mind. The funeral coaches waited in the street; all preparations were halted. At this point, the actors of the Comédie-Française, colleagues old and young who had turned out in the uniform of the *gardes-nationaux*, sped post-haste to the Tuileries to beg the King to intervene. By now a vast concourse of people, scenting excitement, had appeared. The actors had not returned and it was decided to start for the cemetery, abandoning any idea of a service at Saint-Roch. The murmuring indignant populace thought otherwise. The procession reached the narrow rue de la Michodière, where the police tried to halt it, only to retreat before the impassioned cries of the crowd shouting, 'To the church!' When the convoy arrived at the church, its great doors stood closed. The side doors were burst open by the crowd, they entered the church to find that the curé had barricaded himself in the sacristy and, in their wrath, they began to break up the chairs. Outside the church a group of the late actress's friends persuaded the gendarmes to surround the hearse and to conduct it to the cemetery. The dense crowd made such an escape impossible and back once more into the rue Saint-Honoré the hearse was led.[1]

Then began an indescribable scene. The crowd took charge of events. Men fought each other for the honour of carrying the coffin when it was made known that, by order of the King, Mlle Raucourt's remains should receive Christian burial. The great doors of Saint-Roch opened and the crowd with the coffin surged forward. Louis XVIII to his eternal credit sent a priest from his own chapel to conduct the service. With the mortal remains of Mlle Raucourt reposing on the catafalque before the high altar, the erstwhile indignant crowd fell to respectful silence at the mere sight of the priest with crucifix and two choir boys. The funeral rites concluded, the priest conducted the coffin to the church door and a satisfied, orderly crowd followed the hearse to Père-Lachaise.

Thus ended the funeral of Mlle Raucourt, whom Talma

[1] *Notice sur l'enterrement de Mlle Raucourt. Brochure de dix pages*, 1815.

described as the last worthy representative of the mannered school of Mlle Clairon. The scandal surrounding her burial throws into relief not only the Church's intolerant attitude towards actors and actresses but also the forces of reaction that came back with the restored monarchy. Had Mlle Raucourt died under the Napoleonic régime, she would have enjoyed without any question the consolations of her religion. Talma, an ardent and indignant spectator at her funeral, must have recalled how another curé, the cleric of Saint-Sulpice, had refused him the benefits of Christian marriage just because he gloried in his profession of actor.

In the absence of new plays the roundabout of repertory pursued its course for Talma. A revival of *Esther* provided him with an opportunity to have another look at Assuérus with Lafon as Aman receiving good notices. Curiously enough, in *Les Templiers* he reverted to the '*jeune premier*' rôle of Marigny which he had created, discarding the more mature one of Jacques de Molay, by which he had impressed Brussels playgoers. As a reminder of Talma's constant self-examination and his reappraisal of his parts it must be noted at this time that in *Rhadamiste et Zénobie* he gave a completely new reading of Crébillon's hero, charging the recognition scene with added power and fresh significance. This touch of novelty must have brightened those February days when he added *Polyeucte* and, wonderful to relate, *Ninus II* to his tragedies. As far as Talma was concerned, the critics without exception wrote eulogies. Others might abide their question; he seemed free from reproach. Their whips and scorpions were applied elsewhere. They did not spare Mlle Duchesnois because of a bad, drawling, monotonous Pauline in *Polyeucte*.[1] 'I maintain that Mlle Duchesnois' health is not fully restored. Damas and Talma poured life into her listless, boring scenes. Talma especially played with an understanding and a truth wholly admirable Sévère's beautiful scene in the fourth act and, if he was not more tender and loving in the second, the fault undoubtedly lay with his icy partner.'

On March 1st came the electrifying news that Napoleon had ended a ten months exile on Elba and, to the mortification of the restored court, had actually landed on French soil. As the mayor of a little village told the returned hero: 'We were beginning to enjoy peace and prosperity and now you come to upset everything.'[2] These words gravely disturbed Napoleon. How many, he wondered, thought the same. Ney proclaimed his fidelity to Louis

[1] *Journal des Débats*, February, 11th 1815.   [2] Jacques Bainville, *Napoléon*, p. 448.

XVIII. Napoleon however pressed northwards. March 10th found him at Lyons, listening to the reiterated shouts of a frenzied populace. 'Down with the priests! Down with the nobles! Long live the Emperor!' and, to the strains of the Marseillaise, he received a hero's welcome from the soldiers of the local garrisons and from the old campaigners he knew so well how to inspire. In Lyons, the second city of France, Napoleon's followers had swollen to a small army of 14,000 men which Macdonald, under royal command to halt his advance, could no longer restrain. Consternation reigned at the Tuileries. On came Napoleon and Paris heard the rumbling rumour of his approach. On March 19th the King and the royal family took flight to Lille, en route for Ghent. On March 20th Napoleon reached Paris and slept that night in the Tuileries.

The mere appearance of the Emperor, the very incarnation of that military glory France found irresistible, once more cast its magic spell upon the capital. Back came the eagles, the bees and the violets, so propitiously blooming in the woods! What a trampling of the lilies was there! Ever the Emperor's loyal servant, Talma rejoiced in the change. The stimulus of such excitement must have helped him over a revival of Baour-Lormian's *Omasis*, where the actor challenged time itself by his reappearance at fifty-two as Joseph, a *'jeune premier'* lead. The truly great occasion came on April 21st when the Emperor arrived to occupy his box at the Théâtre-Français for a performance of Luce de Lancival's *Hector*. Words fail to communicate the delirious, patriotic spirit that reigned on this occasion, easily the greatest theatrical event of the Hundred Days. The Emperor arrived late but the actors duly went back to the beginning of the play. Even today some idea, however faint, may be gauged of the effect of the following (translated) lines upon a wildly enthusiastic audience, ready to demonstrate a newly recovered loyalty at every possible allusion, however veiled, to the current situation.

HECTOR: I belong not to myself but to the fatherland!
ANDROMAQUE: But your son Astyanax has his claim on life!
HECTOR: Perhaps he will achieve immortality
      If he imitates his father . . .

    . . . .
      Like a mighty Colossus to the stationary army
      Appears a warrior.

PATROCLES: It is he!
ANDROMAQUE: At last he reappears!

What an occasion! Marie-Louise, unlike Andromaque, did not act the faithful wife. The Emperor was alone and his son in virtual captivity. That night Talma and Mlle Duchesnois gave their all and they certainly provided a memory for their beloved Emperor that not even the humiliations of Saint Helena could quench. Napoleon, ever appreciative of their efforts, before leaving the theatre charged the Duc de Montesquiou, his new *surintendant des théâtres impériaux*, to reward the artists in a suitable way. This was the very last occasion on which Napoleon saw Talma act.

Did the returned Emperor welcome Talma to his intimate circle? In those hectic Hundred Days it is hard to speak with any certainty about social engagements. One conversation is repeated by all Talma's early biographers,[1] by the men who claimed to know him intimately, and they all agree upon the precise wording. During his Elban exile Napoleon, who had followed every detail of Bourbon propaganda, was amused to read that, according to his enemies, he had received lessons in deportment from Talma. Napoleon took this stab very lightheartedly, adding that if he recalled Talma's mannerisms his imperial gestures must have proved adequate to any occasion. Then speaking of Louis XVIII he reminded Talma that the King had treated the actor well, that he knew much about the theatre, for he saw Lekain. '*Il a vu Lekain.*' If only it were known in what tone of voice Napoleon said those words.

Then came Waterloo. On that *morne plaine* Victory cheated and Destiny was tired. That fateful eighteenth of June saw the end of the First Empire and its architect, a battle-stained, weary, defeated man, made his way to the Malmaison, where Hortense and Madame Mère awaited him. During that brief respite, when few were allowed to approach the fallen Emperor, Talma, wearing the uniform of a *garde national*, came, not only to salute the 'great man', but to offer him a belt full of his own savings.[2] This was their last meeting and Mlle Cochelet in her *Mémoires* tells how deeply Talma grieved to witness the parting of mother and son. For Talma the Napoleonic contact was now at an end—perhaps

---

[1] Moreau, p. 61. Tissot, p. 40. Regnault-Warin, P. 485.
[2] Mlle Cochelet. *Mémoires sur la Reine Hortense*, Vol. II, pp. 172, 173. Claude Maceron. *Which way to Turn*, Chapter V, p. 47.

not quite. Around his neck for the rest of his life he wore the Emperor's likeness in a medallion bearing the inscription '*tibi semper fidelis*'. After his beloved Emperor died, Talma never acted on the anniversary of his death.

CHAPTER 36

Madame de Staël's Judgment of Talma

The years immediately following Napoleon's exile to Saint-Helena were for Talma, as for all liberal minded Frenchmen, a period of frustration. This time the Bourbons had come back to stay and, with the Corsican ogre firmly chained to his remote Atlantic rock, the reactionary elements in the King's government made no effort to conceal their aim to wipe away revolutionary change and to use the monarchy and the Church as props for a new stability. France welcomed peace with utter thankfulness but resented behind the royal pomp a foreign army of occupation.

For Talma work proved the true anodyne. He filled the Théâtre-Français by his bravura performances of parts that he never allowed to stale. Brunoy offered brief respites where, with his adored mistress and baby son, he tasted the sweets of a relaxed domestic life. Perhaps 'relaxed' calls for some qualification. This country house, aptly named '*Mon Plaisir*', ate up money. Workmen seemed everlastingly occupied in improving it; additional plots were constantly purchased to extend the gardens.[1] Mlle Bazire lacked the business acumen of Caroline Talma and was as reckless as her lover in money matters. With no indulgent Emperor to settle bills and make presents, Talma's finances became more and more involved. Furthermore, in a frantic desire to recoup his losses, he was pursued by ill fortune on the Bourse and at the gaming-table. We are told that he hardly knew one card from another.[2] Before long his rashly incurred debts were to loom large in the actor's dealings with the Comédie-Française.

The autumn and spring seasons of 1815 and 1816 offered the actor but little in the way of novelty. True, Aignan's tragedy *Arthur de Bretagne*, so often postponed because of Mlle Raucourt's illness, finally took the stage on February 3rd, 1816. This inac-

[1] C. Talma, *Quelques Particularités*, p. 303.
[2] C. Maurice, *Histoire anecdotique du théâtre*, Vol. I, p. 378.

curate exercise in English history must have reminded Talma by its very theme of that luckless production of the Ducis *Jean sans terre* far back in his prentice days of 1791. Aignan's feeble example of a dying genre scarcely deserved its brilliant cast. Mlle Mars, now a popular idol, played the young Arthur, Talma the shrewd plotter Rutland and to Mlle Duchesnois fell the Raucourt rôle of the wronged, anguished Constance. It might be said that the play collapsed under the weight of their talents. Aignan had already served Talma by his ultra-classical *Polyxène* in 1804 and had moved sufficiently with the times to seek for a tragic subject in the national mediaeval chronicle.

So back to the old favourites, to the parts the parterre loved so well. The house could always be filled with Talma as Oedipe, Manlius, Oreste, Nicomède, Achille, Cinna, Sévère, Néron, if contemporary dramatists failed. One particular occasion calls for comment. Caroline Vanhove, Talma's lawful wife, who had retired in 1811, decided that she would take her long-delayed benefit on July 20th, 1816. For this occasion she had written a comedy *Laquelle des trois?* which was to share the programme with *Oedipe*. To the surprise of her colleagues, Caroline had decided not to appear. Her comedy turned out to be not only a *pièce à clef* with the three ladies as variations of Caroline herself, Pauline Borghèse and Madeleine Bazire, but a great success as well. Thus passed Caroline Vanhove-Talma from the annals of the Comédie-Française, a cultivated, gifted woman who would find an outlet for her talents in literary pursuits.

While we leave Talma and Mlle Bazire to wait for the birth of their second child, it may not be inappropriate to pause and try to take stock of Talma the actor, now at the critical age of fifty-three. We who come to consider his art after an interval of a century and a half cannot hope to catch even the faintest echo of that vibrant voice which thrilled his generation, or a fleeting glimpse of his handsome features reflecting the agony of tragic emotion. Quotations from critics who saw his performances, often with a jaundiced, partisan eye, have in this compilation played their wearisome part. Even at this distance of time we ask ourselves if it is possible to get a little nearer. Can we fortify our judgment by recourse to a mind that commands universal respect? Can we bring forward a valid analysis of what posterity has accepted as the genius of Talma's acting? Can we, however vicariously, get into the mind of the actor himself?

In 1810 Mme de Staël produced her critical masterpiece *De l'Allemagne*, the whole French edition of which the imperial police destroyed. A great part of this stimulating work deals with a plea for a greater freedom for French tragedy and ridicules the unities, the rigid separation of the genres and the crippling limitation of subject mainly to Greek and Roman themes. Under Napoleon this thought-provoking book was banned and it required the Restoration of 1814 to allow the London edition of 1813 to find its way into the Paris bookshops. Then and only then could Mme de Staël's enlightened and penetrating views about the French theatre be read and discussed. For her the only models worthy of dramatic imitation were Schiller and Goethe, and of course Shakespeare, to whom she always returned. France, she maintains, already had the actor of supreme genius to interpret the new tragedy and that actor was Talma. She had seen him play at Lyons in 1809, when Talma was forty-six, and upon these performances she based her opinions set forth so vividly in Chapter XXVII of *De l'Allemagne*.

Talma was for her the supreme example of an enlightened, imaginative actor. Above everything she admired his bold innovations, his perfect restraint, his naturalness and his dignity. She perceived that in his playing he made use of other arts, modelling pose and gesture upon ancient statuary, wearing his clothes with all the beauty of carelessly assumed classical draperies. His expressive face would repay any portrait painter's study. When his half-closed eyes suddenly opened,[1] their flashing glance seemed to light up the whole stage. His voice thrilled spectators even before the full sense of the words he uttered could excite their emotions. He delivered descriptive verse with a beauty of tone and rhythm so as to throw into relief poetic beauties, just as if Pindar himself had recited his own odes. Other actors seem to require a certain amount of time to move their audience, and see that they possess it, but there is in the voice of this man some inexplicable magic which from his first utterance stirs heartfelt sympathy. The spell cast by music, sculpture, poetry and above everything the effect produced by the language of the heart, there you have his means to generate within the spectator the power of noble and awful passions.

Having pointed the actor's appearance and his superb attack,

---

[1] Bernier de Malagny, one of his pupils, says that Talma kept his eyes half open on his entry and, as the character developed, let fall his glances. Quoted by A. Antoine, *La Vie amoureuse de Talma*.

Mme de Staël proceeds to examine certain of Talma's parts as he played them. By his diction and his facial play, she says, he is the second author. Oedipe, telling Jocaste how he killed Laius, begins '*J'étais jeune et superbe*'. The old actors squeezed every drop out of that word '*superbe*', tossing their heads like chargers champing at the bit. Talma, sensing that these youthful exploits could only lead to bitter remorse, spoke the words timidly, making clear the doubts that assailed him and the self-confidence he had lost. Again, at the critical moment when Phorbas arrives from Corinth, just when Oedipe begins to fear his own origin, he asks Phorbas for words in private. Other actors would turn round and proudly dismiss their followers. Talma, realizing that Phorbas knew the truth Oedipe desperately craved, fixed his eyes upon him, never let him out of his sight and, with an impatient backward movement of his hand, bade his bodyguard depart. Not a word had been said, but his distraught attitude betrayed the disorder of his mind, and when in the last act he cried out as he left Jocaste, '*Oui, Laïus est mon père et je suis votre fils*', it seemed as if the very jaws of hell opened to engulf poor mortals, driven there by treacherous fate.

From Voltaire she passes to Racine, to that terrific moment in *Andromaque* when Hermione in her crazed wrath turned on Oreste for having murdered Pyrrhus without her sanction. Oreste answered:

> . . . *Et ne m'avez-vous pas*
> *Vous-même, ici, tantôt, ordonné son trépas?*[1]

When he recited these lines, Lekain used to hammer out each word as if, like some presiding judge, he were determined to bring home to the prisoner every point in the evidence. Talma showed his love for the woman and for him the dominant emotion was despair at finding her both cruel and unjust. A cry escaped his lips, he pronounced the first few words with emphasis and the following ones with an ever growing despondency. His arms fell limply, his face turned white as death and the audience became more and more moved as he seemed to lose the power of speech. In the rendering of the monologue beginning

> *Que vois-je? Est-ce Hermione? Et que viens-je d'entendre?*

[1] *Andromaque*, Act V, Sc. 3:
'And did not you
Yourself, here, just now, order me to kill him?'

Talma was sublime. He revealed a kind of innocence which was torturing his soul when he reached the line

J'assassine à regret un roi que je révère

and in those words he discovered a pity that even the genius of Racine had not wholly foreseen. Great actors have always regarded the madness of Oreste as a crucial test of their powers; but it was in those scenes that Talma's nobility of gesture and feature enhanced wonderfully the effect of his despair. The intensity of his grief became all the more poignant when it was seen in the true calm and dignity of a noble nature.

Then come under review certain historical characters. Mme de Staël states that Tacitus becomes more understandable when one has seen Talma play Néron. He brought to this part great penetration of mind. She adds that an honest soul always perceives first mentally the beginnings of crime. Nevertheless Talma produced an even greater effect in parts where the spectator, as he listens to him, enjoys surrendering himself to the feelings the actor expresses. In Debelloy's play[1] he did great service to Bayard by purging the part of those swaggering airs other actors felt it necessary to convey. Thanks to Talma, this Gascon hero recovered in this tragedy the simplicity that history accorded him. His costume, his restrained, co-ordinated gestures reminded one of those statues of knights one sees in ancient churches, and one marvelled that a man, who had so completely steeped himself in classical art, could still know how to project himself in the Middle Ages.

Sometimes Talma plays the rôle of Faran in Ducis' Arabian tragedy *Abufar ou la Famille arabe*. Much delightful verse, the dreamy melancholy of an Arabian noontide, the desolation of lands where nature, instead of beautifying, consumes with fiery heat, all this the tragedy admirably communicated. The same Talma, Greek, Roman, mediaeval knight, became an Arab of the desert, energetic yet full of love. His eyes were half closed, as if to shut out the sun's burning rays; his gestures revealed clearly in turn indolence and impetuosity. At times he was overwhelmed by fate, at others he showed himself more powerful than nature itself and seemed to dominate it. The passion which devoured him and which he felt for a woman he believed to be his sister, he kept within his bosom; one might have said, from his uncertain gait,

[1] *Gaston et Bayard*, 1771.

that he wished to flee from his own self. His eyes shrank from looking at what he loved and his hands seemed to push back the vision he believed he saw ever at his side. When at last he pressed Saléma to his heart, saying quite simply, 'I am cold,'[1] he expressed everything at once, the chill within his soul and the devouring passion he had to conceal.

Although alive to many faults in Shakespeare's plays, Mme de Staël admits that it would be unjust to deny their outstanding beauties. Ducis finds his genius in his heart and with such emotions he does well: Talma as a friend brought his talent to the adaptations of this noble old man. In the French version of *Macbeth* the scene with the witches is relegated to a mere recital. Talma has to be seen, giving a taste of his quality with something vulgar yet sinister in the witches' tones and yet preserving in this portrayal all the dignity the theatre demands.

> *Par des mots inconnus, ces êtres monstrueux*
> *S'appelaient tour à tour, s'applaudissaient entre eux,*
> *S'approchaient, se montraient avec un air farouche :*
> *Leur doigt mystérieux se posait sur leur bouche.*
> *Je leur parle, et dans l'ombre ils s'échappent soudain*
> *L'un avec un poignard, l'autre un sceptre à la main.*
> *L'autre d'un long serpent serrait son corps livide :*
> *Tous trois vers ce palais ont pris un vol rapide,*
> *Et tous trois dans les airs, en fuyant loin de moi,*
> *M'ont laissé pour adieu ces mots : Tu seras roi.*[2]

The low, mysterious voice of the actor as he delivered these lines, the way in which he put his finger to his lips like some silent

---

[1] In a letter to Mme de Staël, dated October 14th, 1810, Talma makes the following correction. 'My dear Iphigénie, I have two slight comments to make. Faran in *La Famille arabe* does not say "I am cold" when he falls into his sister's arms, but when he confides his love to a friend. . . . The second concerns the expression *"midi rêveur"* which I confess alarms me.' In the definitive edition of *De l'Allemagne* the offending expression was replaced by *'la mélancolie rêveuse du midi asiatique'*. Guy de la Batut, *Talma: Correspondance*, p. 36.

[2] 'By words unknown, these grisly hags
Called out to each other, then clapped their hands,
Came close, revealed themselves in savage guise;
Their uncanny finger they placed upon their lips.
I speak to them and in the darkness suddenly they escape me,
One with a dagger, another with a sceptre in her hand,
The third with a long snake bound her ghastly shape.
All three towards this palace wheeled in rapid flight,
And all three as they sped far into the air,
In farewell left me these words: Thou shalt be king.'

statue, his features contracted to express an awful repellent memory, everything he did and said conspired to depict a new marvel upon our stage and one which no previous tradition could prompt.

Othello of late has not been too successful in France, says this critic. It seems as if Orosmane stands in the way of our understanding Othello; but when Talma acts this play, the fifth act stirs as if one were present actually at the murder. I have seen Talma in a drawing-room take that last scene with his wife, whose voice and appearance so admirably befit Desdemona. It sufficed for him to touch her hair lightly, to knit his brow in order to become the Moor of Venice and, at two paces from him, terror gripped us just as if all the illusions of the theatre had surrounded the actor.

The reader has already noted the ecstatic praise Mme de Staël heaped upon Talma's Hamlet, a panegyric her contemporaries so fully endorsed that her eulogy became theirs and the incidents she chose to justify her opinion were precisely those that lesser minds —Geoffroy of course excepted—seized upon. What passed in the lack-lustre French version for the Play Scene, the 'To be or not to be' soliloquy, the Closet Scene, Talma by the very genius of his intellect and imagination made completely convincing and lent to these fustian paraphrases of Shakespeare's mighty situations a compulsive tension that overwhelmed his audiences, totally unaccustomed to such a vivid display of romantic feeling. Well might she say that among foreign plays '*Hamlet est son triomphe*'.

This most interesting chapter she concludes with her appreciation of the actor in *Manlius*. The rôle of Manlius has become so identified with Talma she feels, that their names are interchangeable. Before Talma tackled Manlius, the old actors seemed unaware of the really passionate friendship that united the conspirator and Servilius. Mme de Staël, who obviously knew Otway's *Venice Preserved*, underlines the point that in the English play Pierre and Jaffier make plain the strength of this relationship. No shade of Talma's brilliant assumption of Manlius escapes her eye and ear and, like all her generation, she falls captive to the actor's lofty conception of restrained passion.

She sums up in the following words: 'In speaking about Talma in some detail, I do not think I have lingered over matter irrelevant to my work. This artist gives abundantly to French tragedy what Germans, rightly or wrongly, complain it lacks, namely, originality and truth to life. Talma knows how to portray foreign manners and customs in the different characters he essays and no actor embarks upon very powerful effects with more simplicity. In his manner of declaiming verse, he combines artistically Shakespeare and Racine. Why should not dramatists also strive to combine in their plays what the actor has been able to fuse so well in his playing?'[1]

The answer to that question had to wait for the production of Victor Hugo's *Hernani*. This final sentence sets the seal upon the '*pré-romantique*' quality of Talma's contribution to the stage. What did he himself feel about the processes of his own creation? His friend Audibert, during one of his many undated visits to Brunoy, put to him this very question.[2] There was Talma in his garden, wearing a wide straw hat, a striped shirt, white trousers and shod with sabots, declaring that the actor is painter and poet, while from a crystal decanter he watered a tiny oak, ten inches high.

Do I rehearse before a mirror and affright the house with shouts? No. That is a mistake. Meditation takes up much of my time; like the poets I walk up and down or I sit beside my little stream. Yes, I scratch my head and that is the only gesture, not a very noble one as you perceive.

As a rule, when I am studying [*je compose*] a part, whether new or from the repertory, I seek first to soak myself in the character from the historical angle and I do that not only for the character I shall act but also for all those who will be around me, participating in my acting and contributing to the action of the play. I busy myself with dates and give my whole attention to the period.

I become a Roman. I live in Rome as my native city. I get help from looking at statues in museums. I note their stance, even the folds of their cloak. After a performance of *Manlius* David once paid me a flattering compliment. 'When you came on the stage I thought I saw a Roman statue walking'.

When that preliminary study is completed, I then go for the whole character. I feed on its passions. I get accustomed to feel as it feels, I mean as it would feel if it were alive. Then in the evening, before the public, I let my whole being expand, take fire and blaze forth from the great character I have created. What they call my talent is perhaps only a remarkable facility for plunging into the excitement of feelings which are not mine but which, through my imagination, I take unto myself. For a few hours I know how to live the life of others and if I am not granted the privilege of bringing to life historical characters in all their

[1] Mme de Staël, *De l'Allemagne* Chapter XXVII.
[2] Audibert, *Histoire du roman: Talma*, pp. 170–178.

earthly shape, at least I can rekindle their feelings which I force into myself and feel in my very bowels. I am rather like the pythoness. The stage is my Delphic oracle.

In our art there is a mechanical side which one must learn in another way and by a kind of routine. It is only when we have submitted to this discipline that we see arise before us the barrier (where mediocrity comes to a halt) to surmount which requires from us this intensive penetration. I carry this study so far that, by dint of memory, I bring to it the unexpected improvisations of the stage. The inflections of my voice, the expression on my face, the language of gesture, I weigh them all. My mind then subjects any novelties to its own examination, improves them, fixes them in my memory and stores them there for future performances.

Usually in the evening, while I am waiting in the wings, I take advantage of the interval between one scene and the next to review matters in this way. Seldom do I think about the scene to follow but always about the one I have just played. Thus I take stock of my acting almost as I play. If I have done well, I carve that scene in my memory so that I shall always act it in the same way. When I strike a happy effect, this becomes for me a rich possession which I never lose. If on the other hand I have been weak, unconvincing or exaggerated, I take myself to task on the spot and resolve if possible not to fall again into the same defects.

I often seek the opinion of learned men. I question those who remember Lekain, Granval, Clairon, Dumesnil. Monvel confided to me some of the secrets of that great master Lekain.

In this long talk with Audibert Talma admitted that he scored his parts like a musician. 'I am not only actor and poet, I am musician as well.'[1] On his scripts the actor marked modulation and all vocal effects. In a modern play his delicate ear often caused him to alter lines. '*Que mon coeur a de joie!*' he felt must be changed to '*Que mon âme a de joie!*'[2] The close proximity of such harsh sounds as '*que*' and '*coeur*' offended his ear. Once, and in quite another context, Talma was asked by a certain M. Daleg how he would say the line

Soumis avec respect à sa volonté sainte.

In a painstaking letter the actor pointed out the unfortunate sequence of '*avec*' and '*respect*'. To cut out the '*t*' in '*respect*' made the liaison of this noun with the following word ugly and rather

[1] Audibert, *Histoire du roman: Talma*, p. 220.
[2] Ibid, p. 224.

vulgar. If the '*t*' were lightly carried forward, he said, the line would sound less arid and harsh. 'I therefore prefer to say

Soumis avec respectassa volonté sainte.'[1]

These minute points of diction give some indication at least of Talma's aural sensitivity, his care for the speaking of verse and his especial concern to preserve the smooth surface of Racine's harmoniously flowing line.

[1] H. d'Alméras, *Mémoires sur Talma*, p. 337.

CHAPTER 37

Talma Threatens Retirement

This quite fantastic year 1816 still held events that profoundly affected Talma's life. The Parisian mob shouted
'*A bas l'Empereur! A bas les tricolores!*' Banners flaunted
'*la cocarde blanche, c'est la paix*'. The times were indeed grievous for
those who admired Napoleon. Yet in the midst of such manifestations of new-found royalist fervour King Louis XVIII, quite
regardless of Talma's pronounced Bonapartist sympathies,
awarded the actor a pension of 30,000 francs per annum which he
provided from his own privy purse. A similar act of generosity,
in which politics again played no part, endowed Mlle Mars with
an annuity of 20,000 francs. Louis XVIII, both by his tolerance
and his artistic perception, deserved the thanks of all artists for
such signal recognition of two personalities whose position on the
French stage by its very eminence went unchallenged.

For Talma this practical expression of royal favour came at a
time when his recently established ménage with Mlle Bazire made
heavy demands upon his ever dwindling resources. Money he
could always earn, especially in the provinces where Lyons and
Bordeaux would pay him 1,000 francs a performance, but what
with his life in Paris, the ever increasing expenses of *Mon Plaisir*,
the extravagance of a young and sprightly mistress, the hazards of
the gaming-table, his income seemed always to be mortgaged.
With these mounting debts he gave another hostage to fortune.
On September 28th Paul-Louis, a second son, arrived. If joy were
not wholly unconfined, that was merely because the added
expenditure of this happy event increased financial embarrassment
all round. Money must be found and whether the Comité liked
it or not he must ask for a congé, even during these months of
October, November and December, when the Comédie-Française
hoped to play to capacity business. So forth went Manlius to reap
his rich rewards in the northern cities of Lille, Valenciennes, Arras
and to meditate upon the suggestion that he might like to cross

the Channel and play in London. That would indeed want thinking about.

With Hamlet, Oreste and Manlius to occupy his mind Talma, acting in his native department, found life very full. As an *enfant du Nord* he made an especial appeal to Picard, Fleming and Walloon. His remarkable success upon the Brussels and Antwerp stages has already been noted. The French border towns proved no exception. An incident at Arras has passed into legend. During a performance of *Hamlet* in the theatre there, at the very moment when the Prince raised his dagger against Gertrude in the famous *scène de l'urne*, 'there came from a box quite terrible cries.[1]' Its occupant, an artillery officer who had faced death calmly on many occasions, we are told, had become so overwrought by Talma's realistic acting that he had to be removed from the theatre in an unconscious state. When he recovered his wits in the square outside, the poor man's first words were, 'Did he kill his mother?'; and this from no impressionable southerner but from a presumably hardheaded son of the North!

The spring of 1817 saw Talma back at the Comédie-Française where on March 22nd he essayed a new rôle, Germanicus, in the tragedy of that name by A. V. Arnault, whose *Les Vénitiens* had previously served the actor so well. Arnault, an ardent Bonapartist, was living as a political exile in Brussels at the time of the production of this play. Perhaps the subject matter was unfortunate. Germanicus, the adopted son of Augustus and a great Roman general who had won victories in Germany and the East, could hardly fail to stir memories of another great soldier who had fought with a like success over the same ground. Apart from its theme, the absence of women characters until Act III made the play seem an academic exercise, a veritable *tragédie de collège*.[2] The political issues inherent in the action so inflamed a sharply divided audience, composed of *ultras* and *demi-soldes*[3], that what is known as the 'battle of the walking-sticks' ensued and during that fierce fight the actors could communicate but little of the play. However what was heard infuriated the newspapers. *Le Constitutionnel* and *Le Drapeau blanc* pronounced *Germanicus* to be the work of an enemy agent with Talma acting as a willing

---

[1] Moreau, *Mémoires sur Talma*, pp. 61, 62.

[2] Mlle Flore, *Mémoires*, pp. 322–324.

[3] The *ultras* were the extreme royalists, the *demi-soldes* the Napoleonic officers retired on half-pay.

collaborator. Martainville in the *Journal de Paris* so mauled the play and its author that Lucien Arnault felt called upon to avenge his father's honour in a duel with the critic, who incurred, because of the intemperance of his pen, a very slight wound. The acting, even from Saint-Prix, Talma and Mlle Duchesnois, seemed hardly to count. The government immediately stepped in and suspended all further performances of *Germanicus*. What made Arnault's play memorable was the setting up at the theatre doors of a '*dépôt de cannes*' where all such objects had to be deposited, so that no repetition of single stick combat would ever disturb any future performance at the Comédie-Française.

While the rehearsals for *Germanicus* were in progress, Talma had made up his mind that, because of his financial position, he must free himself from the shackles of the Comédie and with liberty assured he could then make money in provincial France, in Belgium and in Switzerland without having to abide by the tiresome regulations of the société. It is not easy to find out what Talma really did earn at this period. Constant, Napoleon's valet, assures us in his *Mémoires*[1] that in 1804 Talma received an annual salary greater than that of a general and gave 60,000 francs as the sum, which included of course money gifts from Napoleon. It is known that Mlle Mars, a highly paid artist, drew at the height of her powers in 1831 55,000 francs a year.[2] If Talma earned in 1804 the sum quoted by Constant, it can be safely assumed that in 1817, with the theatre world at his feet, his earnings would be even more.

On March 20th he addressed a long letter to M. le duc de Duras,[3] *gentilhomme de la chambre du roi*, and asked for his retirement. He pointed out that he was getting on in years, that not only were his finances complicated but that all his earnings were in the control of a third party, without whose permission he could make no monetary transaction. He must at all costs free himself from such bondage.

'I will tell your Grace something more. In the course of my career, perhaps swayed too much by my own goodness of heart, I became of my own free will the sole support of my family. I have brought or am still bringing up six nephews and have other responsibilities with which I shall not weary you. All this puts upon me a heavy expenditure.'

---

[1] Constant, *Mémoires*, Vol. I, p. 329.
[2] E. de Manne, *La Troupe de Talma*, p. 211.
[3] Guy de la Batut, *Talma: Correspondance*, pp. 210–212.

He then came down to brass tacks. He wanted to draw his 'fonds sociaux', a sum of money deposited by a sociétaire in the care of the Comité and to which in the course of service substantial additions were made. Talma's anxiety lest this sum of money should fall into third party hands must have impressed the Duc de Duras. The actor's second point was a request for immediate leave of absence so that he could make up a considerable gap in his fortunes, caused by his numerous responsibilities for which his earnings in the theatre proved insufficient. If these two requests could be granted, he might even consider continuing his service with the Comédie-Français.

He did realize, he said, that the return of his *fonds sociaux* would prove a delicate business, difficult to negotiate. No such payment could be legally made except upon a sociétaire's retirement. This obstacle, Talma thought, could be surmounted by his withdrawal as a sociétaire and his re-engagement as a pensionnaire on a fixed salary basis. If he could draw this sum of money, he would promise to pay the annual interest upon that sum, namely 6,000 francs, so that the Comédie would suffer no pecuniary loss by its premature disbursement. He concluded his letter by reminding his Grace that jealousies existed in the theatre; that without any affectation or false modesty he knew as an actor he was still in possession of his powers and could therefore render useful service to the theatre.

The Duc de Duras had previously assured Talma that his letter would be submitted to the King. At first everything seemed as if Talma would get the money and the freedom he ardently desired. Unfortunately the sociétaires appear to have taken umbrage because Talma's initial request for retirement had not first been broached in their Comité. Better than anyone they knew Talma's worth and their own advantage to keep him bound to his contract. They began to temporize, to ask if he really wanted to retire, in fact to do anything rather than part with the money and the tragedian's services. Talma stood firm on his retirement. On November 27th, 1817, he would have completed a service of thirty years. It would be a wrench of course, *malgré nos légères discordances*, but if he were to go to the provinces he must go at once. Paris audiences would always be indulgent to an actor they had loved and grown up with; provincial playgoers had to be convinced by a taste of quality. 'I have indeed made up my mind.'

Succeeding letters reveal how acrimonious the matter had become. The sociétaires, out to drive a hard bargain, proposed, according to Talma, a very one-sided arrangement whereby they would retain his services for five years beyond the date of his retirement, with an annual congé, the first to last six months and the remaining four three months only. For a long time Talma had enjoyed an almost automatic three monthly leave which he nearly always contrived to extend to four. The new proposal seemed to offer him little and he objected to the arrangement, alleging that it had no legal basis and that while the sociétaires had him bound hand and foot they could at will dispense with his services. Difficult as Talma was showing himself in these negotiations, he dreaded lest the press should get wind of the details. He did not want to see his financial insolvency trumpeted all over Paris and rather naïvely added that such publicity might bring discredit upon the Théâtre-Français. In a further undated letter to his 'dear comrades', almost certainly written in November, 1818,[1] he brought up the question of his health 'very poor, very variable in spite of appearances', pointing out the great fatigue of playing tragic parts in high summer and expressing his doubts about being able to continue with the five-year plan. Warning symptoms made him fear a return of his serious nervous illness. His expenditure far exceeded his income, a terrible source of anxiety. 'I am certain, my dear colleagues, you would not wish, even if you felt you had the right, to keep me among you at the cost of my health, of my well-being, of my peace of mind and of all those who have a claim upon my care and help.' He noted that 'on the 27th of this month'[2] he would have completed his thirty-first year of service and he did not want to enter upon another year. If they required him for a few revivals of plays from the repertory, he would 'oblige' for a reasonable period. As for new plays, in them he could have no part. He went on to say that the reasons he adduced for his retirement were genuine and based upon *la plus exacte vérité*. The sociétaires must realize that only the most urgent causes had led him to cut himself off from their friendship and the public's favour.

Talma's proposed retirement, in a way rather like his divorce case, dragged on until 1820. All sorts of pettifogging details of a legal, quibbling kind were brought into the fray. Was the date of retirement to be based upon the anniversary of the début, November 27th, or must it be reckoned from April 1st, the date upon

[1] Guy de la Batut, *Talma: Correspondance*, pp. 221–224.
[2] November 27th, 1818.

which all actors' pensions were calculated? Behind all these squabbles lurked a harsh, intransigent personality; Chéron, the Commissaire, who had succeeded Bernard in the difficult task of 'controlling' the temperamental sociétaires, had already proved himself a man of battle. He had made things so difficult for Fleury that this brilliant actor had, in 1820, to cede his *emploi* to Damas under circumstances that brought from him the heartfelt cry *'J'en mourrai'*.[1] Such a man would stand no nonsense, not even from a Talma. Meanwhile Paris remained in ignorance of the true position at the Comédie-Française. What lent most colour to the actor's withdrawal from the national theatre was his absence from the cast of two new tragedies. D'Avrigny's *Jeanne d'Arc* and Ancelot's *Louis IX*, both performed in 1819, must have sorely tempted Talma who so long had advocated a 'national tragedy' founded upon the great events of French history. His old time rival Lafon snapped up both leads. Like Henry of Navarre he must often have asked if Paris was worth a mass. The payment he eventually received from the Comédie of a sum of 20,000 francs acted as a *douceur*. But the struggle continued. Talma, with each concession gained, to Chéron's fury increased his demands and went so far as to ask for two and a half shares as the price of his service. This request the sociétaires refused. Economically the Théâtre-Français could not support such a heavy salary for a single artist. Talma's equivocal position began to irk him. Touring certainly offered its triumphs but only Paris could set the seal of ultimate approval. Happily, what every actor finds irresistible, a fat part in a new play, this time by a comparatively new author, lured him back to the Comédie-Française in 1820. But we are taking time too much by the forelock. Let us step back to the morrow of *Germanicus*.

[1] 'It will kill me.' C. Maurice, *Histoire anecdotique*, Vol. I, p. 264.

CHAPTER 38

London Appearance, 1817

The crashing failure of Arnault's play sent Talma back to the North, where he proposed to play a season at Lille. Accompanied by Mlle Féart as his leading lady, he went to the provinces with five plays, *Manlius, Hamlet, Andromaque, Coriolan* and *Oedipe*. He chose the safe *Manlius* for his opening night in Lille, April 16th, and the next day played in *Hamlet*. The actor's arrival in Lille coincided with a period of civic unrest, not unconnected with the inspection then in progress by the Duke of Wellington of France's northern fortresses, of which Lille was a key point. The Lillois as good Frenchmen loathed Wellington, *le tyran de Cambrai*,[1] and showed little patience with what they regarded as the lickspittle Bourbon garrison. It was the old trouble of the ultras against the demi-soldes. Talma was indiscreet enough to get involved in these local squabbles.[2] As a true Bonapartiste he hated France's acceptance of foreign supervision and the humiliation of the heavy indemnity the Allies had imposed. In the *Journal des Débats*, April 30th, 1817, appeared the following paragraph: 'We learn on good authority that Talma was hissed at the Lille theatre on April 26th; this disagreeable experience befell him through causes entirely foreign to his acting ability; but these causes are not sufficiently known for us to comment upon them.' In any case, that government journal, fanatically devoted to the Bourbon cause, would be hardly likely to enlarge upon disturbances in Lille, possibly critical of the monarchy. It was however not unpleasing to record that an actor, known for his loyalty to Napoleon, had been publicly hissed. If the ultras had succeeded in voicing their protest during one particular performance, the citizens of Lille saw to it that Talma departed with all the customary rewards of a highly successful season.

The actor, anything but downcast, proceeded to Dunkirk,

[1] P. Guedalla, *The Duke*, p. 304.
[2] Léon Lefebre, *Histoire du Théâtre de Lille*, Vol. II, pp. 359–362, 390.

where four performances were staged, the last being *Oedipe* on May 4th. Then followed visits to St. Omer, Boulogne and Calais.

Talma decided to accept the English invitation to give readings of excerpts from his great successes in the King's Theatre, Haymarket, at the very height of the London season. The actor took pleasure in the thought of returning to the scenes of his youth. Whenever the political situation permitted, Talma had entertained English visitors to Paris with a lavish hand. When John Philip Kemble visited the city in 1803, Caroline Vanhove tells how her husband wanted to extend his house so that the English actor could be received in a manner appropriate to his eminence.[1] Now he would renew contact with his old friend, who had fixed his retirement from the stage for that very summer.

For this English adventure Talma persuaded Mlle George to join forces with him. A shrewd judge of any theatrical enterprise, he saw that Mlle George, somewhat notorious as the one time friend of Napoleon, would have across the Channel a very definite box-office value, to which the physically less favoured Mlle Duchesnois, better actress though she was, could hardly aspire. He would have Mlle Féart and M. Manivelle as supporting players.

This journey to London fitted in nicely with the conclusion of his tour, on which it would seem that Mlle Bazire and the two children accompanied him. Through the eyes of an anonymous Boulogne friend and admirer we get a delightful glimpse of the actor playing with his two babes on the carpet of a ground-floor suite at the Hôtel d'Europe.[2] Domestically he was care-free but nevertheless was somewhat worried by the smallness of the local theatre. Still he gave there a full-throated rendering of Oreste in *Andromaque*, which he followed the next day with *Hamlet*. The English colony turned out in force for the moody Dane and a certain '*vieux Chevalier B. . . .*' cried out in his enthusiasm: 'It is Garrick back from the dead.'[3] So insistent were the Boulonnais for an additional performance that Talma, delaying his departure for Calais by one day, acted *Manlius* and promised to return after his London engagement. With a jolt one passes from this eye-witness's account of the Boulogne performances to read in the *Journal de Paris*, May 22nd, 'Talma has been playing

[1] C. Talma, *Quelques particularités*, p. 305.
[2] H. d'Alméras, *Mémoires sur Talma*, p. 269.
[3] H. d'Alméras, *Mémoires sur Talma*, p. 277.

Andromaque and *Hamlet* in Boulogne. We are assured that this great actor did not arouse any keen emotion among the Boulonnais.' What is one to believe? Talma himself is reported to have said immediately the curtain fell on *Andromaque*: 'Tiredness has made me cold. They have received me coldly.' Then after that momentary silence, sure indication of an audience deeply moved, the house burst into applause and on all sides came cries of 'Talma! Talma!'

On to Calais. There with the same repertory Mlle Féart pleased the playgoers, who awarded her the same tributes as they heaped upon her incomparably greater partner.[1] On May 26th, Talma took the packet to fulfil his exciting English engagement.

Talma reached London on May 28th when, as the guest of Mr. Howard Payne, he was whisked off to Covent Garden Theatre. There in the foyer, where we are told he lingered long,[2] groups of people anxious to be presented to him learned from the tragedian's own lips in impeccable English how he was born in England and how delighted he was to visit the scenes of his youth. Everywhere he was right royally entertained. The English stage gave a banquet in his honour, at which a toast was drunk to the health of Mrs. Siddons and Mlle George.[3] Such a conjunction of stellar luminaries, one shining with purest ray serene, the other ruddily meteoric, must have aroused somewhere in that bohemian assembly a gentle, tolerant smile.

In London the summer of 1817 was exceptionally hot and the French actors must have harboured doubts as to the financial success of their venture in that blazing sunshine. However, London was unusually full and Queen Charlotte's Drawing Room on June 26th would round off the fashionable season. It says much for English tolerance that, two years after the Battle of Waterloo, London was prepared to welcome, and in the highest social circles of the capital, two French artists who had each been quite intimately associated with the exiled Napoleon. The French did not return the compliment to the English players who ventured upon a Paris stage in 1822.

On or about June 15th, 1817, Talma and Mlle George put up at Brunet's Hotel, Leicester Square. The London newspapers on June 16th and 17th announced a Grand Concert and Recitations

[1] *Journal de Paris*, May 30th, 1817.
[2] *Journal de Paris*, June 16th, 1817.
[3] *Journal de Paris*, 16th June, 1817.

292

for June 19th at the King's Theatre. Tickets of admission, each costing one guinea, could be obtained of M. Talma and Mlle George at their hotel or at the Opera office in the Haymarket. Certain box tickets could be had at £1 5s. od. Applications for seats were requested to be made as early as possible. True to the custom of the day, this Grand Concert was under the patronage of several highly distinguished personages. Music, vocal and instrumental, would be made by the great Mme Pasta and the renowned Signor Crevelli. Their efforts 'would be interspersed' with Recitations extracted from the most popular French tragedies of Racine, Voltaire, Corneille, Ducis and Lafosse.[1]

London's verdict upon Talma's acting has a particular interest. It must be remembered that he was deprived of all those illusions that a full-dress performance in a theatre can provide. As actors say, he opened cold. Here spoke the dramatic critic of *The Times*, June 20th:

The recitations of M. Talma and Mlle Georges [sic] in the concert room of this theatre last night drew a crowded and brilliant audience and excited the most extraordinary expectations. These expectations, high as they had been raised, were more than fulfilled. There was, we believe, but one sentiment of admiration, raised in every person present, mingled with that species of interest and gratification which arises from witnessing an exhibition of excellency not more admirable than it is new. The face of Mlle Georges is handsome and unites grandeur with softness. . . . Of M. Talma's acting we can hardly speak highly enough. Neither his face nor person is much in his favour; the one is flat and round, the other thick and short; nor has his voice much to boast of except a manly strength and depth. He owes everything to the justness of his conception and to the energy of his execution. His acting displays the utmost force of passion, regulated by the clearest judgment. It is the triumph of art but of art still prompted and impelled and kindled into the very frenzy of enthusiasm by the inspiration of nature and genius. The declamation in his performance is scarcely attended to; the measure of the verse is entirely subordinate to the expression, whether slower or quicker, deeper or more vehement, of thought and feeling. In some parts he was electrical, in all impressive and admirable. In Manlius, in Oedipus and in Orestes he equally shewed the master of his art. We shall take the earliest opportunity of referring to some of the particular passages which most forcibly arrested our attention and called forth the enthusiastic plaudits of the audience.

The *Times* critic, in spite of his high note of eulogy, seemed

[1] *The Times*, June 16th, 1817, Advt.

unimpressed by Talma's physical appearance and by the quality of his voice. At fifty-four one can hardly expect to look like a *jeune premier*. With this reservation made, the writer fell completely under the spell of the actor's vital and imaginative playing. In some ways the *Morning Post* of the same day offers the more interesting comment. It very pertinently implied that English acting, when set beside the flamboyance of Gallic transports, must appear a trifle pallid—possibly an understatement as regards the passionately conceived and mannered French style. Surely this is a vital point. Could Irving have permitted himself the extravagances of Mounet-Sully? Could Ellen Terry have treated herself to the showmanship of Sarah Bernhardt? Can John Gielgud indulge in the flamboyance of Jean-Louis Barrault's Hamlet or Peggy Ashcroft in that amplitude of gesture a Frenchman associates with the playing of Marie Bell? When such odious comparisons are made, the continental player tends to appear in English eyes a little larger than life and our critics, not always conversant with the foreign language, so often award excessive praise to his efforts. This is what the *Morning Post* had to say about Talma's performance.

But the grand attraction of the evening was the appearance of Talma and Mlle Georges [sic] in several characters in scenes taken from celebrated French plays. Talma appeared in two scenes from *Manlius Capitolinus* of De La Fosse, the story of which is found in our *Venice Preserved*; in two scenes from the *Oedipe* of Voltaire and in the fourth and fifth acts of *Andromaque* of Racine. In the scenes selected from Voltaire and Racine, Mlle Georges acted with him who also came forward as the principal character of another play by the last mentioned author, *Phèdre*, with a scene from which the performance commenced. In all they undertook they were honoured with the universal applause of a most numerous and splendid assembly: but it was in the scenes from *Oedipe* and *Andromaque* where they acted up to each other that they were most applauded. . . .

The great powers of Talma shone forth with peculiar splendour in every scene. The uninterrupted attention he gives to the business of the stage, and the vivid flashes of feeling which accompany his brilliant declamation, make it impossible for the lover of theatrical merit not to be highly gratified by his exertions. But as there are some plants peculiar to every country, so there are delineations of character in every part of the world, which cannot be transplanted to another soil. Talma finely displayed the despair of Orestes; but had the same noddings and shakings of the head and slappings of the knees, which were deservedly admired in Talma, been ventured upon by an English Orestes, we doubt if the audience would have refrained from laughter. He presented a most interesting picture of wild emotion but it was produced by means to which few English actors could safely resort. For such are the differences between neighbours in matters of taste, that what would seem natural and dignified on one side of the Channel, would be thought extravagance and insanity on the other. Thus on our stage should a performer have to repeat the words 'I am rendered immovable; I know not where I am; my rage has subsided;' he would be very likely to remain riveted to one spot while he uttered them. When Talma as Oedipus came to the speech which begins thus,

> *Ces derniers mots me rendent immobile,*
> *Je ne sais où je suis, ma fureur est tranquille,*

he rushed off the stage as he pronounced the word *'immobile'* and after a lapse of several seconds returned to proceed with the succeeding line. This may be easily explained and we only notice it to mark the varieties of manner which distinguish the two nations, if we are justified in taking up so trifling an incident for such a purpose. In commenting upon some of the peculiarities of M. Talma we are far from wishing to detract from the value of talents like his, which have gained him universal admiration in his own country, and which cannot fail to entitle him to the praise of all the liberal, the polite and the discerning in this.

After a few lines on Mlle George's embonpoint and expressive countenance, the critic continued:

Talma boasts a good figure, a full face which, illumined by a fine eye, is capable of working terrific emotion with prodigious effect, and which is also equal to the portraiture of animated dignity and fervent love.

What conflicting accounts are given of Talma's physical appearance! At one and the same performance, the critics of two important newspapers formed almost diametrically opposed opinions.

The success, both financial and social, achieved at the King's Theatre called for a second Concert with a change of programme on June 26th. Mlle George, in a city where Sarah Siddons had made theatrical history as Lady Macbeth, was imprudent enough to advertise in its press that her assumption of this rôle would produce an extraordinary effect. As this Grand Concert clashed with Queen Charlotte's Drawing Room, proceedings in the Haymarket had to start at nine instead of seven o'clock, with the result that the next morning the French actors' efforts received scant attention from the newspapers, which devoted their columns to describing the dresses of the ladies at the Drawing Room. The *Morning Post* accorded one sentence. 'At the King's Theatre the performances of Talma and Miss [*sic*] Georges were as before crowned with universal applause.' *The Times* did better.[1] 'The performances at the Opera House finished at too late an hour on Thursday night to allow of our saying anything about them in yesterday's paper. We must however seize a little space in our journal today to express the exquisite pleasure which we derived from the recitations generally: but in the passages from *Philoctète* Talma's acting was greater than we can possibly describe: he really penetrated us with horror at the description which he gave, and the semblance he afforded, of a man left wounded, betrayed and forlorn on a desolate island. Mlle Georges was, we think, most happy in the part of Athalie; we wish Md. Georges herself could see Mrs. Siddons in Lady Macbeth.'

Crabb Robinson saw this second performance and in the germanophile's diary[2] occurs this entry for June 26th, 1817:

I took a hasty cup of tea at Collier's and went to the Opera House Concert Room and heard Talma and Mlle Georges recite. I grudged a guinea for payment but I do not regret having gone. Talma performed a scene out of La Harpe's *Philoctète* and out of *Iphigenia in Tauris*. His first appearance disappointed me. He has little grey eyes too near each other and, though a regular and good face, not a striking one. His voice is good but not particularly sweet. His excellence lies in the imitation of intense suffering. He filled me with horror certainly as Philoctète but it was mingled with disgust. Bodily pain is no fit or legitimate subject for drama; and too often he was merely a man suffering from a sore leg. Of his declamation I do not presume to judge. The character of Orestes affords finer opportunities for display. The terror he feels when pursued by the Furies was powerfully communicated and his tenderness towards Pylades on parting was also exquisite. Mlle Georges had more to do but she gave me far less pleasure. Her acting I thought radically bad. . . . If in the same line the words '*crainte*' and '*joie*' occur, she apes fear and joy by outrageous pantomime. . . . Her acting appeared to me to be utterly without feeling.

So much for English opinions on Talma and Mlle George. During their stay in London they received high favours and much

---

[1] *The Times*, June 28th, 1817.
[2] Crabb Robinson, *Diary, Reminiscences and Correspondence*, Vol. I, p. 452.

hospitality from the nobility. The Duke of Devonshire lent Mlle George the keys of his private boxes at Drury Lane and at Covent Garden so that she and Talma could witness, among other performances, John Philip Kemble in *Macbeth* on June 16th and his farewell as Coriolanus on June 23rd. Members of the Royal Family, the Duke and Duchess of Gloucester, the Duchesses of York and Cumberland, had graciously accorded their patronage to the Haymarket Concerts.[1]

Perhaps the social engagement Talma most valued was the pressing invitation to attend Kemble's farewell banquet, which took place in the Freemasons' Tavern, Queen Street, Holborn, on Friday, June 27th, with Lord Holland presiding over a most distinguished company. When the noble chairman rose to propose a toast to M. Talma, there was enthusiastic applause. His Lordship was happy, he said, that they had an actor from a neighbouring nation in their midst and that they were all eager to express their gratification at such a circumstance. He would therefore propose the health of M. Talma and success to the French stage. Talma replied in English. 'Gentlemen, it is impossible for a foreign tongue to express my warm gratitude for the hospitable way in which you have this day received me, (applause) and the honour you have done in my person to the French stage. To be thought worthy of notice on an occasion consecrated to my dear friend Mr. Kemble (shouts of applause) I estimate as one of the highest honours of my life. As I cannot thank you with my words, you will I hope suffer me to thank you with my heart. (Plaudits.) Gentlemen, permit me to drink success to the British nation and to the British stage.' (Thunders of applause.) The account continued: 'These last words, delivered in a clear and powerful voice, with great boldness of utterance and much vehemence of action, had a most surprising effect on the company.'[2] Even in a brief after dinner speech, delivered in a foreign language, Talma's equipment as an actor—voice, vigour and power to sway the listener—was manifest.

Talma little dreamed that his friendly words, uttered on a convivial occasion, would cause him embarrassment on his return to Paris. Of course his request for retirement had not made him popular in the green room, where jealous enemies had been busy

[1] Moreau, *Mémoires sur Talma*, pp. 62, 63.

[2] *Observations on Mr. Kemble and An Account of the Dinner given at Freemasons Tavern*, 1817.

spreading calumny, from the serious charge of traitorous association with the enemy to the petty accusation of smuggling English
goods into France. In a letter addressed to the editor of the *Journal
de Paris*, dated August 2nd, 1817, Talma quickly disposed of the
petty contraband accusation, but the misrepresentation of his
speech at the Freemasons' Tavern called for a longer and more
dignified rebuttal. Thus he answered:[1]

After Mr John Kemble's final performance this leading actor of the
English stage, as rightly esteemed for his noble character as for his
exceptional talents, was honoured by a farewell dinner given by his
friends and admirers who had come together to show him in a truly
remarkable manner their esteem and their regrets at his retirement;
members of the nobility, artists, *savants* and the most distinguished
men of letters were present at this reunion; in accordance with the
English custom toasts were proposed; in the midst of some four hundred guests I was singled out for a particular distinction. The noble lord
proposed a toast in my honour and to the glory of the French stage;
I made reply with a few phrases which were graciously received and in
which I conveyed my gratitude for the kind reception they had been
good enough to accord me and added my wishes for the prosperity of
the English theatre. This polite reply was to some extent a social duty
at which the most rigid upholder of the proprieties could not cavil.

A few English newspapers, which failed to report these extempore
speeches with scrupulous accuracy, did not render mine any more
textually correct than the others and the French rags, by their trans-
lations, showed no greater fidelity.

To add a political slant to the toast which I proposed in the midst of
persons come together to honour the arts and in particular my own
profession would have been, to say the least, a stupid blunder: to forget
in such circumstances that I was a Frenchman would have been more
than mere absentmindedness, and such a lapse from seemly behaviour
would have been tacitly condemned even by those to whom my reply
was addressed.

I take pleasure in making known the truly fraternal reception I
received from the London actors, the flattering favours and friendly
consideration that came my way from the highest classes of society;
but the deep gratitude I retain for these tokens of affection and esteem
(which do honour to the French stage as much as to myself) never made
me nor will ever make me forget that undivided love, that particular
attachment which every well born man must feel for the country of his
birth.

This surely is a dignified reply. In that London atmosphere

[1] Guy de la Batut, *Talma: Correspondance*, pp. 202–204.

Talma felt happy, expansive. Ever a generous soul, his wishes for 'the success of the British nation' sprang spontaneously from the heart without any hint of political flattery or other ulterior motive. If he silenced his persecutors, they could not deny his resounding professional success in London and in the cities of northern France, all of which of course merely added fuel to the fires of jealousy. Things were distinctly difficult for Talma at the Comédie-Française. Another *congé*. This time he went off to Bordeaux, where in October he wrote to Mme Ducis in Paris assuring her that he was still alive and that he intended to defer his death until the very last possible moment. Business was wonderful, the Bordelais delightfully appreciative and only a slight chronic affection of the ear stood in the way of complete bliss.[1] After Bordeaux, Toulouse opened its purse. At Béziers, through which the actor had merely intended to pass, his coach was forcibly halted so that the townsfolk could see him act. Nîmes had to be cut out but Marseilles acclaimed him. Everywhere admiring audiences, garlands, verses and, more precious than all besides, some ready money.

[1] Guy de la Batut, *Talma: Correspondance*, pp. 201, 202.

CHAPTER 39

Lamartine Calls on Talma

Talma's tour of the Midi came to an end on January 18th and he returned to a Comédie-Française exasperated with him, not only for so flagrantly abusing his *congé* but also for what they considered to be a dog in the manger attitude over the question of his retirement. On financial grounds alone his appearance in any of his great classical rôles would always prove welcome. Even Chéron, knowing the difference between packed houses and thinly sprinkled benches, was prepared to be a little more tractable. In addition to Manlius, Oreste, Oedipe and Néron, Talma had recently turned his attention once more to *Athalie*.

When Napoleon encouraged the revival of this fine biblical tragedy Talma, no doubt imbued with the warlike spirit of that generation, saw himself as a dashing military officer in the character of Abner. Tissot, an intimate and longstanding friend of the actor and whose '*souvenirs historiques*' of Talma were compiled immediately after the tragedian's death, has left a most vivid account of Talma in his newly assumed part of Joad the High Priest, that implacable enemy of Jezebel's idolatrous daughter. Perhaps Talma, with his uncanny sense of audience reaction, thought that Abner no longer appealed to a generation which had rewarded the heroic Napoleonic soldier with the pinch of penury. Again, his own years and maturity—fifty-five in 1818— led him to see in Joad a more satisfying rôle. Tissot in his recollections, after enumerating the great services Talma had rendered to the plays of Corneille and Racine, went on to say:[1]

The new method adopted by Talma was even more noticeable when he undertook to act Joad. Instead of applying Corneille's pomp to the poetry of Racine, he gave its natural beauty full play and in no way broke the spell of its harmony. What a religious note he struck when he first appeared! How fervently he urged Abner to defend God and

[1] Tissot, *Souvenirs historiques de Talma*, pp. 30, 31.

the House of David! How burning was his fanatical intolerance of
Mathan, his hatred rival! What tender counsel he gave to the young
prince about to mount the throne! It seemed as if he had caught the
very soul of Brizard, an actor so moving and one he could have seen,
like the rest of us, only in his fading sunset! What exaltation he poured
into his inspired prophecies! What a plucking at the heart and mind!
What overwhelming joy at the vision of the new Jerusalem! What
grief he conjured up as he saw through the future's veil the City's
later disasters! It was just as if immediate truth had overwhelmed his
heart. And what wrath was reserved for Jezebel's guilty daughter!
Talma played his part with integrity, just as Racine had written it. The
effect he created, deriving from the poet's own genius, was at the same
time a lesson for actors and dramatists, instructing both how to draw
from the human heart a moral lesson on the stage. Talma's declamation
and acting of Joad deserves to stand as a model for all time.

This was indeed high praise. Let it not be forgotten that Tissot
reveals himself a sure guide to Talma's later performances, when
the actor wore his years of experience and study like a shining
garment. So many of his colleagues had waited for a decline in
his powers that never came. Talma went on triumphantly, sustained by his faith that to French tragedy he could bring an actor's
fuller and more living conception. Tissot's exact words deserve
to be noted. '*Talma jouait ce rôle de bonne foi.*' The dishonesty of the
cabotin must have no part in his playing; *de bonne foi*, only integrity
mattered.

With a life so vivid in the theatre, Talma often eludes a
biographer where the domestic details of his daily life are concerned. It is with particular gratitude that one savours the
delightful account of the poet Alphonse de Lamartine, who paid
a visit to Talma in the spring of 1818 at 14, rue de Rivoli,[1] where
the actor had set up house with his young family the previous
year. The future author of *Les Méditations*, then a young man in his
twenties, tells how on a fine spring day he set out from his
Burgundian home for Paris, carrying in his valise three carefully
copied out tragedies, of which a biblical effort entitled *Saül* bore
his highest hopes. Upon arrival in the capital he went to the
Théâtre-Français, where he obtained Talma's address; there he
delivered an elegantly written and sealed request that the great
actor would accord him the favour of reading *Saül*. The poet had
not long to wait for a reply which a servant '*en riche livrée de*

[1] Lamartine, *Cours familier de littérature*, III, *Entretien* 14, pp. 86–103. Lamartine
gave 16 or 26; A. Antoine said 14.

fantaisie'—what a lovely sidelight on Talma's vanity and extrava-gance!—brought to his humble lodging in the rue Neuve-Saint-Augustin. That night the actor was playing *Britannicus* and indicated his departure at midday on the morrow for Brunoy, but if his young friend would not be disturbed by too early an appointment he would listen with interest to a reading of *Saül* at eight o'clock the next morning.

Lamartine appeared punctually at Talma's door, which a very beautiful woman opened to him. This '*très belle femme*', from what subsequently transpired, must have been Madeleine-Jacqueline Bazire. 'She wore a cotton wrap with blue flowers, her hair hung over her Clytemnestra neck and the looseness of her belt let me glimpse shoulders and a bosom worthy of some antique statue. Her features showed strength but her expression was kind; her glances, like black velvet shadows, spread over her cheeks. She half smiled as she looked at me but there was no malice in her smile; one could see that she was quite accustomed to ushering in dreams and showing out vain hopes.'

When the poet had established his identity, '*Entrez, monsieur*', she said. Then opening another door, '*Mon ami*', she called out to Talma in caressing yet familiar tones, 'here is the young man you asked me to admit'. Then, gathering up the folds of her dressing-gown, and trailing her slippers, she disappeared. A neat sketch of a reception in a bohemian household.

Then Lamartine stood in Talma's presence. For us his descrip-tion of the tragedian has a documentary value. 'Talma was at that time a heavily built man but very noble in his strength, a man between fifty and sixty. He wore a white silk dressing-gown, slackly bound by a foulard scarf which served as a belt. His neck was bare and one could see his swelling throat with prominent muscles and strongly marked veins, signs of a solid frame and virile energy. His face, which everyone knows, was already deeply graven, recalling by its shape and complexion the imperial bronzes of the Byzantine Empire. But this Roman mask, which seemed imposed upon his features when he was on the stage, fell of its own accord when he was *en déshabillé* and let one see only a wide expanse of face, big gentle eyes, a sad finely drawn mouth, cheeks, inclined slightly to fall away and a little flabby, his facial muscles slack like the untensed springs of some tool. The whole effect of his face was imposing, its expression simple and attractive. One sensed a generous nature beneath his wonderful genius. He sought after no effect; he had enough of that on the stage; he relaxed and at home seemed to be resting his eyes. At once I felt at ease and touched to the heart by the kindness of that face, at once commanding and sincere.'

Lamartine read his play to an attentive, non-committal Talma. At the end Talma rose from his chair and with an affectionate smile said: 'Young man, I wish I could have known you twenty years ago. You would have been my poet. Now it is too late. You are entering the world, I am departing. Your verses are really verses. Your play is well conceived and well constructed. There are scenes capable of producing a great effect and, with a few corrections which I will indicate later, I will make myself responsible for its reception, for playing the leading part and for its success. Here and there is a little too much youth, too much poetic declamation at the expense of dramatic art. That is nothing, merely a few leaves to cut off so that the fruit may form and ripen.'

When he heard from Lamartine of the young man's hopes and struggles, of his ambition to succeed as a dramatist, Talma's eyes filled with tears. He rang. '*Que veux-tu, mon ami?*' asked the now very elegant lady of the house. Breakfast was ordered, a simple meal of eggs and chocolate. After kissing Talma and with a bow to Lamartine, Madeline-Jacqueline Bazire sallied forth until noon. Left alone, the two men discussed poetry and nature, with Talma insisting that his young friend must come and visit him often at *Mon Plaisir*. 'Brunoy will always be open to you. I love the country and always feel better when I am in my woods.' In the course of this conversation, which embraced French tragedy in general, the merits of Corneille and Racine and that 'man of modern genius, Shakespeare', Talma is credited with having said: 'Corneille is heroism, Racine is poetry. Shakespeare is drama. Through him I have become what I am.'

Like a whirlwind in came Mlle Duchesnois. She had the run of the house and entered Talma's study unannounced. 'She was tall, thin, pale and very ugly, with a few touches of coquetry applied to her eyes and cheeks. With a disgusted gesture she threw down her old, silk-trimmed hat, revealing long black hair swathed in bands like a diadem upon her brow.' She was enraged with her colleagues for some real or imagined wrong. (It is known that she wanted another congé, but the astute Chéron had succeeded in getting all sociétaires, except Mlle Mars and Talma, to agree to a self-denying ordinance of no congés for at least two years.[1]) 'That cannot last, that shall not last,' she stormed, all oblivious of young Lamartine, as she threatened the *gentilhomme de la chambre* with a vindictive courage worthy of a Medea. Talma poured oil upon the troubled waters and reminded the actress that the young man in her presence had been reared in Bourbon tradition. Poor Duchesnois! She became all contrition, begging for Lamartine's sympathy. 'I also am a queen and I cannot endure the humiliations they heap upon me.'

Lamartine, after this visit—the truth of which can be checked in every detail—went to Brunoy, but he did not pursue his theatrical dreams. Soon afterwards he set out for the Alps where new scenes, new impressions and a new love inspired thoughts that could be set down only with the intense subjectivity that the lyric muse could permit.

While relations over his persistently demanded retirement remained so prickly with Chéron and his colleagues, Talma found peace at *Mon Plaisir*. Here at least he escaped from the cares of the theatre and the dunning of creditors. In 1817 he had engaged a quite remarkable gardener, Père Louette, who stayed with his master until his death. To Louette we are indebted for a very interesting account of Talma's horticultural activities which, published in the *Revue de Paris*, September 1829, throws a wholly charming light upon his dealings with the actor. 'He was not a master, he was my friend,' wrote Louette. This country house, which Talma bought at the turn of the century, then had a garden of one acre; by constant additions, in Louette's day, the grounds covered an area of sixty-five acres. Here Talma, *'en sabots et en blouse'*, indulged his dreams of nature. If the grounds were extended, so was the house. His architect, Duponchel, was constantly called upon to add a wing, to throw out a room, to put in a staircase *'à la moderne'*,[2] to deflect a stream, to provide an impressive, wrought-iron gateway. Ten thousand francs was a very ordinary bill. Louette saw not only the gratified landed proprietor but the generous family man, as eager to help the surrounding poor as he was to provide Lucullan hospitality for his Parisian friends. No wonder he remarked: 'M. Talma brought up a large family.'

In this vast garden master and man could only find each other

---

[1] E. D. de Manne, *La Troupe de Talma*, pp. 281, 282, 283.

[2] C. Talma, *Quelques particularités sur la vie de Talma*, p. 303.

by means of the whistle each carried. Talma had not the sole right to whistle Louette; the gardener insisted, like a true son of the Revolution, he must be able to whistle his master. Talma of course agreed. Louette reveals a Talma sharing a dish of *pot au feu* in his gardener's cottage, pronouncing that there must be no poor in Brunoy. He, *'le boulanger'*, would see to that! 'M. Talma was so good that I would have served him for the sheer pleasure of carrying out his orders.'[1] Could any master receive a better testimonial? There is one charming incident when Louette came to Paris to Paris to purchase sand, then in short supply, for their garden paths. The same evening Louette was to report to his master at the Théâtre-Français the result of his efforts. When he arrived Talma, made up as Néron, was waiting in the wings. Eagerly he met the gardener. 'Shall we get the sand?' Louette, who had never seen his master so awfully arrayed, merely gasped, unable to utter a word!

The arcady of Brunoy, soothing as its woods and stream must have been to a financially harassed Talma, could not wholly distract him from the ding-dong struggle over his retirement. As has already been seen, he would withdraw his ultimatum, then seek new concessions, shift his ground and create fresh dispute. The plays of the established repertory he still worked at, studying, polishing, perfecting. Relations with the new Court, in so far as a mere actor could penetrate the rarefied, semi-divine surroundings of a Bourbon King, were not uncordial and, throughout his dealings with the sociétaires, Talma always claimed to count upon the benevolence of the Royal Family, to which he professed a devotion that allowed no possible doubt.[2] Yet his Bonapartiste sympathies were all too well known and he showed little patience with the reactionary 'Throne-and-Altar' clericalism of the day. Surprisingly enough, in the early days of February, 1819, Talma in full masonic regalia, accompanied by Mlle Duchesnois *'en costume de bal'*, took a prominent part in a meeting of the Belle et Bonne Lodge, of which he was a member and which was presided over by Mme de Villette, a niece of Voltaire. The occasion attracted much attention because during the ceremonies the two players recited the fourth act of *Oedipe* before the statue of Voltaire.[3] The incident deserves record. At the very least it shows Talma a man

---

[1] *Revue de Paris*, September 1829.
[2] E. D. de Manne, *La Troupe de Talma*, p. 113.
[3] C. Maurice, *Histoire anecdotique du théâtre*, Vol. I, 242, 243.

of robust independence of mind and true to the Voltairean traditions of the Revolution. A trimmer would have walked more warily.

With no new plays to stimulate his creative faculties Talma took advantage of the retiring Mme Thénard's benefit performance to revive Saurin's *'drame bourgeois' Beverley* (1768),[1] a rather old-fashioned variant of Edward Moore's *The Gamester*, which was first played in London in 1753 with such success that the play later attracted the attention of Garrick, who considerably prolonged its life on the English stage. In France Saurin's version had not been acted since Molé's death. On this night of February 13th, 1819, Talma and Mlle Mars appeared as the gamester and his wife. No doubt the idea of playing a gambler appealed to Talma, who would have no difficulty in projecting himself into all the moods and emotions that the hazards of the card table could inspire. Unfortunately, even upon so indulgent an occasion, *Beverley* proved an utter frost; 'the glacial silence of the public, interrupted only once by an outburst of applause which Talma clearly forced revealed how ill-advised he and Mlle Mars had been to lend their talents to such an out-moded play.' The part of Beverley must be set down as one of Talma's failures. Perhaps his own more naturalistic approach to the part than Larive's had been, may have emphasized the play's age and artificiality. Altogether it was a disastrous evening. The inclusion of a comic opera in the programme, as well as a comedy in which Mlle Duchesnois of all people had a part, stretched proceedings almost to breaking point. A public ill-rewarded for its attendance at inflated prices drew little comfort from the news that the one and only beneficiary, Mme Thénard, had netted 16,000 francs. Benefits seemed to be in the air, and on March 8th Talma was accorded such an honour, preliminary to yet another prolonged provincial tour. The occasion is interesting because he himself elected to appear as Joad in Racine's *Athalie*, a part which, while extraordinarily effective in his hands, imposed upon him nothing like the strain of Oedipe or Oreste. From this time Joad was to take its place alongside Talma's major achievements.

Before we leave this year of wandering and wrangles, mention should be made of Talma's appointment as an official examiner, when late in the year the Odéon invited applications from candidates desirous of entering the second Théâtre-Français. This

---

[1] E. D. de Manne, *La Troupe de Talma*, pp. 46, 47. C. Maurice, Vol. I, p. 243.

assignment gives some indication of a rapprochement between the actor and his fellow sociétaires. For this particular test Lafon had prepared a really brilliant young actor, Frédérick Lemaître, who, although he received Talma's vote of approval, was rejected by all other members of the tribunal. Intuitively Talma saw the flash of Lemaître's genius. A little testily he admonished his fellow examiners. 'You were wrong to reject that young man, for he possesses fine qualities that cannot be acquired, beauty, intelligence, the sacred fire. . . . By spurning him, you are condemning him to fall back on melodrama and farce.'[1] Time proved Talma right. Frédérick Lemaître, though driven from the national stages, made history in the boulevard theatres when the new romantic drama of Hugo, Dumas and Vigny found its ideal exponent in this fiery, splendid actor.

[1] Robert Baldick, *Life and Times of Frédérick Lemaître*, p. 32.

CHAPTER 40

'Marie Stuart'

In some respects Talma was an extraordinarily lucky actor. At the moments of real crisis in his career, when jealous enemies inside the Comédie-Française might have consigned him, if not to oblivion, at least to a lowly place, a striking success restored him at one bound to public favour. *Charles IX* had rescued him from a round of insignificant parts which senior colleagues would have imposed upon him for a very long time; *Manlius* had routed the Raucourt-Lafon cabal; Raynouard's *Les Templiers* had removed all possible doubts about his pre-eminence and had set him firmly upon his pedestal as the greatest tragic actor of his day. After the wranglings over retirement and a self-imposed partial eclipse, Talma undertook on March 6th, 1820, his first new part since the ill-fated *Germanicus* of 1817. Such a gap was longer than its counted years. Talma could not afford to be relegated to a mere repetition of his classic successes. That Pierre Lebrun, who had provided on the morrow of the Bourbon restoration a made-to-measure, conventional *Ulysse*, had now come forward with a free adaptation of Schiller's *Maria Stuart*, then unknown to the French stage. With his *Marie Stuart* Lebrun fancied himself quite the innovator. By setting his play in the sixteenth century, where it rightly belonged, he had crossed the tragic frontiers of the antique world; leaning heavily upon the German poet, he had created a hero by no means cast in the uniformly noble mould, but a man who vacillated, even cringed, in base self-interest as love fought out its duel with political power. Leycester presented an acting problem that few tragedians of that day would have wanted to solve. The central situation, the meeting of Mary and Elizabeth, quite unwarranted historically, with Leycester caught between the two fires, had in the German original a certain marrowy strength which Lebrun had taken every care to preserve. Mlle Duchesnois jumped at the rôle of Marie Stuart. To communicate the royal dignity and the disdainful pride of Elizabeth, the exponent should have been Mlle George, who unfortunately had left the Théâtre-Français on May 8th, 1818. A young actress, Mlle Paradol, played the part, which ranked as the greatest of her not too distinguished career.

Triumphantly as the first night ended, the play with its unconventional hero aroused doubts in the parterre that might very easily have become hostile. To make Leycester acceptable to a French audience, the whitewash brush had to be applied. Eyewitnesses noted that during the early scenes, especially when Leycester ordered the guards to arrest Mortimer, some of the spectators showed an ominous restlessness, which the actor, by sheer imposition of his personality, his authority and the intensity of his playing, quelled,[1] 'just as a toothache is cured by pulling out the offending molar'.[2] A grateful author has set down his admiration of Talma's acting in the great encounter between the two queens. 'In the final scene of the play, at the very last verse when the fatal axe falls, Talma cries "*Ah! je meurs*"; that classical "*Ah*" in his rendering became a "*Han*" which seemed to conjure up the executioner. This terrible "*Han*", hitherto unheard in tragedy, completely upset the purists.'[3] Mlle Duchesnois, deeply moving as the Scottish queen, gave Talma all possible support, leaving nothing to be desired. On that first performance one of those unexpected little incidents gripped the audience. As Marie went to the block, the executioner tossed back her lovely dark tresses only to reveal the underlying grey hair, which gave an added touch of heart-breaking drama to an already poignant scene.

The play was a huge success and ran for fifty performances. Martainville in the *Journal de Paris* said briefly what every critic at greater length pronounced. 'As for Talma and Mlle Duchesnois, what advice could I possibly give them? The first acts the part of Leycester with an art unsurpassed in its very depth and Mlle Duchesnois, especially in the fifth act, carries pathos to its highest degree.'[4] The author's manuscript was immediately bought for publication by Barba and Ladvocat for 4,000 francs. Altogether *Marie Stuart* brought Talma back in triumph as *chef d'emploi* at the Théâtre-Français. The play lingered long in the repertory, for the great Rachel some twenty years later bestowed upon it the glory of her genius.

[1] Moreau, pp. 68, 69.   [2] Pierre Lebrun *Oeuvres, Préface*, p. xxv.
[3] *Journal de Paris*, March 17th, 1820.   [4] *Journal de Paris*, March 17th, 1820.

With all Paris crowding to *Marie Stuart*, Chéron, the forceful Commissaire, was not going to have it all his own way. He might get rid of Fleury in characteristically shabby fashion, but Talma was a tougher proposition. The tragedian pressed home his advantage. What about those two shares and a half?[1] On this score Chéron could command support in refusing what he regarded as an outrageous demand. Talma's reply was to take another congé. Late April found him at Rouen, an excellent town theatrically, rather like our own Manchester, a place where money could be made. Thence he proceeded to tour Belgium where in Brussels during May he gave performances of *Manlius* with a new fifth act written by himself. Some critics in Paris expressed strong disapproval of what they regarded as sacrilege. 'Talma is acting in Brussels. He has just corrected Lafosse, changing the dénouement of *Manlius*. Because this temerity has achieved great success, a local journalist advises him to let us see it here in Paris. If the tragedian takes my advice, he will not mutilate in our presence, when he returns, that statue from a pretty good sculptor.'[2]

As far as his actual *rentrée* was concerned, Talma took the hint. He chose *Oedipe* for his opening night at the Théâtre-Français on July 20th, and just to remind us of old scores, if 'the ranks of Tuscany could scarce forbear a cheer' they still clung to a few brickbats as well. 'Talma's return this evening won him great applause. The part of Oedipe is one of those where his tragic powers shine in a high degree. Heroes pursued by the Fates find in him a worthy representative. His eyes indict heaven with a rare eloquence, and no one better than he knows how to give to his whole bearing that mood of despair and of dejection which springs from terror and pity. It is an excess of this power that sometimes leads him to monotony; he emerges with difficulty from prostration when that mood possesses him; but when he bursts forth from this constraining emotion which he narrows too closely he is sublime. Thus, only yesterday, did he have admirable touches of inspiration in *Oedipe*. Never shall we hear better rendered nor in a more noble and natural way

> *Et je ne conçois pas par quel enchantement*
> *J'oubliais jusqu'ici ce grand événement.*[3]

---

[1] A. Augustin-Thierry, *Le Tragédien de Napoléon, Le Temps*, June 3rd, 1938.
[2] C. Maurice, *Histoire anecdotique du Théâtre*, Vol. I, p. 256.
[3] 'And I cannot think by what spell
  Did I forget ere now this great event.' *Oedipe*, Act II, sc. i.

These few words perfectly associate the audience in that search for memories that the character invokes.'[1]

Any glimpse, however fleeting, of Talma at rehearsal has its value. We are told that in this year of 1820 he brought to his work none of the casual lightness of the actor whose interest in the performance is strictly limited to his own part, and who, when not required for his lines, idles and laughs his time away. 'Talma on the contrary takes his responsibilities seriously. Like Fleury and the brothers Baptiste, he studies his part well in advance and the night before a performance, even of plays from the repertory, he is visible to no one. He does everything possible to keep his memory alert. With play-book in hand, he brings it close to his face because of his myopia, reads, mentally recites or walks up and down, and no one would dream of disturbing him by even so much as a glance, let alone a word. Sometimes, with a dreamy look which comes from committing lines to memory, he walks up to someone, fixes upon him his deep eyes, shows clearly but quite unconsciously that he is thinking of something else, goes away slowly to wait for his cue, which he listens for with scrupulous attention.'[2] As ever, even in his off moments, the dedicated artist.

Occasionally the theatre can become the rallying point of popular emotion, a sounding board from which strange vibrations may stir the imagination of the crowd. That popular theatre-loving prince, the Duc de Berri, had been assassinated on February 13th, 1820, while handing his wife into her carriage at the door of the Opéra. In September, the posthumous son of the murdered duke, '*l'enfant du miracle*', was born and in that same month Talma was playing in *Athalie*. The newly born prince, the Duc de Bordeaux, was regarded as the last heir and hope of the Bourbons because his uncle, the Duc d'Angoulême, next in succession to the throne, was childless. When Talma, as Joad, called in Act IV for loyalty to the boy king Joas in the following lines:

> *A ce roi que le ciel vous redonne aujourd'hui*
> *Jurez tous de combattre et de mourir pour lui*[3]

the house rose in wild enthusiasm which, so prodigal were its

---

[1] C. Maurice, Vol. I, pp. 258, 259.
[2] C. Maurice *Histoire Anecdotique du Théatre*, Vol. I, p. 254.
[3] 'By this king, which Heaven today again grants you,
Swear, all of you, to fight and die for him.'

vivats, momentarily halted the acting.[1] To Talma such an ovation must have seemed like the old Napoleonic days, when a performance of *Hector* brought to every mind another miraculous infant, the King of Rome. *Sic transit gloria.*

[1] A. Augustin-Thierry '*Le Tragédien de Napoléon*', Le Temps, May 30th, 1938.

CHAPTER 41

Prize Giving at the Pension Morin

The new romantic ideas in the theatre that Talma had striven for all his life were steadily gaining ground. The classicists, whose outlook and attitude approximated to the spirit of the current reactionary government, still remained a powerful force in the literary world. Their minions in the press did not hesitate to decry any infringement of classical rules and proprieties as evidence of a decayed, revolutionary spirit, dangerous and disrupting. Although Lamartine in the June of 1820 had blazed a new trail for the romantic lyric, the more objective art of the theatre had to wait ten years for its emancipation. A book of poems like Lamartine's *Méditations* could cast its spell upon an individual reader, entranced within his study; a romantic tragedy like *Hernani* had to battle its way to success by a far from peaceful penetration of a massed audience of some thousand spectators. Small wonder that the new romanticism took time to turn its first faltering steps towards the theatre.

With Talma back at the Comédie-Française as an advocate for a truly national tragedy, the Comité, undoubtedly influenced by their greatest and most progressively minded actor, agreed on October 19th to produce Viennet's *Clovis*. Costumes and décor were certainly picturesque and historically accurate and the sociétaires hoped that this cunning, primitive founder of the Frankish kingdom would not upset the high priests of monarchy, then pontificating in the press. In performance Talma's Clovis received only mediocre support from Mlle Paradol, as the heroine Erdelinde; Ligier, a young tragedian, then understudying Lafon, played the showy part of the parricide Clodoric. The play fell between two stools. In conception it was too timid for the liberal minded progressives; its subject merely irritated the conservative classicists. Yet the idea of basing tragedies upon events in French history, despite the semi-failure of *Clovis*, led the sociétaires to put on Formont's *Jean de Bourgogne*, with Talma in the title rôle. This

313

early fifteenth century record of the bitter struggle for territory
and power between the Dukes of Orleans and Burgundy provided
parts all too conventional for Mlle Duchesnois, Damas, Desmousseaux and Ligier. Neither *Clovis* nor *Jean de Bourgogne* counted for
much, even in the inglorious annals of the Comédie-Française for
the last months of 1820. The drama, denied the stage, seemed to
have transferred itself once more to the green room. The sharp
disagreements fast developing into enmity between Chéron and
Talma can be gauged by a very unhappy incident that occurred in
the November of that year. Talma, by virtue of his pre-eminent
position in the company—although it must be remembered that
he was not yet Doyen—had been accustomed to attend, by special
favour, the meetings of the Administrative Committee, where
matters were deliberated concerning the running of the theatre
and therefore in the province of the Commissaire. Talma appeared
as usual at the meeting, only to be ordered out by Chéron who,
to support his action, invoked the Moscow Decree. The bitter
tone of the letters that passed between the two parties brought
out into the open Chéron's growing hatred for Talma.[1]

The tragedian was certainly in the wars and not only at the
Comédie-Française. A matter limited to his private life, one would
have thought, suddenly flared up in the press during the early days
of 1821. Indirectly the actor became involved with the Catholic
Church which, backed by a strongly entrenched clerical party,
le parti prêtre, would brook no criticism from a mere *histrion*.
The unfortunate publicity arose from the following situation.
Talma's two little boys, Alphonse-Alexandre and Paul-Louis,
were pupils at a rather aristocratic pension run by a M. Morin.
Both boys had won prizes which, on the Speech Day, they believed
they would receive from Monseigneur de Quélen,[2] Archbishop of
Paris, who would honour the occasion by his presence. A rather
officious priest, the curé of Notre-Dame de l'Assomption, im-
agining that the prelate would be embarrassed if he were called
upon to embrace and crown the Talma boys in the traditional way,
took it upon himself to change the order of the presentations and
to relegate the actor's sons to the ranks of the 'honourable men-

---

[1] *Archives. Comédie-Française.*

[2] Stendhal, in an article for the London *Evening Standard*, December 1826, affirmed
that the boys were educated at a school conducted by a Monsieur Morion [*sic*] and
that they had been publicly insulted by the Bishop of Hermopolis, M. Frayssinous,
'for being the sons of an actor excommunicated by the Gallican church'. Talma's
correspondence makes clear the true facts of the case.

tions', who of course would not receive such archi-episcopal favours. After the departure of Monseigneur de Quélen, who was certainly unaware of such juggling and who would have condemned it outright had he known of it, the 'mistake' over the Talma boys' prizes was discovered and a kind-hearted priest from Fontenay-les-Roses undertook the belated presentation and made what amends he could.[1]

Talma's feelings over this unhappy incident can be seen in his letter to the headmaster.

Paris, December 30th,
Sir,   1820

It is with unfeigned grief that I find myself compelled to withdraw my children from your school but what happened yesterday at the prize distribution leaves me no other choice, because the insult that my children and I endured at that function we ascribe to your petty action and, in no way, to a prelate so well known for his tolerance and piety. I admit that in order to preserve your school you are compelled to yield to certain pressures; but I for my part, in order to preserve the love and respect of my children, must spare them the humiliation you would have them endure. My life has been free from reproach and when my children bear an honourable name—yes I venture to say this—I do not want harmful prejudices to be implanted in their young minds and cause them to feel ashamed of their father. In order to present their prizes, the school waited until Monseigneur the Archbishop, who distributed the awards, had departed. Then the excuse was made that there had been an oversight, but the whole gathering, your pupils, my children and I received a public insult. I myself could possibly endure without complaint such an undeserved humiliation, but never one that might involve my children. Until then, I was unaware that the Catholic ban upon actors extended to their families. That I learned yesterday in your school. It is useless for one of your masters to say that because they were Protestants they could not receive their prizes from the hands of the Archbishop. The children very properly retorted that other Protestant pupils had been granted that distinction; but your father . . . was the answer. Therefore I, my name, my profession—which the government supports—deprived my children of the honourable distinction they had deserved and which had been accorded to all the others. I conclude, sir. My heart is too full to pursue further comment. I beg of you, dear M. Morin, to forward me your bill for what remains outstanding in my account.

Yours,

J. TALMA.

[1] Fleischmann and Bart, pp. 242, 243.

I ask you to thank on my behalf the good curé of Fontenay-les-Roses who was kind enough to hand the prizes to my children and embrace them.

The press got wind of the affair and, surprising as it may seem to us, Talma received from the journalists some very hard knocks. *Le Journal de Paris* deplored the incident, but the ultra-royalist papers like *Le Constitutionnel* condemned the actor for the above letter to such an extent that Talma felt constrained to write a spirited reply for public circulation. In it he exonerated both the headmaster M. Morin and the distinguished prelate from any complicity in the matter.

I owe it to truth and to my own honour to state that, if my children were not allowed to receive their prizes from Monseigneur the Archbishop of Paris, they were not thrust aside. One of the most distinguished ecclesiastics in the city, no less estimable for his virtue than for his ability, has positively assured me that Monseigneur the Archbishop of Paris, whose truly Christian character is so well known, would have called out my children's names with a degree of satisfaction and that he would not have refused them their rightful due. . . . When the Lawgiver of the Christians called unto Him little children for His blessing, He did not ask them their father's profession. [1]

From this somewhat unusual set of circumstances Talma emerges with dignity. True the old vanity asserted itself. The claim to a blameless life must be viewed with a certain scepticism, but mellowing time had made Talma something of a family man. Two things stand out clearly. He took his responsibilities as a father most seriously and he loved his sons. Although he had professed the Catholic faith in that letter to the curé of Saint-Sulpice just before his marriage with Julie Careau, fundamentally he was materialist and free thinker, much imbued with Voltairian philosophy. A. Augustin-Thierry insists upon a Protestant origin[2] —surely difficult to maintain because members of the Talma family, right from the actor's grandfather, born in 1700, had been baptized in the Catholic Church—but he adds that our Talma had received no religious training of any kind. This may well be true when one remembers his early boyhood spent in Paris and London. Talma's own interest and eminence in freemasonry would remove him from a strictly orthodox Catholicism. And yet he passionately wanted the Church to recognize his beloved pro-

[1] Fleischmann and Bart, pp. 244, 245.
[2] A. Augustin-Thierry, *Le Tragédien de Napoléon*, *Le Temps*, June 2nd, 1938.

fession as one whose devotees might be deemed worthy of salvation. This unfortunate prizegiving at the Pension Morin rekindled the fires of religious conflict. He remembered the difficulties that surrounded his first marriage; more recently he recalled the intolerance that, but for the King's intervention, would have deprived the earthly remains of Mlle Raucourt of the final consolations of the Christian faith. He persisted in his resolve to withdraw his two sons from M. Morin's care and sent them to a Protestant boarding-school at Fontenay-les-Roses.

CHAPTER 42

'Sylla'

Acareer so illustrious as Talma's has its periods of steady glory when the biographer has merely to stand aside and, without further comment, let events take their course. If there was one subject that baffled Talma's rivals and foes, it was that the actor seemed immune from that decline which the passing of years can so often wreak upon the powers of lesser men and women in the theatre. It is a plain and simple fact that Talma never lost his grip upon the Parisian audience, notoriously one of the most exacting in the world, nor his creative impulse towards the new parts that contemporary playwrights might supply. Never did he cease from an endless *labor improbus labor*, where the great rôles of the established repertory were concerned. He himself—and we know he had more than a normal share of vanity—was not oblivious to the perils of advancing age, the thickening figure, the weary voice, the perfunctory gesture, the treacherous memory and, unlike many of his contemporaries, he schooled himself to forgo the raptures of the *jeune premier*. Cinna had to make way for Auguste, Aman for Joad, the young Marigny for the mature Jacques de Molay. Desperately he clung to Hamlet, to Néron, to Oreste and to Achille, because in those parts he had to run the whole gamut of grief, pity and terror, emotions which, he believed, required for their communication a long experience of life and a perfected acting technique. He retained too his share of stately, impressive rôles, Sévère, Manlius, Coriolan, Brutus, where an assumption of great dignity, combined with a restrained but powerful declamation, enabled him to fire the most unresponsive audiences. The mere announcement of his coming to act in any provincial centre aroused such interest as only a royal personage could command. Both in Paris and in the departments, where his four months congé inevitably ran to six, he packed the theatre which was fortunate enough to have him on its stage. Here in Talma was an actor whose physical and intellectual resources

318

stood up to time itself and who, by consummate art and lively imagination, in no way allowed it to stale his infinite variety.

For the actor, May 5th, 1821, would be a point in time ever to be remembered, a date unassociated with any popular appearance or acting triumph of his own. On that day in lone Saint-Helena, lost in the gales of the South Atlantic, his benefactor the great Emperor, whose very memory made these Bourbon puppets seem insignificant indeed, had yielded up his restless, unquenchable spirit to a God he had sought to placate by a Concordat and a coronation. Talma's grief at this world-shaking event was inconsolable. Gone was the prop that had so steadfastly and so munificently sustained him until with *Manlius* he had wrested incontestable laurels from a public corrupted for a time by odious intrigue. Those command performances at Saint-Cloud, the Tuileries, Fontainebleau had proclaimed him Napoleon's favourite actor. There was also that parterre of kings at Erfurt and later at Dresden. If Napoleon excluded his preferred tragedian from the Legion of Honour, he at least saw that imperial bounty wiped out thespian debts. Others might proffer their rewards but for Talma his association with Napoleon Bonaparte would remain in his memory as something consecrated, something quite unique in human relationships.

Even so illustrious a death could not halt life. Most mundane of all experiences at this time was a removal from the rue de Rivoli to a newly built house, 9 rue de la Tour-des-Dames where, in the vicinity of the Église de la Trinité, Talma's new neighbours were indeed old friends. At No. 1 lived the joyous Mlle Mars, who had next door at No. 3 Mlle Duchesnois. Then came two painters, Horace Vernet and Paul Delaroche, at Nos. 5 and 7. By the autumn of 1821 Talma had settled in with Mlle Bazire and their two sons. Every Tuesday mistress and lover went off to Brunoy, where the actor remained until the much frequented week-end performances called him back to the Théâtre-Français. When the boys came on holiday, a more unified, happy domestic life would have been hard to find. True, the creditors did not cease their dunning, but Talma, like every experienced debtor, knew how to temporize and even on occasion to escape.

It must have given him great pleasure to see published in this year of grace 1821, a *Letter to Talma* over the signature of Mlle Vanhove. Caroline, who still remained on terms of close friendship with her husband, had written a classical *épître*, a poem

108 lines long, couched in acceptable rhyming couplets, to applaud
the actor's genius and to celebrate his success in certain well-
known parts. The smooth alexandrines proclaimed a writer of
some literary competence and the note of high eulogy was maintained from start to finish. Thus she began:

> *Illustre enfant des arts, que guida Melpomène*
> *Dans l'enceinte sacrée et de Rome et d'Athènes,*
> *J'ose quand tout Paris t'applaudit à la fois,*
> *Joindre ma voix timide à sa bruyante voix.*[1]

Then, in the stilted, laudatory fashion of the time, she reviewed
as examples of Talma's power his playing of Néron, Manlius,
Coriolan, Oreste and, in her ecstatic admiration, piling Pelion
on Ossa, concluded:

> *Poursuis, ô grand acteur! une course si belle;*
> *Et puissions-nous avec une ivresse nouvelle,*
> *Aller longtemps encor t'admirer chaque soir,*
> *Te voir peindre d'Hamlet le sombre désespoir,*
> *D'Oedipe le malheur, la clémence d'Auguste!*
> *Le Français envers toi reconnaissant et juste,*
> *Toujours plus exalté, brûlant de te l'offrir*
> *Te décerne un laurier qui ne doit périr.*[2]

From a discarded wife this is a fine tribute. As one reads this
generous effusion, one wonders whether Caroline sought in the
power of the pen some justification of her own ego that love and
the theatre had denied. Such a thought would never have occurred
to Talma. For him it was enough to purr in her praise. After all
he had scaled the heights. Furthermore, this poem by Mlle Vanhove was to prove a heartening precursor to a very exciting
theatrical event.

Étienne de Jouy, who had given Talma in *Tippoo-Saïb* an out-

[1] 'Renowned son of the Arts, whom Melpomene
Led to the sacred precincts both of Rome and Athens,
I venture, when all Paris at once acclaims you,
To add my timid voice to its clamorous cry.'
[2] 'Pursue, oh great actor! so fair a course;
And may we, with ecstasy renewed,
Go each evening for a long time yet to admire you,
To see you paint Hamlet's gloomy grief,
The woes of Oedipus, Augustus's mercy.
Frenchmen rightly in their gratitude,
Ever more inspired, burn to offer
And to bestow upon you imperishable laurels.'

Mademoiselle George

standing success, had come forward with a new play, *Sylla*, based upon the life of the Roman dictator (136–79 B.C.). The sociétaires welcomed this return to a classical theme, especially after the disappointments of *Clovis* and *Jean de Bourgogne*. In the part of Sylla Talma saw great opportunities. As rehearsals progressed, more and more did the idea grow within the actor that here was a character whose generalship and unlimited power could keep alive, in the popular imagination, during those lack-lustre Bourbon days, the memory of that vanished god, Napoleon. Ernest Legouvé[1] who frequented the Jouy salon, says that *Sylla* was one of the greatest theatrical triumphs of the century. The author's enemies tried to dismiss it as a '*succès de perruque*' because Talma, greatly daring, astounded the first night audience by appearing in a Napoleonic wig with the celebrated lock upon his forehead. Still more amazing, as he acted he recalled the tone, the stance, the gestures of the late Emperor. The effect was prodigious. Before the very eyes of the parterre the dead Emperor stalked, commanded, raged. It was as if Austerlitz had wiped out Waterloo.

The production required a solution of many technical difficulties, most of them due to the ever encroaching vanguard of new ideas with reference to nature and realism in the theatre. In *Sylla* Jouy used the full dimensions of the stage, which all too often had surrendered its space to confidential duets and lonely monologues. In this play the audience met Sylla first in his study, surrounded by his partisans, then in the midst of his courtiers, later in the animated forum and finally it witnessed the dictator's abdication. Talma welcomed these innovations and for him *Sylla* contained two major problems. There was the terrifying scene where Sylla in his sleep sees his victims pass in procession before him, conjuring up within him awestricken remorse. Everyone counted on Talma to carry off this exceptionally difficult scene. Apart from the acting, which would be poised on the very razor edge of credibility, there was also the technical difficulty of getting the actor to bed in full view of the audience. This was more than a difficulty, it was a danger. Never in the whole annals of French tragedy had any hero or heroine gone to bed on the stage. Such an outrage of the proprieties could not be permitted. Unless this most delicate operation could be accomplished with supreme skill and decency, the parterre would rise in its wrath and that would be the end of *Sylla*.

[1] E. Legouvé, *Soixante ans de souvenirs*, pp. 141, 2, 3.

Talma accepted the challenge. How could he get into that bed? Realism rejected a chair or a sofa, only a bed would do, a Roman bed, not too encumbered with coverlets. How could he avoid giving offence to the spectators? Talma shivered in his bare feet as he thought it out. Let Legouvé explain how the actor solved the difficulty: . . . 'he begins by sitting casually on the edge of the bed. Then he says his first lines, both arms resting on his knees brought close together, then continuing with his speech, he raises his arms and stretches out one of his legs; the other leg then rejoins it; he next bends his body backwards, places his head upon the pillow and there you have Sylla ready for sleep without the public realizing he has gone to bed!' How skilful one had to be, in those days, to become the bold innovator!

We are indebted to this author for another acting detail. In the third act, while the fawning courtiers surround the dictator, shouts are heard from a crowd being slaughtered outside the palace. In the midst of the carnage a rough peasant enters and, going straight up to Sylla, shouts: 'How many do you condemn to death?' Talma's reply, 'I do not know,' depended, we are told, upon the actor's inspiration of the moment. He might, upon occasion, take his tone from the yelling peasant or from the callous courtiers around him. Sometimes it would fall from his lips with casual disdain or with a kind of absent-minded calm, which of course threw into striking contrast the workman's fury. At other times he would hurl it in the man's face like the cry of a wild beast, with a violence that filled everyone with fear. This was an example of the actor's genius. The play was not merely a success, it was a triumph. Let us add quickly, for the poet as well. Thenceforth, M. de Jouy was known as the author of *Sylla*.[1]

That night of December 27th, 1821, when *Sylla* faced the foot-lights, was also Saint-Fal's benefit performance. This actor had long merited the public's favour but even on this great occasion he had to yield the palm to Talma. The press notices of Jouy's play were ecstatic. To begin with, Sylla, the great Roman dictator, whose blood feuds extended to every noble family and whose abdication of supreme power allowed him to die in his bed like an ordinary citizen, had never before been treated as a subject for tragedy. Here was something brand new and no mere refurbishing of a hackneyed classical theme. The staid *Constitutionnel* seemed breathless for superlatives. The construction of the play was

[1] Legouvé, *Soixante ans de souvenirs*, pp. 142, 143.

correct, its colour brilliant, its fidelity to history perfect. After
the terrible dream scene, there came the moment of Sylla's abdication when, surrounded by his enemies, he threw off his purple
robe, snatched from his brow the laurel crown, broke the golden
palm, symbol of his absolute power, and gave himself up to the
people. We are told that hatred was silent; vengeance had
sheathed its sword. In this play, against its two magnificent,
colourful scenes, Talma's acting shone. 'I cannot delay any longer
the pleasure of recording that Talma in the part of Sylla displayed
miraculous ability. On his first entry, his ominous countenance,
his flashing eyes, his piercing glance, chilled the spectators.
Throughout the part, Talma sustained, amplified this baleful impression he had created; in the dream he made one shiver with
horror and in the fifth act he was magnificent. Those advocates
of past days may well boast their Lekain. I never saw him but I am
quite convinced that Talma is the greatest tragic actor who ever
stepped upon the stage.'[1]

The *Journal de Paris* described the play as the panorama of an
epoch rather than a closely knit tragedy and then proceeded with
its panegyrics. So great was the applause at curtain fall that minutes
elapsed before Talma could announce the author's name. 'There
are two fine scenes in the fourth and fifth acts; in rendering Sylla's
dream Talma displays a terrifying power. Finally, at the play's
climax, the abdication scene presents an imposing spectacle which
could not fail to assure brilliant success for the piece.'[2] Martainville came back the next day with another laudatory account,
concluding with the remark: 'Talma contributed powerfully to
the success of the play. It is impossible to imagine Sylla in the
guise of any other actor. Talma seems always to have spent his life
among the great characters of the ancient world.'[3]

The author, Étienne de Jouy, has left also his own impressions:

It is rare that full justice is done to the living, and Talma's admirers
have limited their praise to comparing him with Lekain, with Garrick
and with that illustrious Roscius that I have put in my play and whom
M. Damas represents with so much charm and vitality. By placing
Talma above everything the annals of the stage record as truly great,
I know I am voicing most faithfully the public's admiration. He is not
merely an actor; he wears neither theatrical purple nor paste diadem;

---

[1] *Le Constitutionnel*, December 29th, 1821.
[2] *Le Journal de Paris*, December 28th, 1821.
[3] *Le Journal de Paris*, December 29th, 1821.

he lives every day for two hours the life of the character he portrays; he is Auguste, he is Hamlet, he is Néron, he is Sylla. Never was transformation more complete. Those studied gestures, those sculptured poses, those contrived tones of voice, all conventional art he rejects. He is nature in all her simplicity, passion caught on the wing, feeling in all its surrender; these are the emotions he uncovers before the eyes of an admiring public. He comes forward with a slow stride, his cloak carelessly crossed over his breast, reveals only a drapery severe in style. His face is calm but, at his approach, fear is spread around him. Passive still, how can one explain the impression he creates? He makes no gesture, he utters no word, he looks before him. He sits down, leaning upon the arm of his chair. David might have sketched the felicitous curve of his arm. His strong voice, peremptory and deep, lets fall its pronouncements. By what wondrous alchemy does this actor succeed in expressing such terrifying disdain, such frightening irony? How comes it that his flashing eye seems at once so eager for glory, blood and repose? By what miracle does one read on those features the weariness of power in a soul heinous yet proud, the political machinations of a most versatile mind, the courage of a warrior and the fears of a frightened child?'[1]

Then he added by way of afterthought:

Roscius, whom Cicero calls the most virtuous man of his time, was the idol of Roman youth, a favourite of the dictator. By a strange coincidence that will not have escaped my readers, Talma like Roscius enjoyed the honoured friendship of the most distinguished personalities of his day and lived close to the man who for fourteen years was the monster of Europe.

Thus wrote Jouy of that first night when Mlle Duchesnois, Damas, Firmin and Ligier added all their combined art to make the play one of Talma's greatest successes. *Sylla* retained its place in the bill as long as Talma lived. The actor's lock of hair and Napoleonic stance made history and, although the government had police in readiness to deal with any possible Bonapartist disturbances at the Comédie-Française, such a force was never used. The ministry had the good sense to ride out the storm. Neither was *Sylla* banned nor did it become a subject for legal action. It merely packed the theatre whenever it was performed.

When this resounding success allowed Talma to take his annual *congé*, a condition he had imposed upon his return to full service at the Théâtre-Français, it was to Belgium he took his repertory of plays. In some respects Brussels offered greater rewards than

[1] E. Jouy, *Sylla*, p. 23.

Paris. The Belgian actors welcomed him not only in their capital, but also in Ghent, Liège and Antwerp as well. For them his presence on their stages proved a wonderful stimulus and a precious link with the Parisian dramatic scene. Apart from the affection and adulation with which he was regarded by his beloved Belgian audiences, the pleasant fact that *Hamlet* would draw 3,600 francs at the doors for a single performance in Brussels,[1] in addition to seats paid for by the regular subscribers, made the journey across the frontier, despite the difficulty of getting theatrical costumes and properties through the customs,[2] a financially exciting project. Talma, a son of the Nord, understood the lively Belgian mind. In Belgium too he renewed contact with many friends, exiled Bonapartists, not least among them David. Such enthusiasm did he arouse among all classes of society that King William I of the Netherlands awarded the actor a pension of 10,000 francs, on condition that for the next five years he would visit annually the Royal Theatre at Brussels and there play his latest successes. This kingly gift served magnificently to underline the actor's prestige and popularity.

[1] Frédéric Faber, *Histoire du Théâtre-Français en Belgique*, Vol. II, p. 264.
[2] Guy de la Batut, *Talma: Correspondance*, p. 199.

CHAPTER 43

Talma fights for a Comedy Part

T
alma returned to Paris in May only to find a disgruntled
Chéron prepared to subject him to all the little pinpricks
which French official life seems to abound in and to enjoy.
He resented particularly Talma's comings and goings, and the
urgent requests for the star's appearances in the great provincial
centres he was determined to oppose. On May 22nd, Talma had
even refused an invitation to act in America, giving as his main
reason that he did not wish to be separated from his family.[1] The
actor's fame had never stood higher. Damas, whose friendship
with Talma went back to the days of the Théâtre de la République,
had very definitely become the minion of Chéron who, after his
shabby treatment of Fleury, found it very necessary to bolster
up his by no means adequate successor. The combination of
Chéron and Damas could spell trouble for Talma. There was
always the endless friction of comedy and tragedy, especially
when the Bourbon court, like Marie-Louise in her time, tended to
prefer the lighter form of dramatic entertainment. Talma's vanity,
blinded by King William's pension, did not see or pretended not
to see the alliance that was building up against him. In no way
discomfited, Talma applied his mind to a new play.

Into rehearsal went Lucien Arnault's tragedy, *Régulus*. Lucien
was the son of that Arnault who had written *Les Vénitiens* and
Germanicus, and although the father had been allowed to return
from exile in 1819, a certain atmosphere of Bonapartism surrounded them both. The ultra-royalist press had put every
obstacle in the way of Lucien's literary career and openly accused
the father of writing plays signed by his son.[2] Although by no
means a maiden effort, *Régulus* was Lucien Arnault's first play to

---

[1] Fleischmann and Bart, *Lettres d'amour de Talma*, p. 246. Talma's letter with
romantic Chateaubriand touches first appeared in the *Gazette anecdotique*, pub. by
G. Heylli, April 30th, 1882, p. 261.

[2] L. Arnault, *Oeuvres dramatiques*, Vol. I, Intro. p. vii.

reach the boards of the Comédie-Française, which it did on
June 5th, 1822. The following day, Martainville in the *Journal de
Paris* acclaimed the tragedy a brilliant success. He particularly
praised the style, stressing its severe yet energetic quality, its
noble and lofty sentiments, its core of solid yet sublime thought.
The verse also had a lapidary quality. 'Carthage has soldiers,
Rome has citizens'; 'Without laws, there can be no fatherland'[1]
appeared in the notice as evidence of the fact. However much we
may raise our eyebrows today, *Régulus* with its tale of integrity
and patriotism gripped its generation by the throat. 'Talma is
admirable in the rôle of Régulus. Mlle Duchesnois in the part of
his daughter Attilie has her share in his success.' The author was
rapturously acclaimed and his father, who appeared in a box,
became the object of loud cheering. Martainville attended the
second performance on June 7th and again wrote of the play's
great success. 'Talma was called for again and again and forced to
reappear. We regret being unable to enter into full details of that
fine performance.'[2]

More can be learned from Alphonse François, who undertook
the editorship of Lucien Arnault's collected dramatic works:[3]

His début was a brilliant success. The tragedy of *Régulus*, inspired
by a courageous patriotism and remarkable for the speed of its action,
its powerful situations, the strength of its verse, received unanimous
applause. Talma played the illustrious martyr of Carthage and in every
way the play was worthy of such an interpreter. The part of Régulus,
abounding in vigour and vitality, was specially written for Talma who,
by the natural eloquence of his delivery, by the authority of his virile,
powerful voice, his compelling by-play, by that glance so expressive
and so penetrating, by all his resources seemed to bring to life this hero
of the ancient world. All the prestige of his talent was displayed in
Régulus. With what patriotic and sublime hatred he sounded that final
call 'To Carthage!' Cato himself would use the same tones for '*delenda
est Carthago*'. On this prophetic and terrible note, one thought one heard
crumble the walls of Rome's rival city.[4]

Fortune smiled on Talma. With *Marie Stuart*, *Sylla* and *Régulus*,
three thumping great successes in a row, she might be said to have
laughed. Tragedy seemed to be itself again and Alexandre Soumet,

---

[1] '*Carthage a des soldats. Rome a des citoyens.*' '*Sans lois, point de patrie.*'
[2] *Le Journal de Paris*, June 9th, 1822.
[3] L. Arnault, *Oeuvres dramatiques*, Vol. I, Intro. p. vii.
[4] L. Arnault, *Oeuvres dramatiques*, Vol. I, p. xxxviii.

very prominent in that little circle presided over by Émile Deschamps which was destined for literary fame as the Premier Cénacle, had persuaded the sociétaires to read his *Clytemnestre*. One asks how many times this baleful lady had trodden the stage of the Comédie-Française since its foundation in 1680. The permutations of the tragic incidents which involved the wife of Agamemnon should, one might have thought, have reached their ultimate conclusion by 1822. But no! Soumet's play in its unfolding of the woeful tale brought a touch of distinction, mainly discernible in his verse which, a little more flexible and daringly poetic, caused the young progressives to cheer it at least to a modest success. Mlle Duchesnois, no doubt persuaded that the more things change the more they remain the same, again donned the peplum to striking effect and fifty-nine-year-old Talma, as her son Oreste, disentangled emotions he had already explored in the same character in a number of other tragedies. Soumet, for all his romantic stirrings, adopted the standard form of five acts, and, when one reads the play today, Diderot's dictum that 'nothing was so easy to write as a French tragedy provided one could count up to five on one's fingers'[1] comes forcibly to mind. The fervent subscribers to *La Muse Française*, who called him '*le grand Alexandre*', endorsed the praise Victor Hugo had bestowed upon *Clytemnestre* in *Le Moniteur*. The classicists approved the play's theme but objected to the freedom and colour of the verse. Nevertheless, the acting of Talma and Mlle Duchesnois, ranging over very familiar ground, contrived to give the play a semblance of life, sufficiently so for it to be chalked up as a success for the new ideas.[2]

During this rewarding year of 1822 mention should be made of a revival of Kotzebue's very sentimental comedy, *Misanthropie et Repentir*. Mlle Mars whose hold upon the Parisian playgoers was very great saw herself as Eulalie, the heroine. Provided the part of old Uncle Meinau were strongly cast, the play could prove a money-maker. In 1798, Saint-Fal had enjoyed the success of his life in this very part and, although this veteran had taken his farewell benefit on that auspicious night of *Sylla*, he was still playing in the theatre. Mlle Mars wanted no Saint-Fal; she insisted that if *Misanthropie et Repentir* were to be revived Talma must play Meinau. The thought of supplanting an old colleague, still on the active list, in his greatest part went sorely against the Talma grain.

---

[1] Quoted by Fleury, *Mémoires*, p. 307.
[2] H. Girard, *Le Centenaire du Premier Cénacle Romantique*, pp. 48–51.

Mlle Mars, scenting rich rewards with herself and Talma in the cast, renewed her importunities, but the great actor would appear only with the consent and approval of Saint-Fal. In this play, which belongs to that hybrid genre, *le drame bourgeois*, and a very sorry example at that, Talma acted an old man part quite outside his normal range and succeeded in bringing to his portrayal all that melting pathos that twenty-four years earlier had been so highly praised in Saint-Fal's performance.

So many tales are told of Talma's ability to hold an audience and keep it unaffected by those occasional accidents or private exchanges which occur from time to time between players. Damas, who used to play Pylade to Talma's Oreste in *Iphigénie en Tauride*, always rejoiced in telling how, in those moments of torment when the Furies pursued him, the actor by a sudden movement once lost his wig in full view of the spectators, and how he, Damas, picked it up and threw it into the wings.[1] Even Geoffroy chronicled: 'No one laughed and that is the highest praise of Talma's talents; a whole volume of panegyrics could not confer upon the actor as great an honour as the serious attitude of the public with regard to the loss of his wig.'[2] During a performance of *Oedipe* on February 26th, 1823, Talma in the title rôle was playing a scene with Desmousseaux as Icare. The younger actor had made up his face in an exaggerated and unconvincing way. The scene went as follows:

OEDIPE: 'Is it you I really behold? . . .'
            (Heavens, how black you are!)
ICARE: (I, sir?)
OEDIPE: 'You, wise guardian of my tender years. . . .
            (How could you smear yourself so)
ICARE   (It's just as usual, M. Talma.)
OEDIPE: 'You, worthy henchman of Polybius, my sire. . . .
            (Dear friend, you look awful)
ICARE: (I can't do it otherwise)
OEDIPE: 'What vital matter brings you amongst us?
            (Go and take out those wrinkles)
ICARE: (I'll go up to my dressing-room)

We are told that Talma, reassured by this promise, continued the scene without looking at Desmousseaux![3] One can almost hear

[1] Lanzac de Laborie, *Le Théâtre Français*, p. 56.
[2] Geoffroy, *Journal des Débats*, December 1st, 1803.
[3] C. Maurice, *Histoire anecdotique du théâtre*, Vol. I, pp. 290, 291.

today's actor murmur 'timing'. Years after Talma's disappearance from this world, Sarah Bernhardt, as she played Phèdre, found time between her lines to give instructions to electricians and, during her flying matinées of any play, breathed orders from the stage to her maid about her packing. *Tempora mutantur*.

As soon as Talma could be released from his round of successes at the Comédie-Française, he took the road to Brussels, there to carry out his obligation to the King of the Netherlands and delight his subjects with *Sylla* and *Régulus*, as well as with stock pieces from his repertory. A letter from Rouen, dated March 25th, to a Genevan friend[1] stated: 'The commitments I have with the King of the Netherlands to devote all my *congés* to the Court at Brussels deprive me of any hope of seeing you.' The royal pension of 10,000 francs tended to tie Talma to the cities of the North. For a man no longer young, the fatigue of lengthy coach journeys to Lyons and Bordeaux imposed a serious handicap and one notes that in these later years Talma's tours covered only the northern departments.

He returned to Paris for Ancelot's tragedy *Le Maire du Palais*, given on April 16th, 1823. The author's shadowy evocation of Ébrouin, an unscrupulous king-making mayor of the palace, yet another example of a 'national' subject, flickered to the end of an overlong first performance, when it was greeted with only polite applause. Martainville, bewailing the play's length, praised the careful writing, particularly the 'elegant and pure versification'. After the second performance the same critic wrote: 'Talma acts the part of Ébrouin with energy, but even he cannot altogether disguise the play's monotony.'[2] *Le Maire du Palais* lasted for only five performances.

The failure of Ancelot's tragedy enabled Chéron to take a strong line with Talma over a serious dispute that had arisen between Damas and the tragedian. A young poet from Le Havre, Casimir Delavigne, had offered to the Comédie-Française in 1818 a tragedy entitled *Les Vêpres siciliennes*.[3] The play dealt with an underground Sicilian rising against a foreign oppressor. The Comité, fearing the effects of staging the play at the national theatre, with the allied army of occupation still on French soil, refused a piece so provocatively patriotic. The author took his

---

[1] Munier Rouilly; Guy de la Batut, *Talma, Correspondance*, p. 174.
[2] *Le Journal de Paris*, April 19th, 1823, April 21st, 1823.
[3] E. Legouvé *Soixante ans de souvenirs*, Vol. I, p. 21.

play to the Odéon, where the student audience acclaimed the tragedy with such fervour that the applause went on continuously throughout the interval between the fourth and fifth acts. After this, the sociétaires felt they ought to look very closely at any work this immensely popular young man, still in his twenties, might submit.

By the spring of 1823, Delavigne had in his portfolio a new five-act comedy in verse *L'École des vieillards*. The very title recalled the great days of polished classical comedy that Fleury knew how to present. The Comité accepted the play with unanimous delight. It would go into immediate rehearsal. Delavigne confessed to Legouvé that, for his central character Danville, a sixty year old shipbuilder from Le Havre with a married son and whose second wife Hortense was a young Parisienne of twenty-one, he had Baptiste *aîné* in mind. As he left the reading, he was overtaken in the corridor by Talma who, having heard the play read, said to the young author: 'M. Delavigne, I will play Danville, for I am Danville.'[1] The author, like everybody else, knew that Talma was wildly jealous of his own young mistress. He was quite overcome by the proposal. Mlle Mars and Talma in the same play, here indeed was a fine start for his new comedy. Yes, a comedy! Joad in evening dress, Hamlet a substantial bourgeois! Surely all the ingredients for an overwhelming success were there. Talma had played comedy parts, witness *Shakespeare amoureux*, *Pinto* and *Plaute*. The part of Hortense would fit Mlle Mars like a glove. The elegant Armand, who had partnered her in so many successes, would bring a raffish charm and impeccable manners to the ducal seducer, d'Elmar.

Everything was nicely shipshape in Talma's and his author's mind. Unfortunately Damas, who had made life difficult in the green room for his team[2] asserted in a most unpleasant way his rights to all leading comedy rôles. Talma's wish to play Danville was unorthodox, to say the least. He might try to justify his desire on the grounds that Damas had never really filled Fleury's place, but there could be no gainsaying the fact that his old versatile colleague was *chef d'emploi*. Damas immediately enlisted the militant support of Chéron, ever spoiling for a quarrel with Talma. The dispute took on a bitterness that only a closed and jealous community could engender. For their part, the majority of the

[1] E. Legouvé, *Soixante ans de souvenirs*, pp. 22–32.
[2] E. de Manne, *La Troupe de Talma*, p. 173.

sociétaires saw in this stellar conjunction of Mars and Talma rich rewards. The public, apprised of the squabble, awaited the outcome with feverish impatience. Damas, as a protest against this attack upon his rights, sent in his resignation.

On April 15th Chéron took action. He wrote to the Baron de La Ferté, *Intendant des Menus Plaisirs du Roi.*[1] He begged this courtier to forbid M. Talma to play Danville in *L'École des vieillards*, pointing out that the actor had imposed his services upon the author and expressing as his view that, had not M. Damas persisted so long in offering his resignation, Talma's demand to play the part would have come to nothing. He stated categorically that M. Delavigne had assured him personally that he had always intended M. Damas to play Danville. He would also point out that as M. Damas had withdrawn his resignation, those actors who had previously supported Talma's claim to the part had now changed their minds. There were even more serious reasons. With the tragic lead playing comedy, tragedy would suffer neglect; the actors' functions would become confused; authors' rights would be sacrificed. The Théâtre-Français had conceded much to M. Talma's advantage, but let it be understood such concessions were made to the first tragedian and not to an actor free to play any part. The casting of M. Talma for Danville could only prove prejudicial to the best interests of the sociétaires. Finally, he thought M. Talma himself might run a grave risk of compromising his great reputation as a tragedian by a doubtful success in this comic rôle.[2]

Chéron had gone all out to obtain the necessary injunction. The Baron, after some prevarication and subsequent consultation with the Duc de Duras, who alone could make the final decision, understandably refused to intervene. The courtiers were in a difficult position. Both Talma and Mlle Mars enjoyed signal marks of royal favour and in Talma's case a neighbouring monarch's gesture had added to a prestige that required some courage publicly to affront. Mlle Mars, a power to be reckoned with, supported Talma wholeheartedly in his determination to play Danville.

This miserable fray dragged on painfully. Delavigne must have

---

[1] Lit. Major-domo of the King's Minor Pleasures—a high official in the department of the Duc de Duras, in charge of the Royal Theatres. E. de Manne, *La Troupe de Talma*, pp. 107, 108, footnote.

[2] E. de Manne *La Troupe de Talma*, pp. 107, 108.

had some black moments over rehearsals begun, postponed, suspended. The summer months saw a scattering of the cast all over the provinces; delay followed delay. Chéron and Damas did their utmost to prevent Talma from playing in *L'École des vieillards*. A letter from Talma to Charles Maurice, dated as late as November 9th, throws some light upon the general unhappiness in the green room. From it we learn that the tragedian had again threatened resignation.

Whatever distress the gratuitous insults I have endured may leave in my mind, if my colleagues apologize I will continue with my service. I will put aside my just resentment for the sake of my duty to the public and to M. le duc de Duras, who in this matter had acted only as the benevolent mediator. I will also make this sacrifice for the sake of the friendship of most of my colleagues who had no part in this deplorable quarrel, and in the interests of the author who offered me a part in *L'École des vieillards*, his first comedy at the Théâtre-Français, a part he persists in assigning to me and in which I will try to justify the favours the public has always shown me and which console me for all the shameful insults heaped upon me. Talma. [1]

He won the fight. On December 6th, 1823, an excited, expectant and highly critical audience assembled for *L'École des vieillards*. 'The day of this first performance,' wrote Legouvé,[2] 'the house was as stormy as an equinoctial gale. The curtain rises, a door upstage opens and the first person to appear is Talma, Talma laughing, Talma making an entrance arm in arm with a comic actor, Devigny. He wore a white wig with a more silvery lock of hair upon his brow, a blue coat with gilt buttons, a white waistcoat, black silk breeches, white silk stockings. The metamorphosis was complete. Voice, facial expression, gestures, bearing, everything about him breathed a joyous, candid good nature. He was charming!' Here indeed was a very different entry for one who had so often struck terror in the minds of his beholders.

At this distance of time it is quite impossible to appreciate the dangers this comedy ran by its defiance of accepted conventions, conventions not merely of writing but also of behaviour. Hortense, the young wife, is persistently pursued by the young Duc d'Elmar who, late at night and in her husband's absence, calls upon her in her bedroom. Quite unexpectedly the husband returns and is informed by a faithful servant of this nocturnal visit.

[1] C. Maurice, *Histoire anecdotique*, p. 309.
[2] Legouvé, *Soixante ans de souvenirs*, Vol. I, pp. 22, 32.

Hortense, hearing her husband's approach, hurriedly consigns the Duke to a closet, when Danville enters. A terrible interrogation and embarrassed replies from Hortense, who in a moment of anxiety betrays the ruse by a frightened glance at the closet door, stir the fires of the old man's jealousy. Talma's whispered *'Il est là'* seemed to defy all the rules. No shouting, no melodramatic coup, merely an indication of smouldering fires. He persuades Hortense to retire, withdraws himself, only to return precipitately to call forth the Duke. The nobleman, stressing the difference between their ages, tries to refuse Danville's challenge to a duel. Stung by the husband's taunts, the Duke agrees. 'I will await you.'[1] Danville's 'You will not be incommoded by a long wait,' ends a very bold act. Of course the old man is disarmed in the sword play and when in the fifth act Hortense reads a most revealing letter proving that she never sought the Duke's attentions and that, for the love of her husband, she had dismissed him from her life, the play achieved a happy ending. Throughout its course there were some delightful scenes in which Danville and his old friend Bonnard discuss the problems of youth and age. Legouvé summed up: 'It is poetry in evening dress.'

The play won an immediate and emphatic success. *Le Constitutionnel* could not wait for its critic's report and the next morning stated that 'Mlle Mars had been delightful and Talma sublime'.[2] The full notice on December 8th praised the play highly and summed up the major acting contributions as follows: 'The author had the good fortune to find two interpreters like Talma and Mlle Mars who seems born to play Hortense. . . . Talma, a little uncertain and diffident at first in the difficult character of Danville, quickly summoned up all his perfection of playing to which he has accustomed us in his finest tragic parts. This rôle puts another feather in his theatrical cap, perhaps the finest of them all.' Évariste D., the newspaper's critic, concluded with the belief that *'L'École des vieillards* will make stage history'.

Martainville[3] distributed his favours immediately. 'As for Talma, who played the principal part, his personal success in no way fell below that achieved by the comedy. With Mlle Mars he was recalled again and again and we believe he will earn even greater praise in subsequent performances, if he will try to conceal

---

[1] *'Je vous attends.' 'Vous n'aurez pas l'ennui de m'attendre longtemps.'*
[2] *Le Constitutionnel*, December 7th and 8th, 1823.
[3] *Le Journal de Paris*, December 7th and 8th, 1823.

more effectively the efforts he makes to rid himself of tragic power. In all the strongly dramatic scenes, his acting tingled with a heart-stirring beauty.' The following day the same critic published: 'We shall return constantly to the talented way in which Talma plays the part of Danville, a talent just a little constrained in a few places but admirable everywhere else.'

Sufficient for the day was the success thereof. In the flush of so much adulation it must have been a pleasurable experience to act before the King and the Royal Family, who came in force on December 10th to see Corneille's *Le Cid*. Talma, forsaking the ardours of Rodrigue, contented himself with the rôle of the dwarfish Don Sancho, Chimène's rejected suitor. We are told that, by reducing his own inches, Talma bestowed a greatness of stature upon the character he played.[1]

[1] C. Maurice, *Histoire anecdotique*, p. 310.

CHAPTER 44

A Spell of Failure

On this flood-tide of success Talma turned more and more to the young, progressive writers of the day. Stendhal had recently compared Racine, perhaps a little unfairly, with Shakespeare in a critical treatise[1] destined to make literary history. Talma adored Racine whose harmonious verses he loved to declaim and to whom as an actor he owed Oreste, Achille, Néron and Joad. The great poet's successors with their machine-turned alexandrines, their repetitive rhymes of *lauriers, guerriers âme, flamme, lieux, dieux*, never provided that *épanouissement*, that full-throated outpouring which Talma confessed to Fleury[2] to be an indispensable quality of dramatic verse. Also their wan, blood-less characters had never satisfied the actor. Shakespeare could offer in his plays not only the enchantment of his poetry but the glorious sweep of life itself, where laughter and tears might mingle and where, at every social level, the red blood of humanity asserted itself by appropriate word and deed. Anyone who takes the trouble to read the prefaces of the published plays in which Talma appeared, cannot fail to be impressed by their authors' acknowledgement of indebtedness to Talma, not only on the score of his interpretation but also because of the helpful sugges-tions he made during the actual writing of their tragedies. Talma had so often tried to stir tragic embers to dancing flame, to plead for nature and truth in dramatic writing, to seek heroes a little closer to his own century than those fitful shades, dragged to the light from the darkness of antiquity.

He had always insisted upon the accuracy of costumes, in design as well as in materials, of properties, of décor, in fact upon what the Romantics were soon to call local colour. Of course the battle was by no means everywhere won. Even on June 15th, 1823, Lafon appeared in *Alzire* dressed as for a contemporary Parisian

---

[1] Stendhal, *Racine et Shakespeare*, 1823. Enlarged 1825.
[2] Fleury, *Mémoires*, p. 317.

carnival to make love in sixteenth-century Peru.[1] It was good to note that the critic of *Le Courrier des Théâtres* had slated him for such culpable carelessness. Still, the ideas Talma had always stood for were gaining ground. He hoped that this young Dumas with so many ideas in his woolly, negroid head or perhaps that debonair Victor Hugo would bring life to a failing theatre. Hugo certainly felt the full force of Talma's influence. Did he not ascribe to the actor, to whom he had shown his early drama *Cromwell*, the significant comment 'Truth! That's what I've been looking for all my life'.[2] No wonder Hugo underlined a little later in his famous *Préface de Cromwell*, *'le caractère du drame est le réel'*.

It was a progressively minded Talma who listened to the reading of *Jane Shore*, a tragedy by Népomucène Lemercier, based upon the English hunchback king, Richard III, and owing not a little to Nicholas Rowe's play of the same name. The part of the sinister Duke of Gloucester appealed to the actor who of course knew of Garrick's memorable portrayal and of Kean's later success in the rôle. If tragedy were to achieve complete reality, what could be more challenging, more illustrative of the new ideas than a hero infamous as a misshapen, evil tyrant? This theory of the grotesque, where in one and the same character the Romantics would combine the most opposing attributes, might have become practice in *Jane Shore*. The reading committee accepted the play and Talma, anxious to repeat the success of *L'École des vieillards* with a spectacular tragic performance, threw himself heart and soul into the study of Richard III. By a strange coincidence[3] the author was completely paralysed on one side of his body and in his delineation of Richard had been at pains to show that the King's distorted frame did not rule out the grace and elegance of the courtier. He sedulously coached Talma in what might be called the deportment of a graceful deformity, in the stance of the hunchback, in the movement of Richard's paralysed right arm. So wholly did Talma submit himself to Lemercier's tuition that for days afterwards he endured acute muscular pains in his shoulder. By the time of *Jane Shore's* first performance, April 1st, 1824, Talma had learnt Lemercier's lesson, that innate elegance could overcome the handicap of outward physical disfigurement.

---

[1] C. Maurice, *Histoire anecdotique*, p. 304.
[2] *V. Hugo raconté.* Vol. II, p. 160.
[3] Legouvé, *Souvenirs de soixante ans*, Vol. I, pp. 67, 68.

He moved through the play with the feline grace of a tiger, hideous without being ill-bred, retaining even in his most ferocious moments something of the prince and the courtier. This picture of a deformed but elegant prince did not wholly convince the Parisian playgoers. Martainville, almost echoing Geoffroy, affirmed: 'Unfortunately the Paris public is not yet sufficiently won over to the dramatic taste of London's citizens . . . The play therefore failed.' At curtain fall derision was so widespread in the theatre that the author did not appear. 'It is a pity to see Talma and Mlle Duchesnois display all in vain their great talents and their whole ardour in such an unfortunate play.'[1] Sad to relate, this first performance had been earmarked for Talma's benefit and all Paris had turned out to do honour to its favourite. The press, usually anxious to announce the receipts of such performances, seemed always to refrain from mentioning the figure reached at a Talma benefit. Was the actor hiding his rewards from his horde of rapacious creditors? One wonders. Lemercier had certainly not repeated with *Jane Shore* the success of *Agamemnon*, nor even of *Pinto*. Kinder critics voted the play a '*demi-succès*', but such faint praise did not keep it in the playbill.

Before *Jane Shore* is consigned to the limbo it no doubt fully deserved, an incident must be recorded which occurred during its second performance and which throws a ray of light upon Talma's integrity as an artist as well as upon audience reaction at that time. Mlle Brocard, in the rôle of Hastings' mistress Alicia, had a scene with Talma where she had to endure the hunchback's insults and to run the gauntlet of Richard's wrath. On this second night her bracelet became unclasped and fell on the stage. Immediately Talma broke off his stormy tirade, bent low to recover the bracelet and with exquisite courtesy restored it to Mlle Brocard's arm. Then at once he renewed his anger to finish the scene 'with the impetuous fury of an executioner'. The effect upon the audience of this sudden change of mood was so overwhelming that his colleagues, no doubt catching at any straw to bring popularity to a poor play, requested Talma to repeat the 'accident' the following day. This he steadfastly refused to do. 'In our art,' he said, 'there are accidental moments of inspiration which, if one were to make a habit of them, would become mere commonplace routines.'[2] That such a moment should have stirred a French audience in 1824

[1] *Le Journal de Paris*, April 2nd, 1824.
[2] Legouvé, *Soixante ans de souvenirs*, pp. 67, 68.

shows how near playgoers were to accepting the facile and irrational sensationalism that was to characterize the later romantic drama. To more modern minds this sudden break in Talma's playing seems a quite unwarranted hiatus, tantamount to sacrilege.

The months following the failure of *Jane Shore* the actor spent between Paris and Brunoy, snatching what rustic peace he could in his round of highly successful appearances in *Marie Stuart*, *Sylla* and *Régulus*. The success of Arnault's son's dramatic exercise on the rivalry of Rome and Carthage had quite surprisingly rekindled an interest in the father's *Germanicus*, that play of stormy memories in 1817. Phoenix-like it rose from the ashes of presumed failure and gave Talma an opportunity to recreate the Roman conqueror. During the hot August days, Manlius and Sévère in *Polyeucte* afforded the actor some respite from his more exacting rôles.

The death of King Louis XVIII on September 16th closed all the royal theatres. The lying-in-state at the Tuileries and the subsequent pomp and ceremony of the monarch's funeral, with the ensuing gloom of prolonged court mourning, made entertainment in the subsidized playhouses a social matter of secondary importance. During this period however dissension was again rife at the Comédie-Française.

This time the trouble centred round Mlle Mars, who was most anxious to extend the scope of her acting by an appearance in a tragic part. Pierre Lebrun, who had won such an emphatic success with *Marie Stuart*, had written a Spanish play, *Le Cid d'Andalousie*, about a valiant Don Sanche of Seville, a warrior hero not to be confused with Corneille's Don Rodrigue who, two centuries earlier, had added his meed of glory to the title *Le Cid*. Lebrun whom Dumas *fils* described as 'a man of tradition, the end of one phase and the beginning of another',[1] like a true forerunner of Victor Hugo, had concocted a tragic drama, remarkable at least for its spectacular scenes, which included exotic gardens, an opera house and a throne room, also for a wealth of detail about Spanish life and betrothal customs. The sociétaires wanted to produce the play, but felt in duty bound to respect the vested interests of Mlle Duchesnois, to whom by her playing of Marie Stuart the author had already owed much. Talma, having triumphed in comedy with Mlle Mars, saw great possibilities in their partnership in a tragedy. *Le Cid d'Andalousie* might well become a money-

[1] Stewart and Tilley. *The Romantic Movement in French Literature*, Footnote 2, p. 71.

maker like *L'École des vieillards*. The sociétaires, whether their shares were whole or fractional, could not resist the prospect of another Pactolus pouring its golden stream into the theatre coffers. In the ensuing squalid squabbles, rancorous jealousies were exacerbated. They bade fair to repeat that unhappy situation when Talma and Damas had struggled for a part; now Mlle Mars and Mlle Duchesnois prepared to battle. Lebrun's own preface to the printed play indicates the cause and the bitterness of the quarrel. He had conceived a heroine whose lighthearted manner would carry 'high comedy into the tragic domain'.[1] The trouble with Mlle Duchesnois, in the author's opinion, was that she did not *speak* her lines. On the other hand 'Mlle Mars who did not know how to declaim possessed, in addition to this great advantage, gifts to which Mlle Duchesnois could not pretend. She therefore appeared to me to be indispensable to my work. . . . That was why I told the actors that without Mlle Mars *Le Cid d'Andalousie* could not be played.'

With such unqualified support from her author Mlle Mars stood firm in her resolve. Talma, despite his sixty-two years, would play the young warrior lover. While these casting troubles were being straightened out, Lebrun's enemies whispered without any real substance that *Le Cid d'Andalousie* was politically a dangerous play. The censorship, now called upon to safeguard the divinely royal rights of a Charles X, a king much more reactionary in thought and attitude than his brother Louis XVIII, required little persuasion to maul the author's text. In fact, only the efforts of Chateaubriand, then a minister, succeeded in rescuing the manuscript from such clutches. The first night of the play, March 1st, 1825, brought together a stormy restless audience which, in addition to any partisan spirit it might show, had suffered some inconvenience by the unexplained late arrival of the door-keepers. The play had actually started while furious spectators were noisily taking their seats. The critic of *Le Journal des Débats*[2], although impressed by its spectacle, thought little of the play. 'Talma had two or three opportunities to be tragic and on these two or three occasions he was sublime. But when he had to sigh out his languorous love, no longer was he Talma. The same thing happened to Mlle Mars. She was excellent in the scenes where Talma was weak; she became ineffective when the tragedian gathered his

---

[1] P. Lebrun, *Oeuvres complètes*. Préface, *Le Cid d'Andalousie*, p. xxxii seq.
[2] *Le Journal des Débats*, March 3rd, 1825.

forces; so that the most important parts of the play were performed with the same inequality the author had given them.' The critic proceeds to tell us that the fifth act was scarcely heard and in a din that lasted ten minutes Talma had to wait patiently before he could announce the playwright's name.

Le Journal de Paris[1] showed itself a trifle piqued by the pretentiousness of Lebrun's title. The paper made much of the erring doorkeepers. Neither the acting nor the play pleased. 'The first acts, thanks to Talma's talent, and Mlle Mars' charm and sensitivity, were warmly applauded. Towards the end, the long-winded dialogue, the touches of everyday life that had been lavishly expended upon the principal characters and, above all, the multiplicity of useless detail, spelled victory for the enemies of the romantic cult. In a word, the play was hissed.' However, the critic did add. 'Talma, plaintive and monotonous in a few passages of love and dalliance, had elsewhere moments of compelling beauty.' The Duchess d'Abrantès attended the first night[1] and entered her impressions in her journal. 'For the first time the Comédie-Française gave voice to romantic lines.' Here, she continued, was no rehash of Corneille's *Le Cid*. The author had caught remarkably well the life of the period. 'No, there are great beauties in this play.' In commenting upon its failure, she concluded: '*C'était une cabale.*' The critic of *Le Journal de Paris*, clearly a faithful admirer of Talma, with a laudable persistence went to the play's third performance. In his notice[3] one sentence deserves quotation. 'Talma, the worthy inheritor of the celebrated Baron, makes one forget by sheer acting talent that his age is no longer Le Cid's.' Very rarely indeed occur references to Talma playing parts unsuitable to his age. Of course theatre-goers in those days viewed with a tolerance greater than would an audience today the spectacle of a mature actor in *jeune premier* rôles. But they had to be seen in great parts where the technique of a life-time could suspend that disbelief which the burden of years might try to impose. Talma certainly possessed this technique in a superlative degree. He could in some plays defy time but not the fustian of *Le Cid d'Andalousie*.

Lebrun ascribed the failure of his tragedy, which registered only five performances, to illness in the cast. Talma brought back

[1] *Le Journal de Paris*, March 2nd, 1825.
[2] *Mémoires de la Duchesse d'Abrantès*, Vol. VI, p. 170.
[3] *Le Journal de Paris*, March 6th, 1825.

Régulus to the bill as his main attraction until he journeyed north-wards in April to Belgium. By his contract with the King the actor had to play his current successes at the royal theatre in Brussels. Clearly *Le Cid d'Andalousie* could not be numbered in that category, but the ingenious Talma found a happy way out of his dilemma. In a letter to Lebrun, tantalizingly headed 'This Monday the First', he wrote: 'The idea has occurred to me to take your manuscript to Brussels to read your *Cid* to the King and the Queen at a small private reunion. It would give me great pleasure and provide for the King and the Queen one of the most agreeable evenings in the world.'[1] This is the last we hear of this unfortunate play, whose author, utterly disgusted with the Comédie-Française, abandoned the theatre. Talma's death the following year deprived him of support in the Comité as well as of his ideal interpreter and led him eventually to accept the respon-sibility of directing the royal printing press.

When Talma returned from Brussels in May, he found Paris caught up in preparations for the new King's coronation. To celebrate this national occasion an ultra-royalist gentleman from Montpelier, M. Draparnaud, who in the difficult Hundred Days had helped the Duchesse d'Angoulême to resist the returned Napoleon, had written a tragedy in three acts entitled *La Clémence de David*. At that time, to write a tragedy was deemed something of an accomplishment, particularly if the author stood outside the narrow circle of professional purveyors of the genre. M. Drapar-naud could not by any stretch of the imagination be included in that august band and one can only conjecture that royal pressure must have persuaded the sociétaires to accept this biblical exercise for the free performance to be given to the citizens of Paris on June 7th, 1825.

Talma's intelligence must have kicked against this outrageous tissue of nonsense. To the most superficial reader it became clear that M. Draparnaud's knowledge of Old Testament events was of the scantiest, and his chronology grievously at fault. The play abounded in anachronisms. Many must have wondered whether the usurper David, fighting a divinely anointed king, could be considered an appropriate choice for the coronation of a monarch who before everything proclaimed himself the champion of hereditary right. More awkward still, to Talma fell the rôle of Abiathar, the High Priest, a feeble caricature of Racine's mighty

[1] Guy de la Batut, *Correspondance*, p. 90.

Joad, a character still closely identified with the actor. Both the part and the play seemed an abuse of the royal occasion and of the talents of the Théâtre-Français.

The action couched in naïve, pseudo-biblical language concerned the proposal of the conspirator Thamar that Isbaäl, a young warrior, should assassinate David the King. Isbaäl refused, preferring as a loyal adherent to Saül to fight David in hand to hand combat. Thamar, fearing the consequences of his suggested treason, threatened to denounce Isbaäl if he refused to carry out the murder. Isbaäl killed Thamar and was magnanimously pardoned by David. There we have *La Clémence de David*, served up of course with high priestly trimmings for Talma and an outburst of distraught mother love for Mlle Duchesnois as Jésabel. The *Journal des Débats*[1] remarked: 'Rarely has one seen a new play exposed to such constant expressions of the audience's disfavour. . . . The united talents of Talma, Lafon, Mlle Duchesnois availed nought against the monotony of this composition or against the clumsiness of style which aroused laughter not only in the auditorium but on the stage as well. One even saw the High Priest Abiathar (Talma) laugh stealthily at some particularly silly expressions put into Isbaäl's mouth when he embraced his mother in the person of Mlle Duchesnois.' The *Journal de Paris*,[2] equally scathing about the play, culled this gem from its poverty-stricken alexandrines.

> . . . *Entraînés dans un péril égal,*
> *Isbaäl par David, David par Isbaäl.*[3]

which surely deserves remembrance beside that English bathetic jewel,

> 'Oh! Sophonisba! Sophonisba! Oh!'

Yet, according to this paper, 'the public called loudly for the author and Lafon, who played the part of David, came forward to announce the name of M. Draparnaud.'

The play achieved only two performances. Its total failure can best be gauged by the official visit to the Théâtre-Français in a round of coronation engagements of the newly anointed Charles X, accompanied by the Duchesse d'Angoulème and other

---

[1] *Le Journal des Débats*, June 11th, 1825.
[2] *Le Journal de Paris*, June 8th, 1825.
[3] 'Swept into a like danger,
Isbaäl by David, David by Isbaäl.'

members of the royal family on June 11th when, *par ordre* Alexandre Soumet's *Clytemnestre* was acted. Had *La Clémence de David*, the official *pièce d'occasion*, won a modicum of success, it would surely have been performed in the presence of the author's patroness. Prudence counselled the Soumet tragedy in which Talma of course played Oreste. 'The moving quality of Talma's acting appeared especially to create a deep impression upon the mind of the King and of the princes who took pleasure in giving the public the signal for applause.'[1]

[1] *Le Journal de Paris*, June 12th, 1825.

Part 4

Apotheosis

CHAPTER 45

Léonidas ·

D uring a summer when a monarch is crowned, particularly when the scene is laid in the mercurial city of Paris, joy reigns unconfined and entertainment becomes the order of the day. For the theatres it was a season of great prosperity and the tragedy team of the Théâtre-Français, if a little shaken by the failures of *Le Cid d'Andalousie* and *La Clémence de David*, could still offer as comparative novelties *Sylla* and *Régulus*. To provide the new tragedy which the times seemed to require, Jouy's *Bélisaire* went quickly into rehearsal. The piece, although written seven years previously and long accepted by the Comité, owed its constant postponement to a belief that it was politically tactless to depict an all-conquering general in those 1818 days, when Bourbons and Bonapartistes publicly wrangled. Apart from censorship considerations, the production of *Bélisaire* had yet another claim to popular interest. The theatre's commissioner, Chéron, contemplated retirement and with him would go Damas. Talma's relief can almost be sensed in his generous action when, to speed the parting Damas, he offered to play for the first time the rôle of Bélisaire at his farewell benefit performance on June 28th, 1825. It would prove a good opportunity to wipe away all the unhappy memories that their disputes over *L'École des vieillards* had occasioned. Damas must to some extent have forgiven Talma, otherwise he could never have accepted so signal a favour from his great colleague. The sociétaires in their joy at this reunion had announced in the Paris press that they would guarantee M. Damas should receive as a result of this performance at least 10,000 francs.

When the curtain rose on *Bélisaire*, the theatre was barely half full. The parterre looked thinly sown with spectators and only 120 seats had been sold in the boxes and galleries. Yet on this night Talma was to appear in a new play by an author who had given him *Tippoo-Saïb* and *Sylla*. The fact that the new play had been once deemed forbidden fruit ought surely to have added to its attraction. Nor could the weather be blamed. Those late June days were distinctly cool. Damas' popularity went unchallenged. How came it that the takings, even at the customary raised prices, reached only 2,500 francs? The Comédie-Française, by its much trumpeted guarantee of 10,000 francs to Damas when all Paris knew that on such occasions greater sums were the rule, had undermined public confidence. Paris asked where the money would go. Like Molière's Géronte, the French playgoer wants to know what he is paying for and to whom.

Jouy had been at great pains to invent an original plot around Justinian's great general, efforts which would remove his play from any possible comparison with still remembered tragedies on the same subject. In the Jouy version Bélisaire's daughter, Eudoxe, loves the Romans' bitter foe, a Bulgar King, Thélésis. The old general, by his wise military counsel, secures for his Emperor, but at no little domestic cost to himself, a complete victory over the Bulgars. The generous Bélisaire, mortally wounded in battle, intercedes with his master for the life of Thélésis who, when pardoned, takes Eudoxe as his bride on condition that he becomes the ally of Rome. After this convenient settlement of all disputes, Bélisaire plucks from his breast the fatal shaft and with due solemnity expires.

The critics found *Bélisaire* cold, slow in action and often prolix, but judged it not unworthy of the success it achieved. Talma received his usual meed of praise.[1] 'We applauded all Bélisaire's part, but most loudly of all the by-play which recalled David's picture.' 'Talma took the part of Bélisaire really well. He received an ovation when he came forward to announce the author's name.' The same verdict could not be pronounced upon his colleagues. 'A gentle mediocrity informed the other acting. Mlle Bourgoin did not shine as Eudoxe and, to the great handicap of the play, Mlle Paradol had been called in to replace Mlle Duchesnois as the general's wife, Antonine. Only Lafon, who by some self-denying ordinance agreed to play a minor rôle with one effective scene, earned the epithet "brilliant".'[2]

Jouy's play, if not a spectacular success, nevertheless kept a steady place in the bill until August. September found Talma in

[1] *Le Journal de Paris*, June 29th, 1825.
[2] *Le Journal des Débats*, June 30th, 1825.

Brussels. Touring now meant northward tracks, and Talma never concealed the satisfaction and pride he felt in the compulsive experience of a royal command to appear on the Brussels stage. During that autumn, a Dauphinois playwright named Pichat, whose romantic leanings caused him to alter his patronymic to the more mediaevally sounding Pichald, had aroused great hopes in the mind of the reading committee with his *Léonidas*. In the opinion of Victor Hugo this Pichald stood with Soumet as the 'two future kings of our theatre'.[1] Leaving out of the question any merits the play might have, Pichald had certainly struck lucky over his theme. Lord Byron by his heroic death at Missolonghi had fired all Europe with an interest in the Greek struggle for freedom against the Turkish despots. With French opinion firmly behind the Greek cause, it did not require much imagination to estimate the effect of such rousing lines in Pichald's play as:

> . . . . . . *leur gloire vengeresse*
> *Dans l'avenir encore ressuscite la Grèce.*
> *Oui vaincus, opprimés, dans les siècles lointains*
> *Les Grecs ne seront pas déchus de leurs destins*
> *Tant que de notre gloire entretenant leurs villes*
> *Vous resterez debout, rochers de Thermopyles!*[2]

With so topical a theme and with such high-sounding verse, success, elusive goddess in the theatre, seemed almost assured.

For once prophecy realized fulfilment. If there was any doubt in the minds of the audience assembled on November 26th, it was dictated by a curiosity to know how M. Pichald would spin out five acts long the heroic stand of Léonidas in the Pass of Thermopylae. Like the true romantic he was, the author for the opening of his play had imagined the arrival of two young Greeks, who came into the Persian camp to offer their lives for two Persian envoys who had been murdered by the Greeks. This device permitted scenes in both camps with much rhetorical verse, threw in for good measure the motive of mother love and served to some extent as a unifying thread between Greeks and Persians.

It is of interest to compare the notices the play received in three

---

[1] H. Girard, *Le Centenaire du Premier Cénacle Romantique*, p. 43.

[2] ' . . . their avenging glory will yet in times to come quicken Greece to life. Yes conquered, oppressed, in centuries afar off, Greeks will not have fallen from their destined greatness, so long as their cities draw strength from our glory and you remain erect, rocks of Thermopylae.'

national newspapers. *Le Journal de Paris*[1] observed that the author, in order to lend drama to his scenes, had to give his imagination free rein, but 'by energetic painting, tendentious verses, sentiments which faithfully recall the heroes of Lacedaemon, this tragedy is really a kind of Spartiana in which no tributes glorifying Léonidas and his brothers in arms have been omitted or marred. But we saw no construction, no action, no mounting tension. The Greek cause largely contributed to the success, and the verses of the new Léonidas yield in no way to Byron's lyrical stanzas. Talma, Mlle Duchesnois, Lafon, Firmin, David and Victor each according to his means contributed wondrously to the play.'

Le Constitutionnel[2] had similar reserves about the structure of the tragedy. 'The *Léonidas* of M. Pichald is one of those works which on the score of its dramatic interest cannot suffer without scathe the test of analysis and of careful scrutiny. The action hardly exists. . . . The scene is laid in ancient Greece but in reality we are transported to a contemporary Greece.' Mlle Duchesnois 'who lacked force' and Lafon 'who played for mere effect' did not please the critic. 'As for Talma, his great talent is ill at ease in the passive and really on-looking rôle of Léonidas; but his physical appearance alone suffices to maintain the immense superiority which distinguishes him; in painting I know of nothing more beautiful than the face of Léonidas in David's canvas and Talma brings it to life.'

Le Journal des Débats[3] on November 27th hailed the play as a triumph and regaled its readers with the extract on Greece's destiny already quoted. The acting exceeded praise. Mlle Duchesnois had moments of inspiration as the mother. Lafon was all that could be desired; Firmin and David comported themselves ideally as the two young heroes. 'What really assured the evening's success was the team spirit with which this tragedy was acted . . . and Talma was without exaggeration and without any qualification above his own standards in the part of Léonidas. Only after applause lasting five minutes did Talma succeed in making M. Pichald's name heard, a name that was received with renewed bravos. A complete success which gives every indication of being sustained.'

The critic proved right. Between its first night, November 26th,

---

[1] *Le Journal de Paris*, November 27th, 1825.
[2] *Le Constitutionnel*, November 28th, 1825.
[3] *Le Journal des Débats*, November 28th, 1825.

and December 31st, 1825, no fewer than twelve performances of *Léonidas* were given. In a repertory theatre like the Comédie-Française, where comedy and tragedy divide the bill, such a demand for a new tragedy was quite exceptional and, let it be remembered, *Léonidas* went triumphantly on into 1826.

CHAPTER 46

Talma on Lekain, 1825

During this year of 1825 Talma, in response to many requests that he should write something about his great predecessor, Lekain, put pen to paper and produced his *Quelques réflexions sur Lekain et sur l'art théâtral*. It must be remembered that Talma had never seen Lekain act. All his early acting life Talma had lived in the shadow of a grudging comparison with the great interpreter of Voltaire's plays, constantly enduring the denigration an older generation heaped so prodigally upon his reforms, and learning what he could of Lekain from senior colleagues like Molé, Larive and Monvel who of course had played with him. By 1825 the name of Lekain held no terrors for Talma. His own position as the greatest tragedian of his generation was now unassailable and from this theatrical eminence he could survey the past with something akin to a calm objectivity. It must be confessed that, although Talma was asked to set down something of Lekain's contribution to the French theatre, the larger and infinitely more interesting part of his book illustrates his own reforms both of declamation and costume, his own philosophy of acting and what he wanted still to see accomplished.

Mme de Staël had told him that one day he must write. Here is his book, which demolished Diderot's thesis, set out in *Le Paradoxe du Comédien*,[1] where the philosopher affirmed that 'extreme sensibility makes middling actors; middling sensibility makes the ruck of bad actors; in the complete absence of sensibility lies the possibility of a sublime actor'. Talma made clear that he held quite the opposite view. For him the first and basic qualification of an actor was sensibility, which he regarded as the very source of imagination. He wrote: 'To form a great actor like Lekain the union of sensibility and intelligence is required.' More than half a century later, when Henry Irving began to consider 'the true

---

[1] Although written in 1773, Diderot's essay was not published until 1830, after Talma's death. His ideas were of course current among actors of Talma's day.

inwardness' of his work, he had Talma's study translated and published in a Victorian magazine, *The Theatre*, contributing to it a preface in which he fully endorsed the Frenchman's views. Talma had no doubts about these fundamental qualities. Between two persons destined for the stage, one gifted with extreme sensibility and the other endowed with profound intelligence, he would without any question prefer the former.

Talma followed the career of Lekain from the goldsmith's bench to those seventeen months of débuts, an indication of his prodigious success at the Comédie-Française, where history relates he made a resistant Louis XV weep. 'I who never weep,' protested the King.[1] Sympathetically, Talma noted Lekain's early exaggerated acting style, the shouting and the stamping, and made clear the young actor's belief that the mannered pompous delivery of Grandval or Clairon might be modified in favour of a warmer and more moving utterance. He paid Lekain the tribute of humanizing tragedy without any loss of its inherent nobility. Innovation in Lekain's day ran the risk of giving offence to the court. The changes that the small, ugly, harsh-voiced Lekain succeeded in effecting, especially in matters of costume, struck Talma as all too timid, and when the writer began to speculate upon theatrical reform, there was no holding his impetuous enthusiasm or restraining his own vain pretensions. He, Talma, wrought the changes that Lekain had but dimly glimpsed.

Nevertheless Talma gave without stint the honour that was due to his great predecessor. 'Lekain displayed supreme intelligence in the tempo of his delivery, which he made more or less rapid, more or less slow, according to the emotional state of the character, whose lines he would often break up with studied pauses.' Then he passed obviously to matters of his own practice.

There are indeed certain occasions when the actor must needs meditate before putting into words what he feels within him or what his intelligence prompts. In such a case the actor must appear to think before speaking; he must, by means of pauses, seem to take time to consider what he is going to say, but he must also by his facial expression eke out those silences and, by his bearing and the play of his features, indicate that during such pauses his mind is deeply preoccupied. Without such by-play these gaps in the delivery of his lines would seem merely a cold hiatus due rather to a lapse of memory than to any cogitation.

[1] All ensuing matter on Lekain and the new conception of theatrical art is taken directly from *Quelques Réflexions sur Lekain et sur l'art théâtral par Talma.*

There are also situations when a human being, deeply stirred, feels that his excess of emotion cannot wait for the slow combination of words. The feelings which sway him before his own voice can express them suddenly slip out in dumb show. Gesture, bearing, facial expression, must of necessity forestall words as the lightning flash precedes the thunder clap. This method heightens expression to a remarkable degree in that it lays bare a mind already deeply affected and impatient to declare itself by the most immediate means available. These artifices constitute what has properly been called dumb show, so essential a part of the art of acting and one so difficult to attain, to possess and to control; by it an actor conveys to his words a touch of everyday life, of truth itself, thus depriving it of any resemblance to something learnt by heart and recited. [1]

Throughout the study we pass constantly from Lekain's achievements to Talma's own thoughts about the art of acting. He saw in the terrible experiences of the French Revolution a great release from the formal, courtly conventions that had bedevilled the actor's task. That great upheaval showed how aristocrat and workman in moments of intense passion felt and expressed themselves in much the same way. The bereaved mother before the empty cradle suffered as did a duchess enduring a similar plight. [2] The great emotions of the soul brought out the best in man. The cause of the *sans-culottes* made even street orators sublime. There spoke the '*enfant de la Révolution*'.

As he surveyed the past Talma took the view that it required twenty years of hard work to perfect an actor, one who could be relied upon to produce night after night the same groupings, the same effects, the same tones, inflections, gestures, movements, with the same exactitude, the same vigour, the same abandon. Any difference between an actor's performances should be to the advantage of his last.

What did he deem necessary for a beginner? He headed his list of desirable qualities with memory, 'an indispensable tool'. Then came physical qualities, build and countenance to make possible for the player a wide range of parts. A voice, flexible and capable of being easily modulated. As an essential background the aspirant must have had a really good education with some stress upon the study of history, in order that events, personalities, the way of life of different peoples and what we should call today a sense of period might be fully understood. Graceful deportment and fencing skill had their place; he also saw in drawing a valuable aid

[1] Talma, *Quelques Réflexions*, p. 542.   [2] Ibid. p. 525.

to the actor. If he admitted that comedy and tragedy might require the same fundamental gifts, he believed that for tragedy they had to be more in evidence.[1] Talma contested the idea that the comic actor offers a greater variety of human types and foibles. He pointed out that the painting of passion is of all time and that society in varying ages and at different levels may modify the degree and manner of its emotional expression. In his view there fell to the tragic actor a greater moral responsibility.

Lekain, the perfected artist, had mastered the art of communicating the pathetic and displayed, for all to see, his power to run the whole gamut of human emotion, from hatred to love, from nicely tempered thought to that specialized fanaticism, the hallmark of Voltaire's plays. More generally Talma believed that every actor must himself have experienced the extremes of passion and must remember in his own playing the impressions he received so that he can evoke in simulated emotion standards of nature and truth. He confessed, not without a hint of shame, that upon one occasion when he was overcome with genuine grief the actor within him noted the change his tears wrought in his voice and the spasmodic quality of his sobs. These observations he turned later to professional profit. On the subject of weeping on the stage Talma showed himself possessed both of judgment and technique. Tears, he tells us, must be controlled; they tend to push the voice into a high register where sounds assume a shrillness, a thin quality, and have little carrying power. For shedding tears the actor must keep his voice strictly to the middle register. Only within this range are tears really noble, touching and sincere. Thus can the actor draw from his own personal sufferings a professional advantage that will serve him well in his efforts to attain perfection in his art.[2]

He concluded:

I have jotted down these ideas without much arrangement, just as they have come to my pen. I could not refuse myself the pleasure of rendering homage to the memory of the greatest actor who has appeared on our stage nor of developing in the process a few ideas on the art of the theatre which my own experience has been able to provide. I am not unaware how incomplete these must seem. Far be it from me to imagine that I can make good what he has left undone, but if my abilities match my desires and if my busy life leaves me a little leisure,

[1] Talma, *Quelques Réflexions*, pp. 541, 542.
[2] Talma, *Quelques Réflexions*, p. 547.

I should like later on to assemble in quiet and repose the memories of a long experience and to end in this way by an account perhaps of use to those who will come after me—of a career, adorned by some success and wholly dedicated to the art I have loved so much.

So much for Talma on Lekain and the art of acting. Caroline Vanhove in her miscellany of memoirs pays tribute to the actor as a writer. She refers to her late husband's exquisite literary taste, how playwrights asked him to correct their verses, to his re-writing of the fifth act of *Manlius* and she even hints at collaboration between Ducis and Talma. Among his papers he left behind outlines and sketches of at least two comedies, *La Méprise* and *L'Erreur agréable*, but these were sold and dispersed after his death.[1] Mme de Staël, who had perceived in Talma something of a writer's talent, proved to be not wholly wide of the mark. The trouble was that the niceties of literary composition stood little chance of exercise in a life so teemingly full of stage experience.

With his ideas on acting so firmly stated in his Lekain memoir, it must therefore come as rather a shock to the reader to learn that, in the latter days of March of this selfsame year, 1825, Talma's technique as an actor was roundly attacked by Charles Maurice who, through his somewhat gossipy column in *Le Courrier français*, insisted that the tragedian's performances had deteriorated on the score of his age and that his acting had become mechanical by a constant use of six gestures. This was a serious charge and one cannot do better than let Charles Maurice make it and comment on the consequences.[2]

In my last article I refer to the six gestures, the recurrence of which forms the basis of Talma's postures; raising his belt, rubbing his hands, crossing them to touch his shoulder, wiping his brow, lifting his eyes to heaven and a trembling in his left leg as he bends it. I end by saying with justice that the name of Talma has become almost national. . . . I stop writing. Talma himself is announced. What is going to happen? . . . He was deeply moved; but his fine features did not convey anger, rather did they denote a kindness, restrained by the fact of his intrusion. At once he said: 'You have not the power to deprive me of my talent. That is a gift of nature and the fruit of my study; but you take from me my confidence. You reduce my gestures to six . . . perhaps it is true. I think about it when I am on the stage, I want to put it right, clumsiness slips in and my memory goes! I have

---

[1] H. d'Alméras, *Mémoires sur Talma*, p. 340. C. Talma, *Quelques Particularités*, p. 314.

[2] C. Maurice, *Histoire anecdotique du théâtre*, Vol. I, pp. 347–350.

come to tell you that if you intend to continue (these articles) I shall leave the stage. I would rather do that than end up by justifying your criticisms still further.' Struck by the nobility of his opening words and almost overcome by the touching inflection he imparted to the last, I said to him: 'When an artist like you speaks to a man like me, he can only make this reply,' and taking advantage of the fact that he was sitting near my armchair, I took his hand, bending my knee towards him. I was about to complete my action when he drew me towards him to mingle the emotion we both felt in a close embrace. 'I expected it,' he added when he had recovered himself. 'Thérèse[1] had often told me so. Come round to her place tomorrow, she will give us a dinner to celebrate our reconciliation.' I shall never forget that scene which made me realize what compensations one may expect in the pursuit of such a difficult profession and I shall retail it tomorrow to Mlle Bourgoin's guests without any concealment at all.

Had Talma become so mechanical a player? Every actor has certain mannerisms which may betray him in voice or gesture. Let the date of this interview be noted, March 28th, 1825, when in that very month Talma had miscast himself as Lebrun's youthful lover, Le Cid d'Andalousie. Against an actor so intelligent, so versed in his profession, so sensitive to audience reaction, it seems almost impossible that this serious charge could ever have been brought. Charles Maurice had not as a critic the stature of a Geoffroy or even of a Martainville. In all the material that has been read to produce this book, only one other reference to a mechanical gesture by Talma can be cited. It goes back a long way, in fact to the days when the tragedian and Geoffroy were on terms of amity. Talma in July 1802 had appeared as Tancrède, a great Lekain part, and as a returned exile spoke this opening line:

A *tous les coeurs bien nés que la patrie est chère!*[2]

Geoffroy[3] meeting Talma one evening as a guest of Lainez the singer, told the tragedian how his admired Lekain took that opening scene. 'As soon as he appeared,' he said, 'all the chivalry of knighthood came on with him. You come on like a mere passer-by, a commercial traveller, a herbalist, anybody. You hand over your shield on the right, your lance on the left to the two supers who act as your squires; then you come down to the footlights, say as best you can, "*A tous les coeurs*".' Of course this

[1] Mlle Bourgoin.
[2] 'To every highborn heart how dear is the fatherland!' *Tancrède*, Act III, Sc. i.
[3] Lanzac de Laborie, *Le Théâtre-Français*, pp. 50, 51.

is not really a comment on a personal gesture of Talma's. Rather does it serve as evidence of mechanical stage business. Yet it remains as the only parallel passage to Maurice's criticism of the six gestures. The Tancrède incident happened in 1802, refracted through the partisan mind of Geoffroy. Talma never enjoyed playing Tancrède for, like so many of Voltaire's heroes, there was little poetry in the part and too many of its creator's propagandist ideas. Can the charge of a monotonous, artificial, mannered technique be sustained against Talma on such evidence? When Maurice brought the charge of '*les six gestes*', Talma had served the Comédie-Française for thirty-eight years, he had created seventy-two rôles supplied by contemporary dramatists, he had brought astonishing life and beauty to the great tragedies of Corneille and Racine, he had opened French eyes to the glories of Shakespeare, he had won the plaudits of the greatest men and women of his time, Mirabeau, Napoleon, Mme de Staël, Chateaubriand, Stendhal, Lamartine, Victor Hugo, and the utter devotion of Revolutionary, Napoleonic and Restoration audiences. No mere puppet actor, relying on a few tricks, could have achieved all this. The man's own communings on his art proclaim the sensibility, the imagination and the intelligence of the great artist. No, the charge of mechanical acting cannot be sustained. The defendant stands acquitted.

CHAPTER 47

The Final Triumph

It was a weary Talma who celebrated his sixty-third birthday on January 15th, 1826. He had passed through a strenuous year with four new parts, a season in Brussels to keep faith with the King of the Netherlands and a constant return to old and favourite rôles, so often undertaken to help some fledgling Hermione or budding Jocaste called to make a critical début. In addition he had written his memoir on Lekain. At No. 9 rue de la Tour-des-Dames all went well. Madeleine-Jacqueline Bazire, domestically minded and faithful beyond the world's idea of mistresses, kept house, received amiably her lover's legal wife Caroline and presided over those lavish entertainments the actor provided all too frequently for his friends. The boys were at school at Fontenay-les-Roses and little Virginie, born in 1823, was the darling of the ménage and certainly the apple of her father's eye. Finances of course created their customary problems, but the actor's renown, the admiration in which he was held by all classes of society seemed at once a bulwark against undue persecution and, alas! a source of credit for ever newly contracted debts. No, it was a strange bodily weariness that assailed the actor. His medical adviser, Dr. Tanchon,[1] began to fear for his patient and had protested against the heartless way the Comédie-Française had overworked him. Like every true artist of the stage, Talma was irresistibly drawn to the theatre. How could he be expected to close his ears to the applause of the multitude? Why must he withdraw just when new playwrights were asking him to act in tragedies where his own ideas of nature and truth saw something of fulfilment? Before everything he was an actor, a true servant of a noble and beloved profession, whatever doubts Holy Church might have about its dignity. He was also the father of a young family. How could he obey his doctor's orders? Yet there was this constantly recurring trouble in the abdomen. No wonder Dr. Tanchon, in his *Histoire*

[1] The name appears in some records as Tanchou, in others as Tanchot.

médicale de Talma, wrote when early in 1826 he diagnosed an intestinal irritation, 'He had at this time his body so upset and natural needs so pressing that, even on the stage, he had barely time to reach his dressing-room.'

Strange to relate, despite the pain and discomfort of this physical trouble, Talma could or would not bring himself to believe in his illness. The public clamoured for him; that sufficed. He had so much to act, both old and new. Stendhal had again set them all talking about Shakespeare. He must revive *Macbeth*, such a contrast with that *Léonidas* that everybody liked so much. Then he had a new play on the stocks, *Charles VI*, Delaville's '*tableau historique*' of a disordered France under an old, mad king. Surely at long last here was tragedy on a national theme. Work, work, the only anodyne. Messieurs, the stage waits.

It is of interest to see what Talma was doing on the eve of this new production, destined to be his last creation. January and February found him much occupied with *Léonidas* and with *Macbeth* in which Mlle Duchesnois shared honours as the guilty thane's lady. This ailing man, refusing to face the gravity of his physical condition or to heed the advice of his doctor, while rehearsing for *Charles VI*, due on March 6th, played *Macbeth* on February 28th and *Léonidas* on March 2nd and 4th, allowing himself the respite of a single day before he faced in a new and most exacting rôle the critical parterre of the Théâtre-Français.

What a first night that was! Everything in the play conspired to rouse the patriotism of the crowd. The evil Queen, Isabelle, taking advantage of her husband's infirm mind, marries her daughter to the English conqueror, Henry V, and disinherits her own son, the Dauphin. The rightful heir meets his father in secret; the old King during a lucid interval recognizes his son and with him takes stock of the national situation. Isabelle treacherously connives at the Dauphin's arrest by the English. Charles VI, in his fitful moments of sanity, shows his love for his people, tries to implement his good intentions then, realizing all the human misery around him, dies with a pathos that only Talma could command.

The critics praised the clever way in which the author had managed to convey the sudden, strange transitions from the darkness of madness to an almost prophetic enlightenment of mind in the rôle of the King. The first two acts opened coldly and slowly, but[1] 'Happily the arrival of Talma immediately stirred the public and the three following acts in which he appeared drew forth the loudest applause. One cannot imagine a more moving picture of human suffering. For this evening let us take pleasure in saying that this tragedy or rather this historical tableau, thanks to the skilful delineation of the part of Charles VI and above all thanks to Talma's admirable talent, appears to us certain to draw crowds for some considerable time.'

Le Constitutionnel[2] also noticed the play's sluggish start. 'Then towards the middle of the third act the play begins to disclose its numerous dramatic beauties. Once there . . . the arrival of the Dauphin and his interview with his father, the complications that spring from these situations, in fact everything helps to surround the character of Charles VI with the most pathetic interest. What contributes to this interest are the tones of Talma's voice. One can say that never before has he carried so far his imitation of nature; his virile handsome features bear the impress of grief, dejection, bewilderment; his voice speaks to the soul. One cannot conceive of art progressing farther.'

Tissot[3] who saw him as Charles VI reports that for Talma to pass from a tyrant like Sylla 'to the character of Charles VI, old, oppressed by infirmities, sometimes reduced to direst poverty, finding reason only in flashes in order to shed tears of blood over the misfortunes of France, was mere child's play. Not only was it impossible to recognize him under the mask and costume he assumed but, more remarkable still, he let fall from a heart deeply stricken pangs of grief and of fatherly love which hitherto he had never divulged. He brought tears to every eye and at the same time won golden opinions by his complete regard for truth. Every man would say: 'I have seen Charles VI as he must have been when, bowed beneath the burden of misfortune, he stirred the pity of his poor subjects who laid the blame for their own miseries only on their monarch's sickness." '

One could multiply quotations of this kind. Through all the emotion and admiration which stirred his contemporaries one thing stands out clearly. He created this last part with a compelling imagination and intelligence that released from the bonds of treacherous, mortal flesh the deathless spirit of a great artist.

[1] *Le Journal de Paris*, March 7th, 1826.
[2] *Le Constitutionnel*, March 13th, 1826.
[3] Tissot, *Souvenirs historiques de F. Talma*, pp. 31, 32.

Happily these last months at the Comédie-Française carried with them an aura of happiness, bringing peace to the green room. Chéron's departure which had first been bruited in the press on June 29th, 1825, meant few regrets for Talma, who saw in M. le baron Taylor a more sympathetic commissaire. In an undated letter from Le Havre to his friend Coupigny in San Domingo he wrote about this time.[1] 'What shall I tell you about the theatre? It is always in a rather sad state. Only Mlle Mars and myself are making any money. We have now a young man to lead us as *commissaire royal*, the baron Taylor, much in love with the theatre, an artist, a designer, full of zeal, of ability, himself an author of a book about his extensive and picturesque travels in France. If he does not make the theatre a success, then we must give up. Since your departure I have created several rôles which earned for me a great measure of success, among others Régulus, Oreste (*Clytemnestre*), Sylla, which came after your leaving, Richard III in *Jane Shore* by Lemercier, *L'École des vieillards* and lastly Charles VI. Finally, dear friend, since you left us, my reputation has grown to double its size, at least that is what they say. But we who are princes must beware of flatterers.' As he cast a backward glance Talma recalled so well the eager, unassertive direction of Mahérault, who reintegrated at Napoleon's behest the Comédie-Française, the more competent reign of the thrustful Bernard, who really drafted the Moscow Decree for 'the great man', then the days of the mean-spirited Chéron, who loved him not. M. le baron had romantic leanings and for him it was a joyous experience to number among his early successes Delaville's *Charles VI*.

With this play established in the repertory Talma set out for Normandy on what was to prove his last provincial tour. With him went Madeleine-Jacqueline, their little daughter Virginie, Mme Firmin a friend and two servants. This little caravan with all the impedimenta of Talma's costumes and properties made its way first to Rouen, where Holy Week was spent. The spare framework of French classical tragedy must have been a blessing to actors on tour. Any provincial theatre could provide the conventional peristyle or the ante-chamber to a palace, as well as a local company of players prepared to support any star at the shortest notice in the customary masterpieces which of course Talma offered, *Manlius, Britannicus, Cinna, Athalie, Iphigénie, Oedipe*. The tragedian's later

[1] Guy de la Batut, *Talma: Correspondance*, p. 160.

successes, often ruled out by scenic complexities, carried the disadvantage of being unknown to stock companies in the smaller towns. The exceptions to this rule, strangely enough, were Ducis' adaptations of Shakespeare plays. Talma's Hamlet was acclaimed everywhere. During this particular congé, *Macbeth* served him especially well.

From Rouen Talma proceeded to Le Havre and here a shattering domestic tragedy overtook him. His small three-year-old daughter Virginie was suddenly seized with meningitis and despite all medical effort died. The actor in any reference to himself and his children is always described as an excellent father and his grief can be imagined. This little girl, the joy of his latter years, had, though so briefly, brought to that fashionable bohemian round which constituted Talma's Paris life the sweetness of babyhood and the joy of family ties. Ill himself and quite overcome by this cruel bereavement, the actor however asserted himself when arrangements for the child's burial were made. Virginie, the daughter of an actor, excluded by the Roman Church from the communion of the faithful by her father's exercise of his profession, was buried in the Protestant cemetery at Sainte-Adresse, where, on the word of Baron de Cottenson writing in 1901, her grave still exists.

The tour went on. Talma played at Caen,[1] where he found time to pay his respects to Malherbe's house, to indulge in sea-bathing at Luc-sur-Mer, which seemed to do him good, and to boat on the Orne. On one occasion, when his frail craft reached the Channel waters, it was stopped by the customs officers. Talma without his passport quickly established his identity by reciting snatches from *Manlius* and *Oedipe*, to the great joy of the superintendent, who remembered that uniquely tragic voice and instantly apologized for any inconvenience the actor might have suffered at the hands of his subordinates. It was during this Caen visit that Talma made the pilgrimage to the chapel of Notre-Dame de la Délivrance and bought there for himself and his friends the silver flower sprays that were sold to the faithful. This tiny point deserves recording. Talma was never vindictive; here he behaved like a good Catholic visiting a hallowed shrine.

Paris of course called him insistently. The sociétaires wanted him to play Virginius in a new tragedy which Alexandre Guiraud had written on a subject that Sheridan Knowles the English play-

---

[1] E. Duval, *Talma. Précis historique*, pp. 122, 123.

wright had used for Macready at Covent Garden in 1820. Also Alexandre Duval's play on the Italian poet Torquato Tasso, scheduled for production in the autumn, promised him a rare acting opportunity.

The register of the Comédie-Française[1] records that M. Talma returned to play *Charles VI* on Monday, May 8th, to a rapturous house worth 3,516 francs 80 centimes. He repeated this performance on May 10th. By this time he was a very sick man. The grip of a malignant disease had become tighter. Thus did Dr. Tanchon report on his patient: 'His colour is leaden, his skin dry, his pulse formicant, his abdomen hard and swollen, with sudden evacuations following periods of persistent constipation.' The actor found consolation in the fact that his torso, the firm lines of his handsome neck, his expressive face, remained unimpaired. If his complexion looked a little dry, white lead and rouge, saffron and powder, discreetly applied, would soon mask that defect. He threw himself into his parts in a way that positively alarmed his doctor, who never ceased to rail against the Comédie-Française for the exceptionally heavy load it imposed upon a man suffering from an incurable complaint. No doctor could have had a worse patient. Rather sadly Tanchon tells us that Talma had always suffered from an excess of doctors, whose conflicting advice he often turned to suit his own purpose and that purpose was ever to serve the stage.

A mere glance at his appearances during his last season at the Comédie-Française astonishes to the point of incredulity. Those two opening performances of *Charles VI* he followed with Néron in *Britannicus* May 13th, *Charles VI* again on May 15th, Achille in *Iphigénie* May 16th, *Léonidas* May 17th, *Charles VI* May 19th, *Hamlet* May 23rd, *Sylla* May 27th, Danville in *L'École des vieillards* May 30th, *Léonidas* June 1st and on Friday June 3rd, came his final appearance in *Charles VI*. The theatre register, in chronicling this performance, carries the following note. 'Talma played this rôle for the last time. He fell ill.' What a herculean task he had accomplished in those summer days of 1826! Twelve performances covering seven plays, given by a dying man, which included Néron, Achille, Hamlet and his amazing comedy success Danville. To the end, to the very end, he held his audiences enthralled. For *Léonidas* on June 1st the box-office returns amounted to 2,657 francs 60

[1] I am indebted to Mme Sylvie Chevalley, Bibliothécaire-archiviste of the Comédie-Française, for details of Talma's final performances.

centimes. On June 2nd the sociétaires put on *Iphigénie* without Talma to a house that drew 246 francs! The following day Talma returned for his final curtain in *Charles VI*, when the takings rose to 2,704 francs 80 centimes. Even in summer sunshine he could attract a good audience.

Moreau has left a moving comment on Talma's last performance.[1] 'I remember the last performance of *Charles VI*. The pathetic scene of the play's climax stirred me to heartbreaking grief. The old King, worn out by the suffering and misfortune, who for one moment regained his reason before dying; that voice which uttered a snatch of sound so terrible and then faded away; that fiery eye which suddenly closed, that royal hand which grasped for the sceptre only to let it fall, that scene so beautiful and so brief saddened me deeply, not because of the character but because of the actor. I thought of his age, of the ravages of the disease he already endured. I felt I was present at the last contest of a vigorous athlete.'

Only an actor, and one accustomed to bear the burden of principal parts in classical and modern plays, will fully realize the heroism of these last appearances at the Comédie-Française. No layman, however devoted to the stage, can hope to estimate the outpouring of nervous energy and the strain upon memory for an ailing tragedian of sixty-three years of age that such a varied display of acting power would demand from a dedicated artist. One's heart aches to see recorded in the register during Talma's enforced absence the faithful parterre's persistent requests, voiced from the auditorium, for the latest bulletin of their beloved favourite's health.

In the midst of these final performances it must have rejoiced Talma to learn that the aggregate receipts of the Comédie-Française for the previous year, April 1st, 1825, to March 31st, 1826, amounted to the unprecedented sum of over a million francs. No wonder the press followed his illness with such close attention. On June 12th in *Le Journal de Paris* appeared this notice. 'Talma's indisposition has delayed the first performance of *Virginius*, postponed until next week. Our great tragic actor will spend a few days in the country to regain his health. We hope to see him next Sunday in *Macbeth*.' One can really only gasp. On top of those heavy May performances the actor, who had to keep a strict guard on his memory, contemplated a new rôle, Virginius, and a

[1] Moreau, *Talma*, pp. 71, 72.

return in *Macbeth*. Could devotion to the theatre and to the public go further? If ever a man served the stage with every fibre of his being, mind and body, surely it was François-Joseph Talma.

At this point the doctors arrive to take up the tragic tale. Wisdom after the event is a human vanity. In a medical case so completely documented as Talma's one tends to affect omniscience and to jump to conclusions fortified by accomplished events. So ill had the actor become during the period June 10th to June 12th that Dr. Tanchon called in as consultant Dr. Biet,[1] a rather opinionated man who fought always to get his own way, heedless of any knowledge of the patient's condition that Dr. Tanchon could supply. Talma was at once removed to Brunoy for a short stay and brought back to Paris on June 25th. Dr. Biet, now at complete variance with Dr. Tanchon, whose opinions he disdainfully set at nought, counselled rest at Montmorency, some twelve kilometres north of Paris. Thither Talma went on July 2nd and, to Dr. Tanchon's disappointment, a newly invoked practitioner, Dr. Pitaro, supported Dr. Biet in his diagnosis of a simple case of stoppage. It must be remembered that the science of diagnosis was at that time not very advanced. Biet and Pitaro agreed upon the treatment, a generous application of leeches, a low vegetable diet, plenty of enemas and constant purges. Pitaro even prescribed castor-oil. On July 5th Tanchon, Biet and Pitaro consulted with Dr. Breschet, a pupil of the great surgeon Dupuytren, when a wrathful Tanchon heard the pundits debate the relative value of calomel and castor-oil. On July 9th another medical adviser, Dr. Husson, insisted that the greatest surgeon of the day, Guillaume Dupuytren, should be summoned to Talma's bedside. This most distinguished specialist quickly changed the treatment and diet but stopped short at surgical operation. Whether such action would have proved much too experimental or whether he deemed the patient's case hopeless we do not know. Talma responded immediately to Dupuytren's treatment, which two doctors of his choosing, Braissais and Faquier, scrupulously carried out. So obvious was the patient's improvement, that his condition raised false hopes of complete recovery and of a return to the stage. Throughout the month of August Talma, given nourishing food and a respite from purges, seemed to

---

[1] The name of this doctor who plays such an important part in Talma's illness is variously spelt. It occurs as Biette, Biett and Biet. The last form has been chosen because this is how it appears in the records of the Comèdie-Française.

regain his strength to such an extent that he could return to Brunoy for a few days before proceeding to Paris. Back in the capital a relapse occurred. The patient hiccoughed, showed a swollen tongue, vomited pus and blood and became quite skeletal save in the upper part of his body. On September 19th the actor was transported to Enghien-les-Bains, quite close to the Montmorency retreat. The Paris newspapers followed the progress of the malady with an interest and detail they reserve for the great ones of the earth.

While Talma suffered at Enghien, he received a visit from Firmin, a younger tragedian and fellow sociétaire. Let Regnault-Warin take up the thread.[1] 'During the short stay he made at Enghien just before his death, M. Firmin went to see him. In the midst of his cruel sufferings Talma spoke only of the new ideas that had inspired his passionate love for the theatre. "Ah, my friend," he said to him, "how far we still are from truth! So you are going to play *Le Tasse*?" It was a part intended for Talma before his illness. "There is a fine scene in the fifth act, the one where, in the hope of restoring poor Torquato's reason, they tell him of the honours that await him, of the crown that will grace his brow." At the word "crown" he seems to rally. "A crown for me! Alphonse will not then refuse me his sister!" They present the crown to him and, looking at it with great sadness, he says, "It is not made of gold! It is only laurel. Oh, her brother will never give his consent." "Look!" continued Talma, "this is how I would have played his dull prostration." Then rising with difficulty from his bed of suffering, he struck an attitude so true. His face expressed so well the last stage of madness that it seemed as if the mighty shade of the Italian poet had stepped forth from his tomb.' Even in those pain-racked closing days the actor, ever seeking nature and truth, still affirmed his artistic creed.

[1] Regnault-Warin, *Talma*, pp. 495, 496.

CHAPTER 48

Suffering and Death

Talma did not tarry long to take the waters at Enghien-les-
Bains. He was removed to his house in Paris where his
nephew, Dr. Amédée Talma, hearing of his uncle's
alarming state, arrived from Brussels on October 9th. Three days
later no fewer than eleven doctors deliberated on his case, but
only very few held out any hope. Mercifully by their prescriptions
they relieved the patient of any acute pain. The least emotion,
even the least movement, brought on severe attacks of vomiting.
To the very last he retained clarity of mind but from his own
statement and his actions it was clear that his vision had greatly
deteriorated. Now Amédée Talma took charge of the household
and before long had to decide a very delicate matter.[1] Monseigneur de Quélen, Archbishop of Paris, whose connection with the
Pension Morin Prize Distribution will be remembered, called at
the actor's house on October 16th, ready to offer his ministrations
to the dying man. Dr. Amédée Talma, fearing the effect of such a
visit, took it upon himself after consultation with those closest to
the actor to deny the prelate admission to the sick-room. The
Archbishop retired, but not before he had assured Talma's family
that he would hold himself in readiness day and night to obey any
wish to see him the invalid might express. The zealous Monseigneur called again the following day, but Amédée Talma
advised another postponement. However, at the urgent request
of Dr. Dupuytren, he did inform his uncle of these visits. Talma,
who had met the Archbishop at the house of the one time minister
Decazes, when he heard of the prelate's concern, remarked: 'The
good Archbishop! I am very sorry not to be able to receive him.
As soon as I get better, my first call will be upon him.'

Tissot in his account of Talma's illness[2] warned his readers not

---

[1] These last days of Talma are fully described in *Journal des derniers jours de Talma,
tenu par M. le docteur Amédée Talma, médecin-dentiste à Bruxelles*, reprinted by Regnault-
Warin in his *Mémoires*, pp. 501–510.
[2] Tissot, *Talma*, p. 53.

to accept these stories of the Archbishop's zeal. He himself did not believe a word of them and, although it can be established that Monseigneur de Quélen called upon Talma, his persistence over wanting to see the sick man, which in some accounts came near to menace, certainly seems to accord ill with a Prince of the Church who had won a great reputation for his tolerance. One thing is certain. No priest approached Talma's death bed.

There is yet another puzzling matter in all these accounts of Talma's last days. No direct mention anywhere is made of the actor's beloved companion, Mlle Bazire, who had lived with him for more than twelve years. Caroline, his legal wife, was certainly present at the end. In the fierce light of publicity that surrounded Talma's illness the strict conventions of the day would find no place for a mere mistress. In France the sense of family ties has always been so strong that the silence surrounding the equivocal position of Madeleine-Jacqueline Bazire need occasion no surprise. It was a time for relatives to appear. Charles Jannin,[1] another nephew, had arrived from Brussels on October 16th. The actor's two sons, Alphonse-Alexandre and Paul-Louis, were fetched from Fontenay-les-Roses. Amédée Talma in his record of these last days spent by his uncle's bedside reports conversations which, by their very vigour of thought and speech, seem ill-placed on the lips of a dying man. Charles Jannin must have had some contract with the royal playhouse in Brussels for, on October 18th, prior to Jannin's departure for Brussels, Talma talked theatre with him and, mindful of his obligations to the King of the Netherlands, bade his nephew communicate with M. van Gobbelschroy, Minister of the Interior. That same evening a sister who lived in London reached Paris. Then about 6 a.m. on the 19th Talma saw his faithful friend and gardener, Louette, to whom, it transpired, he owed two months' wages. 'You must tell Madame,' said the actor. Here surely, under the courtesy title of Madame, might be a reference to Mlle Bazire, for so long châtelaine of Brunoy. Even here caution must be exercised. If Amédée Talma's account is to be trusted, immediately after the words to Louette came the question, '*Où donc est Caroline? Elle m'abandonne.*' Caroline, who had been snatching a little sleep, appeared. '*Te voilà, Caroline! Il faut porter toutes ces affaires là-haut, entends tu?*' Perhaps the Madame, to whom Louette had to apply

---

[1] Name occurs as 'Jamin' in Fleischmann and Bart.

for his wages, may after all have been the legal wife. One hopes not.[1]

Let Amédée Talma take up the story:[2]

It is nine o'clock. The notaries have come as well as M. Davilliers.[3] Talma gave them his hand and wished them good-day. More and more his speech became incoherent. He speaks very softly but we do not understand what he is saying. MM. Arnault and Jouy arrive. The first embraces him very tenderly and lets fall the word *'adieu'*. My uncle comes out of his somnolence and, recovering all his faculties, says to me, 'You are really going away?' 'Yes,' I replied briskly. 'M. Arnault is also leaving for Brussels as well as M. Jouy.' I brought forward the latter, who dared not approach the bedside for fear of exciting the sick man still further. These gentlemen embrace him; he says to them *'Adieu'*. They had already moved away slightly when my uncle, turning his head in their direction, said to them with a wave of his hand. 'Farewell, my friends, yes, go quickly, for that gives me the hope of seeing you again.' After this incident he became very weak, spoke often without our being able to understand him, then in a conscious moment he pointed to his eyes. His children are brought. He gives them his hand which they kiss. A little later he enunciates very distinctly these words. 'Voltaire! . . .' he lifts his eyes heavenwards, then continues, 'like Voltaire! always like Voltaire!' It was turned eleven o'clock. He uttered his very last words. 'The hardest thing of all is not to see.' A moment afterwards, at a fairly loud sound coming from a piece of furniture, he turned his head in our direction. A lady who had just arrived took his hand and said to him: *'Talma! c'est moi, Mlle Hénocq.'* He made a slight movement with his eyes and clasped her hand. Half-past eleven chimed, my uncle took his handkerchief with both hands, placed it slowly to his mouth which he wiped, then put it behind his head, still holding it with both hands. Soon these dropped to his side. I grasped one which he gently pressed, then no further movement; his breathing became almost imperceptible. Finally, at thirty-five minutes past eleven, he drew his last breath without the

[1] The identification of this Caroline creates a problem. In the Fonds Lebrun papers, Carton 29, exists the confirmation of Louette's whistle story with *renseignements donnés pour la plupart par Mme Caroline Bazire et par M. Ducis.* M. Ducis is Talma's nephew, son of that sister who married the dramatist's painter son. Again, there is a letter written by Talma to a dear friend M. Bis from Rouen on April 23rd, 1826, in which he says Caroline *joint ses remercîments aux miens pour ta bonne et touchante attention.* We know Mlle Bazire was with Talma on that last tour. It seems odd that Mlle Bazire, usually referred to as Madeleine-Jacqueline, should appear here with the name of Talma's legal wife. In this context it looks as if Caroline is the mistress and not the wife. Yet it is Caroline the wife who appears in Fleury's painting *Les Derniers moments de Talma.*

[2] Amédée Talma's account quoted by Regnault-Warin, pp. 508, 509.

[3] Executor of Talma's will.

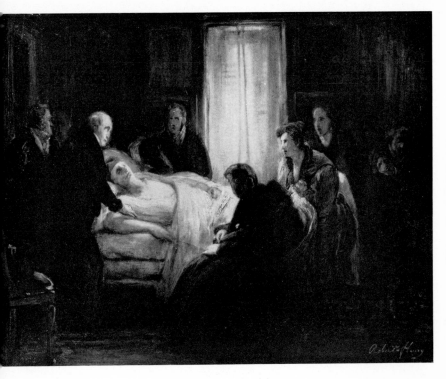

Les Derniers Moments de Talma
Painting by Robert Fleury

(It was the obstinate Dr. Biet who summoned so quickly the painter Robert Fleury to Talma's death-bed. The original cartoon of *Les Derniers Moments de Talma*, catalogue No. 38, hangs in the Foyer des Travestissements at the Comédie-Française. The picture, completed in 1827, No. 49, hangs in the Salle du Comité. In it are to be seen Amédée Talma, Jouy, Arnault, Firmin, Caroline Vanhove, Biet, Davilliers, Nicault the notary, Marchais and, in the foreground kneeling by the bedside, are the two little boys. Our illustration shows Fleury's second effort, from which he eliminated Talma's sons.)

slightest tremor or any facial contraction. Later, two artists made sketches of his head. M. David[1] the sculptor took a cast for a bust. Another painter drew the room, the bed and marked the positions occupied by those who were present at the last moments.[2]

By three o'clock that afternoon no change had occurred in the actor's features. As he lay dead he was still Talma from his breast upwards, the noblest and the greatest tragic masque the stage has ever known.[3]

On October 20th there appeared in all Paris newspapers the letter Amédée Talma had circulated to the press. He asked that the fullest publicity might be given to the dead tragedian's expressed wish that his body should be conveyed directly and without religious ceremony to its final resting place.

---

[1] Pierre-Jean David d'Angers, sculptor, not to be confused with the painter Jacques Louis David, who died in 1825.

[2] It was the obstinate Dr. Biet who summoned so quickly the painter Robert Fleury to Talma's death-bed. The original carton of *Les Derniers Moments de Talma*, catalogue No. 38, hangs in the Foyer des Travestissements at the Comédie-Française, The picture, completed in 1827, No. 49, hangs in the Salle du Comité. In it are to be seen Amédée Talma, Jouy, Arnault, Firmin, Caroline Vanhove, Biet, Davilliers, Nicault the notary, Marchais and, in the foreground, kneeling by the bedside, are the two little boys. Our illustration shows Fleury's second effort, painted early in 1827, from which he eliminated Talma's sons.

[3] Tissot, p. 55.

CHAPTER 49

Burial at Père-Lachaise

The French have a wonderful sense of all the pomp and panoply of death. That twenty-first day of October 1826 would long be remembered as a great occasion, when representatives of all classes, soldiers, writers, musicians, painters, bankers, actors, as well as humble folk from the working classes, paid with touching dignity and grief the last tribute to their beloved Talma. All too recently in their minds had lingered the memory of an unseemly scuffle that took place over the body of the favourite boulevard actor, Philippe, in an attempt to secure for his mortal remains the offices of Christian burial. In Talma's case such a disgraceful scene could not be repeated. Amédée Talma had not minced his words; he left no doubt about the disposal of his uncle's body. It would be taken from 9, rue de la Tour-des-Dames to the cemetery of Père-la-Chaise.

From eight o'clock that morning an immense crowd filled the streets adjacent to the actor's house. The coffin bore one laurel wreath adorned with the red ribbon that had served the actor as a fillet during those ninety performances of *Sylla* he had given at the Comédie-Française.[1] The procession formed and at ten o'clock began to move off. Around the hearse and led by M. le baron Taylor, commissaire royal, were grouped the sociétaires and the pensionnaires of the Théâtre-Français; to join this band MM. Saint-Fal and Saint-Prix had emerged from their retirement. The pall bearers were MM. Baptiste *aîné*, Lafon, Cartigny, Monrose, Michelot, Armand, Devigny and Firmin. Immediately behind the body walked Amédée Talma and, led by M. Davilliers, the tragedian's young sons. Every theatre in Paris sent its mourners, whether it bore the *imprimatur* of the State establishments like the Opéra, the Théâtre-Italien, the Opéra-Comique, the Odéon, or whether it belonged to a more popular category like the Variétés, the Palais-Royal or the Ambigu. The stage, true to its tradition,

[1] H. d'Alméras, *Mémoires sur Talma*, p. 335, footnote 2.

rose to a great occasion. In that vast concourse could be glimpsed writers like Béranger, Mignet, Thiers, Lebrun, musicians of the quality of Rossini, Meyerbeer, Cherubini, Paër, painters like Delacroix, Gros, Fleury, an early photographer Daguerre, the Brunoy architect Duponchel and, as more official mourners, Vatout the secretary of Mgr le duc d'Orléans and Beauchêne the private secretary of the Ministre des Beaux Arts.

Then followed in all its lonely emptiness Talma's own carriage, behind which came the carriages of Mlles Duchesnois and Mars. To these must be added twenty mourning coaches mostly empty because those who should have occupied them preferred to walk behind the hearse.

It was a long and tiring walk that faced Talma's mourners. Eastwards they marched along the rues Blanche, Saint-Lazare, des Trois-Frères, Taitbout, then through the boulevards until at the end of the rue du Chevron-Vert the cemetery gates were reached. At this point another huge crowd awaited the procession and, when the hearse drew up as near as was possible to the open grave, the young students of the Conservatoire who had known Talma as a teacher insisted upon replacing the actors of the Comédie-Française as bearers of the coffin to its resting-place near by. So dense was the press of people that it took nearly an hour before these young student actors could deposit their burden in the open grave. All accounts of these proceedings insist upon the reverent behaviour of the crowds who waited in a hushed silence for M. Lafon, sociétaire du Théâtre-Français, to deliver in the name of his colleagues the funeral oration.

That generous tribute, declaimed in ringing tones and inter-rupted only by the sobs of the mourners, reviewed Talma's career, emphasizing his Paris rather than his London origins, and the speaker's own happy associations with a great and lamented master. He dwelt upon Talma's early success in *Charles IX*, his reforms in the matter of accurate costume, his scrupulously historical exactitude. Lafon awarded Talma the palm both in comedy and tragedy. To name the excellence of his parts would require a list of all the works of Corneille, Racine, Crébillon, Voltaire, Ducis, Chénier and Legouvé. Nor could the speaker pass over in silence the delicate and subtle emotional shades Talma had imparted to the fatalism of Oreste and Oedipe, to the adul-terous love of Néron, to Faran's incestuous passion, to the weak criminality of Macbeth, to the murderous Agamemnon, to noble

Germanicus, to stoic, rugged Régulus. After this eulogistic catalogue Lafon paused over what he, his colleague, regarded as
Talma's finest achievements, Joad in *Athalie*, Sylla and Charles VI.
Deeply moved, Lafon referred to his own association with his
beloved chief.

'Full twenty-six years have I shared with you, I will not say
your glory, but the daily round which our close contact made so
perilous; and you often encouraged my efforts; by your friendship
I was sustained against a competition which no one feared so
much as I. More than once have I known your generous indulgence support my weakness, giving me liberal opportunities to
play your parts, to follow in your footsteps however far behind.
Ah! let me now drop upon your coffin a few of those laurel leaves
which you have harvested for so long, in such abundance and so
continuously.

'It is the modest tribute of a boundless gratitude and admiration. Honoured and beloved spirit, if you are still aware of earthly
things, if, as we are allowed to hope, as I believe and hope, like to
that Achilles whose great soul more than once I have tried to raise
up, you have not wholly descended into the tomb; receive this
sorrowful, solemn farewell; it comes from a voice known to you.'

Lafon's final words went straight to the hearts of his hearers.
'His memory will live for ever in all those countries of the world
where the sacred flame of the arts is tended. As long as there
exists a single one among you who have had the honour of being
associated with the glory he gave the French stage, for such a one
will it be a duty to visit this burial place and to draw from it that
warming glow which quickens talent and to pay homage, constantly renewed, to the excellent man who was our friend and
who will be for ever our exemplar. Adieu, Talma!'

The second speaker was M. Arnault *père*, the author of that
Germanicus which Lafon numbered among Talma's acting
triumphs. He began by modestly excusing himself as Lemercier's
quite unworthy understudy.[1] Arnault had been Talma's friend
since the days of Julie Careau and he spoke especially of the actor's
political tolerance, how much he loathed the revolutionary
excesses, how generous and steadfast he was to his friends. 'In his
noble improvidence he heaped upon friends money that he was
obliged to borrow in order to satisfy his own needs.' The orator
waxed eloquent over Talma's contacts with the great names of the

[1] Arnault replaced Lemercier who was unable to attend.

century, Mirabeau, Dumouriez, David, Lesueur,[1] and of course
the man of the century, Napoleon. 'What has become of all those
famous men? Dust and ashes like Talma but he like them enjoys
an immense reputation, an immortal glory as durable as civilisation
itself. In the capital of Art the death of a great artist is a public
calamity.'

M. Jouy, the author of Talma's sensational success *Sylla*,
wearing the uniform of an Academician, concluded the set orations. Possibly with more rhetoric than actual substance M. Jouy
referred to the genius of the actor, piling up his exclamations,
posing the dramatic question, fortifying his argument by impressive quotation. All he said he epitomized in a brief conclusion. 'No, Talma! Your name will not perish. It belongs to our
time and bears its character and impress. . . . Adieu, Talma! Our
sorrow will fade only with our life but time will never erase your
memory from the minds of men.'

One might have thought that after three such formal orations
nothing required to be added to their accents of deeply felt grief.
But no! M. Firmin stepped forward to read some verses composed
in honour of Talma. Then came M. Guilbert de Pixérécourt,
director of the Opéra-Comique and a popular writer of melodramas, to strew laurel branches, uttering as he did so a few
touching words. Finally over the open grave M. Toulotte, an
eminent Roman historian, improvised these last words. 'Endowed
with nature's fairest gifts, favoured by a sound education, finding
the great inspired examples of antiquity in the freedom of his
country, filled with love of liberty and with admiration for glory,
Talma was upright as a citizen, great beside the modern Trajan,
sublime in the theatre, delightful in society. His life leaves behind
an example for artists to follow and his death, which brought
grief to every heart, was that of a wise man.'

After those final words the crowds dispersed in the same silence
in which they had assembled. Never with greater dignity had a
popular idol been laid in his grave. The next day in some sections
of the Paris press comparisons were made with Garrick's inter-
ment in Westminster Abbey, when peers of the realm held it a
high honour to act as pall-bearers. Talma had occupied the same
position in France as Garrick had won in England. It was the
absence at Talma's funeral of any member of the aristocracy or of
the government that aroused critical comment. The orderliness of

[1] J. F. Lesueur, French composer of Napoleon's Coronation March.

the crowds, their attitude of sober grief, uncontrolled by any police, excited wonder.

To attempt to evaluate the press tributes paid to the late actor would be in very truth to ascend the highest heaven of invention. Eulogies such as those composed in verse or prose to mark Talma's death outstripped all superlatives and often, by a florid fulsomeness, induced a touch of weariness in the readers. A great actor had taken his final curtain call. The grief at the passing of a beloved personality, the assurance that he must be numbered with the finest artists of all time, the glowing memories of his famous parts and the affection he had won from all classes of society filled the newspaper columns which their writers, sensible of an irreparable loss to the French stage, clothed with all the deferential trappings reserved for the truly great. Very rarely did an astringent comment appear. Charles Maurice[1] ever ready to apply the ferula, bemoaned the fact that Talma's 'premature death' resulted from the demands made upon him in his later years by a life of pleasure. 'Gambling especially, with its excitement and late hours, had become for him who never knew one card from another, his normal and most dangerous recreation. . . . On that score I have certain information.'[2] That Talma's finances were complicated by his gambling debts none will deny, but it should be remembered that Dr. Tanchon ascribed the final deterioration of his health to work and not to play.

Stendhal, who contributed through the medium of an anonymous English translator to the *New Monthly Magazine*, wrote of Talma in its December 1826 and January 1827 issues.

As a general rule he had no more than the normal degree of pretentiousness, without which it is impossible nowadays to succeed in Paris. He was the last of our great men formed by the beneficent Revolution. . . . Talma owned a beautiful country residence at Brunoy near Paris, on which he expended enormous sums of money. In spite of this he left only 10,000 pounds to his sons. He was very charitable to the poor; and what is rather strange, gave a great deal to the Catholic priests who were always applying to him for money for church repairs and other similar purposes. He spoke English very well and frequently read Shakespeare in the original. Before performing in Ducis' version of *Hamlet*, he read the original play and often remarked, 'This Shakespeare electrifies me.' Nature had endowed him with handsome features and a finely proportioned figure. When he performed the

---

[1] and [2] C. Maurice, *Histoire anecdotique du théâtre*, Vol. I, pp. 377, 378.

part of Oreste in *Clytemnestre* nobody would have supposed him to be more than twenty-five years old. He never came nearer to perfection than in 1821 when he performed in *Sylla*. He presented in this rôle a striking resemblance to Napoleon.

Talma had no idea of his physical deterioration. During his last long illness the only circumstance that caused him anxiety was that his extreme thinness would disable him from impersonating certain youthful characters where he was obliged to reveal his neck. His forte lay in the depiction of Terror, for he was indifferent on the stage as a lover. In spite of this, it was love that dominated his entire existence. He was loved by some of the most distinguished women of his time; and even at the time of his death he was said to be in love with and jealous over his last wife.[1]

In the January number of the *New Monthly Magazine* Stendhal would seem to refute Maurice's charge that Talma was brought low by the excesses of social life. 'The constant object of Talma's ambition was not to shine in society but to excel in his profession. He devoted himself entirely to the advancement of dramatic art. This feeling for one's profession, a feeling without which no proficiency in the fine arts is possible, is becoming more and more rare. The arts are now cultivated merely as a means of making money. . . . It is a contagion from which Talma escaped and, escaping from which, derived his own profound feeling for the art of the tragedian.'

In the theatre's own world, as a mark of respect for the deceased actor, playhouses closed. The Comédie-Française for three successive nights gave no performance. The other State theatres in Paris, likewise those in the large provincial centres, Lyons, Marseilles, Bordeaux, went dark for one night. Even greater emotion showed itself in Belgium, where the actors of the Brussels, Antwerp and Ghent stages wore mourning for forty days and in the month of November produced their elaborate, commemorative rituals. The *Hommage à la Mémoire de Talma*[2] in which verse speaking and music were enhanced by a series of *tableaux emblématiques*, devised by M. Petipa, Maître de Ballet, showing Immortality leading Talma dressed as Roscius to take his heavenward flight to the outstretched arms of Lekain and Garrick, gives some idea of what constituted in the Brussels of that day a seemly act of dignified remembrance. If such romantic fancies cause a smile today, they summoned up tears enough in 1826.

[1] *New Monthly Magazine*, December 1826.
[2] A. Delavault, Éditeur, *Notice sur Talma*, 1827, p. 46.

The presence at Talma's funeral of bankers and money-lenders served as a signal for the gathering of the vultures. In such disorder were the actor's finances and his debts so pressing that it would require a Balzac adequately to render this alarming conflict between the improvidence of the artist and the greed of the Gobseck clan. At Brunoy stood *Mon Plaisir*, Talma's greatest asset, which took an unconscionable time to sell. Bertrand, manager of the Funambules and Madame Saqui, a circus performer, vied with each other, offering 240,000 francs in protracted negotiations which a third party terminated with a more ready and acceptable offer. On March 24th, 1827, at his Paris home in the rue de la Tour-des-Dames began a three days' sale. All his pictures, drawings and *objets d'art*, which he had collected with such pride, went under the hammer and saddest of all was to see assembled forlornly in lots his expensive costumes and personal properties for parts he had made so famous. The wig he wore for Charles VI fetched 43 francs and Sylla's famous lock of hair and costume another 160. For ridiculously low sums went Oreste's gleaming white pallium and robe,[1] also Hamlet's customary suit of solemn black.[2] Delaistre, an obscure player of the barn-storming kind, bought up Talma's theatrical wardrobe. On provincial playbills soon appeared: 'M. Delaistre will act this evening in costumes worn by Talma.'

The sale of his books *chez* Nève began on April 17th and it took eight days to dispose of a library that would have done credit to a savant. English readers will note with pleasure the inclusion of Flaxman's Designs, the poetry of Ossian, Young and Byron, Shakespeare's plays, Hazlitt's criticism, the tragedies of Robert Southey, the biographies of Garrick and Kemble. A substantial section on agriculture and gardening attested to his care for the Brunoy estate. Books on costume, classical and oriental, alongside tomes of historical memoirs and volumes of plays proclaimed the actor's intellectual interests. To these were added works on travel, theology and belles-lettres.

The education of Talma's two boys, one aged twelve, the other ten, posed something of a problem. Caroline, the legal wife, without fuss or performance, made herself responsible for the future of her husband's natural sons. With a generosity that transcended ordinary standards, she had both boys transferred to

[1] 100 francs.
[2] 236 francs.

the Collège Sainte-Barbe, where they would be prepared for a career in the army or navy. There were difficulties because the sons of Talma and Mlle Bazire had no clearly defined civil status. Alphonse-Alexandre 'as the natural son of Mlle Bazile' entered the army in 1832 as *élève-trompette*, saw service in Algeria and was decorated in 1845 with the Chevalier's Cross of the Legion of Honour. He died in 1882. Paul-Louis chose the navy and in 1832 became a cadet at the *École navale*. He retired from the sea in 1876 with the rank of *capitaine de vaisseau*. Thus neither boy bore his father's honoured name. Both however under the name of Bazile served France with distinction.

Of Madeleine-Jacqueline Bazire, later through her sons Bazile, no information at present seems available. She came from the shadows into the blaze of Talma's life, lived with him for fourteen years and bore him three children. Who was she? Reference has been made to her possible identification with an unsuccessful actress, Florine Bazire. Could she by any chance be related to that faithful Rosalie Bazire, who worked in the royal linen room and performed that act of mercy by bringing clean linen to Marie-Antoinette in the Conciergerie? There was also Claude Bazire, a member of the National Convention, who went to the scaffold in 1794, leaving behind a wife and young daughter, *en bas âge*, to whom three years later the Directory awarded a pension. Could there be any substance in the suggestion that she was a kins-woman of Comte Lecourbe of Lons-le-Saulnier who became Lieutenant-General and was finally promoted by Moreau to be his Général en chef in 1800? Surely this is difficult to accept. Friend-ship with the Moreau faction would spell disloyalty to Napoleon. Talma would run no risk of losing the great man's favour. In the state of our present knowledge we can be sure only of one fact; she was Talma's mistress. The rest is darkness.

Caroline on the other hand walked in the sunlight. On May 31st, 1828, she married Jacques-Antoine, Comte de Chalot, formerly a colonel of a cavalry regiment, who lived in the rue de Vaugirard. Her third venture into matrimony proved a great success and only in 1836 did she emerge from her comfortable bourgeois life as the author of a book which contained much sound advice on acting, followed by her own fragmentary memories of Talma. The title page bore the words '*par Madame Veuve Talma, née Vanhove, maintenant Comtesse de Chalot*'. During a life of considerable literary production Caroline survived her third husband by a few years and died in Paris on April 10th, 1860, in her ninetieth year, mentally alert until the end.

Talma's remains, placed in ground belonging to the Davilliers family, were exhumed on October 19th, 1827, and transferred to the vault which, surmounted by a cenotaph, can be seen today in Père-Lachaise.[1] A public subscription had been opened to provide a statue which was originally intended to grace his tomb. The Comédie-Française subscribed 10,000 francs and when David d'Angers had completed his work, realizing that the cenotaph ruled out any adornment, presented his work on March 29th, 1837, to the sociétaires, who added a further 4,000 francs to the theatre's subscription. Thus David d'Angers' remarkable effort, entitled *Talma studying a part*, stands in the Premier Vestibule of the Comédie-Française. The great sculptor saw Talma 'in the costume and the attitude of Caesar pondering the destinies of his empire'.[2] This superb statue greets the playgoer as he enters the theatre. This indeed is holy ground, for it was here that Talma by his incomparable art stirred the heart and mind of France.

[1] The Comédie-Française possesses the heart of Talma enclosed in a polished mahogany Empire casket. The lid bears a metal plaque with the following inscription: *Cette boête renferme le coeur de Talma*. The actor's heart had been removed during the autopsy carried out by his nephew, Dr. Amédée Talma. The remains are contained in a heart-shaped metal receptacle. The relic is authenticated by a parchment certificate dated October 19th, 1827.

[2] René Delorme *Le Musée de la Comédie-Française*, pp. 48, 49.

CHAPTER 50

The Glory that was Talma

It is an impossible, hopeless task to try to catch the accents of a dead actor, to glimpse his slightest gesture, even if he be a great, much recorded and universally admired artist in the theatre like Talma. Over two centuries time has cast its all-enveloping silence to hush Talma's agonized cries and its mortal chill to reduce to cold ashes the fiery passion that once burned within his manly torso. How fragile, tenuous and vain are these ghostly shadows that the flickering torchlight of stage history casts upon posterity's wall. In all the reading that has been undertaken to make this book, only rarely, very rarely could the straining ear and the searching eye grasp for one fugitive particle of a second the glory that was Talma. A sulky, casual Néron, arrogantly fingering the pattern of his robe as a hectoring Agrippine pours out her complaints, Danville's laughing entrance in *L'École des vieillards*, the heartbreak of the urn scene in *Hamlet*, a few fleeting incomplete impressions may linger in the mind and truth must be on its guard lest self-deception magnify such moments into irrefutable evidence of acting quality.

There remains another problem. An actor lives two lives; his imaginary characterizations on the stage and his existence as an ordinary individual. In some ways, the greater the actor the less important becomes his private life. Talma lived and loved generously outside the theatre, but urgently necessary as were to him the affections of Julie Careau, Caroline Vanhove, Pauline Borghèse and Madeleine-Jacqueline Bazire, in the final count only the stage with its compulsive, simulated emotions could hold him completely in thrall. With Talma who can tell where the fictions of the theatre ended and the reality of life began? The wealthy landed proprietor, the intrepid gambler, the reckless spendthrift, the gracious generous host, the family man, in what proportions, one may ask, are here mingled folly and sincerity, fiction and fact?

Yet Talma's life deserves some record. However theatrical

fashions may change, great acting remains in essence fundamentally the same and is immediately recognizable by connoisseurs as such. Lekain, Garrick, Talma, Kean and Irving, to go no further, possessed within them that daemon, that spiritual and emotional power which enabled them to conjure their very souls and, by the exercise of sheer imagination, to project to an audience with an equal conviction the noble aspirations and the craven weakness of mankind. Talma held his position as an outstanding actor during three succeeding régimes in France, the Revolution, the Napoleonic Empire and the Bourbon Restoration. Throughout those thirty-nine years he shared his triumphs with the famous leading ladies of the day, Vestris, Desgarcins, Vanhove, Raucourt, George, Duchesnois and, outside the tragic genre, Mars. Perhaps of all these, ill-featured Duchesnois gave him finest support, she who as Marie Stuart was unsurpassed even by the great Rachel herself. His authors, ephemeral as they were, numbered every contemporary dramatist of note, ever eager to enlist his services not only as actor but as play doctor as well. To the great parts of the classical repertory he gave a new life. Well might Chateaubriand say: '*Sans Talma une partie des merveilles de Corneille et de Racine serait demeurée inconnue.*'[1] Into Ducis' cold adaptations he breathed something of true Shakespearean fire. Of his efforts to reform a meaningless, incantatory declamation, to ensure historical accuracy of costume and décor, to establish nature and truth as the ultimate criteria of theatrical performance, this study has provided many examples.

Historians, political and literary, seize upon Talma's achievements to illustrate the by-ways of a formative period. The friend of Mirabeau did yeoman service for the revolutionary cause by his portrayal of tyrant kings like Charles IX. With the advent of Napoleon to power, the conquering general, Cyrus or Hector, became fashionable as the type of tragic hero. Some researchers will pounce gleefully upon Talma's performance of Assuérus in *Esther* which led the Emperor to accord a recognized civil status to Jews in France.[2] Others, more literary minded, will see something of Bonaparte's intellectual quality in the advice he gave the

---

[1] *Mémoires d'outre tombe.* II, p. 275.

[2] E. Duval, *Talma*, pp. 92, 93. The day following *Esther*, early July 1806, at one of his informal luncheon parties, Napoleon, criticizing the character of Assuérus, turned to Champagny, Minister of the Interior, and asked for a report on the Jews in France. On July 26th, 1806 the Jewish notables met and their position was duly ratified by law. Regnault-Warin, *Mémoires*, p. 501.

actor on the playing of some of his rôles. Then too there remains the remarkable friendship between the two men which, even when the Emperor had fallen, a faithful Talma greatly daring did not scruple to keep alive in his own heart and in the public mind by his portrayals of Germanicus and Sylla. If the story of the Napoleonic legend in France is to be fully told, then Talma must take his place among its earliest creators. In the sphere of literature Talma was a romantic *avant l'heure*. All the reforms of French tragedy that Stendhal had urged in *Racine et Shakespeare*, that Victor Hugo had advocated with such earnest persuasion in *La Préface de Cromwell*, Talma had fought for all his life. If Talma's acting has vanished over the centuries, his ideas on the French theatre can be proved as revolutionary as the times through which he lived, and to talk of 'local colour', the mingling of comedy and tragedy, and all the romantic box of tricks as something startlingly new in 1826 is to forget those amazing stage directions for *Abufar* set down by Ducis at Talma's prompting in that year of disgrace 1794. The glowing pages of Mme de Staël, inspired by those performances at Lyons in 1809, endorsed Talma's passport to posterity. Honour to whom honour is due and the emancipation of French tragedy from the mummified wrappings of an old outworn literary tradition and acting technique owes much more than grudging pundits admit to the enlightenment of François-Joseph Talma, artiste sociétaire and, from 1824 until his death, Doyen de la Comédie-Française.

APPENDIX A

List of parts created by Talma from 1788 to 1826

CLÉANDRE, in *La Jeune Épouse*, comedy in three acts in verse, by Cubières. (July 4th, 1788.)

LE CHEVALIER TRISTAN, in *Lanval et Vivianne, ou Les Fées et les Chevaliers*, heroic comedy by André Murville. (September 13th, 1788.)

LE COMTE D'ORSANGE, in *Le Présomptueux ou L'Heureux Imaginaire*, comedy by Fabre d'Églantine. (January 7th, 1789.)

LE GARÇON ANGLAIS, in *Les Deux Pages*, comedy by Dezède. (March 6th, 1789.)

LE CHEVALIER DE SABRAN, in *Raymond V, comte de Toulouse, ou Le Troubadour*, heroic comedy by Sedaine. (September 22nd, 1789.)

CHARLES IX, in *Charles IX ou La Saint-Barthélemy*, tragedy by Chénier. (November 4th, 1789.)

JUAN, in *Le Paysan Magistrat*, drama by Collot d'Herbois. (December 7th, 1789.)

D'HARCOURT, in *Le Réveil d'Épiménide à Paris*, comedy by Flins des Oliviers. (January 1st, 1790.)

LE COMTE D'AMPLACE, in *L'Honnête Criminel*, drama by Fenouillot de Falbaire. (January 4th, 1790.)

DORVIGNY, in *Le Comte de Cominges*, drama by Darnaud Baculard. (May 14th, 1790.)

J. J. ROUSSEAU, in *Le Journaliste des Ombres, ou Momus aux Champs-Élysées*, heroic play in one act in verse, by M. Aude. (July 14th, 1790.)

HENRI VIII, in *Henri VIII*, tragedy by Chénier. (April 27th, 1791).

CLÉRY, in *L'Intrigue Épistolaire*, comedy by Fabre d'Églantine. (June 15th, 1791.)

JEAN, in *Jean sans Terre*, tragedy by Ducis. (June 28th, 1791.)

LASALLE, in *Jean Calas*, tragedy by Chénier. (July 6th, 1791.)

LE PRINCE ÉPOUX DE ZULÉÏMA, in *Abdelazis et Zuléïma*, tragedy by André Muville. (October 3rd, 1791.)

ALONZO, in *La Vengeance*, tragedy adapted from the English, by M. Dumaniant. (November 26th, 1791.)

MONVAL, in *Mélanie*, drama by La Harpe. (December 7th, 1791.)

FULVIUS FLACCUS, in *Caius Gracchus*, tragedy by Chénier. (February 7th, 1792.)

OTHELLO, in *Le Maure de Venise*, tragedy by Ducis. (November 26th, 1792.)

DELMANCE, in *Fénelon*, tragedy by Chénier. (February 9th, 1793.)

MUTIUS SCÉVOLA, in *Mutius Scévola*, tragedy by Luce de Lancival. (July 23rd, 1793.)

NÉRON, in *Épicharis et Néron*, tragedy by Legouvé. (February 3rd, 1794.)

TIMOLÉON, in *Timoléon*, tragedy by Chénier. (September 11th, 1794.)

SERVILIUS, in *Quintus Cincinnatus*, tragedy by M. Arnault. (December 31st, 1794.)

PHARAN, in *Abufar*, tragedy by Ducis. (April 12th, 1795.)

QUINTUS FABIUS, in *Quintus Fabius*, tragedy by Legouvé. (July 31st, 1795.)

JUNIUS, in *Junius ou Le Proscrit*, tragedy by M. Monvel, fils. (April 3, 1797.)

ÉGISTHE, in *Agamemnon*, tragedy by M. Lemercier. (April 25th, 1797.)

KALEB, in *Falkland*, drama by M. Laya. (May 25th, 1797.)

MONCASSIN, in *Les Vénitiens*, tragedy by M. Arnault. (October 15th, 1798.)

THAULUS, in *Ophis*, tragedy by M. Lemercier. (December 22nd, 1798.)

ÉTÉOCLE, in *Étéocle et Polynice*, tragedy by Legouvé. (October 19th, 1799.)

PINTO, in *Pinto*, comedy by M. Lemercier. (March 22nd, 1800.)

MONTMORENCY, in *Montmorency*, tragedy by M. Carrion-Nisas. June 1st, 1800.)

THÉSÉE, in *Thésée*, tragedy by M. Mazoyer. (November 15th, 1800.)

PHAEDOR, in *Phaedor et Waldamir*, tragedy by Ducis. (April 24th, 1801.)

DON PÈDRE, in *Le Roi et le Laboureur*, tragedy by M. Arnault. (June 5th, 1802.)

OROVÈZE, in *Ysule et Orovèze*, tragedy by M. Lemercier. (December 23rd, 1802.)

SHAKESPEARE, in *Shakespeare amoureux*, comedy by M. Alexandre Duval. (January 2nd, 1804.)

ULYSSE, in *Polyxène*, tragedy by M. Aignan. (January 14th, 1804.)

HAROLD, in *Guillaume le Conquérant*, drama by M. Alexandre Duval. (February 4th, 1804.)

PIERRE LE GRAND, in *Pierre le Grand*, tragedy by M. Carrion-Nisas. (May 19th, 1804.)

CYRUS, in *Cyrus*, tragedy by Chénier. (December 8th, 1804.)

MARIGNY, in *Les Templiers*, tragedy by M. Raynouard. (May 24th, 1805.)

HENRI IV, in *La Mort de Henri IV*, tragedy by Legouvé. (June 25th, 1806.)

OMASIS, in *Omasis*, tragedy by M. Baour-Lormian. (September 13th, 1806.)

PYRRHUS, in *Pyrrhus*, tragedy by M. Lehoc. (February 28th, 1807.)

PLAUTE, in *Plaute, ou La Comédie latine*, comedy by M. Lemercier. (January 20th, 1808.)

HECTOR, in *Hector*, tragedy by Luce de Lancival. (February 1st, 1809.)

LE DUC DE GUISE, in *Les États de Blois*, tragedy by M. Raynouard. (June 22nd, 1810.)

MAHOMET, in *Mahomet II*, tragedy by M. Baour-Lormian. (March 9th, 1811.)

TIPPO-SAÏB, in *Tippo-Saïb*, tragedy by M. Jouy. (January 27th, 1813.)

NINUS II, in *Ninus II*, tragedy by M. Briffaut. (April 19th, 1813.)

DUGUESCLIN, in *La Rançon de Duguesclin*, heroic comedy by M. Arnault. (March 17th, 1814.)

ULYSSE, in *Ulysse*, tragedy by M. Lebrun. (April 28th, 1814.)

RUTLAND, in *Arthur de Bretagne*, tragedy by M. Aignan. (February 3rd, 1816.)

GERMANICUS, in *Germanicus*, tragedy by M. Arnault. (March 22nd, 1817.)

LEICESTER, in *Marie Stuart*, tragedy by M. Lebrun. (March 6th, 1820.)

CLOVIS, in *Clovis*, tragedy by M. Viennet. (October 19th, 1820.)

JEAN DE BOURGOGNE, in *Jean de Bourgogne*, tragedy by M. de Formont. (December 4th, 1820.)

SYLLA, in *Sylla*, tragedy by M. Jouy. (December 27th, 1821.)

RÉGULUS, in *Regulus*, tragedy by M. Lucien Arnault. (June 5th, 1822.)

ORESTE, in *Clytemnestre*, tragedy by M. Soumet. (November 5th, 1822.)

ÉBROÏN, in *Le Maire du Palais*, tragedy by M. Ancelot. (April 16th, 1823.)

DANVILLE, in *L'École des Vieillards*, comedy by M. Casimir de Lavigne. (December 6th, 1823.)

GLOUCESTER, in *Jane Shore*, tragedy by M. Lemercier. (April 1st, 1824.)

LE CID, in *Le Cid d'Andalousie*, tragedy by M. Lebrun. (March 1st, 1825.)

ABIATAR, in *La Clémence de David*, tragedy by M. Draparnaud. (June 7th, 1825.)

BÉLISAIRE, in *Bélisaire*, tragedy by M. Jouy. (June 28th, 1825.)

LÉONIDAS, in *Léonidas*, tragedy by M. Pichat. (November 26th, 1825.)

CHARLES VI, in *Charles VI*, tragedy by M. Delaville. (March 6th, 1826.)

APPENDIX B

Mme Sylvie Chevalley, Bibliothécaire-Archiviste de la Comèdie-Française, has estimated that during 1787–1791 and 1799–1826 Talma gave at that theatre 2,814 performances in 195 plays old and new, playing 247 parts. His greatest successes were:

ORESTE	in *Andromaque* (Racine)	108 performances
MANLIUS	in *Manlius Capitolinus* (Lafosse)	102 ,,
NÉRON	in *Britannicus* (Racine)	95 ,,
SYLLA	in *Sylla* (Jouy)	90 ,,
MARIGNY– MOLAY	in *Les Templiers* (Raynouard)	82 ,, (M.66 Molay 16)
CINNA– AUGUSTE	in *Cinna* (Corneille)	74 ,, (C.45 A.30)
HAMLET	in *Hamlet* (Ducis)	69 ,,
DANVILLE	in *L'École des Vieillards* (Delavigne)	66 ,,
OEDIPE	in *Oedipe* (Voltaire)	65 ,,
LEICESTER	in *Marie Stuart* (Lebrun)	56 ,,

Appendix

Selected Bibliography

ABRANTÈS, DUCHESSE d'. *Mémoires.* Paris, L. Mame, 1831–35.

ANDRÉ, ANTOINE. *La Vie amoureuse de Talma.* Paris, E. Flammarion, 1924.

ANON. *An Account of the Dinner given at the Freemasons' Tavern,* London. D. N. Shury, 1817.

ANON. *Mémoire sur Lekain précédé d'une notice sur la vie de Talma.* Bruxelles, A. Delavault, 1827.

ANON. *Souvenirs historiques sur la vie et la mort de Talma.* Bruxelles, Tarbier, 1826.

ANON. *Talma dans le Nord.* Lille, Lefebre-Ducroq, 1888.

ARNAULT, A. V. *Les Souvenirs d'un sexagénaire.* Paris, Duféy, 1833.

AUDIBERT. *Histoire du roman: Talma.* Paris, Duféy, 1834.

AULARD, A. *Paris sous le Consulat.* Paris, Léopold Cerf, 1903–09.

AUGUSTIN-THIERRY, A. *Le Tragédien de Napoléon.* Paris, 30 feuilletons du Temps, du 5 mai au 8 juin, 1938.

BABEAU, ALBERT. *Les Anglais en France après la Paix d'Amiens.* Paris, Plon, 1898.

BAINVILLE, JACQUES. *Napoléon.* Paris, Arthème Fayard, 1931.

BALDICK, ROBERT. *Life and Times of Frédérick Lemaître.* London, Hamish Hamilton, 1959.

BAPST, GERMAIN. *Essai sur l'Histoire du théâtre.* Paris, Hachette, 1893.

BEAUVAIS, ROGER DE. *Mémoires de Mlle Mars.* Paris, Roux et Cassanat, 1849.

BERVILLE, ST. A. ET J. J. BARRIÈRE. *La Vie et les mémoires du Général Dumouriez.* Paris, Baudoin Frères, 1822.

BOURRIENNE, L. A. F. *Mémoires sur Napoléon.* Paris, Ladvocat, 1829.

BURY, J. P. T. and J. C. BARRY. *An Englishman in Paris,* 1803. London, Bles, 1953.

CAMPAN, MME. *Mémoires sur la vie privée de Marie-Antoinette.* Paris, Baudoin Frères, 1822.

CAMPARDON, ÉMILE. *Les Comédiens du Roi.* Paris, H. Champion, 1870.

CHARPENTIER, JOHN. *Napoléon et les hommes de lettres de son temps.* Paris, Mercure de France, 1935.

CHATEAUBRIAND, FRANÇOIS-RENÉ. *Mémoires d'outre tombe.* Paris, Krabbe, 1851.

CHEVALLEY, SYLVIE. *Talma, Comédien français.* Paris-Revue d'Histoire du Théâtre, Oct.—Déc. 1962.

COCHELET, MLLE. *Mémoires sur la reine Hortense.* Paris, Ladvocat, 1858.

CONSTANT, BENJAMIN. *Mélanges de Littérature et de Politique.* Paris, Pichon et Didier, 1829.

CONSTANT (né LOUIS-CONSTANT WAIRY). *Mémoires de Constant, premier valet de Napoléon Ier.* Paris, Ladvocat, 1830.

COPIN, ALFRED. i. *Talma et la Révolution.* Paris, L. Frinzine, 1887.
ii. *Talma et l'Empire.* Paris, L. Frinzine, 1887.

COTTENSON, BARON DE. i. *Talma et sa famille militaire.* Paris, Le Carnet 4me année novembre, Émile Paul, 1901.
ii. *Militaires, fils d'acteurs.* Paris, Plon, 1911.

CUNNINGHAM, G. H. *London, A Comprehensive Survey.* London, Dent, 1927.

DESGRANGES, C. M. *Geoffroy et la critique dramatique.* Paris, Hachette, 1897.

DELORME, R. *Le Musée de la Comédie-Française.* Paris, Ollendorff, 1878.

DUMAS, ALEXANDRE. *Mémoires de Talma.* Paris, Souverain, 1850.

DUVAL, ÉMILE. *Talma, précis historique.* Paris, Monsat Fils, 1826.

ÉTIENNE, CHARLES. *Histoire du Théâtre-Français.* Paris, Barba, 1802.

FABER, FRÉDÉRIC. *Histoire du Théâtre-Français en Belgique.* Bruxelles, Olivier, 1879.

FLEISCHMANN, H. et PIERRE BART. *Lettres d'amour inédites de Talma à la Princesse Pauline Bonaparte.* Paris, Charpentier et Fasquelle, 1911.

FLEURY, (A.-J. Bénard, dit). *Mémoires avec notices et notes par Henri d'Alméras.* Paris, Société parisienne d'édition, 1904.

FLORE, MLLE. *Mémoires. Paris, Société parisienne d'édition,* 1894.

FUSIL, LOUISE. *Souvenirs d'une actrice.* Paris, Dumont, 1840.

GEORGE, MLLE. *Mémoires inédits.* Paris, Cheramy, 1908.

GIRARD, HENRI. *Le Centenaire du Premier Cénacle.* Paris, Éditions des Presses Françaises, 1926.

GONCOURT, E. et J. i. *Histoire de la Société française pendant la Révolution*. Paris, Dentu, 1854.
　　　　　ii. *Histoire de la Société française pendant le Directoire*. Paris, Dentu, 1855.

GREEN, F. C. *Minuet*. London, Dent, 1935.

GRIBBLE, FRANCIS. *Romances of the French Theatre*. London, Chapman and Hall, 1912.

GUEDALLA, PHILIP. *The Duke*. London, Hodder and Stoughton, 1946.

HÉDOUIN, PIERRE. *Talma à Boulogne*. Paris, Ladvocat, 1827.

IRVING, HENRY. Preface to 'Talma on the Actor's Art'. London, Bickers and Son, 1883.

IRVING, LAURENCE. *Henry Irving*. London, Faber and Faber, 1951.

KOTZEBUE, AUGUSTE. *Souvenirs de Paris, 1804*. Traduction de l'allemand, G. de Pixérécourt. Paris, Barba, 1804.

LAMARTINE, ALPHONSE DE. i. *Cours familier de littérature*. Paris. Chez l'auteur, 1857.
　　　　　ii. *Saül*. Paris, Société des Textes Modernes, Hachette, 1918.

LANSON, GUSTAVE. *Esquisse d'une histoire de la tragédie française*. Paris, Hachette, 1920.

LANZAC DE LABORIE, L. DE. *Paris sous Napoléon; Le Théâtre-Français*. Paris, Plon, 1911.

LAS CASES, E. DE. *Le Mémorial de Sainte-Hélène*. Paris, La Pléïade, 1935.

LAUGIER. *Documents historiques sur la Comédie-Française*. Paris, Firmin Didot Frères, 1853.

LEGOUVÉ, ERNEST. *Soixante ans de souvenirs*. Paris, Hetzel, 1886–7.

MADELIN, LOUIS. *Histoire du Consulat et de l'Empire*. Paris, Hachette, 1939.

MANCERON, CLAUDE. *Le Dernier choix de Napoléon*. Paris, Laffont, 1960.

MANNE, E. D. de. *La Troupe de Talma*. Lyon, Scheuring, 1866.

MANNE, E. D. de et C. Ménétrier. *Galerie historique de la Comédie-Française*. Lyon, Scheuring, 1876.

MAURICE, CHARLES. *Histoire anecdotique du théâtre*. Paris, Plon, 1856.

MAXWELL, CONSTANTIA. *The English Traveller in France*. London, Routledge, 1932.

MOREAU, M. *Mémoires historiques et littéraires sur F.-J. Talma*. Paris, Ladvocat, 1826.

NICOLSON, HAROLD. *Benjamin Constant*. London, Constable, 1949.

PERNOUD and FLAISSIER. *The French Revolution*. London, Secker and Warburg, 1960.

POUGIN, A. *La Comédie-Française et la Révolution*. Paris, Gaultier, Magnier et Cie. Undated, believed 1902.

REGNAULT-WARIN. i. *Mémoires historiques et critiques sur F.-J. Talma et sur l'art théâtral*. Paris, A. Henry, 1827.

    ii. *Mémoires sur Talma avec notes et nombreux documents collationnés par Henri d'Alméras*. Paris, Société parisienne d'édition, 1904.

RÉMUSAT, MME DE. i. *Mémoires de Mme de Rémusat 1802–1808*. Paris, Calmann-Lévy, 1881.

    ii. *Memoirs of Mme de Rémusat*. Published by her grandson, Paul de Rémusat. Trans. by Hoey and Lilly, London, Sampson and Low, 1880.

ROBINSON, HENRY CRABB. *Diary, Reminiscences, Correspondence*. Ed. Thos. Sadler, London, Macmillan, 1869.

SAUNDERS, EDITH. *Napoleon and Mlle George*. London, Longmans Green, 1958.

SCOTT, JOHN (of GALA). *Journal of a Tour to Waterloo and Paris, 1815*. London, Saunders and Otley, 1842.

SCOTT, JOHN BARBER. *An Englishman at Home and Abroad*. London, Heath Cranton, 1830.

STAËL-HOLSTEIN, MME DE. *De l'Allemagne*. Paris et Londres. Édition chez Colburn, 1814.

STRICKLAND, GEOFFREY. *Stendhal*. Selected Journalism. London, Calder, 1959.

TALMA, F.-J. i. *Correspondance avec Mme de Staël*. Introduction de Guy de la Batut. Paris, Éditions Montaigne, 1928.

    ii. *Quelques réflexions sur Lekain et sur l'art théâtral*. Paris, Tétot Frères, 1826.

(Originally this work appeared as a preface to Bernard Cain's collection of his father's memoirs entitled '*Mémoires sur l'Art dramatique*', published by Ponthieu in 1825. Talma's contribution was separately printed in 1826 by A. Henry and by the firm named above. It was also included by Regnault-Warin as an Appendix to his *Mémoires*, pp. 511–549).

TALMA, CAROLINE, *née* VANHOVE. i. *Épître à Talma*. Paris, Petit, 1820.

ii. *Études sur l'art théâtral, suivies d'anecdotes inédites sur Talma et de la correspondance de Ducis avec cet artiste*. Paris, Feret, 1836.

TALMA, JULIE. *Lettres de Julie Talma à Benjamin Constant avec des notes de la baronne Constant de Rebecque*. Paris, Édition de la Palatine, Plon, 1933.

TALMA, le SIEUR. *Instructions nécessaires pour l'entretien des dents*. Paris, Louis Collot, 1770.

THOMPSON, J. M. *The French Revolution*. Oxford, Blackwell, 1947.

THIERS, ADOLPHE. *Histoire du Consulat et de l'Empire*. Paris, L'Heureux, 1845–52.

TISSOT, P.-F. *Souvenirs historiques sur la vie et la mort de Talma*. Paris, Baudouin Frères, 1826.

VITRY, AUBERT de. *Particularités remarquables sur Talma par son plus grand ami et camarade d'enfance*. An account dated and signed 1827. Printed in *L'Artiste*, Paris, 1857.

WELSCHINGER, HENRI. *La Censure sous le Premier Empire*. Paris, Charavay Frères, 1882.

WHEATLEY, HENRY B. *London Past and Present*. London, John Murray, 1890.

Index

Index

Geoffroy, Julien-Louis, 21, 115, 133–44, 147, 150, 151, 158, 166–8, 170, 174, 175, 180–2, 184, 190, 200–2, 208, 211, 216, 218–20, 222, 235–41, 243, 251, 252, 264, 280, 329, 338, 357, 358
Geoffroy, Mme, 140, 238
George (Marguerite-Joséphine Weimer), 141, 146, 149, 152, 153, 161, 168, 169, 178, 182, 186, 190–2, 245–7, 251, 253, 259, 266, 291–7, 309, 382
George III, 23
Gérard, actor, 92
Germanicus (A.-V. Arnault), 285, 286, 289, 308, 326, 339, 374
Ghent, T. at, 325
Gielgud, Sir John, 294
Giguet et Michaud, publishers, 170
Girodet, Anne-Louis, 45
Gironde Faction, 72, 77, 81, 82, 93, 95, 101
Gloucester, Duke and Duchess of, 297
Gobbelschroy van M., 369
Goethe, Johann Wolfgang, 194, 196, 276
Goncourt, Edmond et Jules, 104, 111
Grammont (Jean-Baptiste-Jacques Nourry), 56, 61
Grand-Théâtre, Bordeaux, 66, 245
Grand-Théâtre, Lyons, 139, 185, 203
Grandmesnil (Jean-Baptiste Fauchard), 66, 77, 123, 191
Grandval (François-Charles Racot), 282, 353
Greatheed, Bertie, 145, 146, 165
Greatheed, Squire, 145, 146
Green, F. C., Prof., 77
Gribble, Francis, 225
Grimm, Friedrich Melchior, Baron, 38, 55
Grimod de la Reynière, Laurent, 52, 352
Gros, Antoine-Jean, 45, 373
Gros, Mme, actress, 123, 161, 193, 198
Guerre Ouverte, La (Dumaniant), 24
Guillaume le Conquérant (Duval), 152, 153
Guillaume Tell (Lemierre), 22, 46, 78, 95, 100, 103
Guiraud, Alexandre, 363
Gustave or *Gustavus Wasa* (Piron), 173

H., Sulpice, 21
Halkin St., London, 20, 23
Hamlet (Ducis), 27, 29, 98, 157–61, 200–2, 204, 205, 211, 227, 230, 247, 267, 268, 280, 285, 290–2, 325, 364, 376, 381

Harcourt, George Simon, Earl of, 23–5, 28
Hardenberg, Charlotte von, 203
Hardy, Marie-Cathérine, 18
Hazlitt, William, 25, 378
Hector (Luce de Lancival), 202, 215, 224, 238, 271, 312
Helvetic Republic, 46
Hénocq, Mlle, 370
Henri VIII (Chénier), 67, 68, 74, 162
Héraclius (Corneille), 163, 178, 186, 259
Héritiers, Les (Duval), 199
Hirsch, Robert, 262
Holland, T. in, 223
Holland, Lord, 297
Hommage à la mémoire de Talma, 377
Horace (Corneille), 107, 161, 182, 186, 196, 216
Hugo, Victor, 142, 160, 180, 307, 328, 337, 339, 349, 358, 383
Husson, Dr., 366

Impératrice, Théâtre de l', 184
Imperial Theatre, St. Petersburg, 258
Intendant des Menus Plaisirs, M. l', 44, 332
Intrigue Épistolaire L' (Fabre d'Églantine), 77
Iphigénie en Aulide (Racine), 32, 64, 120, 132, 141, 178, 185, 186, 190, 195, 212, 213, 254–6, 266, 362, 364, 365
Iphigénie en Tauride (La Touche) 32, 34, 187, 208, 236, 245, 296, 329
Irving, Sir Henry, 176, 294, 352, 382
Ivry, 39

Jacobin Club, 82, 91
Jacobins, 81, 82, 88–90, 93, 96, 98, 99, 112
Jallu, financier, 185, 186, 188
Jaloux sans Amour, Le, 64
Jane Shore (Lemercier), 337–9, 362
Jane Shore (Rowe), 337
Jannin, Charles, 369
Jansénistes, 74
Jean Calas (Chénier), 79
Jean de Bourgogne (Formont), 313, 314, 321
Jean sans Terre (Ducis), 77, 86, 275
Jeanne d'Arc (D'Avrigny), 289
Jeune Épouse, La (Cubière), 46
Jeunesse de Henri V, La (Duval), 237, 258
Jeunesse de Richelieu, La (Duval et Monvel), 219

Index

Index

Vanhove, Charles-Joseph, 32, 39, 44, 45, 77, 88, 92, 97, 112, 122, 151, 204
Vanloo, Jean Baptiste, 45
Vaperot, pedagogue, 21, 28
Varennes, actor, 168, 193, 198
Variétés-Amusantes, Théâtre des, 66, 83, 372
Varon, Art Commissioner, 46
Vatout, Jean, 373
Vaudeville, Théâtre du, 243
Védel (Alexandre-Louis Poulet), 172, 173
Venceslas (Rotrou), 129, 190, 215
Vengeance, La (Dumaniant), 79
Venice Preserved (Otway), 173, 174, 280, 294
Vénitiens, Les (A.-V. Arnault), 109, 110, 119, 120, 124, 1○7, 285, 326
Vêpres siciliennes, Les (Delavigne), 330
Verdier, pedagogue, 21
Vergniaud, Pierre-Victurnien, 72, 101
Vergy, Gabrielle de (Debelloy), 253, 266
Vernet, Horace, 319
Vestale, La (Spontini), 253
Vestris, Auguste, 202
Vestris (Rose Gourgaud), Mme, 40, 49, 52, 56, 62, 66–8, 82, 97, 103, 112, 114, 122, 123, 382
Veuve du Malabar, La (Lemierre), 34, 242
Victor (Antoine-Victor Lerebours), 350
Vie amoureuse de Talma, La (Antoine), 260
Vigny, Alfred de, 85, 307
Villette, Mme de, Reine-Philiberte, 305
Virginius (Knowles), 365

Vitry, Aubert de, 22
Vivandiers, Les, 89
Volnais (Claudine-Placide Croizet), 140, 149, 150, 152, 181, 197, 201, 218
Voltaire (François-Marie Arouet), 17, 25, 27, 41, 44, 51, 66, 76–9, 89, 90, 102, 124, 125, 136, 139, 195, 203, 206, 224, 266, 277, 293, 305, 352, 355, 358, 370, 373

Wairy, Louis-Constant; *see* Constant
Wales, Prince of, 23–5, 28
Watteau, Jean-Antoine, 45
Wattier-Ziegenis, Mme, 223
Weimer, Georges, 141
Wellington, Duke of, 245, 290
Westphalia, King of; *see* Bonaparte, Jérôme
Winckelmann, Johann Joachim, 43
Würtemmburg, Catherine of, 186, 187
Würtemmburg, Frederick II, King of, 194
Würzburg, Grand Duke of, 187

Ximénès, Marquis de, Augustin-Marie, 52, 172

Yates, Richard, 145
York, Duchess of, 297
Young, Edward, 378
Ysole et Orovèze (Lemercier), 142

Zaïre (Voltaire), 25, 124, 132, 133, 178, 194, 202